RELIGIOUS ORGANIZATIONS AND DEMOCRATIZATION

Religious Organizations and Democratization

Case Studies from Contemporary Asia

TUN-JEN CHENG and DEBORAH A. BROWN, EDITORS

An East Gate Book

LONDON AND NEW YORK

An East Gate Book

First published 2006 by M.E. Sharpe

Published 2015 by Routledge
2 Park Square, Milton Park, Abingdon, Oxon OX14 4RN
711 Third Avenue, New York, NY 10017, USA

Routledge is an imprint of the Taylor & Francis Group, an informa business

Copyright © 2006 Taylor & Francis. All rights reserved.

No part of this book may be reprinted or reproduced or utilised in any form or by any electronic, mechanical, or other means, now known or hereafter invented, including photocopying and recording, or in any informati on storage or retrieval system, without permission in writing from the publishers.

Notices
No responsibility is assumed by the publisher for any injury and/or damage to persons or property as a matter of products liability, negligence or otherwise, or from any use of operation of any methods, products, instructions or ideas contained in the material herein.

Practitioners and researchers must always rely on their own experience and knowledge in evaluating and using any information, methods, compounds, or experiments described herein. In using such information or methods they should be mindful of their own safety and the safety of others, including parties for whom they have a professional responsibility.

Library of Congress Cataloging-in-Publication Data

Religious organizations and democratization: case studies from contemporary Asia / edited by Tun-jen Cheng and Deborah A. Brown.
    p.cm.
  "An East gate book."
  Includes bibliographical references and index.
  ISBN 0-7656-1508-8 (hardcover : alk. paper); ISBN 0-7656-1509-6 (pbk. : alk. paper)
  1. Religion and politics—Asia. 2. Democracy—Religious aspects. 3. Democracy—Asia.
I. Cheng, Tun-jen. II. Brown, Deborah A.

BL1033.R45 2005
322′.1′095—dc22
                                                           2004024679

ISBN 13: 9780765615091 (pbk)
ISBN 13: 9780765615084 (hbk)

In memory of Julia Ching

Contents

Preface		ix
1.	Introduction: The Roles of Religious Organizations in Asian Democratization *Tun-jen Cheng and Deborah A. Brown*	3
2.	The Falun Gong: Religious and Political Implications *Julia Ching*	41
3.	"Buddhism for the Human Realm" and Taiwanese Democracy *André Laliberté*	55
4.	New Karma: Buddhism and Democratization in Thailand *David Ambuel*	83
5.	The Presbyterian Church in the Formation of Taiwan's Democratic Society, 1945–2004 *Murray A. Rubinstein*	109
6.	Christian Churches and Democratization in South Korea *Hyug Baeg Im*	136
7.	The Limits of Conservative Church Reformism in the Democratic Philippines *Coeli M. Barry*	157
8.	Hong Kong's Catholic Church and the Challenge of Democratization in the Special Administrative Region *Deborah A. Brown*	180
9.	Islam and Democratic Transition in Indonesia *Greg Barton*	221

10. Democracy, the "Islamic State," and Embedded Realities in Malaysia
    Patricia Martinez 242
11. The Soka Gakkai's Critical Role in the Rapidly Changing World of Postwar Japanese Politics
    Daniel A. Metraux 267

About the Editors and Contributors 287
Index 293

Preface

This project began as a special issue for the *American Asian Review* in the winter of 2001, when we were intrigued by the resurgence of religious movements in China and the lack of comparative studies on religious organizations in newly democratizing Asia. Touring Williamsburg in 2000, Julia Ching, late eminent scholar of Chinese religion and philosophy, was inspired and promptly responded with pen in an article on the Falun Gong. She enthusiastically marshaled evidence from the public domain as well as from her own eyewitness observations to define the nature of this essentially spiritual movement and to insightfully shed light on its political implications. To provide a comparative framework, we consigned three case studies within the Confucian cultural zones, Deborah A. Brown's study of the Roman Catholic Church in Hong Kong, a region that is struggling to safeguard its limited democracy, Murray A. Rubinstein's study of the Presbyterian Church in newly democratized Taiwan, and André Laliberté's study of Buddhist organizations, also in Taiwan. In addition to these three cases, David Ambuel agreed to contribute an "out-of-region" case centered on Thai Buddhist organizations. All five papers went through normal referee processes. The output was so well received that we were convinced of the need to broaden the scope. Indeed, when we revisited the literature on Asia's democratization, we instantly found a gaping hole, the role of religious organizations in democratic transition and consolidation. We quickly realized that a full-blown study and a comparative volume on this topic were in order.

In addition to asking the existing contributors to revise their essays, we decided to embrace paired comparisons as the main research method and added five more cases: two comparable Muslim cases, Malaysia and Indonesia (by Patricia Martinez and Greg Barton, respectively); the Filipino Roman Catholic Church (by Coeli M. Barry)—a counterpoint to the Hong Kong case; the Korean Christian Churches (by Hyug Baeg Im)—seemingly in parallel to the Taiwanese Presbyterian case; and the

Japanese Soka Gakkai (by Daniel A. Metraux)—arguably a contrast with the Falun Gong.

Our introductory chapter provides theoretical, comparative, and historical perspectives. Aside from circulating it to contributors, the introductory chapter was presented to the International Studies Association's meeting in Budapest in June 2003. At the panel meeting there, we were excited to learn that Gregory Gleason at the University of New Mexico was going to launch a similar study of Central Asian cases, and John Anderson at St. Andrew's University in Scotland was assembling a group of scholars to work on East and Central European cases. We look forward to their publications, which will offer important opportunities for interregional comparison.

It is commonly true that a study such as this in the pages ahead is made possible only through the gracious help of many persons. First and foremost, we are grateful to each of the contributing authors for his or her substantial efforts and timely responsiveness. Collectively, they not only created the substance of this volume but also immensely facilitated its evolution in other ways. Additionally, we are indebted to the College of William and Mary and Seton Hall University for travel and summer research grants that lightened the financial burden of our work. For other help, we owe many thanks to Chuck Brown, who came to our aid whenever technical difficulties arose. Assistance not specified here is no less important. The endnotes of the individual chapters identify many persons who were interviewed or otherwise provided valuable information and analysis, and whose contributions to our group research are vast.

As all authors know, when a book has been completed, it is time for celebration. Yet, a central scholar is missing from our moment of closure. We express profound sorrow that Julia Ching cannot see her labors and those of colleagues come to fruition. With enduring admiration for her friendship and scholarship, we count ourselves and readers fortunate that this volume is graced with her insights. We are in debt to her as a motivator, scholar, and adviser. We dedicate this book to her memory and to her many achievements.

Tun-jen Cheng
Williamsburg, Virginia

Deborah A. Brown
Allendale, New Jersey

June 2005

Religious Organizations and Democratization

1
Introduction
The Roles of Religious Organizations in Asian Democratization

Tun-jen Cheng and Deborah A. Brown

Religious organizations are yet to be fully included in the studies of Asian democratic transition and consolidation. The literature of Asian democratization initially focused on the role of the middle class in democratic fermentation, the interaction between the political opposition and the military or the ruling party, and the relevance of labor and capital to the transformation of the political arena. Scholarly attention subsequently has shifted toward institution building, constitutionalism and electoral rules, and economic conditions that hinder or facilitate democratic consolidation. The newest round of research is particularly directed at how nonreligious social organizations inject new concerns, such as environmental preservation, social welfare, minority rights, and gender equality, into "normal politics."

Little attention has been paid, however, to how religious organizations are affecting democratization in Asian societies. Yet, some religious organizations have played a decisive role in democratic transition, while others have been dormant, and still others have acted in alliances with conservative politicians and business interests to block democratic development. Protestant churches in Korea, the Presbyterian Church in Taiwan, the Catholic Church in the Philippines, some Islamic organizations in Indonesia, and personality-based Buddhist movements (rather than institutional, or *sangha*-oriented, Buddhism) in Thailand were instrumental in activating democratic forces. Further, the Falun Gong—an eclectic movement that blends Buddhist ideas with partly Taoist-inspired practices—has been relentlessly persecuted in China since 1999, precisely because authorities see it in the long shadow of China's democracy movement, which erupts periodically, most recently (but now sixteen years ago) in the 1989 demonstrations at Tiananmen Square.

The Buddhist organizations in Taiwan and Korea, institutional Buddhism (centered on the sangha, or monastic community that is central to Theravada Buddhism) in Thailand, Christian organizations in Hong Kong, and Islamic organizations in Malaysia, in general, have been politically mute.

Some religious organizations that once were active and instrumental to democratic change lost their political vitality and relevance to politics as soon as civil liberty was successfully introduced, elections were regularized, democratic politics were routinized, and separation of church and state had become the norm. The Filipino Catholic Church, the Presbyterian Church in Taiwan, and the Protestant churches in Korea, practically speaking, retreated to their institutional niches, and are barely audible, even regarding areas of their special interest, such as abortion and social welfare. However, other religious organizations—irrespective of their roles in the process of democratic transition—have emerged as key political forces in the civil societies of Asia's newly created democratic environments. Indonesian Islamic organizations, Soka Gakkai in Japan, and a devoted lay Buddhist in Thailand organized political parties and plugged themselves directly into the core of electoral politics and coalition government.

This introductory chapter attempts to explain the variations among the postures of major religious organizations in Asia concerning their political involvement in democratic politics. We seek to uncover the factors that have led some religious organizations to "step into" democratic politics and others to eschew it. In so doing, we selected ten religious organizations or groups for comparison. The case selection was not based on an organization's behavior or decisions, but instead on its importance in each society, and, therefore, on its potential to influence a society's political development. The cases that were selected are Islamic organizations in Indonesia (active) and Malaysia (dormant); Buddhist organizations in Thailand (active), Taiwan (inactive), and Japan (active); one Protestant denomination in Taiwan (active, then dormant), and the Protestant community in Korea (also active, then dormant); the Catholic Church in the Philippines (dormant, then active, then relatively dormant), and Hong Kong (dormant, but now increasingly active); and finally Falun Gong (suppressed) in China.[1] This chapter compares eight cases, and introduces both the Falun Gong and Soka Gakkai, the former as an example of a religious organization that is severely persecuted by an authoritarian regime, and the latter as an illustration of participation by a religious group that has become accepted as part of mainstream politics in an established democracy.

First, we contend that religious doctrines do not predetermine the involvement of a religious organization in the politics of democratic transition. Doctrines may constrain or inspire, but they do not preclude or determine. Most religions are multivoiced; their doctrines could be and have been interpreted in ways that permit, if not encourage, political action for the cause of democracy. Monks can be radicalized, as the case of South Vietnam shows. Some pro-status-quo Catholic dioceses underwent cultural revolution once liberation theology spread, while presumably reformist Protestant organizations sometimes have sided with the authorities against democracy, using separation of church and state as a justification. Further, there are elements in Islamic law and tradition that promote tolerance, pluralism, and cooperation with secular forces, even in the face of today's widespread radical Islam.

We next advance three observations. First, political exclusion versus inclusion prior to democratic transition and the legitimacy formula of the prior regime have strong implications for politicization of religious organizations. A regime may co-opt, suppress, or simply leave alone religious organizations, depending on its legitimacy formula. Different political strategies will have divergent impacts on the capacity and motivation of religious organizations to "go political." For instance, even benign marginalization (deemed an insult) of a religious organization by a regime can prompt its political leaning either toward or away from democracy in the future. While this leaning may not be expressed by overt political action, it exists to subtly sway many members of society who are followers. In other cases, a new and direct threat to a church's ability to wield influence in society, and even to survive, can motivate its leaders to try to effect political conditions that are favorable to the preservation of its previous stature, while there is a perceived brief window of opportunity to do so. Second, while the coalescence between religious organizations and the political opposition is a crucial variable in the process of democratic transition, the political opposition usually initiates the united front, but religious organizations do not necessarily respond. A religious organization can be an important incubator of a political dissident movement. Whether the organization will harbor or even promote the cause of democratic change directly hinges on strategic action (or inaction) between the religious leadership and the political dissidents. Close preexisting ties with an authoritarian regime might constrain religious leaders from responding to the call from prodemocracy political activists for a blessing, support, or even a partnership. Highly motivated, even self-righteous, political opposition is predisposed to try to work through a religious organization when it aspires to mobilize support from civil society for its political reform. Facing this maneuver, religious leaders must make a strategic choice. In deciding how the religious institution or group will position itself, the most prominent determinant seems to be organizational interests, rather than the personal beliefs or preferences of the organization's leader. Third, whether a religious organization participates in "normal" democratic politics depends on whether its leaders are able to justify doing so and are willing to spend their organizational resources for political participation. Doctrine makes it natural for Islamic forces to "stay on" in democratic politics, while Buddhist and Christian forces bear the burden of their continual involvement. Rhetoric aside, rationalization against participation in the political arena is never a barrier to political engagement. Separation of church or temple and state never prevented sustained political activism, as vividly shown by Japan's Soka Gakkai and Western Christian democratic parties. Leaders' preferences and the public's receptivity to a religious organization's participation in public affairs probably have shaped the way that a religious organization redefines and fine-tunes its role once democratic transition has been completed.

Table 1.1 lists the eight religious communities that are considered in paired comparisons in this volume, and identifies their ties to the authoritarian regime prior to democratization. It also classifies the religious organization or group's involvement in the democratization process.

Religious Doctrines

Religious doctrines do not explain the variations among the calculations of religious organizations about whether to directly engage themselves in politics.

Buddhism

Buddhists are popularly perceived as introspective, meditative, and inclined to shun worldly affairs. The scripture has much to say about society, but little commentary about political institutions. The traditionally common distinction between worldly pursuits and spiritual seeking, albeit

Table 1.1

Religious Communities and Political Involvement

Community	Percent of population	Ties to authority	Involvement in democratization
Thai Buddhists	99	Included	Noninstitutional organizations, very vocal/active
Taiwan Buddhists	34	Excluded	Mute throughout
Taiwan Presbyterians	Under 5	Suppressed	Voiced in transition; mute subsequently
Korean Protestants	25	Suppressed	Voiced in transition; mute subsequently
Hong Kong Catholics	About 5.2	Excluded*	Mute, then voiced
Filipino Catholics	97	Included	Mute, then voiced
Indonesian Muslims	90	Included	Mute, then participatory
Malaysian Muslims	60	Excluded, then included	Voiced

Source: Compiled by authors.

*Many churches, including the Catholic Church, had contractual arrangements with the British Hong Kong government to provide education, health, and social welfare services. However, none of these churches was a political partner.

often rejected by Buddhist scholars, is akin to the divide between Caesar and God. Buddhist writings display a fundamentally individualistic orientation. This does not mean that Buddhist dharma does not encourage people to care about society, but rather that attainment of enlightenment is essentially an individual undertaking.[2] If one is in the Theravada branch of Buddhism, achieving enlightenment is decidedly a self-help effort. However, while a Mahayana Buddhist must strive on his or her own to achieve enlightenment, the believer understands that one's own salvation is tied to the fate of others. Consequently, a devout Mahayana Buddhist seeks to do good for others without wishing for something in return.

Therefore, Buddhist leaders and followers can be very engaged in social and political issues and crises, despite the contemplative nature of Buddhism. One ordained Buddhist leader, the fourteenth Dalai Lama of Tibet, and one lay devout Buddhist leader, Aung San Suu Kyi of Myanmar, were Nobel laureates (in 1989 and 1991, respectively) for their nonviolent efforts to motivate others toward supporting peace and social justice. Yet, sometimes extreme actions have been taken by engaged Buddhists, including self-immolation and street protests by South Vietnam's monks against both sides of the 1960s and 1970s belligerence, or in the case of India, direct action and participation in a liberation movement among India's untouchables (who include Buddhists), who were guided by Dr. B.R. Ambedkar,[3] himself an untouchable. Still, other Buddhists have engaged in less dramatic activities, such as social service and participation in village rejuvenation by Sri Lankan monks. Engaged Buddhism usually begins with the emergence of a high-profile, charismatic leader with privileged education, who often straddles East and West and reads old dharma in a new way. Thus, he or she provides a charter for change and a model for emulation, becoming a symbol of a new order and triggering dauntless activism, while being honored as a saint or bodhisattva.[4] The founders of such worldly asceticism have provided a foundation for political and social action. This is quite a departure from Siddhartha Gautama (c. 563–483 B.C.E.), the historical Buddha, who advocated that each person should live a rationed life to help cultivate individual enlightenment, not social reform (although he opposed entrenched Brahmin traditions and India's caste system). He advised that an individual must work out his or her own salvation with diligence. In contemporary society, however, the road to individual enlightenment can merge with the one that is traveled by political activists to achieve democracy. As the current Dalai Lama has written,

> I do not find alien the concept and practice of democracy. At the heart of Buddhism lies the idea that the potential for awakening and perfection is present in every human being and that realizing this potential is a matter of personal effort. The Buddha proclaimed that each individual is a master of his or her own destiny . . . not only are Buddhism and democracy compatible, they are rooted in a common understanding of the equality and potential of every individual. . . . In theory at least, even the teachings of the Buddha can be altered under certain circumstances by a congregation of a certain number of ordained monks.[5]

Thus, many Buddhists share values with other democrats and are straightforward friends of democracy.

Islam

Doctrinaire-wise, political Islam seems to be the mirror image of otherworldly Buddhism. Islamic organizations are said to be innately political, while the presumed fusion of politics and religion under Islam and the supposed intolerance toward non-Islamic believers are often regarded as inimical to the making of democracy. On Islam, Samuel P. Huntington writes that "no distinction exists between religion and politics or between the spiritual and the secular, and political participation was historically an alien concept."[6] Larry Diamond also points to a doctrinal mismatch between Islam and democracy.[7] However, doctrinaire political Islam does not help us to differentiate an Islamic organization that dances with an authoritarian regime from one that opposes it. Moreover, the alleged doctrinaire restriction on democracy under Islam probably is overstated. Like other great religions, Islam is multivoiced. "Although Islamic fundamentalists are attempting to appropriate political Islam, there are also other voices . . . in the Koran, in scholarly interpretations of the Koran, and among some major contemporary Islamic political leaders."[8] Take, for example, the call for a "Protestant Reformation" within Islam coming from some quarters within Iran. One fallacy is to regard a religion as static, reading too much into "unique founding conditions."[9] As Bernard Lewis writes, there are democratic concepts that are alien to Islam, but there are elements in Islamic law and tradition, emphasizing contractual and consensual features, that are conducive to the development of democracy.[10] Eickelman and Piscatori put it most bluntly: the union of politics and religion under Islam is overstated, while religious politics elsewhere is overlooked.[11] Majid Tehranian points out, while Islamic doctrines envisioned the unity of religion and state, periods of unity later gave way to periods of separation, and, in the contemporary world, the relationship between the two takes many forms, from their convergence, to their coexistence, to suppression of mosques by the state.[12]

Certainly, Islam itself embraces significant political dimensions. Like all of the great wisdom traditions, Islam has had its schisms. The most important historical division centered on the debate over the proper successor to Muhammad. Sunni Muslims, constituting some 80–85 percent of the world's Muslims, are the mainstream of the faith. Thus, Sunni Islam often is regarded as orthodox Islam, although within Islam, there is no central, doctrinal authority to establish this.[13] Sunnis are followers of the *sunna*, or the "way" of the Prophet. This branch of Islam might be considered more "democratic" than Shia or Shiite Islam, which is the largest minority faction among Muslims. This is so because, historically, Sunnis have believed that the leadership of the community should be bestowed on an individual by means of community consensus. Most Muslims in the Middle East (e.g., Egypt, Palestine, and Syria), Africa, the Indian subcontinent, Pakistan, Bangladesh, Indonesia, and Malaysia are Sunni.

In contrast, Shiites are dominant in Iran, where Shiism became paramount by decree in the sixteenth century. About a third of Lebanon's population, half of Iraq's, and one-sixth of Pakistan's are Shiites. Shiites also are found in significant numbers in the Eastern Province of Saudi Arabia,[14] and small populations of them are in India, Syria, Yemen, and elsewhere.[15]

Shiites are set apart from Sunnis by several consequential factors. One is their comparatively undemocratic approach to selecting leadership. Shiites are followers of Ali, a resolute warrior, who was Muhammad's cousin and son-in-law, and whom Shiites claim was designated by Muhammad to be his successor. Rejecting the concept of leadership selection by community consensus, Shiites assert that leadership is correctly derived only from relationship to Muhammad, who was divinely appointed. Thus, they regard the successors to Muhammad before Ali as usurpers and adhere to the belief that authority can rest only with Ali and his descendants in the Hashemite line, who are Allah's receiving stations of temporal and spiritual authority. After having been passed over three times, Ali finally was appointed leader of the community upon the assassination of the third caliph in 655 C.E., only to be assassinated himself in 661 C.E. Shiites maintain that Ali is the vanished Imam, who nevertheless remains alive. He continues his rule through earthly representatives. The Imamate, then, distinguishes Shiites from Sunnis, who contend that divine law bestows on the community the right to establish leadership authority through consensus. Fazlur Rahman observes that, to Shiites, the Imam is,

> both sinless and absolutely infallible in his supposed pronouncements on the dogma and indeed in all matters. In fact whereas in classical and medieval Sunni Islam the office of the caliph is recognized as only a practical necessity, belief in the Imam and submission to him is, according to the Shia, the third cardinal article of faith, after a belief in God and his apostle.[16]

Thus, Shiites view the Imam as an infallible guide to human affairs, who acts as an intermediary between God and Muslims. Leadership of the community is regarded as a divine right through descendance from Ali, his wife Fatimah (Muhammad's daughter), and their sons Hasan and Husayn (Hussein). Husayn was beheaded after being defeated in 680 C.E. by Umayyad forces at the battle of Karbala, in present-day Iraq, and is regarded by Shiites "as a martyr whose heroic death is a redeeming sacrifice that invites imitation."[17]

Today, no living person is held by Shiites as the rightful successor of the line stemming from Ali. The Twelvers,[18] who are dominant in Iran, recognize Muhammad al Muntazar as the twelfth and last legitimate successor, who mysteriously disappeared through a process of occultation sometime between 872 C.E. and 878 C.E. He is thought to continue to live in a supernatural state that allows him to communicate with believers, and his return is awaited as the *Mahdi*, or messianic figure, who will preside over a perfected society.[19]

Thomas W. Lippman speculates that there is a linkage between the violent deaths of Ali and his son Hussein and the proclivity of Shiites for martyrdom in the cause of Allah. They fight, he says, "to establish the primacy of Islam and they believe that death in the cause . . . [earns] them a place in Paradise and the veneration of their companions."[20] Shiism, then, is said by some to be distinguished from Sunni Islam by "'the centrality of the passion motive.'"[21] Lippman further observes that Shiism encourages emotion, which must find outlets, and does so in a variety of ways, ranging from pilgrimages to tombs of Shiite saints, to self-flagellation, to revolution, as in the case of Iran.[22]

In Sunni society, all believers are viewed as equals in the sight of God. Among Shiites, however, certain individuals are raised above others as servants to the Imam. This privileged group enjoys an elevated status, as in Iran. Independent of the government, their power has outpaced that held by other Muslim leaders, such as those in Malaysian states, where religious figures are dependent on the government for their appointments and compensation.

Christianity

The history of reformation suggests a dichotomy between, on the one hand, the challenges to the status quo and the participatory and egalitarian approach to religion and society of the Protestant Church, and, on the other hand, the more hierarchical and authoritarian Catholic Church, which traditionally has been inclined toward preservation of the status quo. Huntington was quick to observe that democracy first occurred in Protestant societies, and later spread to Catholic countries.[23]

Is Christianity inclined toward democratic beliefs? Despite Jesus' determined engagement in society, his desire for a new social order, and his tenacious teachings about kind and just treatment of others, some scholars have asserted that Jesus, in fact, was weak when it came to democratic-minded social activism.[24] Paul's emphasis, they note, was less on the historical Jesus and more on the cosmic Christ, whose self-sacrifice made possible a reunion between God and sinful humankind. Perhaps imposing a modern understanding on an ancient time, these critics are perplexed that Jesus did not champion nineteenth- and twentieth-century causes, such as the abolition of slavery and the eradication of systemic oppression of women. Yet, others see in the teachings of Jesus democratic tenets that call for justice in the social order and freedom and rights for all individuals who are held as equals in the eyes of God. There is debate, then, whether Jesus was a dedicated proponent of democratically leaning systemic practices in society.

Regardless, few argue that the Christian Church itself retained its initial democratic character. Indeed, by the fifth century, Pope Leo I asserted that all popes were apostolic successors to Peter, to whom Jesus had given the keys to the kingdom of heaven. This led the emperor to pass an edict that all Christians must submit to the pope's authority. By the eleventh century, Pope Gregory VII had declared that every pope was divinely appointed. The pope could not be ruled by any human, moreover, he could depose kings and emperors. Not surprisingly, the matters of legitimate authority and broader democratic practices had become the central focus of the first major schism within Christendom in 1054 C.E. The church in the more democratic Byzantine East refused to recognize the pope's claim to universal authority over all Christians and championed historical considerations and the rights of individual churches. While the rigidly legalistic and hierarchical Roman Catholic Church stressed that dogma came from the pope, in the Eastern Church, a more democratic leaning would lead to God's truth being disclosed by means of consensus among officials of independent churches who gathered in ecclesiastical councils to speak as equals.

The sixteenth-century Protestant Reformation was the second major schism among Christians. Fed up with corruption and abuses of power among his Catholic ecclesiastical brethren, Martin Luther nailed his ninety-five theses on indulgences to the church door at Wittenburg in 1517, beginning a major reform movement. Beyond the sale of indulgences, relics, and masses for the dead to earn spiritual merit, other factors, including the rise of nationalism, business, and new ethical and moral interests among Europe's emerging bourgeoisie prompted Protestants to deemphasize the role of the clergy and, instead, to stress the individual believer's immediate communion with God. What had been categorical in the Roman Catholic Church now was open to scrutiny. "Armed with the spiritual battle cry *sola scriptura!* (scripture alone),"[25] Protestants turned away from the authority of the pope, and thus began their inward struggle to see whether they could hear God's will correctly. In many cases, Protestants heard God's call for freedom and justice and other democratic aims. Nevertheless, while Protestants justifiably have earned a reputation for their democratic spirit, ironically, in some places, Protestant leaders and churches have been charged with being in an "unholy alliance"[26] with conservative businesspersons and politicians to try to prevent democratization, and where modest democratic advances have been made, to try to eliminate them.

Most observers would agree that, historically, Protestant churches have had greater democratic leanings than the Roman Catholic Church and that this Protestant persuasion would not begin to be matched by Catholics until the Second Vatican Council of 1961–1965, which offered the first major reforms in the Catholic Church since the Council of Trent between 1545 and 1563. Not until then would the groundswell for personal discernment that so marked the Protestant Reformation begin to affect Catholics.

New debates over traditional Catholic practices paved the way for the growth of liberation theology, which had begun in South America in the 1950s. Here, some clergy and other Catholics realigned themselves with the poor, and against landowners and powerful politicians, the very secular power bases with whom, historically, Catholic leaders had been friends. Indeed, the rise of liberation theology in Catholic countries is said to have been instrumental to democratic transition in Latin American countries. "The liberation theology movement attacked injustice, inequality, oppression, and corruption by formulating a Christian message that emphasized the need to organize politically at the lower reaches of society."[27]

However, the inclination of Latin American liberation theologians to broadly identify with the poor was not the disposition of other Christians, for instance, the Catholics and Protestants in the Philippines and Hong Kong. As in the Philippines under Marcos, Christian mainline churches in Hong Kong under British rule were reticent to act as counterwitnesses in society against the government. This was so in Hong Kong because churches were heavily dependent on government subvention for their educational and social service programs. For example, some 40 percent of Hong Kong's primary schools and 56 percent of its secondary schools even today are affiliated with religious organizations, chiefly Christian.[28] For these and similar circumstances in the field of social service, Hong Kong's Christian churches almost instinctively have sought to avoid any conflict with officials that could pit them in a power struggle with the coercive authority of the government. Likewise, although the Catholic Church in the Philippines held an influential position in society, it was not in its interest to oppose the Marcos authoritarian regime. There is no sustained history of social activism among Hong Kong's or the Philippine's Christian churches. Rather, historically, they have found it judicious to be cozy with governmental authority, and to help to preserve the status quo of which they have been a part.

Yet, a certain amount of adaptability is essential to survivability, and, therefore, church leadership allows for flexibility when applying principles to practice. For instance, although Pope John Paul II sided with the poor and downtrodden during his papacy, he undercut the liberation theology movement, which threatened the church and its political establishment. His East European background and personal experience with communism made him wary of the Marxist bent of the movement.[29] Nevertheless, while alert to a dangerous drift away from the established order, the Vatican managed to co-opt the issues that the movement brought forward, and promoted many of its recommended reforms to protect the Holy See's authority. The Vatican did not yield, however, on the maintenance of its centralized authority, nor did it concede on issues of its concern (e.g., "birth control, homosexuality, a celibate and male priesthood, women's rights, and abortion").[30]

Regimes, Religious Organizations, and Political Opposition

The first key factor accounting for variation among religious organizations' involvement in the making and consolidation of democracy is their ties to preexisting regimes. An authoritarian regime can include (co-opt) religious organizations in its ruling coalition, subsidize them, regulate them, and make them its "political partners." Alternatively, the regime can leave religious organizations alone (exclusion), or suppress them. Largely molded during the founding period of a regime, the relationship between the regime and religious organizations is conditioned extensively by a regime's effort to legitimize its rule. The legitimacy formula, in turn, is related to the nature of the regime and the social demography. Other matters being equal, a monarchy (e.g., Saudi Arabia) in the contemporary world needs religious legitimization of its political power more than a military regime (e.g., Suharto's Indonesia), which, in turn, is on shakier ground than a regime that is rooted in a political party (e.g., Mahathir's Malaysia). An authoritarian regime also tends to co-opt or suppress, but not to leave alone, religious leaders if a society is highly homogenous in its religious belief (e.g., Indonesia, Thailand, and the Philippines). Conversely, in a multireligion society, there is less imperative for an authoritarian regime to pursue political inclusion. In this case, the regime is more inclined to suppress specific groups that pose a threat to its authoritarian control.

A regime's political strategy can crush the capacity of a religious organization to hold sway in society, or heighten it so that a religious body assumes perhaps more influence in and respect from the public sphere than its leaders on their own otherwise might be able to command. Falun Gong is not permitted to organize in China, nor is it officially recognized as a spiritual movement. Its members are rooted out by governmental authorities and severely punished, imprisoned, and ill-treated by additional means.[31] In a smaller way, some Christian organizations in South Korea and Taiwan were suspected of inciting political opposition and their leaders were persecuted. In sharp contrast, Buddhist organizations in Thailand and Islamic organizations in Malaysia and Indonesia almost acquire the status of state religions. The regimes acknowledge a special standing for these organizations, aware that their favoring of them bolsters their own governing legitimacy in the public domain. That a religious organization chooses to be a cooperative friend of the government is a choice that the religious leadership must make. Yet, a symbiotic relationship with the governing power tends to diminish the religious group's capacity to speak against the government when the desire or need to do so arises.

Another key factor shaping a religious organization's choice in the political arena is its ties to the political opposition. Ellen Lust-Okar has convincingly shown that the absence of a coalition between Muslims and the political opposition is the single most important reason for the lack of democratic transition in the Middle East and North African (MENA) countries. The regime, be it military, monarchical, or a personal dictatorship, has been able to make use of the Iranian case to instill in society a pervasive fear of a totalitarian, theocratic state if radicalized Islamic forces are allowed to dominate political space. The secular political opposition, with either a liberal democratic or leftist leaning, hence, is deterred from striking a tactical alliance with the Islamic force.[32] This fear factor is much less intense in our two Muslim cases, where Islam either is less fundamentalist (thanks to its amalgamation with indigenous folk belief systems in Indonesia), or not as predominant (the case of multiethnic and multireligion Malaysia).[33] In other cases, the fear is not whether the religious force would overwhelm and digest the political opposition after jointly dislodging the authoritarian regime. Rather, the political opposition is more concerned with political inaction of religious forces.

In most instances, it is political opposition that expects, if not prods, religious organizations to rise up against an authoritarian regime. As political opposition pushes for democratic change, it must decide whether to bypass or march through religious organizations. For their part, religious leaders must make their own calculations as to whether and when to act, and which side to support, especially when it comes to a critical democratic moment in a nation's history. Will a religious leader be apolitical, rendering to Caesar what is Caesar's and to God what is God's, or will he follow the path of deliberate confrontation with the government, as in the case of Latin American liberation theologians? The decision may be vital to a religious organization's survival. Some religious organizations side with the underdog early on. Others may want to work from within the existing regime, a more conservative approach. Yet, a church or other religious organization can tip the balance toward democracy if it or its members choose to become engaged in the promotion of human rights, freedoms, and civil liberties. It can choose to be a counterwitness in society against the government or its individual policies. Conversely, as noted above, a religious organization may have vested interests in protecting the status quo, and thus side with the regime to resist change.

Finally, how a religion defines (or redefines) its role in civil society is a question with which a religious organization must deal after normal democratic politics is established. Separation of church or temple and state is not a difficult issue when the state is in the wrong hands. When an authoritarian regime abuses its power, and when freedom and justice are lacking, "going political" to help to bring about democratic transition may well be the call of religious duty. However, as soon as liberal democracy is installed, the matter of separation of the spiritual from the mundane quickly returns. If a religious organization that has directly partaken in democratic transition does not confront this issue itself, its political adversary certainly will raise it.

Here, Islamic organizations have a less onerous task than their Buddhist and Christian counterparts in justifying their presence in normal politics, thanks to their scripture. However, as we assiduously contend, religious doctrines may constrain or inspire, but do not determine or preclude. Noninstitutional Buddhist groups in Thailand did follow the Japanese Soka Gakkai in sponsoring a political party, which no longer exists but whose spirit lives on under a new party configuration. And, no one can rule out the formation of other Buddhist parties in the future. Elsewhere, Christian organizations, Catholic and Protestant alike—most notably in continental Europe—have at least tacitly endorsed, if not organized, Christian democratic parties. None of our cases has opted for this journey. Indeed, the Christian organizations in South Korea and Taiwan are not even active in the legislative process regarding matters of their concern, interest, and expertise, such as family planning, abortion, welfare, and education. It is likely that, once democracy is installed, the default position for Buddhist and Christian organizations is to abstain from politics, especially when there are whistle-blowers against religion in political domains. If a religious organization chooses to "stay on" rather than to abdicate from politics, its leaders will have to redefine the organization's role from one of incubator of democracy to one of representative in the political market. Regarding this choice, we submit, public attitude carries much weight. We do not have hard data to substantiate this, but circumstantial evidence shows that preference and stance of religious leaders on the linkage between religion and politics are quite conditioned, if not completely swayed, by the public's receptivity to them.

Paired Comparisons

Buddhist Organizations in Thailand and Taiwan: A Vivid Contrast

The Thai authoritarian regime exercised control over the sangha of institutional Buddhism, for it was "a system of legitimating practices and discourses."[34] Akin to the meritocratic civil service examinations of China's imperial past, the Thai priesthood is an examination-based hierarchy that is administered and financed by the state. Political authority obviously pursued a strategy of inclusion and control, initially for nation building and integration, and subsequently for further development.[35] In Thailand, where some 90 percent of the people are Buddhist, a family believes it earns spiritual merit if a son becomes a monk. Unlike Mahayana Buddhists, Theravada Buddhists believe that reaching nirvana comes by means of meditation and self-help in a setting (the sangha) of detached, unworldly living. Spiritual attainment is most likely for the monks and nuns and the perfected disciple, or *arhat*, one who has moved alone toward nirvana. This is why it is particularly ironic that, since Thailand's adoption of Theravada Buddhism in the fourteenth century, the sangha has tied itself to wealth and secular power.

However, domestication of a religious organization has its hazards. Thailand's remarkable economic development in the 1980s gradually became the raison d'être for authoritarian rule. One consequence of political inclusion is that institutional Buddhism could not easily dissociate itself from political authority (barring the regime's collapse) and side with democracy activists. The co-opted clergy had neither the capacity nor the propensity to endorse or join Thailand's democracy movement.

In the 1990s, state control lessened, permitting the rise of religious movements—often personality-based, disconnected from the sangha, and diversified—that catered to the needs of different social groups. Having deviated from institutional Buddhism, charismatic clergy, such as Buddhadasa Bhikkhu and Sulak Sivaraksa, used universal language, and addressed human suffering and compassion to achieve spiritual liberation. Buddhadasa founded the temple-retreat-training conference center of Suan Mokkh in Chaiya, Thailand. Based on this foundation, lay Buddhists began to engage followers in democratic politics. As individual, non–sangha-connected Buddhist groups gained stature, Buddhism ceased to be a tool to bolster the legitimacy of authoritarian rule, and, instead, became relevant to the democratic process. For one thing, endorsement of a charismatic monk with democratic leanings is an effective campaign strategy. For another, Buddhism could legitimize societal criticism of the government, the centralist state bureaucracy, and the expanding influence of the capital.[36]

Democratization in Thailand proceeded intermittently, with students and urbanites taking the leading role. However, in "purifying" politics (corruption having been a key factor and justification for military intervention), non–sangha-affiliated Buddhist organizations have been instrumental. Chamlong Srimuang, an ascetic ex-general and a devout Buddhist who is closely associated with the Santi Asoke Sect, launched a Buddhist party, the Palang Dharma Party (Moral Force, or PDP), to champion the cause of clean politics. In the 1980s, he introduced a new type of politics to Thailand, and in the early 1990s, he and his party were a major political force. Indeed, "Chamlong fever" and Buddhist criticism of the establishment provided a significant impetus for arguably the most important constitutional amendment during the protracted process of democratization in Thailand.[37] Although the most decisive factor for the 1998 constitutional change was the 1997 Asian financial crisis, which began in Thailand, the Buddhist social mobilization against Thailand's corrupt politicians provided a major thrust for political transition.

Yet, clerical political activism may not be sustainable, as it is widely perceived as tainting spiritual authority and transgressing the proper role of a Buddhist ascetic.[38] Buddhist social criticism centers primarily on issues such as consumerism and materialism, and does so in a nostalgic way, while rarely embracing a political reform agenda.[39] Thus, Buddhist political activism served the purpose of promoting democratization only at a critical juncture, like a flash in a pan. Chamlong's political career illustrates this. He organized a party and took to the streets to restore democracy in Thailand and he continued to preach clean politics. But his party did not do well by the mid-1990s election; he ran as Palang Dharma's candidate in the June 1996 elections for the governorship of Bangkok, but was defeated.

Thailand is widely marked by a Buddhist ethos that has permeated the society and polity. On the streets, Thais try to earn spiritual merit by giving money to the needy and by offering food and other necessities to monks. Moderation, harmony, rectitude, modesty, charity, and many other virtues are held in high regard, but because the principal focus is on the religion, Thai Buddhism itself does not provide a code of conduct for specific political activities.[40] The political role played by Thai Buddhists was more as facilitators of political transition than as a steady prodemocracy phenomenon within the state. Nonetheless, it remains noteworthy that Thai Buddhism, even though it was tightly controlled, played an instrumental role in Thailand's democratic transition. Of continuing significance is that its "purifying" influence on democratic politics may continue to linger.

Different from the case of Thailand, political inclusion of Buddhist organizations was more apparent than real in Taiwan. The state-sponsored, -supported, and -controlled Chinese Buddhist Association (CBA), which was relocated from the mainland to the island and officially was the only legitimate Buddhist association, was in principle used by the Kuomintang (KMT) government to prevent the formation of any rival religious group. Nevertheless, the CBA was quickly surpassed by two vibrant grass-roots Buddhist organizations, which were tolerated, but not dominated by the state. The KMT's historical task of retaking the mainland from the communists, the associated national emergency, and later on, Taiwan's economic development and local elections, were used to legitimize the KMT's political power. Reliance on religious institutions was not necessary. Although the bulk of society practices Taoism and Buddhism, the people of Taiwan are not typically characterized as ardently religious. Identification with Buddhism and "supporting" the clergy, therefore, were not crucial to maintaining political legitimacy and popular acquiescence to the KMT regime in Taiwan as they were to the authoritarian rulers in Thailand, a devoted and almost exclusively Buddhist polity.

For their parts, the two new Buddhist organizations claimed to be apolitical. Hence, they were left alone by the KMT to grow, and unhindered, became very large. With Taiwan's democratic transition in the 1980s and 1990s, the two organizations suddenly found themselves in a position to play politics and, indeed, were courted by political parties and aspiring as well as entrenched politicians. Members of the Fuoguanshan Buddhist organization were in demand and their leader, Master Hsing-yun, was said to be supportive of an insurgent KMT candidate during the 1996 presidential election. However, by and large, this organization has remained nonpolitical. The other organization, the Buddhist Compassionate Relief Tzu-Chi Foundation, under the leadership of Dharma Master Cheng Yen, has been explicitly neutral politically.[41] It should be noted that both organizations, especially Tzu-Chi, are extremely well endowed and generously supported by highly educated members of the middle class and numerous successful business owners. For over thirty years, the Tzu-Chi Foundation has focused its energies on charity, education, culture, international relief, and medicine, including bone marrow donation,[42] earning admiration internationally for its charitable and disaster relief work. Master Cheng Yen received the "Asian Nobel Prize," the Philippine Magsaysay Award, in 1991. Tzu-Chi, centered in Hualien, undoubtedly is the most respected nongovernmental organization based in Taiwan. Neither the Fuoguanshan nor the Tzu-Chi organization is dependent on the government's fiscal support for its active social welfare activities.

If democratization upset the equilibrium of state-clergy interdependence in Thailand, the delicate balance and mutual noninterference between the state and leading Buddhist organizations have been well maintained in Taiwan. Political inaction has marked the relationship between the government and Buddhist groups. The KMT authoritarian regime followed a policy of benign neglect toward the surge of new Buddhist organizations, and they, in turn, abstained from siding with the emerging prodemocracy political opposition. Political élites in the newly democratized polity did not attempt to blatantly mobilize Buddhist support for electoral gains, nor did they organize a Buddhist party or a Buddhist wing under any existing party. While Buddhist leaders give audiences to all political leaders who care to pay courtesy visits, they never counsel their devoted followers to act in a particular way in any political arena, election poll, legislative hearing, or bureaucratic corridor.

Protestants in Korea and Taiwan: Catalysts for Change

In Korea, Christianity won ideological legitimacy, while official Confucianism lost it as the Yi dynasty crumbled from the late nineteenth century forward under the weight of Japanese pressure. During Japan's brutal colonization of Korea from 1910 to 1945, Christians sided with the oppressed Koreans. Unlike other nations in the region, Korea had a strong nationalist movement against Japanese colonialism, and Christianity was a vehicle for it. Thus, Christianity rapidly won support because it was perceived not only as a "modernizing" factor, but also as a "liberating" force.[43] Indeed, the rise of Christianity went hand in hand with the rise of nationalism in Korea, a country that politically has been sandwiched between China and Japan for centuries.[44] The civil war caused most Christians in North Korea to move to the South, and the prolonged wartime misery as well as political suppression by military regimes also helped to expand South Korea's Christian population. About 25 percent of South Koreans are Christians (compared to 5 percent in Taiwan and less than one percent in Japan), making South Korea more Christian (predominantly Protestant) than other peoples in East Asia. (In Southeast Asia, the Philippines is a notable exception for its Christian majority.)

However, a number of Protestant churches in Korea have had to weather suppression by military authoritarian regimes, even when the ruler happened to be Christian. The founder of South Korea's authoritarian regime, Brigadier General Park Chunghee, considered himself a pious Buddhist. During his rule (1961–1979), Park renovated Buddhist temples; however, he also managed to control Buddhist organizations, and forced declarations of allegiance from believers, drafted monks into the military services, and disciplined dissenting monks.[45] Probably due to South Korea's dependence on security support from the United States and to the strongly conservative (viz., anticommunist) bent of most South Korean Christians, the regime did not attempt to manipulate the churches as it did the Buddhist temples. Using South Korea's miraculous economic performance, the long arms of intelligence apparatus, and the cause of national security to legitimize its rule, the regime made no effort to construct any corporatist structure for political support.[46] However, the regime did not hesitate to suppress any church. Many ministers were imprisoned for their antigovernment and antiauthoritarian stance.[47] The two most well-known opposition leaders, Kim Young Sam and Kim Daejung—who both eventually became Korean presidents after the country's democratic transition—were Christians. After 1979, the new president, Chun Doohwan, himself a Presbyterian, perceived Buddhism to be backward and conservative, and, consequently, undermined and restrained Buddhist activities.[48] Also, and ironically, leaders and followers of Protestant churches were arrested even more frequently under Chun than under Park, for the dissident students had begun to forge a united front with labor and young churchgoers in support of the political opposition movement. Exiled opposition leaders in the United States also had the effect of drawing a significant number of overseas Koreans—75 percent of them Christian—into the democratic camp. While detailed studies are yet to be done, it is plausible to contend that Protestant churches contributed to the making of Korean democracy. Churches in Seoul, Kwangju, and overseas Korean communities were especially important incubators of prodemocracy activists (as important as higher education and freshman orientation camps[49]).

However, it is interesting to note that, following Korea's democratic transition, Christian organizations themselves have not been involved in Korea's electoral process, albeit some religious leaders and Christian activists participate extensively in the electoral arena through nongovernmental organizations or on an individual basis. While Roh Taewoo (president, 1988–1993) was from a Buddhist family and assiduously promoted Buddhism and encouraged Buddhist organizations to engage in social activities, his two immediate successors, presidents Kim Young Sam (1993–1998) and Kim Daejung (1998–2003), were both Christians, and, indeed, were beneficiaries of Christian churches that daringly harbored political dissidents. The Christian churches have been very active in some matters concerning governmental policies, for example, they organized a massive political rally in support of the United States on March 1, 2003, and they have been involved in policy making in areas such as social welfare. However, they have ceased to be a significant political force in day-to-day mainstream politics since South Korea's transition to democracy.

The trajectory of the churches' involvement in Taiwan's democratization has been quite similar to that in South Korea. While the supreme leader of the KMT regime, Chiang Kai-shek, belonged to the Methodist Church, there was no incentive or imperative for the regime to embrace the Christian community for the purpose of building political legitimacy. As mentioned above, only some 5 percent of Taiwan's residents are Christian, and the regime used historical projects (retaking the Chinese mainland and modernizing the national economy), rather than the blessing of religious organizations, to justify its monopoly of political power. Retreating to Taiwan after losing the mainland, the KMT regime did manage to install a corporatist structure to mobilize public support for the military project of retaking power from China's communists and the political project of running local elections. However, while the regime extended its reach into many corners of society, the churches were left alone, thanks to their international connections and financial independence.

Yet, one denomination, the Presbyterian Church, was quickly suppressed as soon as it began to side with the prodemocracy opposition movement. The church's southern chapter consisted predominantly of Minnan people (who represented some three-quarters of the local population). These people's ancestors had come from southern Fujian and succeeding generations had lived in Taiwan for centuries. Beginning in the 1970s, the Presbyterian Church had become a significant source for prodemocracy activists. Leaders of this church were among the pioneer advocates of the principle of self-determination, under which the residents of Taiwan would have the final say about their own future and their relations with mainland China—options that the authoritarian KMT regime and the communist regime in the People's Republic of China (PRC) opposed.[50] To the Presbyterian Church, advocacy for self-determination (subsequently, advocacy for an independent Taiwan that is delinked from mainland China) and the push for democratization were two sides of the same coin.[51] While not the core of Taiwan's democratic activists, church leaders and many of their followers threw their support to the democracy movement, helping to propagate the dissidents' views, promoting human rights, endorsing protests, and even providing cover for opposition leaders whom the regime was hotly pursuing. Obviously, most of the opposition's activities were not routed through the church, and most of Taiwan's democratic activists were not churchgoers. However, the church unconditionally acted on behalf of, not at the behest of, the democratic opposition, as if the church were its political ancillary unit.

The conflation of the pursuit of Taiwan democratization and independence was even more evident in the Presbyterian Church that served the overseas Taiwanese community in the United States. Community leaders and church leaders often were intermeshed; their organizations existed side-by-side, if they were not fused, and their political stands were compatible, if not identical. The political overtones of the overseas Taiwanese Presbyterian Church were unmistakably in favor of liberalization, democratic change, and the independence of Taiwan. The nexus of overseas Taiwanese associations and Taiwanese community churches, as well as the overseas Taiwanese students, whom, in part, these two sectors served, provided political dissidents inside Taiwan with financial support and links to persons within the international community who were willing to hear their case.[52] Beyond the reach of the KMT regime, overseas networks were extremely instrumental to the recovery and revitalization of the democratic movement inside Taiwan that had to endure periodic suppression from the authoritarian regime.

As Taiwan's democracy became more and more consolidated in the second half of the 1990s, and especially after the pro-independence Democratic Progressive Party (DPP) successfully dislodged the KMT from power in March 2000, the political activism of the Presbyterian Church in Taiwan quickly tapered off. This church seems to have largely withdrawn from the political arena in which it was involved for decades. It participates little in the discourse on welfare, education, language, and other policy areas where it has either a stake or strong preference. While democracy has been adopted, the pursuit of an independent Taiwan not associated with mainland China—a goal that the Presbyterian Church leadership so vehemently promoted—has become more treacherous following the DPP's ascent to power. This is a result of China's greater fear of Taiwan's drift toward independence than when the KMT, which consistently advocated eventual cross-Strait unification, governed. Ongoing activism by the Presbyterian Church would invite potentially crippling criticism from political adversaries, who most likely would cite the principle of separation of church and state as the reason that the church should retreat from the political arena. It is ironic that the Presbyterian Church, formerly in the vanguard of democratization, has had to undergo greater role contraction in public affairs than other religious organizations in the region.

The Roman Catholic Church in the Philippines and Hong Kong: Belated Assertion

Homogeneous religious belief in the Philippines induced the Marcos regime to include the Catholic clergy in its strategy to legitimize its political power. Nearly everyone is a Catholic in the Philippines. Consequently, the blessing of the Catholic Church is crucial to any leader who has abused or lacked a popular mandate. Ferdinand Marcos, an authoritarian ruler, forced the church to be involved in politics. Initially, the church in the Philippines stood in the way of democracy, but due to public pressure (especially from the church's broad constituency), it had to change its stance and side with democratization. Infused with liberation theology in the 1960s, the grass-roots priests of the church underwent a role change by expanding their concerns from salvation to social injustice, and, unlike the military, became the critics and opponents of the authoritarian Marcos regime. The church's top leadership, however, continued to dance with the regime and was seemingly more concerned with the violence in peasant society than with the causes of the tumult.[53]

Although the political opposition was not well-organized, human rights lawyers and some unionists, intellectuals, and reformists from the military joined the antiauthoritarian movement. At times, the movement was articulated in church activities. Often, there was a confluence between church and anti-Marcos pursuits. Thanks to liberation theology, lower-level clergy permitted or facilitated the continuation of the synergy between the movement and the church. Consequently, Cardinal Jaime Sin was forced to reverse his stand with Marcos. He did so principally to save himself and to prevent the church from being marginalized, therefore, potentially being swept into a dustbin of irrelevance.

Upon the collapse of the authoritarian regime as a result of a "People Power" overthrow of Marcos and the redemocratization of the Philippines, the church faced a choice between returning to its traditional role, and continually being entangled in politics. The attempted coups against the Corazon Aquino government released some pressure from the church's role contraction. Lack of significant social reform also led religious activists to stay engaged in politics.[54] However, the church did not continue to play a significant political role after the people's revolution. The Filipinos elected Fidel V. Ramos, a Protestant, as their president in 1992. The church intervened only on the issue of family planning, but even then the government did not budge. The church did step directly into politics, once again, in 2000. Ramos was succeeded in 1998 by Joseph Estrada, who was forced from office in 2001, plagued by charges of having received more than $8.5 million in bribes from illicit gambling syndicates. In October 2000, Cardinal Sin and seventy-five senior priests had called for Estrada to resign in the following public statement: "In light of all the public scandals that have besmirched the image of the presidency in the last two years, we stand by our conviction that he [Estrada] has lost the moral ascendancy to govern."[55]

As in the Philippines, the indigenous Catholic Church was late in its outspoken support of democratization in Hong Kong. Given the heterogeneous religious beliefs in Hong Kong, the authority in Beijing and its agent, the chief executive officer of the Hong Kong Special Administrative Region, would hope to co-opt major religious organizations to prevent them from being allies of the prodemocracy opposition. Yet, it turns out that the Roman Catholic Church in Hong Kong is now an outspoken advocate of democratization, and, consequently, its bishop, Joseph Zen Ze-kiun, is in great tension with the Special Administrative Region and Central People's governments. The forthright position of the Roman

Catholic Church under Bishop Zen's leadership is very different from other religious organizations in Hong Kong. The largest Buddhist organization, headed by the Reverend Sik Kok Kwong, is very much on the side of Beijing, as has been the Anglican Church, headed by the Right Reverend Peter Kwong.

Protecting their religious organizations probably looms large in the minds of religious leaders. Bishop Zen may not be trying to promote a democratic movement, per se. However, his activities and statements are conducive to the making of democracy and political liberty. He emphasizes constitutionalism and human rights, and his church has been assertive about the protection of freedoms, especially of religion, peaceful assembly, and speech. Bishop Zen is not a political participant. Also, the Roman Catholic Church is hierarchical (and hence structurally undemocratic). Nonetheless, Bishop Zen works toward creating the conditions that can pave the way for democratization.

Indonesia and Malaysia: Deradicalization Versus Co-optation

Indonesia is an overwhelmingly Islamic society, but the Muslim forces in Indonesia have been internally divided between landowner-aristocratic traditionalists in the inland areas, represented chiefly by Nahdlatul Ulama (NU), Indonesia's largest Muslim organization, and the reformist-modernists in coastal and commercial areas, represented primarily by Muhammadiyah, founded in 1912, and the oldest and second largest Muslim organization.[56] Historically, NU has been quite apolitical and syncretic in its outlook (there has been a blending of Hindu-Buddhist and Islamic views). Ever since its establishment in 1926, NU has avoided a direct political role, and, instead, has chosen to stress social welfare. It was forced to join hands with other Muslim groups in 1973 to form the Development Unity Party (Partai Persatuan Pembangunan, or PPP), but after a decade, chose Abdurrahman Wahid (Gus Dur) as its leader and returned to its apolitical stance.[57]

There has been a historical tension between NU and Muhammadiyah. These tensions include accusations that, under Wahid, many NU members burned Muhammadiyah mosques and schools.[58] Muhammadiyah, known for its scripturalism and strict religious mission, is viewed as an organization of educated persons and professionals in academic circles, in contrast to NU's membership, which historically has been farmers.

Muhammadiyah's constituent base is mostly urban, orthodox Muslims. Amien Rais, its former leader, who was educated at Notre Dame and the University of Chicago, rejected the Muslim Brotherhood's religious justification for violence and religious fundamentalism as the guide for modern Muslims.[59] However, his anti-Chinese, anti-Christian sentiments[60] have tainted the organization in other circles.

Having crushed the leftist secular forces, most notably the communists and their sympathizers, Suharto's military regime subsumed all Islamic forces under the umbrella organization, the PPP, in 1973, obviously a strategy of political co-optation. By accommodating an Islamic cultural revival in the 1980s and its demands concerning education, the Islamic Bank, family law, and the court, the regime was able to favor one group over another, and, hence, to perpetuate old cleavages and create new tensions within both the traditionalist and modernist groups. Political co-optation also enabled the regime to monitor newer religious intellectuals and reformers, who were urbanized, educated, and professional.[61]

When Indonesia's economic crisis deepened and the military regime's legitimacy waned, the modernists, under the influence of Amien Rais, plunged into an opposition movement directly, but Rais was not truly followed by his own supporters. Furthermore, leaders of the traditionalist camp under Wahid remained undecided until the imminent collapse of the Suharto regime. Then there were three responses: Wahid and his loyalists had a "wait-and-see" approach; senior *ulama* (religious specialists and scholars) in the provinces insisted on continued support for Suharto; and the younger generation wanted to embrace *reformasi*.[62] Eventually, both Nahdlatul Ulama, led by Wahid, and Muhammadiyah, led by Rais, launched a struggle against Suharto. Rais's role was especially crucial in mobilizing students for peaceful protests and demands for democratization.

Indonesia's democratic opening provides the opportunity for political forces, Islamic groups included, to recraft the Indonesian state. Meanwhile, the fledgling democracy has been confronted with an array of problems, including economic difficulties, separatist movements, sectarian violence, and the shattering of Indonesian nationhood. One approach to reshaping the polity and rebuilding national confidence and identity is to forge an Islamic state, with a constitution based on Islamic law. This is the way forward that is advocated by some fundamentalists, for example, Nursanita Nasution, a University of Indonesia economics lecturer and an activist in the Justice Party. An alternative is to maintain a secular state that is compatible with most Islamic values, a condition that is necessary for coexistence between mosques and the state, and one under which Islamic parties still can be active, even dominant.[63] However, not only has an Islamic state failed to emerge in post-Suharto Indonesia, but also Islamic forces have not become even the mainstay of Indonesian political society.

As Indonesia embarked on democratic transition, its Muslim leaders did not abdicate from politics, unlike most of the cases with which we have dealt above. Both Rais and Wahid organized new political parties. However, Rais's party included non-Muslims in its leadership and was not explicitly Islamic, and Wahid unequivocally campaigned against establishing an Islamic state. Islamic fundamentalist parties did not have significant numbers of followers. Indeed, the two most extreme Islamist parties won only a combined 3 percent of the votes in the July 1999 presidential election.[64] The fragmented Indonesian Muslim community failed to form a united front and lost the opportunity to place Islam on the agenda during the regime change. Various Islamist parties collected only 35.06 percent of the votes in the 1999 election (compared to 43.9 percent in 1955, the previous election), far fewer than the first two secular-nationalist parties combined, which was 56.58 percent.[65] Islamist parties accounted for less than one-quarter of the seats in the parliament. Islamist forces did play coalition politics, but as a veto player, rather than a dominant force. In any case, an Islamic state does not appear to be on the horizon. The prospects for this were further dimmed by the Bali bombing of October 12, 2002, and the trial of the fundamentalist leader who instigated it.[66]

Unlike Indonesia, Malaysia is a religiously heterogeneous society. Racial, linguistic, and religious divides overlap and run deep, although the Malays, the majority of the population, are predominantly Muslim. Dominated by the United Malays National Organization (UMNO), the Malaysian polity is often characterized as a semi- or quasidemocracy, as it displays a strong bent toward authoritarian control in many key policy areas (including education and the economy) and its civil liberty has been, at best, "partially free."[67] Since the 1980s, there have been increasingly strong signs of Islamic revival in Malaysia, manifested not just in social behavior, but in politics as well, namely, in the formation and advancement of the Malaysian Islamic Party, or PAS. The revival has had less to do with external factors, such as the Iranian revolution and the power of oil-producing Islamic states, than with internal developments. These changes include the New Economic Policy (NPC) that empowered Malays, creating an element of disorientation among urban Malays and a raised demand for identity among rural Malays who increasingly were in tension with non-Malays.[68] The Islamic revival might threaten to create a theocratic state and undermine Malaysia's already limited, even flawed, democracy. But the politically activated Islamic forces might also help the democratic forces to combat the authoritarian tendencies of the one-party dominant UMNO regime.

To UMNO, the political challenge posed by the Islamic revival has been quite formidable. For the first time, a significant opposition party (and a religion-based one), PAS, has been formed within UMNO's social base, the Malay community. In addition, behind this opposition party lies a social force that is entrenched in the Malaysian educational system. Ulama are mostly educated abroad in Cairo, and are especially influential in primary and secondary private education, which still is quite prevalent. This means that the state is not the only, or the most powerful, socializing agent. Further, the regulatory and legislative power over religious affairs is dispersed and diffused, resting more in the hands of state governments than in those of federal authorities. The clergy's influence is manifested most clearly in opposition (Islamic) party-controlled states. PAS members, indeed, are numerous (some 800,000), highly homogeneous, and spread across many social groups. They abound not just among ulama, but also among religious teachers, fishermen, farmers, and Malays who are not benefiting from the New Economic Policy.[69] PAS's supporters have been frustrated by UMNO's illiberal policies, and they are searching for a moral compass, conscious of the issue of justice, receptive to Islamic custom (such as wearing a *tudong*, the Malay word for the traditional Muslim headscarf), but not really aware of civil rights.[70] If the trend continues, we may see an Islamic state in the making, a state where Muslims would govern, control all sectors of society, enforce law, and shape jurisprudence.

Yet, if we examine what sort of power the clergy can bring to bear on the Malaysian polity, we can see that the making of a true Islamic state in Malaysia is more apparent than real. First, the influence and persuasive power of the clergy and PAS frequently are overstated. The Islamic organizations in Malaysia are so diffused, thanks to the colonial policy of power dispersion, that the clergy, collectively, at present, are not an effective or coherent actor. Moreover, religious and political movements often are and have been conflated. Both PAS and UMNO regard PAS's votes as an endorsement for a theocratic state that is run by the ulama. However, both parties say so for "strategic" reasons: PAS can draw a line to distance itself from UMNO, while UMNO can alert swing voters to side with it to curtail the growth of PAS. As Patricia Martinez's attitudinal study shows, PAS supporters do not seem to really want to create a theocratic state; rather, they appear to be chiefly angered and frustrated by the perceived widespread corruption of the ruling coalition Barisan Nasional (BN) state governments.[71]

Second, the federal government's power over the Muslim clergy should not be underestimated. The government has attempted to control and contain personnel policies regarding the ulama that the opposition-party-controlled state governments have been hiring and paying. The central government can use many civil laws, including the Internal Security Act and the Penal Code, to discipline the clergy.[72] All of these factors assist the ever-vigilant UMNO party regime to co-opt Islamic forces away from PAS. Lack of fusion between Muslim Malays and non-Muslim Chinese further has helped UMNO to manipulate Malaysia's religious sector. Since the ruling coalition moved to incorporate religious organizations into its power base, it has had to continually outflank the fundamentalist challenge by appearing "holier than thou."[73] Nonetheless, UMNO seemingly has dislodged PAS as the standard bearer for Islamic forces. Former premier Mahathir's declaration that Malaysia is an Islamic state may turn out to be more symbolic than substantive.[74] Islamic political forces have neither fostered a theocratic state nor thawed the authoritarian UMNO regime.

The Chapters That Follow

Chapter 2 addresses the rise of Falun Gong in post–Deng Xiaoping China and the Chinese Communist Party (CCP) regime's assiduous attempt to repress it. Based on her personal experience, the late university professor Julia Ching showed how a quasireligious movement—essentially based on Buddhist ideas and Taoist-inspired spiritual and physical practices—took hold of China like a wildfire. Falun Gong's expansive, soft organizations and its well-demonstrated capacity for mobilization have posed a more resilient, enduring, and pervasive, though less intense, threat to the CCP regime than the Tiananmen student movement in 1989 that demanded free speech. However, Julia Ching contended in her chapter that the Falun Gong is not political, and will remain one (although not necessarily the most popular) of the underground spiritual groups in China that will loom even larger after the onset of democratization. Whether the relentlessly persecuted Falun Gong will indirectly contribute to democratic change in China through its efforts to gain freedom of religion is a moot question. The never-ending protests and, indeed, lawsuits filed by Falun Gong members overseas against specific Chinese leaders have brought world public opinion to bear on the CCP regime, a "lateral" pressure that may help to nudge China toward political liberalization eventually. Yet, whether the Falun Gong as a loosely coalesced, quasireligious organization will serve as a platform or incubator for a democracy movement is more difficult to conjecture.

Chapters 3 and 4 by André Laliberté and David Ambuel, respectively, show that Buddhist organizations can be aloof from and wary of democratic processes (the case of Taiwan) or integral to them at least at some historical critical junctures (the case of Thailand). Laliberté submits that the democratic transition and electoral politics in Taiwan have been so overwhelmingly structured along the subethnic divide (among various "Taiwanese" groups and the "mainlanders") and subsequently around the national identity issue (Taiwan permanently independent of the PRC, or eventually unified with it) that the island's two leading Buddhist organizations have neither the credibility nor propensity to weigh in. Instead, their leaders have aimed to transcend the ethnic divide on the island and avoid the fallout of political tension across the Taiwan Strait, a prudent strategy that is manifested in the institutions' all-inclusive ethnic memberships and global charity efforts, and designed to protect their organizational interests well. In contrast, Buddhist organizations, old and new, as Ambuel demonstrates, have left their deep imprints on Thai politics. The institutional Buddhist organizations legitimized authoritarian power in the past, not because the monks did not respect the division between the here and now and the spiritual world, but because the ruling élite needed endorsements—hence the trinity of "nation, monarchy, and religion." The rise of reformist Buddhist movements eroded the traditional sangha-political élite symbiosis and helped to propel democratic change in Thailand. However, democratic reform—epitomized by a crucial constitutional amendment in 1997—did not really move the Thai state away from Buddhist-sanctioned authority to rule and procedure-based governance. Because the sangha still has much political standing, Thai society has not secularized and individual charismatic monks, as Ambuel reiterates, continue to command national attention; indeed, politicians still seek their association, if not their endorsement.

Chapters 5 and 6 by Murray A. Rubinstein and Hyug Baeg Im, respectively, present a welter of parallels between Taiwan and South Korea regarding the critical role that a few specific Christian institutions—most notably, the Presbyterian Church in Taiwan and the Korean National Council of Churches and the Korean Student Christian Federation in Korea—played in democratic transition. The trajectory of their involvement in the process of democratic change was almost identical: politically motivated regulations, blatant persecution, and human rights abuse compelled these religious institutions to exploit their resources and positions to either harbor or sponsor political dissident activities. Their Western connections and religious status did not provide any shield against waves of targeted and orchestrated suppression. Religious organizations that were willing to challenge the governments, however, were a minority. Both Rubinstein and Im stress that most members of the Christian community were either "adapters" or "conformists," gingerly safeguarding their organizational interests, and only passively observing the escalation of conflict between the authoritarian regime and democratic activists. There are differences between the two countries, though. A small number of Korean Catholic churches also were active "resisters," though less visible or less directly confrontational than their Protestant counterparts. In Taiwan, Catholics by and large were spectators during the process of regime change. The pursuit of selfhood and political autonomy by Han-Taiwanese fueled the Presbyterian Church's drive to side with the democracy movement, while the military regime's political suppression motivated the select Korean Christian churches to join the political opposition for democratic change. The Presbyterian Church has now retreated to its niches, charity and medical care. It remains to be seen if the previously active Korean churches will turn their attention to the issue of Korean nationalism and the unification of the two regimes on the peninsula.

Chapters 7 and 8 by Coeli M. Barry and Deborah A. Brown, respectively, examine the Catholic Church in the Philippines and Hong Kong during two critical periods, the restoration of Filipino democracy in the late 1980s, and the reversion of Hong Kong to China in the late 1990s. Barry urges readers to look beyond Manila to see the long years of opposition by priests and nuns in the provinces to the authoritarian Marcos regime, a contrast with the eleventh-hour transformation of the Catholic

Bishops' Conference of the Philippines (CBCP) from "critical" collaborator of the regime to an ally of liberal and democratic dissidents. However, although these efforts by dissidents led to the ouster of the Marcos government, which ended authoritarianism, they did not usher in mass democracy. Instrumental to Corazon Aquino's landslide electoral victory and the protection of her presidency against several coup attempts, the conservative, male-exclusive CBCP was entrusted to provide "moral leadership" to the new government. The CBCP chose to reflect Aquino's much watered-down, only marginally redistributive Land Reform program, arguably missing the most precious historical moment to recast its association with the deeply entrenched and election-savvy agro-business élite. In the end, the church hierarchy helped to regain civil and political rights but also helped to reestablish Filipino élitist, patrimonial democracy, an equilibrium that may drive the vocal minority of bishops and younger priests and nuns to endorse the evangelical Catholic movement and advocate a radical social agenda. The story in Hong Kong, as Deborah Brown's chapter meticulously catalogues, is on a different thread. The leadership of Hong Kong's Roman Catholic Church was historically cautious about the delicate church-state ties. The church came to rely on government resources to support its extensive educational activities; however, it also has empathy with democracy activists that, unlike the pro-Beijing business élite, diligently guard the freedom and civil-political rights of Hong Kong's residents. For many reasons, including that the Special Administrative Region government attempts to wrest from church leaders their approval of and participation in an undemocratic political system, rebuffs public demand for democracy, and has launched efforts to erode Catholic influence in the educational sector, the church is becoming more and more disenchanted with the ruling establishment, and less and less hesitant to put its imprimatur on political and social movements against authoritarianism, both local and that increasingly coming from outside—specifically, from Beijing.

Chapters 9 and 10 by Greg Barton and Patricia Martinez, respectively, direct our attention to non–Middle Eastern Islamic organizations in newly democratized Indonesia and ethnically divided Malaysia. Barton contends that the two leading, mass-based Islamic organizations in Indonesia were central to peaceful transition to democracy in post-1997 Indonesia, not simply owing to their charismatic leadership, but also due to their strategic location and practical activism in Indonesian civil society. The bifurcation of the Islamic community has largely fallen on the urban-rural divide rather than on sectarian schism or the fundamentalist-secular split as in many Middle Eastern nations, thereby exempting Indonesia from the curse of "Balkanization," and keeping it a Muslim society tolerant of democratic experiment. Barton draws an interesting parallel between the elections in 1955 and 1999, the first and second free and fair elections in Indonesia. In both "founding" elections, the share of votes garnered by all Islamist parties was 38 percent, suggesting the normal watermark that Muslim voters might reach, an indication soon to be confirmed in the 2004 election. Barton's conclusion is well taken: Islamic parties will be key players (coalition partners) in Indonesian democratic politics, but are not in a position to turn this nation into an Islamic state. Patricia Martinez's chapter highlights the centrality of the one dominant party system to our understanding the relations between the political society and Islamic organizations in Malaysia. Organizational interest of the UMNO requires that it maintain a multiethnic and multireligious framework to prevent any centrifugal tendency from developing within the coalition. But, it is also imperative that the UNMO nurtures institutional affinity with Islamic organizations and, if necessary, reinforces the ties with them so as to preempt the challenge from fundamentalist Islamic parties. As the leadership shuttles between the two concerns, the relationship of the state to Islamic organizations fluctuates accordingly. This balancing act has been one of the defining features of Malaysian democracy. However, whether a democratic constitution—a "social contract" hammered out at the founding of a postcolonial state among ethnic communities and religious groups—can be a safeguard against the Islamization of the Malaysian state remains to be seen. Political and social groups representing non-Muslim minorities harbor concerns about the possible erosion of constitutionalism. Extensive interviews led Patricia Martinez to conclude that the drift to an Islamic state is not impossible, given that the majority of ordinary Muslim Malaysians would not favor, but would not oppose, the creation of such a state, and that the rising opposition Islamic party, acting like a political entrepreneur, is equating an Islamic state with good governance and justice.

Chapter 11, by Daniel A. Metraux, analyzes the political activism of the Soka Gakkai, a lay Buddhist mass-based movement in postwar Japan, the first industrial democracy in Asia. Imposed by the victors of World War II, the Japanese democratic system has been for four solid decades dominated by the conservative Liberal Democratic Party (LDP).

Through its political arm, the Komeito, Metraux contends that the Soka Gakkai has been a voice on behalf of millions of alienated, less-fortunate, downtrodden Japanese who might otherwise have opted out of maturing Japanese democracy. Espousing a reformist agenda, the Soka Gakkai and Komeito raised the ethical bar in highly corrupted Japanese politics, and together with other progressive forces, prevented the LDP from amending Japan's pacifist constitution and helped to consolidate Japanese democracy, which otherwise might have suffered from a violent confrontation between two ideological camps. The Soka Gakkai and Komeito officially separated in 1970, but elective affinity between the two has remained, a relationship akin to that between unions and labor parties in Europe. The difference is that the Soka Gakkai, as a religious movement, tenaciously adheres to morals and other values, continuously updates its reformist agenda, and remains an avid participant in electoral politics. As an extension of Metraux's observation, we can probably conclude that the Soka Gakkai has reinvented itself and maintained its political relevance to democratic politics, a dire contrast with some other religious organizations covered in this volume among which political barometers dropped sharply once the political parameters transpired.

Notes

1. Reference is made in this volume to the Catholic Church in Korea and other Protestant churches in Taiwan, as they also provide good benchmarks for comparison.

2. David Ambuel, "New Karma: Buddhist Democracy and the Rule of Law in Thailand," *American Asian Review* 19, no. 4 (Winter 2001): 145–46.

3. See Christopher S. Queen, "Introduction: The Shapes and Sources of Engaged Buddhism," in *Engaged Buddhism*, ed. Christopher S. Queen and Sallie B. King (Albany: State University of New York Press, 1996), 1–43.

4. Ibid., 23–24.

5. Dalai Lama, "Buddhism, Asian Values, and Democracy," *Journal of Democracy* 10, no. 1 (January 1999): 3–4.

6. Samuel P. Huntington, "Will More Countries Become Democratic?" *Political Science Quarterly* 99, no. 2 (Summer 1984): 208.

7. Larry Diamond, "Introduction," in *Political Culture in the Developing World*, ed. Larry Diamond (Boulder, CO: Lynne Rienner, 1993), 2.

8. Alfred Stepan, "Religion, Democracy, and the 'Twin Tolerations,'" *Journal of Democracy* 11, no. 4 (October 2000): 48.

9. Ibid., 44.

10. Bernard Lewis, "Islam and Liberal Democracy: A Historical Overview," *Journal of Democracy* 7, no. 2 (April 1996): 55.

11. Dale Eickelman and James Piscatori, *Muslim Politics* (Princeton, NJ: Princeton University Press, 1996), 56.

12. Majid Tehranian, "Disenchanted Worlds: Secularization and Democratization in the Middle East," in *Democratization in the Middle East: Experiences, Struggles, Challenges*, ed. Amin Saikal and Albrecht Schnabel (Tokyo: United Nations University Press, 2003), 82, 97.

13. Thomas W. Lippman, *Understanding Islam: An Introduction to the Muslim World*, 2d rev. ed. (New York: Meridian, Penguin Books, 1995), 137.

14. Ibid.

15. Michael Molloy, *Experiencing the World's Religions: Tradition, Challenge, and Change*, 3d ed. (New York: McGraw Hill, 2005), 456.

16. Fazlur Rahman, quoted in Lippman, *Understanding Islam*, 141.

17. Michael Molloy, *Experiencing the World's Religions: Tradition, Challenge, and Change*, 2d ed. (Mountain View, CA: Mayfield, 2002), 429.

18. Shiites are not unified in their beliefs. Seveners, or Ismailis, recognize descent from Muhammad only to the seventh Imam as legitimate. Influential historically in North Africa, Seveners are remembered for the brutality of the groups that they spawned, including the Syria-based Assassins, known for their wanton murders. Their descendants are found today mostly in Pakistan, and they look to the Aga Khan as the Imam.

19. Lippman, *Understanding Islam*, 142.

20. Ibid., 138.

21. Fazlur Rahman, quoted in Lippman, *Understanding Islam*, 138.

22. Lippman, *Understanding Islam*, 138–39.

23. Samuel P. Huntington, *The Third Wave* (Norman and London: University of Oklahoma Press, 1991), 75.

24. See, for example, Molloy, *Experiencing the World's Religions*, 328–29.

25. John Corrigan, Frederick M. Denny, Carlos M.N. Eive, and Martin S. Jaffee, *Jews, Christians, Muslims: A Comparative Introduction to Monotheistic Religions* (Upper Saddle River, NJ: Prentice Hall, 1998), 185.

26. This characterization was first made by Emily Lau, formerly a reporter for the *Far Eastern Economic Review*, and now a directly elected member of Hong Kong's Legislative Council and the leader of the Frontier. The Frontier is an activist, prodemocracy group that runs candidates for office but claims not to be a political party.

27. James A. Bill and John Alden Williams, *Roman Catholics and Shi'i Muslims* (Chapel Hill: University of North Carolina, 2002), 123.

28. Ng Tze-min Peter, "Education in Hong Kong: A History of the Churches' Involvement in Schools," *New and Views*, Hong Kong Christian Council (Spring 2000): 4, in Deborah A. Brown, "The Roman Catholic Church in Hong Kong: Freedom's Advocate Struggles with the SAR Government in Electoral Politics and Education," *American Asian Review* 19, no. 4 (Winter 2001): 48.

29. Bill and Williams, *Roman Catholics and Shi'i Muslims*, 124–25.

30. Ibid., 126.

31. According to the *Economist*, 28 percent of the inmates in China's labor camps are followers of the Falun Gong spiritual movement. See "A Jail by Another Name," *Economist*, December 21, 2002, 52.

32. Ellen Lust-Okar, "Why the Failure of Democratization? Explaining 'Middle

East Exceptionalism,'" mimeograph. Also see her article, "Divided They Rule: The Management and Manipulation of Political Opposition," *Comparative Politics* 36, no. 2 (January 2004): 159–79.

33. This is how the *Economist* puts it: "Muslims in South-East Asia have long been renowned for their tolerance." See "Islam in South-East Asia: Incense, Silk, and Jihad," *Economist*, May 31, 2003, 37–38.

34. Peter A. Jackson, "Withering Centre, Flourishing Margins: Buddhism's Changing Political Roles," in *Political Change in Thailand*, ed. Kevin Hewison (London: Routledge, 1997), 75.

35. Ronald K. Swearer, "Centre and Periphery: Buddhism and Politics in Modern Thailand," in Ian Harris, *Buddhism and Politics in Twentieth-Century Asia* (London: Pinter, 1999), 229–53.

36. Jackson, "Withering Centre, Flourishing Margins," 85.

37. For the importance of the Thai constitutional amendment in 1998, see Tun-jen Cheng, "Political Institutions and the Malaise of East Asian New Democracies," *Journal of East Asian Studies* (March 2003): 1–41.

38. Jackson, "Withering Centre, Flourishing Margins," 93.

39. Ambuel, "New Karma," 150–62.

40. Donald Baxter, professor emeritus, College of William and Mary, interview by Tun-jen Cheng, December 13, 2002.

41. See André Laliberté, "Buddhist Organizations and Democracy in Taiwan," *Asian American Review* 19, no. 4 (Winter 2001): 97–130.

42. See Gertraude Roth Li and Douglas Shaw, eds., *The Thirty-Seven Principles of Enlightenment: Lectures by Dharma Master Cheng Yen*, trans. Norman Yuan, Lin Sen-shou, E.E. Ho, W.L. Rathje, May Gu, Kitty Liu, Sylvester Young, and Low Siew Kheng (Taipei: Tzu Chi Cultural Publishing, 1999).

43. Correspondence between Byung-Kook Kim, professor of Political Science, Korea University, and Tun-jen Cheng, April 20, 2003.

44. Donald Clark, *Christianity in Modern Korea* (Lanham, MD: University Press of America, 1986).

45. Henrik H. Sorensen, "Buddhism and Secular Power in Twentieth-Century Korea," in Ian Harris, *Buddhism and Politics in Twentieth-Century Asia* (London: Pinter, 1999), 138–39.

46. Tun-jen Cheng, "Political Regimes and Development Strategies: Korea and Taiwan," in *Manufacturing Miracles*, ed. Gary Gereffi and Donald Wyman (Princeton, NJ: Princeton University Press, 1990), 159.

47. Correspondence between Eun Mee Kim, sociologist and dean of International Studies, Ehwa Womans University, Seoul, and Tun-jen Cheng, April 2003.

48. This led a monk to self-immolation in 1980, and drove monks and nuns from the Chogye Order to join the popular uprisings against the government in 1986. See Sorenson, "Buddhism and Secular Power in Twentieth-Century Korea," 140.

49. For more than two decades following the student uprising in 1960, student leaders organized orientation camps to brief incoming students on experiences and outlooks. Thus, the tradition of political dissident movements among college students was transmitted from one generation to the next.

50. Murray Rubinstein, "The Presbyterian Church in the Formation of Taiwan's Democratic Society, 1945–2001," *American Asian Review* 19, no. 4 (Winter 2001): 63–96.

51. For the political preference of the Presbyterian Church in Taiwan, see Yang-sun Chou, "Democratization in Taiwan" (Ph.D. diss., Columbia University, 1989).

52. On the contribution of overseas communities to Taiwan's democratic transition, see Tun-jen Cheng, "Democratizing the Quasi-Leninist Regime in Taiwan," *World Politics* (April 1989): 487–88.

53. David Wurfel, *Filipino Politics* (Ithaca, NY: Cornell University Press, 1988), 261–64. Cardinal Sin treaded the papal line on liberation theology. Wurfel notes that, in a much publicized visit in 1981, Pope John Paul II "lauded the church's efforts to protect human rights and stand up for social justice, but also warned against class struggle and the use of violence."

54. Gretchen Casper, *Fragile Democracies: The Legacies of Authoritarian Rule* (Pittsburgh: University of Pittsburgh Press, 1995).

55. "Cardinal Sin Tells Estrada to Quit," *BBC News*, Internet edition, October 11, 2000, news.bbc.co.uk/hi/english/world/asia-pacific/newsid_967000/967115.stm-32k-.

56. The division was largely a result of "the uneven process of Islamization throughout the archipelago," and subsequently was accentuated by specific colonial policies that attempted to use local Islamic authority and Javanese aristocracy to cope with the threat from the modernists. See Suzaina Kadir, "The Islamic Factor in Indonesia's Political Transition," *Australia Journal of Political Sciences* 7, no. 2 (December 1999): 23–24.

57. Eickelman and Piscatori, *Muslim Politics*, 55.

58. Syafii Ma'arif, president of Muhammadiyah, quoted in the United States Indonesia Society, *USINDO Brief* (Washington, DC: USINDO Open Forum on Islam and Democracy in Indonesia, April 8, 2002).

59. Theodore Friend, *Indonesian Destinies* (Cambridge, MA: Belknap Press, Harvard University Press, 2003), 389.

60. Ibid., 390.

61. Kadir, "The Islamic Factor in Indonesia's Political Transition," 26–28.

62. Ibid., 32.

63. See Jay Solomon, "Mosque and State: Two Models of Islam Vie for Shot at Curing Indonesia's Many Ills," *Wall Street Journal*, January 8, 2002, A1, A8.

64. Stepan, "Religion, Democracy, and the 'Twin Tolerations,'" 49–50.

65. Kadir, "The Islamic Factor in Indonesia's Political Transition," 35–38.

66. "An Ace in the Hole," *Economist*, April 26–May 2, 2003, 35–36.

67. Zakaria Haji Ahmad coined the term "quasidemocracy." See his "Malaysia: Quasi Democracy in a Divided Society," in *Democracy in Developing Countries: Asia*, ed. Larry Diamond, Juan J. Linz, and Seymour Martin Lipset (Boulder, CO: Lynne Rienner, 1989), 347–82. In Freedom House's rating in recent years, Malaysia has bordered on the "not free" category.

68. See Harold Crouch, "Malaysia: Do Elections Make a Difference?" in *The Politics of Elections in Southeast Asia*, ed. R.H. Taylor (New York and Cambridge, UK: Woodrow Wilson Center and Cambridge University Press, 1996), 126, and Judith Nagata, *The Reflowering of Malaysian Islam* (Vancouver: University of British Columbia, 1984).

69. Patricia Martinez, "The Islamic State of the State of Islam in Malaysia," *Contemporary Southeast Asia* 23, no. 3 (December 2001): 481.

70. Ibid., 483–85.

71. Ibid., 480, 486. There is a significant silent segment that embraces religiosity, but does not want to see a theocracy.

72. Ibid., 478–80.

73. Judith Nagata, "Religious Correctness and the Place of Islam in Malaysia's Economic Policies," in *Culture and Economy: The Shaping of Capitalism in Eastern Asia*, ed. Timothy Brook and Jy V. Luong (Ann Arbor: University of Michigan Press, 1997), 90.

74. Shad Faruqi astutely denotes that Malaysia is neither a full-fledged Islamic state nor a wholly secular state, as "there can be many beliefs in the same God." Cited in Martinez, "The Islamic State of the State of Islam in Malaysia," 494.

2

The Falun Gong

Religious and Political Implications

Julia Ching

The Falun Gong (literally: The Wheel of the Law Exercise, now called the "Buddhist Law" movement), first surprised world media when ten to fifteen thousand followers surrounded the Zhongnanhai compound, the seat of the Chinese government, on Sunday, April 25, 1999. Many came to Beijing from far away. They were mostly middle-aged; they first stood shoulder-to-shoulder and then sat down to meditate in lotus position with their legs crossed. It was in startling contrast to the noisy student demonstrators of spring 1989. The Chinese government appeared surprised. Premier Zhu Rongji met with a few of the movement's leaders—actual or retired senior officials themselves—who complained of official harassment, especially as several of their fellow followers had been arrested in Tianjin, after criticisms of their movement were voiced by a scientist, He Zouxiu, a theoretical physicist of the Chinese Academy of the Sciences. The group wanted rehabilitation or legal status to ensure protection, especially from regional authorities who sometimes refused to give them permission to assemble. They also wanted the ban lifted on their founder's books. (The group's leaders were later identified as Wang Zhiwen, a retired official with the Railways Ministry, and Wang Youqun, an official at the Ministry of Supervision, which oversees the Chinese Communist Party.)

Three months later, on July 22, it was the Chinese communist government's turn to surprise the West by outlawing this spiritual movement that combines Buddhist meditation and Taoist *qigong* exercises for the sake of promoting physical and mental health. At that time, too, tens of thousands of persons protested the decree in ten cities, including Beijing. The police took away thousands in busloads to schools and sports stadiums. Most were later released, although about seventy to a hundred leaders were arrested.[1]

The author visited China precisely in late July, and watched with boredom the daily television news that orchestrated the criticism of Falun Gong and its founder, Li Hongzhi. The leaders of China's officially approved religions appeared on television to denounce Falun Gong. Followers who recanted were also there to register their contrition and add to the criticisms. Falun Gong was accused of all kinds of crimes, including leading the sick astray and forbidding them to see physicians, thereby causing deaths. Following such media outcries, local Chinese friends were likewise bored and dismayed. For them, it was as though the Cultural Revolution were coming back. The problem is, years later, these media criticisms continue.

So, what is the matter with Falun Gong and with the Chinese government? Why does the one refuse to go away quietly and the other continue such high pressure tactics, including arrests, imprisonments, and long and harsh sentences against those individuals who refuse to give up their faith and practice? These questions bring to mind the basic questions: What is Falun Gong, anyway, and why does the government hate it so?

To answer these questions, this chapter incorporates conversations with intellectuals watching what is happening in China and with Falun Gong members in Canada and the United States. It also turns to some of Li's books, especially *Zhuan Falun* [Turning the wheels of Buddhist law], which allegedly outsold Deng Xiaoping's biography at a national book fair. And it reflects the news, including the *People's Daily*, and information provided on Web sites maintained by the government and by Falun Gong.[2] The last question is addressed first, and then attention is turned to the others.

The Falun Gong

As a term, *Falun* is hard to translate. The *New York Times* (April 27, 1999) calls it "Buddhist Law." This is technically correct, except that the term "law" in Buddhism refers to doctrine rather than to rules or decrees. The best translation may be "Dharma Wheel." *Dharma* is a word of Sanskrit origin, a Buddhist term meaning teaching, or truth. The "Wheel of the Dharma" refers to teaching Buddhism. The word, *gong*, literally, practice, is used also in Taoism, especially to refer to its yoga practice of qigong, which includes a range of physical/spiritual exercises, all of which have meditative components. The Falun Gong shows itself to be an eclectic movement, blending Buddhist ideas with partly Taoist-inspired practices. Its emblem displays both the Buddhist Dharma wheel and the circular Taiji symbol that represents Taoism. But the Buddhist symbol is more prominent, placed in the middle as well as on the sides.

The Founder and His Teachings

Li Hongzhi, originally from Jilin, founded the movement in 1992 when he was barely forty years old. It happened at a time when qigong exercises were very popular, especially for their health effects. Li's own claim is that he started learning qigong at age four from a Buddhist master, and a bit later from Taoist masters. He joined the People's Liberation Army after middle school and worked first on a stud farm. Then he served as a trumpet player with a musical troop of the Jilin provincial forest police. After that, he worked especially as a clerk in the provincial grain bureau in the northeastern industrial city of Changchun. He became a popular qigong teacher but ran into difficulties with the official Qigong Research Association of China. In 1994, Li withdrew his movement from this association. Sensing trouble, Li himself left China in 1995, just three years after starting the movement. His group made the amazing claim of having more than one hundred million followers (seventy million in a country of 1.2 billion, and thirty million elsewhere—all recruited in seven years). Others say the number is somewhere between twenty and eighty million (the former figure is given by an enemy; the latter might be closer to the truth). Some in China maintain that Falun Gong was the biggest qigong group in the country, and that many professors of Peking University practiced the exercise every day on the campus grounds until the movement was banned.

The Falun Gong was careful not to make itself into a religion. In China, it had no temple, no official headquarters, no formal rituals, and it exacted no fees from its followers. Its gatherings were always in public. Apparently, many senior cadres, retired military personnel, and well-known intellectuals had written to Zhu Rongji in support of the group. Some said that Falun Gong was saving the people money in medical fees, and even that Premier Zhu Rongji was very happy about that. "The country could use the money right now," they reasoned.[3] When the suppression began, it came from Jiang Zemin, who allegedly was unhappy that "theism" should triumph over "atheism" and, therefore, decided to act swiftly.[4]

Li's books are not easy to read, even in Chinese. He does not write systematically. Ethically, he advocates the cultivation of "truthfulness, benevolence and forbearance"—referring especially to the endurance of hardship—in order to transform one's karma (*ye*).[5] Spiritually, he speaks of taking people to a higher level of mystical consciousness and supernatural feats, asserting that qigong means spiritual cultivation or *xiulian*. Using Buddhist language, he explains how one can cultivate the "third eye" of mystical vision and understanding, which he calls the "heavenly eye" (*tianmu*). He locates it in the pineal gland, hidden between the eyebrows. This is also an important acupuncture point. Li both uses Taoist language and criticizes certain Taoist teachings, such as those about the "three cinnabar fields." For him, any part of the body can serve as a cinnabar field during meditation, without need of distinctions. But he relies on established Taoist practices when he talks about completing a microcosmic and macrocosmic orbit while guiding energy through the body.[6] However, the real goal is to transform the whole human being, so that every part of the body becomes pure and supple, while the spirit is completely enlightened.[7] In keeping with Buddhist beliefs, he opposes the killing of life, without obliging followers to become immediate vegetarians. He opposes drinking liquor and smoking. Supposedly, his aim is to purify the body, a purification that becomes healing.[8] For these reasons, he expressly forbids disciples to serve as "healers."[9]

Healing, especially faith-healing, has been popular in China, where visits to the doctors are expensive for those without high income. There are accounts of so-called Christian faith healing, practiced in the countryside since the late 1970s. In the case of Falun Gong, the healing sessions are not unlike those one witnesses elsewhere, including in the West. Followers go on the stage, confess their sins, describe their ailments, and give thanks for the healing power they experience, frequently from reading Li's books. The opposition decries this as dangerous and unhealthy, and encourages conventional medicine instead.

One concept Li discusses is that of the "primal spirit" (*yuan shen*). According to him—and this is Taoist belief—our primal spirit, which we all have, is indestructible. To prove this, however, he turns to the indestructibility of the body. Using the language of physics, he speaks of atoms and electrons, indeed, material elements too small for the microscope to see. They are also full of energy, dynamic, always in motion. At death, these elements still remain, with their energy, so that if the body appears dead in one kind of space, it is really alive somewhere else. With the heavenly eye, he asserts, one can see this better.[10]

Here, it should be mentioned that Li is often misunderstood for speaking of himself as part of the cosmos, of the "primal spirit." Apparently, he does not claim this exclusively, but believes rather in a kind of universal participation in this spirit, showing a certain pantheism. He also speaks of a catastrophic "end of the world"—a common Buddhist notion, referring to our age as a final age before this end.

The Opposition

In China, every group is required to be registered in an officially approved category. The Falun Gong movement developed in a legal limbo, as the government refused to permit registration under any category other than qigong. It was, however, loosely affiliated with the State Sports Administration. But Falun Gong was without adequate political protection, and thus exposed to attacks or criticisms from all quarters. Indeed, the Public Security Department conducted many investigations over the years that remained inconclusive until recently. According to Falun members, the Tianjin police arbitrarily arrested forty practitioners, following the publication of an article by He Zouxiu in a university journal criticizing the movement.[11] He Zouxiu asserted that he did not wish to see the young practice qigong, urging rather that they take up as many athletic sports as possible to help their bodies develop properly.

Qigong is practiced to cease human thinking. As a result, a monk can sit in meditation without moving for five or six hours. Critics argue that such practice is not good for the health of young people.[12]

He Zouxiu claims that, while qigong is supposed to help spiritual and physical health, he knows many people whose practice led to their placement in mental institutions with various kinds of ailments. He attacks Li Hongzhi, saying, while the movement claims to help practitioners enjoy better health, live longer, and even attain preternatural or supernatural skills, such practice actually has resulted in several reported deaths. In conclusion, he refers to historical disasters connected to qigong practice.[13] True, secret religious societies always were feared by the traditional Chinese state, starting at least with the Yellow Turbans (Taoists) who rebelled against the Han dynasty in the second century. In the mid-nineteenth century, the Taiping rebels, of Christian inspiration, nearly brought down the Manchu government. Fifty years later came the Boxers, who sought to help the Manchu dynasty with their allegedly invincible techniques but who instead brought foreign invasions and havoc to the country. After all, the popular Iguangdao, a syncretistic traditional Chinese religion, was legalized in Taiwan only after democracy gained ground. It remains underground in China. Add to it, of course, the communist opposition to spiritual and religious movements: even the approved religions are only tolerated, not encouraged. Besides, as a one-party government without a popular mandate, the communist leadership remains always afraid of its own people.

At the end of January 1999, China banned another qigong group, the Zhong Gong, raiding its headquarters in Beijing. Could this be another confirmation that the present Chinese government is opposed to its citizens practicing much qigong? One should avoid speculation. Ye Jianying, a now deceased head of state, allegedly had his life prolonged by qigong. But China's third-generation leadership, with engineers like Jiang Zemin and Li Peng, did not appear to be of the same mind.

On July 22, 1999, the Ministry of Interior declared that Falun Dafa and the Falun Gong it manipulated were illegal organizations, to be at once banned. Actually, hundreds of practitioners already had been detained during home arrests in the early hours of July 20. The official ban meant that, unless they recanted, Falun Gong members would lose their party memberships, jobs, educational opportunities, and pensions—not to mention that those arrested faced severe jail sentences. It is no great surprise that Falun Gong was in a legal limbo.

On October 25, 1999, the government identified Falun Gong as an "evil cult" (*xiejiao*). And the characteristics of *xiejiao* were spelled out for the first time: the worship of the cult leader (as in the case of the Aum Shinrikyō in Japan); spiritual manipulation of members; the spreading of evil teachings ("end of the world," and so on); illegal collection of funds (from teaching qigong and selling Li's books); the secrecy of its organization (with 29 main stations, 1,900 supplementary stations, 28,263 training points in the entire country, and an alleged following of 2.1 million); and its harm to society, including its political ambition (here Falun Gong is compared with Jim Jones's People's Temple and the collective suicide of nine hundred followers).[14] On October 30, special legislation against this "evil cult" passed the Standing Committee of the National People's Congress assembled under Li Peng.[15]

The accusation of Falun Gong's being an "evil cult" made previous arrests and imprisonments "constitutional." Of course, the accusation was made after the government already had started to crack down on Falun Gong members. The enumeration of features of an "evil cult" was done by political officials on political premises, not by any religious authority. It was an atheistic, communist government handing down an executive decision by the pronouncement of an "evil cult," without an explanation of what would be its opposite: a good cult, or a good religion.

The government appears in the right when it describes the tight organization of the group, which Li Hongzhi characterizes as spontaneous. Still, the Chinese Constitution of 1982 protects freedom of assembly (under certain conditions). It also protects freedom of religion. Here, however, China officially acknowledges only five religions: Buddhism, Taoism, Islam, and Protestant and Catholic Christianity. Falun Gong is outside sanctioned religious practice, and, for that reason, never claimed to be a religion. Ironically, this made it more attractive to Chinese Communist Party members, who are not permitted to belong to religious groups.

The state pronounced, and it acted swiftly. In more than thirty cities, police rounded up over thirty thousand members. At the same time, police security was tightened around Zhongnanhai, the seat of communist power. Although many of those who were detained were released later, the show of force indicated the determination of the regime.[16] The surprise, however, is that the banned group did not take it all lying down. Quiet vigils by young followers were made at Tiananmen for four days, concluding with a petition to the state asking for greater tolerance. With this, the police removed the youth. There were other demonstrations as well outside China: for example, a hundred followers demonstrated at the United Nations headquarters in New York, asking for intervention in the name of human rights and on reports of torture applied to those in prison.

The ban included a government and party purge. Some 1,200 government officials who were members were taken over a weekend to schools in a city in northern China, to study communist party documents and renounce Falun Gong allegiances.[17]

The Reactions

From the beginning, Falun Gong members did not take the ban passively. Their followers in Hong Kong protested at once in late July, and also thereafter. Within China, while some recanted, others continued to protest. In late October 1999, many assembled at the capital, seeking to influence the National People's Congress that was in session. They found safe houses in the city, offered by fellow members or sympathizers.[18] For six days, many carried out silent protest at Tiananmen, until they were forcibly removed. Indeed, some thirty of them held a daring, clandestine press conference in a suburban hotel for seven foreign journalists, appealing for international pressure. Those Falun Gong members present included former communist party members and former police officers, as well as an aerospace researcher and a factory manager.[19] A woman explained how she had been tortured after her arrest, and an eleven-year-old how he had been expelled from school. Falun Gong publications were collected from voluntary surrender or after the raiding of homes, and many were burnt in public, in a gesture that once more brought to mind the events of the Cultural Revolution. As of June 2001, there had been thousands of arrests and about two hundred deaths under custody.

Now formally outlawed, the Falun Gong followers in China have become desperate. Within China, they have nothing to lose, and in prison, can always practice forbearance and perhaps gain new converts. By December 1, 1999, the state had tallied thirty-five thousand run-ins with Falun Gong members.[20] Outside of China, the media have helped to publicize their cause. Nine hundred Falun Gong members met in Hong Kong, renting the Hong Kong Convention and Exhibition Centre for $13,000, paid with personal checks. They also meditated outside China's state news agency, at the end of a quiet march on December 12, 1999. Some of these members came from Canada, the United States, Australia, and Ireland, although most were Chinese. Without a doubt, new converts now are being won every day in Europe as well as in North America.[21] Today, Falun Gong followers in China are especially challenged to practice forbearance. One wonders whether Li Hongzhi knew what might happen when he said:

> What is the heart that possesses the greatest forbearance? For a practitioner, it means first of all to reach the stage of not hitting back when hit, not yelling back when yelled at, that is, be forbearing. Some may say to practice such forbearance is cowardly, making members prey to bullying. I say, this is not cowardice ... but the demonstration of a strong will.[22]

Political and Religious Implications

Why has the Falun Gong been such a phenomenal success only to face destruction? This question has been asked many times. Many believe that Falun Gong is different from other qigong groups because it offers a set of beliefs, called nonreligious, but nevertheless, beliefs about life and the hereafter. They are based on traditional Chinese beliefs, and they remain very powerful. After all, communist ideology has lost its hold over people's minds since the Cultural Revolution (1966–1976), and many Chinese remain unsatisfied with the quest for material gain alone. In a communist state, the official religions all have witnessed revival and unprecedented growth. But there are those who prefer more traditional beliefs combined with practices, which shows the strong hold of tradition even today.

Why does the government hate Falun Gong so? The press suggests that the communist government was completely surprised by the Zhongnanhai demonstrations, a surprise that led to fear, animosity, and suppression. The overseas Chinese-language press has suggested that the Zhongnanhai demonstrations were actually organized in part by the government, to help trump up charges against the Falun Gong, which it had observed and monitored for years through its infiltrators. It even gives the name of a high official, Lo Gan, as being the chief communist organizer of the Zhongnanhai gathering.[23] As secretary general of the State Council, Lo had been investigating Falun Gong and had wanted it banned since 1996 but could not find any legal basis for transgression. In that case, it is not certain where the Falun followers intended first to make their petition, but Lo had the police direct them to Zhongnanhai, in order to create an incident with which they afterward could be charged. Contacts from mainland China agree that the crackdown was to be expected, as the party cannot tolerate a mass movement. The party itself, after all, has only fifty-five to sixty million members, and fears infiltration, as many Falun Gong members were also party members.[24] According to communist propaganda, the Falun Gong was "competing for popularity with the party." This is an unpardonable crime.

Within the government, Jiang Zemin, as China's president, seemed to be leading the charge against Falun Gong, with Li Peng helping him in the National People's Congress. The Falun Gong demonstrations at Zhongnanhai became the basis for the official repression. They have been officially compared to the Tiananmen demonstrations of 1989 as a threat to political stability. Besides, it is reported that Jiang had received a letter defending Falun Gong from a high-ranking official in the 301 Military Hospital, which treats top leaders. He was further enraged to find out that the PLA Navy was the publisher of Li's book, the *Zhuan*

Falun, and that possibly seven hundred thousand party members were involved with the Falun. Jiang emphasized the need for people, especially party members, to study politics. He accepted the threat of Falun Gong as an ideological one: spiritual beliefs against militant atheism and historical materialism. He wished to purge the government and the military of such beliefs. His decision was in line with the suspicion of religious protest by the traditional Chinese state. As it turns out, the government's campaign against "evil cults" includes popular folk cults, as well as underground Christians—Catholics and Protestants—who meet at house churches.

In a country where many people are tired of Marxist ideology and hungry for religious and spiritual influences in their lives, cults can prevail, including the so-called Supreme Deity cult in which Liu Jiaguo, supposedly with a Christian mother, claimed to be a deity himself. He attracted ten thousand followers and swindled large sums of money, only to be hunted down and condemned to death. In his confession, Liu said: "People do not know what gods are. But if you flaunt a divine banner, people believe in you and are willing to dedicate everything to you."[25]

Li Hongzhi has not claimed divinity. But he often speaks as a mystic and a pantheist, in a language difficult for those who know little about Buddhist or Taoist thought to understand. When he claims to be part of the *qi* or energy, he is not just speaking of himself; he is speaking of all practitioners, although not all may have the transformed consciousness. He also claims to have certain preternatural gifts, such as making himself invisible or seeing through another's body for healing purposes. These are claims made by others, too; they are hard to prove. However, being a mystic and a teacher of morality does not elevate him necessarily to ethical superiority. A charismatic man, he has human failures and might have, as the government claims, changed his birth date to make it fall on the same date as the historical Buddha's to attract more believers. Does that mean he is claiming to be the Buddha himself? In Mahayana, the belief is that everyone is a Buddha potentially. It is not certain if Li Hongzhi means to claim that he already has become one in this life, but clearly, he seeks to demonstrate that he has special gifts and status.

The overarching issue is religious and spiritual freedom associated with human rights. In a dictatorship where so much of life is regulated by the state, the people need spiritual solace and individual freedom to practice meditation and qigong. However, they are being told that the most popular form of qigong is illegal and evil. Besides, qigong should be practiced in open air, and in the case of Falun Gong followers, home practice itself is difficult and dangerous. Believers are forbidden to read Li's books. They can keep what they have, and circulate these in secret, but risk official punishments. The government, indeed, is looking into their inner souls, and rendering judgments of good and evil, as well as of legality or illegality.

The Political Confrontation

This chapter has pointed out how the government has acted against both the letter and spirit of its own constitution: first, by arresting some leaders of the movement, then by banning the movement, and finally by declaring it an evil cult. In China, there is no real vehicle of expression for the people to communicate with their leaders, since ballot boxes do not count. The only means of mass protest is petition of the government. And yet, mass petitions become the basis for mass suppression. Herein lies the tragedy of the Tiananmen incident and of the Zhongnanhai incident.[26]

However, Falun Gong's response was surprising. It not only complained to the public, to Amnesty International, to various overseas governments, and to the United Nations. It also launched what may be called basically a civil disobedience campaign within China by sending followers to Tiananmen to unfurl the Falun Gong flag and then await arrest in front of the public eye. The world was shocked once more on January 23, 2001, when Tiananmen witnessed the self-immolation by fire of five persons, male and female—a child included—who made meditation gestures in the Falun Gong style as they committed suicide. A controversy ensued after this event, however, with the Chinese government asserting this to be a crime committed by Falun Gong followers, while the Falun Gong overseas denied that any member took part in the episode, quoting the movement's opposition to violence and suicide.[27] Isolated incidents elsewhere in Beijing followed. What should the world say? On the one hand, history has recorded Buddhist self-immolations by monks during the Vietnam War, and also much earlier in traditional China. Buddhist scriptures, like the Lotus Sutra, recount with approval myths of self-immolations. But the immediate and vehement denials by Falun Gong have deflected criticism from the group, while the deaths of all the participants make it nearly impossible to establish in the near future how these suicides were planned and enacted. If the Chinese government staged the gruesome event in order to discredit Falun Gong, it did not make any lasting impressions on account of the controversy.

Yet, what we find is a continuing political campaign on the part of the Falun movement to counterattack the government for its human rights record, even to the point of lobbying the United Nations Commission on Human Rights, and, later, demonstrating in Hong Kong during the Fortune Global Forum that Jiang Zemin attended.[28] It does appear that the Falun Gong has become a political force that is seeking justice for itself by pressuring China to democratize. However, it does not appear to have any agenda other than freedom for its following.

Still, there is an irony accompanying the political metamorphosis of the mass qigong movement. This paradox is not just that Falun Gong fulfills the incipient fears of the Chinese government. Nor is it the continual denial of the Falun members that they are not an organized movement. Such assertions are beyond credibility. The real irony is that, given such assertions, why should the movement fight so hard for its survival in China and worldwide? Would it not be more appropriate for the leader to ask his followers to stop public acts that would lead to instant arrest and possible death under torture? After all, the movement promotes physical and mental health, and the leader should protect his own, rather than have them suffer. What, otherwise, is he looking for?

In itself, Falun Gong is not political. However, under persecution, members have developed an astonishing political consciousness. To protect their own group survival, they have become a political force to be reckoned with. There are millions of Christians, both Catholics and Protestants, in China. Some practice in private. But they are not a political force. In contrast, Chinese Muslims easily could be, and in some cases—in Chinese Central Asia—they already have a political agenda. So do some Tibetan Buddhists. These groups want greater autonomy, if not separate statehoods. The deprivation by the government from the people of the freedom to practice breathing exercises and meditation is a serious infringement on personal liberty. Such infringements, in the long run, will work against the government. More respect and tolerance on the government's part is needed. The communist leadership will not gain more loyalty without them. In the case of the Falun Gong, it is difficult for the government to back down under pressure. But it could treat the followers with less harshness. Early in 2001, President Jiang Zemin talked of practicing more "virtuous" governance or *dezheng*, a term reminiscent of Confucian teachings. One could only hope this would happen.

The Future

What future has the Falun Gong? With persecution in China, and in spite of the boldness of many individuals, one must hesitate to speculate. But the Chinese government's decree to have Li Hongzhi arrested by Interpol has had no effect. Elsewhere, the number of followers is growing in Japan, Taiwan, Malaysia, Canada, the United States, and Europe. The members in China have diverse backgrounds and tend to be middle-aged and retired; but some of them are expert enough with electronic mail and Internet surfing to stay in constant connection. The members overseas include many younger people. It would appear that Falun Gong's future is that of an underground cult in China, and that of an ascendant Eastern spiritual group in the West. But it will be one group among many—not necessarily always the most popular. It likely will attract some intelligent people who are searching for truth and meaning. But it is unlikely to become mainstream. The movement, after all, is going against the tide in Western culture. It appears to expect followers to believe totally in the leader; however, most intelligent people are not ready to surrender themselves so completely. Such loyalty is more like that required by so-called cults and by the Chinese Communist Party itself. Falun Gong is not another case of Aum Shinrikyō, or of the Jonestown cult—unless other developments set in. And last, whether it claims to be a religion or not, Falun Gong obviously has religious features.

In the case of modern Japan, many new religions became recognized only after World War II. Before that, their founders suffered official persecution and imprisonment. With democratization, China might eventually enjoy true freedom of religion. Many underground cults would then reemerge, including Falun Gong. However, we do not know how long political liberalization will take. It could be a very long time, at least decades.

Notes

1. See *Ming Pao* (Hong Kong), July 22–26, 1999; *South China Morning Post*, July 22–26, 1999.
2. Found at www.chinese-embassy.org.uk/news/pr9907221.html (no longer active), and www.fmprc.gov.cn, the latter for its May 2000 response to the United States Human Rights Commission on international religious freedom. The Falun Gong maintains many Web sites around the world; see, for example, www.falundafa

.org and http://faluninfo.net (accessed January 9, 2005), although they frequently change their names.

3. *U.S. News & World Report*, February 22, 1999, 46.

4. *People's Daily*, June 20, 1999, offers Jiang's comments at a government meeting without referring to Falun Gong.

5. Li Hongzhi, *Zhuan Falun* (Hong Kong: Falun Dafa Publication, 1998), 14.

6. Ibid., 360.

7. Ibid., 53–70.

8. Ibid., 301–12.

9. See ibid., 99.

10. See ibid., 34.

11. He Zouxiu, *Tianjin qinshaonian keji bolan*, no. 4, Tianjin, April 1999.

12. Translated from German, *China Heute* 18, nos. 3–4 (1999): 81.

13. See He, *Tianjin qinshaonian keji bolan*, 82.

14. *People's Daily*, overseas edition, October 28, 1999.

15. *People's Daily*, overseas edition, October 31, 1999, http://english.peopledaily.com.cn/english/199910/31/enc_19991031001013_TopNews.html.

16. *Globe and Mail*, July 22, 2000, A13.

17. *New York Times*, July 27, 1999.

18. *New York Times*, October 28, 1999, A3; October 30, A4.

19. *New York Times*, October 29, 1999, A10.

20. *New York Times*, December 1, 1999, A13.

21. *New York Times*, December 13, 1999, A12.

22. *Zhuan Falun*, 419–20.

23. *World Journal*, American edition, June 20, 1999.

24. *Economist*, May 1, 1999, 39–40; *Asian Wall Street Journal*, April 28, 1999, 10.

25. *New York Times*, September 8, 1999, A5.

26. Julia Ching, *Probing China's Soul: Religion, Politics and Protest in the People's Republic* (San Francisco: Harper and Row, 1990), chap. 7.

27. See www.CNN.com, January 24, 2001.

28. See www.CNN.com, May 4, 2001.

3

"Buddhism for the Human Realm" and Taiwanese Democracy

André Laliberté

The relevance of religious institutions to the process of democratization in Taiwan represents a marginal area of study in Western scholarship, with the exception of the literature on the Presbyterian Church.[1] This perhaps reflects the fact that, until recently, research in Chinese has not paid much attention to the role of religious movements in the transition toward democracy.[2] One of the most glaring gaps in our knowledge, curiously, involves one of the most important religious traditions of Taiwan, Buddhism, and no scholar has written extensively on the involvement of organizations belonging to that tradition in contemporary Taiwanese politics. This may be about to change, in the wake of new research on the history of Buddhism in Taiwan since the Qing dynasty,[3] and studies on large lay Buddhist organizations emerging during the period of democratic transition.[4] Some important questions about the significance of these organizations to the political process deserve to be addressed. In particular, not only were all Buddhist organizations of importance in Taiwan silent during the period of martial law (1947–1987), but also their voice was conspicuously unheard during the process of democratization ushered in throughout the 1990s. Considering that some other religious institutions, such as the Presbyterian Church, expressed clearly their views during the martial law period and after, why have most Buddhist organizations shunned political involvement? What factors prevent Buddhist organizations in Taiwan from joining other actors in the process of democratic consolidation? Finally, assuming that these organizations might become engaged politically, what kind of policies would they promote and what kind of ideals would they propagate?

Taiwanese Buddhist Organizations and Democratic Transition: Silence and Absence

The behavior of Buddhist organizations in Taiwan in the past two decades can best be described as indifferent to politics, in general, and to the process of democratization, in particular. Buddhist leaders have avoided opposing the government since the Nationalist Party (the Kuomintang, or KMT) established its control over Taiwan in 1945 and they have maintained that attitude toward the Democratic Progressive Party (Minjindang, or DPP) government. Sometimes, this indifference was of a clearly conservative, if not outright reactionary, nature: this much was clear when the leaders of the Buddhist Association of the Republic of China (ROC)—the BAROC or Zhongguo Fojiaohui—in 1982, criticized calls for the lifting of martial law and the creation of political parties.[5] Since the beginning of political reforms in the mid-1980s, only a few Buddhist individuals have joined other actors in the consolidation of democracy. One of the most noted among them, Zhaohui (Chao Fei), is a famous nun who has criticized the authoritarian tendencies she observes in Chinese societies.[6] Chen Lü'an (Chen Li-an), a lay Buddhist who served as the first civilian national defense minister in 1990, left the KMT and ran as an independent candidate in the 1996 presidential election.[7] Wu Boxiong (Wu Po-hsiung), currently head of the ROC chapter of the Buddha Light International Organization (BLIA, or Guoji Foguanghui),[8] is a popular Hakka politician who served before as interior minister and KMT secretary general under successive Li Denghui (Lee Teng-hui) administrations. Besides these individual initiatives, no major Taiwanese Buddhist organization has expressed support for the process of democratic consolidation currently under way. Yet, this indifference to politics should not be construed as proof that the monks and nuns heading Taiwanese Buddhist organizations are aloof from this-worldly concerns. Quite the contrary. The spiritual leaders of the two largest Taiwanese Buddhist organizations, Foguangshan and the Buddhist Compassion Relief Tzu Chi Foundation (hereafter Ciji, or Ciji Gongdehui), have, in fact, overseen over the years the growth of their monastic communities into large institutions, running their own hospitals and clinics, universities, publishing houses, and television channels.[9] With a membership exceeding one million people for Foguangshan[10] and two million for Ciji,[11] in a Buddhist population of 4.9 million,[12] these organizations represent a formidable source of political capital.

The main Taiwanese Buddhist organizations did not oppose the government when it enforced its authoritarian rule up to 1989,[13] and they did not come forward to support democratic consolidation, either by sponsoring candidates or by voicing their opinions on public policies. They did not come forward publicly to express support or their compassion for the victims of the government's repression during the major events that marked that process of democratization, such as the Gaoxiong (Kaohsiung) incident in 1979. However, they did not oppose the founding of the Democratic Progressive Party in 1986. Two gestures by Xingyun (Hsing Yun), the founder of the Foguangshan monastic order, briefly suggested that some Taiwanese Buddhist organizations were about to join other popular movements in pushing for the consolidation of democracy: the support lent to the candidacy of Chen Lü'an in the presidential election of 1996,[14] and participation in a grass-roots campaign that led to the downfall of the Lien Zhan (Lien Chan) cabinet in 1997.[15] Subsequent events, however, would reveal that this involvement of Foguangshan was meant not to oppose an authoritarian regime (by 1995, after all, Taiwan was entering the stage of democratic consolidation) but, rather, to express reservation toward liberalizing trends that seemed to go too far in the eyes of Xingyun and his followers. Hence, after the resignation of Premier Lien Zhan, Xingyun did not oppose the KMT and continued to work closely with the KMT Central Committee—on which he had served since 1986—and even accepted an appointment by the cabinet-level Overseas Chinese Affairs Commission (OCAC, or Qiaoweihui) in 1997.[16] Xingyun did not sponsor any opposition candidate during the presidential election of 2000, and after Chen Shui-bian won the election in March of that year, the new president made certain he would pay a visit to Foguangshan. This was recognition from the DPP leadership that Buddhist voters are an important constituency to woo. After the DPP won a plurality of the vote in the Legislative Yuan election of 2001, and after Taiwan became a truly multiparty system with the consolidation of four parties, Buddhist organizations found a new structure in which they could exercise considerable influence if they wished to do so.

The limited success of candidates who have been endorsed by Buddhist leaders leaves open the question about the influence of the latter on their followers' political behavior and electoral choices. Although BLIA members were briefly mobilized in 1997, they have refrained from intervening openly in politics in the following years. Xingyun has maintained good relations with the KMT since Lien Zhan's resignation, and has never intervened in subsequent electoral campaigns to sponsor either independent candidates or candidates affiliated with parties that have maintained or developed good relations with the BLIA, such as the New Party (NP, or Xindang), or, more recently, the People First Party (PFP, or Qinmindang). Meanwhile, Xingyun has never publicly criticized either the DPP or the Taiwan Solidarity Union (TSU, or Taiwan Tuanjie Lianmeng), the party sponsored by Li Denghui. The impact of Xingyun on the political behavior of lay Buddhists remains difficult to pinpoint because his views have not been consistent over the years and two important figures close to him, Chen Lü'an and Wu Boxiong, were involved in opposite camps during the 1996 election.[17] With respect to Ciji, no influence can be inferred from its leader, except, perhaps an indifference toward the entire process of electoral competition. For instance, the background of its leader, Zhengyan (Cheng Yen), as a "person from this province" (*Benshengren*),[18] has never translated into the suggestion on her part that she is somewhat closer to the "pan-Green" camp of the DPP and TSU, identified with Benshengren assertiveness, than she is to the two parties of the "pan-Blue" camp, the KMT and the PFP, which stand for the status quo. Opinions expressed by Ciji workers, volunteers, and commissioners over the years reflect this: They express a wide diversity of views concerning the DPP, Taiwanese independence, and other issues. This profession of neutrality reflects the belief expressed by Zhengyan herself that politics are too "complex." Clearly, an involvement in the emotional issue of national identity could prove threatening for the organization's cohesion and reputation of impartiality vis-à-vis the population.

The neutrality or the indifference expressed so far, however, should not lead to the conclusion that Taiwanese Buddhists are irrelevant to the politics of the island: The assiduity with which politicians court their leaders, after all, demonstrates otherwise. The absence of surveys on voting preference according to religious beliefs precludes for the moment the profiling of average Buddhist voters and the policies they would likely prefer. Could survey data on electoral choice, party identification, and candidate preference, in light of various demographic attributes such as class, gender, ethnic and regional origins, education, and age group, help predict the political behavior of Buddhist organizations when the demographic attributes of each become known? Even if these figures were available, such information might not produce a portrait representing the views of most Buddhist voters, because, as Ding Renjie's (Ting Renchieh's) study of Ciji illustrates, there exist different categories of membership in such organizations, associated with varying degrees of commitment.[19] Keeping in mind this caveat, one fact can nonetheless be asserted: The demographic characteristics of Foguangshan and Ciji do not appear to differ significantly from each other, and both organizations appeal to the same mainstream constituencies of middle-class Taiwanese. The two organizations rely on massive lay support all over the island, women are very active in both organizations, and both attract Taiwanese of all ethnic backgrounds.[20] Overall, these demographic characteristics of the two organizations raise an intriguing paradox: They are not distinct enough to explain the difference between the BLIA's greater political assertiveness in 1996 and 1997 and the period before or after those two years. This issue, however, is too complicated to be discussed within the limits of this chapter. Therefore, the following sections focus on the motives behind the generally tacit support that Buddhist organizations gave to previous authoritarian regimes and the organizations' current absence in the ongoing process of democratic consolidation.

Understanding the Attitude of Buddhist Organizations

The extreme prudence displayed by contemporary Taiwanese Buddhist organizations contrasts with the more assertive, if not outright radical, attitude exhibited by other Buddhists on the Chinese mainland and Taiwan since the turn of the twentieth century. Even the most revered figure among the Buddhist mainstream in Taiwan, Taixu (Tai Hsu), a noted monk, was politically active during the Republican era. Considered, today, in the People's Republic as a Chinese Buddhist equivalent to Martin Luther,[21] he befriended in his lifetime socialists and anarchists, opposed conservative élites within the Buddhist monastic order, encouraged the development of a strong laity, and favored internal democracy within Chinese Buddhism.[22] Many other lay Buddhists living in Taixu's time also believed that their faith represented a source of renewal for China and an alternative to the declining Confucian order of the late Qing dynasty. Individuals such as Zhang Bingling,[23] Liang Qichao,[24] and the young Liang Shuming[25] had reflected on important political problems faced by their compatriots, if not by humankind as a whole, on the basis of their own knowledge of Buddhism. Although nationalism and socialism would quickly supersede the idealist views of these thinkers and hold sway among most Chinese intellectuals, their effort demonstrated that Buddhist philosophy does not, a priori, shun vigorous discussion of down-to-earth political matters. The same could be observed for Taiwan, even when it was under Japanese colonial rule. Some individuals did not shun controversies that could even endanger their lives, such as the monk Zhengfeng (aka Lin Qiuwu), who went as far as espousing Marxism and Taiwanese self-determination.[26] However, after the Republic of China asserted its authority in Taiwan in 1945, and after Taixu himself passed away in 1947, no prominent Buddhist leader has come close to adopting such views. Throughout the period of martial law and since the transition to democracy got under way, no contemporary prominent Buddhist leader has emerged to hold views that resemble the activist stance of Taixu, despite the claims made by most of them that they follow his theological orientations.[27] Buddhist theology, "Chineseness," or authoritarianism cannot account for this behavior.

Buddhist theology has not prevented adherents of that faith in other parts of East Asia from becoming involved in the politics of their societies. Buddhists in many Asian countries have used their faith as a justification for their advocacy of social change, if not the establishment of a new political order. Many of them, from Thailand to Japan, even have gone so far as to create their own lay organizations or political parties for that purpose.[28] Their faith has inspired political goals that vary from country to country. In Thailand, Sulak Sivaraksa has attempted to launch a critique of unfettered consumerism in his project of Dhammic socialism.[29] In Japan, the Society for the Creation of Value (Soka Gakkai) represents a support group for the New Party for Clean Politics (Shin Komeito, or New Komeito), the third largest party in Japan, and works to promote legislation emphasizing peace, environmental protection, and social welfare.[30] In Vietnam, the United Buddhist Church has led mass resistance against corrupt authoritarian governments and American intervention.[31] These different groups' behaviors serve to demonstrate that Buddhism is not indifferent to this-worldly concerns. In fact, Buddhist theology does not inspire any specific policy: Although most of the politically active Buddhist devotees pursue their objectives through peaceful means, some others, in Japan, Sri Lanka, and other countries, have adopted aggressive behavior in the promotion of their objectives. During the first half of the twentieth century, for instance, Suzuki, a Zen Master, condoned the aggressive policy of the Japanese militarist government.³² Even more recently, Buddhist monks have been involved in the Sri Lankan civil war.³³ Thus, Buddhist theology does not preclude or encourage political participation, but it also does not provide guidance about the direction taken by Buddhists who would become involved in politics.

Putative characteristics of Chinese culture are not more convincing than Buddhist theology as explanations for the apolitical behavior of Taiwanese Buddhist organizations. Besides the question of defining the characteristics of "Chineseness," the behaviors of other religious institutions refute that claim. Although one may argue that politically active religious organizations, such as the Presbyterian Church in Taiwan, represent an exception because of their privileged transnational connections and the support they can gain from coreligionists in the West,³⁴ the political involvement of other organizations without this type of external linkage rebuts the suggestion that Chinese religious institutions, in general, are not interested in politics. A major trend of Chinese politics well known to historians is the pervasive involvement of traditional religious institutions in politics: This participation has ranged from the support bestowed to the state by the institutions of local diffused religions to the toppling of dynasties with the help, if not at the instigation, of sectarian movements.³⁵ Taiwan has not experienced any such religious-inspired upheaval since 1945, but one major religious institution entirely indigenous to China, the Yiguandao (Way of Pervasive Unity),³⁶ played a significant role in the process of democratization in Taiwan during the 1990s that remains largely ignored in the West: Mobilization of voters by the sect has helped KMT candidates belonging to the reformist factions led by Li Denghui to win local elections that thereby ensured consolidation of the reformist wing of that party.³⁷ This case, as well as growing evidence emerging from the People's Republic about the role of religious institutions in local politics, demonstrates that the Chinese identity of Buddhist institutions in Taiwan cannot explain their quietist attitude.³⁸

The legacy of an authoritarian government—such as the four decades of KMT rule under martial law—can leave many different kinds of imprints, ranging from the nostalgia for previous arrangements, in which specific institutions stood to benefit in terms of authority, to the mistrust of any government, which results from an institutional memory of persecution. Clearly, this double bind is relevant to Taiwanese Buddhist organizations. Hence, until 1987, the BAROC benefited considerably from the corporatist structure imposed by the KMT because it was illegal for any other Buddhist institution to be established outside of its authority.[39] The leaders of that organization, not surprisingly, had no reason to support the unraveling of a structure that had favored them until then and it is not surprising that, throughout the 1990s as the process of democratization unfolded, the BAROC leaders consistently asked for more control by the central government over religious affairs, hoping to strengthen their declining position within the Buddhist community by maintaining their role as custodians of the faith.[40] The effect of the institutional memory of authoritarianism on the Buddhist organizations' lukewarm support for democratization, however, may not emerge as a convincing explanation when one keeps in mind that state repression of religious activities, primarily through the provincial government's police administration, affected Yiguandao, the Soka Gakkai, the Presbyterian Church, and so on, but not Buddhist organizations, per se.[41] Evidence of this high degree of tolerance from the KMT for Buddhism is the fact that other Buddhist institutions were established following 1966, along with the BAROC, despite the corporatist arrangement enforced in Taiwan. Another legacy left by authoritarianism, however, may have had a more lasting effect: the structure of Buddhist organizations.[42] Hence, the leadership of Ciji is based entirely on the charismatic leadership of Zhengyan, who is helped by a board of directors accountable to no one else.[43] The Foguangshan monastic order, which supervises the BLIA, is also a hierarchy: Leadership succession is determined by the deliberations of the eleven-member Committee for Religious Affairs.[44] This adoption of authoritarian structures by Buddhist organizations suggests that important elements of the explanation for their political behavior may reside within the organizations themselves.

To sum up, theology, "Chineseness," and authoritarianism are all insufficient, when each is taken alone, to explain the lack of enthusiasm displayed by Taiwanese Buddhist organizations toward democratization; however, the ways in which the leaders of these organizations have interacted with these factors may provide a better explanation. Studies undertaken about the behavior of religious organizations in the United States have suggested that the political stands they adopt are shaped by the preferences of their leaders, who are granted a legitimacy that transcends external constraints, and, therefore, are able to mediate for their followers concerning the impact of theology, the social environment, and political circumstances.[45] Yet, these findings have left open one important question: To what extent have social and political contexts shaped the preferences of these leaders? Hence, in the context of Republican China, the reformist ideas of Taixu and the modernist views of lay Buddhists emerged in the conditions of social upheaval that arose during the time in which they lived. Conversely, the conservative climate in which the KMT exercised its rule in Taiwan following 1945, and the concern of many Buddhists for the survival of their religion in China, especially during the Cultural Revolution, contributed together to encourage a drift toward a more cautious attitude on the part of Buddhists in Taiwan, who looked at the island's society as the repository of Chinese traditions.[46] The acceleration of democratization in Taiwan, while not changing the strategic situation of the island vis-à-vis mainland China, has nonetheless significantly transformed the domestic situation and offers considerable opportunities for any group that wants to become involved politically. As discussed above, however, the significant changes in Taiwan's political system have not led to a noticeable change in the political behavior of Buddhist organizations. Is it because the changes are too recent? Or is it because the leaders of Taiwanese Buddhist organizations believe that the current transformations are only cosmetic and fail to address their concerns? In other words, under which conditions could the interests of these organizations' members and the ideas of their leaders change? In an attempt to answer this question, the next section looks at the ways in which recent changes in Taiwanese society and in its political system affect the political views of the leaders of Buddhist organizations.

Understanding the Muted Response of Buddhist Organizations to Democratization

While theology, the cultural environment, and political culture may have shaped over decades—if not centuries—the range of options available to Buddhist leaders when they select their preferences, including their preference for democratization, factors pertaining to socioeconomic conditions and the political context, which could influence their choice for the best strategies available to achieve these goals, have yet to be examined. In particular, more needs to be known about the extent to which economic growth, by creating new opportunities for the expansion of religious institutions and the proliferation of new ones, may present well-established institutions with competition that they did not have to face under an authoritarian regime. In short, prosperity and democratization may not necessarily be an advantage for them. Among political factors, at least three stand out for their possible impact on shaping the preferences of Taiwanese Buddhist leaders. First, and with respect to democratization per se, it is possible that the leaders of Taiwanese Buddhist organizations find that many of the fundamental premises of democracy are incompatible with the tenets of their religious worldviews. Second, it is not clear to what extent the divisive nature of ethnic cleavages within Taiwanese society may compel Taiwanese Buddhist leaders to avoid engagement in politics, lest it have a negative impact on the growth of their memberships. Finally, it is worth asking to what extent Taiwan's strategic situation compels these leaders to adopt prudent positions.

The impact of social change on the behavior of religious institutions in Taiwan has been abundantly documented, and a growing literature exposes the relationship between the "economic miracle" and the explosion of religious expression that comes in its wake. However, this effect on Buddhists' views of democratization has yet to be clearly understood. Data on the growth in the number of Buddhist temples between 1960 and 1989 show the congruence between economic growth and the expansion of religious activities.[47] The wealth of publications in Chinese and Western languages attests to the positive impact of economic growth on the expansion of religious institutions.[48] This phenomenon, however, comes with two drawbacks. First, the simultaneous expansion of the economy and of religious activities often coincides with a commercialization of religion, which, in turn, puts the credibility of established institutions to the test. The case of Foguangshan is illustrative of this predicament: Victim of its own success, the organization has been severely criticized for its positive valuation of material wealth.[49] Second, and in relation to the problem of commercialization, the "this-worldly" orientations of established organizations, such as Foguangshan and Ciji, leave unsatisfied many people who are looking for a more esoteric religious practice, thus providing the incentive for the development of new cults. The proliferation of new religious movements, such as Forshang Buddhism (Foshengzong), the Way of the Children (Haizidao), the Wheel of the Law (Falun Gong), and the like, suggests the existence of that demand in Taiwan.[50] To what extent organizations belonging to more orthodox traditions welcome this development remains to be seen. The attitude of the BAROC in this regard is instructive:

Throughout the 1980s and the 1990s, the organization pushed in vain for legislation on religion that would, in effect, limit the number of legalized religions.[51] Although the BAROC's proposals for a law on religion was resisted by a few small Buddhist organizations then, as well as many individuals belonging to other faiths,[52] Xingyun and Zhengyan did not oppose the effort, thereby suggesting their indifference, if not their hostility, to freedom of religion from state intervention that is inherent to democratic consolidation.

Among political factors, the workings of democracy themselves may not necessarily appeal to the promotion of the interests and the ideals of the large Taiwanese Buddhist organizations: In particular, the proliferation of organizations allowed by democratic institutions makes the advocacy of Buddhist interests under one leader much more difficult, and competition among political parties representing antagonistic interests contradicts the goal of harmony they are supposed to nurture. The argument that democracy may not serve the interests of Buddhists may seem counterintuitive in light of the absence of legal existence for any Buddhist organization besides the BAROC until 1989, when new legislation ended that privilege. Yet, a closer look at the history of Foguangshan and Ciji—which were both established in 1966—reveals that the leaders of both organizations managed to take advantage of the legal structure prevailing during martial law.[53] Xingyun developed his organization under the umbrella of the BAROC, and was indeed a high-ranking member of that organization.[54] Zhengyan set up her own institution as a charity, and, therefore, never competed with the BAROC for the representation of Buddhist interests: In fact, her organization is not even registered with the Ministry of Interior's Bureau for Religious Affairs.[55] In light of these circumstances, the process of democratization, which allows younger Buddhist monks to create their own representative organizations, not only diminishes severely the authority of the BAROC secretary general but also prevents charismatic leaders, such as Xingyun, from rallying a majority of Buddhists under his guidance. This has resulted in many different voices speaking for Buddhism today in Taiwan. Competition among Buddhist institutions, in turn, refutes the impression of harmony in society and disinterest in politics that leaders like Zhengyan have so successfully nurtured over the years. Although differences of opinion among Taiwanese Buddhists do not lead to acrimony, they are important enough to prevent the creation of an organization representing a majority of them.[56] The 1996 presidential election taught Buddhists one important lesson in this regard: The results achieved by Chen Lü'an showed that a candidate supported by a major Buddhist organization such as Foguangshan, who also relied on other sectors of civil society, as shown by his choice of Wang Qingfeng (Wang Ching-feng) as his vice-presidential candidate, could not garner more than 10 percent of the vote, and that many Buddhist voters preferred to cast their vote for more established parties.[57] Therefore, it is not surprising that neither Foguangshan nor Ciji showed interest in supporting any of the contenders for the 2000 presidential election, lest political backing would further increase division among Buddhist organizations.

A second political factor, the communal cleavage between the Benshengren and Waishengren or "those from outside the province," [58] which is based on places of origin,[59] is also likely to exercise an impact on the preferences of Taiwanese Buddhist leaders that could bode ill for their active support of democracy. Successive KMT governments controlled by the minority Waishengren ruled the island until the late 1980s, even though the Benshengren represented a majority of the population. While the late president Jiang Jingguo (Chiang Ching-kuo) promoted Benshengren in the party and in public administration during the 1980s, Taiwanese politics continues to be influenced by this cleavage, which resonates with the issue of national security.[60] The leaders of both Foguangshan and Ciji have always sought to transcend these divisions. Xingyun has demonstrated throughout his career the political acumen of selecting Benshengren for positions of importance in his organization.[61] Zhengyan, although identified as a Benshengren herself, has never expressed in her numerous discourses either a sense of entitlement for Benshengren or resentment toward Waishengren. Nor do Buddhist leaders play up other communal cleavages based on ethnicity among the inhabitants of Taiwan, separating aboriginal people and ethnic Chinese, Hoklo and Hakka among the Benshengren, or Buddhists and adherents to the other fifteen faiths recognized by the law. This attitude, which may help in nurturing a sense of national identity that is devoid of ethnic or communal dimension and is based on citizenship, is certainly commendable. However, by refraining to speak against the suffering that was experienced by the Yuanzhumin at the hands of ethnic Chinese settlers, and by Benshengren élites who were harassed by the Waishengren-controlled KMT during the period of martial law, Buddhist leaders have deprived themselves of adopting a principled stand on the ethnic divide. Lacking credibility on this sensitive issue, it is not surprising that they would hesitate to become involved in politics, and thus refrain from making pronouncements on any dimension of democratic consolidation.

Finally, a third political factor, the strategic situation experienced in Taiwan, also indirectly influences the attitude of Buddhist organizations. In relation to the cleavages mentioned above, the status of Taiwan as a de facto independent state, either as the Republic of China or the Republic of Taiwan, divides Taiwanese and presents another reason for Buddhist organizations to keep their distance from politics. The members of the KMT and the supporters of the People First Party, together known as the "Blue Camp," support the continuation of the Republic of China, while members of the DPP and the TSU, who constitute the "Green Camp," lean toward the formation of the Republic of Taiwan. Parties may paint each other as more extremist on the issue of Taiwanese independence or reunification with China, but they all fundamentally seek votes from the same constituency. The vast majority of the population, which is satisfied with the status quo, agrees with the popular slogan, "not pressing for independence, but not pressing for reunification."[62] On this issue, Taiwanese Buddhist organizations have clearly preferred the existing situation and have never openly supported Taiwanese independence, fearing its consequences in terms of interstate violence. Would the leaders of Taiwanese Buddhist organizations, then, consider subordination to the People's Republic of China a lesser evil than armed conflict? Any answer to this question is a matter of speculation, but it is clear that Taiwanese Buddhist organizations have gone very far in trying to establish good relations across the Taiwan Strait. Ciji, in particular, has offered relief to provinces affected by floods and other natural disasters since 1991. Taiwanese Buddhists may take some comfort from the experience of their coreligionists in the Chinese Buddhist Association (CBA, or Zhongguo Fojiao Xiehui) in the People's Republic of China (PRC), who have weathered traumatic events since 1953,[63] but are now experiencing a remarkable revival. If the PRC tried directly to impose its authority on the island, it is not inconceivable that mainstream Taiwanese Buddhist organizations would revert to the practice that was adopted by the BAROC when the KMT implemented martial law in Taiwan. The rationale would be the same as then: concerns for self-preservation—whether of the organization or the faith itself. That is, cooperation with those who favor PRC sovereignty over Taiwan may appear a better guarantee for the survival of Taiwanese Buddhist institutions in the long run, as long as the stands of the opposition are interpreted in Beijing as support for Taiwan's independence.

Although prudence, if not approval of the official ideology, has explained the indifference of most Buddhist leaders to democracy during the period of martial law, the absence of state repression in the current climate of democratic consolidation and the diversity of views upheld by legislators and officials of all parties may compel the leaders of Buddhist organizations to become more proactive. The lack of concern for democratization by the large Taiwanese Buddhist organizations represents an increasingly untenable position to adopt because politics on the island is becoming more polarized, and taking refuge in passivity may simply be perceived as cooperation with the adverse camp. This situation presents Buddhist organizations with the opportunity to act as disinterested third parties. However, assuming Buddhist leaders might decide to intervene in politics, what kind of politics would they be likely to endorse for their lay followers? Although Taiwanese Buddhists have yet to produce any systematic reflection comparable to the Catholic Church's social doctrine—not to mention its Liberation Theology—or inspire any movement that could be associated with a trend of "engaged Buddhism," the political leanings of Buddhist organizations in Taiwan can nevertheless be surmised by an examination of the specific political concerns raised by their leaders over the years.

An Outline of Taiwanese Buddhist Political Philosophy

The pace of democratization and the uncertainties it presents for the continuing growth of Buddhist organizations may help explain the organizations' attitude toward democracy, but do not say much about the political values they might stand for if they decided to become involved in politics. Two points can be asserted with confidence about the political orientations of Buddhist organizations. First, with respect to their beliefs, the writings of Xingyun, Zhengyan, Yinshun (Yin Shun), and others suggest that most of the popular Buddhist leaders subscribe to political philosophies that try to reconcile socially conservative values with the acceptance of neoliberal economic policies. Besides this fundamental element of convergence, however, important disagreements among them arise about two issues: Buddhists' participation in politics and their relationship to wealth. These divergences point to the difficulty inherent in the establishment of a Buddhist political doctrine that is supported by most adherents of the faith. In particular, the contrasting views of Xingyun and Zhengyan on political participation, as well as their variant opinions on wealth, discussed below, illustrate the obstacles preventing the constitution of a specifically Buddhist political stand. Second, looking at the practice endorsed by Taiwanese Buddhists' approaches to politics from a comparative perspective, their embrace of mainstream society demonstrates that none of them approves radical theologies. However, they also differ from the large, mainstream religious institutions found in Western Europe and Japan that have worked with confessional parties to reconcile their support for market economies and policies of redistributive social justice. Taiwanese Buddhist institutions prefer to quietly exercise their influence through informal channels within existing institutions, in line with their conservative theology. The following two subsections elaborate on these two points.

Taiwanese Buddhist Perspectives on Politics: A Diversity of Conservative Views

The political views embraced by the leaders of Buddhist organizations do not differ in most respects from the positions adopted by the conservative politicians affiliated with the KMT, the PFP, or the NP who support the status quo in cross-Strait relations, sanction the market economy, approve the principle of a minimum welfare state, and who still dominated the ROC legislature in the summer of 2005.[64] Until the lifting of martial law in 1987, Buddhist organizations aligned themselves with KMT governments in international forums and in domestic politics, but since the middle of the 1990s, they have distanced themselves from the party, which was suspected of covertly leaning toward greater Taiwanese assertiveness on the international stage under the leadership of Li Denghui. In retrospect, this should not come as a surprise. Studies of the KMT ideology by Thomas Metzger suggest that the "revolutionary" legacy of the party, which embraced the three principles of nationalism, democratization, and social welfare,[65] was bound to be less—not more—conservative than the worldviews embraced by Buddhist leaders in the second half of the twentieth century. This became clear in the 1990s, when the KMT, under the influence of a growing number of Benshengren, became more lukewarm on the issue of reunification with China, in contrast to many of the important Buddhist monks, who, born on the mainland, continued to support that goal. To the extent that they oppose socialism and have expressed reservations toward political liberalism—but not toward neoliberal economic policies—most leaders of the Taiwanese Buddhist organizations can be defined as conservatives.[66] That is, they agree with worldviews critical of the belief that volition is powerful enough to remold human nature by the creation of a new social order, and assert that the appropriate analogy for people within a polity is not the contractarian model of liberal theory, but the family. Perhaps not surprisingly for people who uphold an old tradition, they agree that allegiance to authority is part of a convention, not a matter for negotiation. In their behavior and in their writings, Buddhist leaders such as Xingyun, Zhengyan, and Yinshun agree with these classical definitions of conservative political philosophy in which the ultimate value is not individual liberty, but established authority, and in which there exists no natural right transcending the citizen's obligation to be ruled.

The values advocated by the leaders of the BAROC, Foguangshan, and Ciji, nevertheless, differ from those of the conservative factions within the KMT in one important respect: They are derived from a theological view of the world. They mirror in some respects the ideologies of the West European conservatives for whom, in the words of Noel O'Sullivan, "everything has a place to it assigned by God."[67] In that sense, the leaders of BAROC, Foguangshan, and Ciji differ radically from the KMT conservative old guard, whose ideas rest on a belief in the existence of historical laws and objective barriers to human volition, such as passions and emotions, of which German romanticism represented a good example.[68] In other words, the conservative views of Taiwanese Buddhist leaders, premised on theological ideals that emphasize harmony within society, moral rectitude from the political leadership, and altruism from the population, differ from the perspective of the KMT old guard on revolutionary nationalism. But while the KMT conservative leanings are not necessarily incompatible with democracy—as the evolution of the past decade demonstrates—democracy appears problematic for many Buddhist leaders. From the perspective of Xingyun and Zhengyan, the competition for votes between the "pan-Green" and the "pan-Blue" parties implies fierce and bitter struggles that demonstrate the divisive nature of democracy. In that respect, they agree with conservative KMT figures such as Hao Bocun (Hau Po-tsun) and his supporters—who have joined the NP and the PFP—who believed that the enforced unanimity and the semblance of harmony prevailing during the martial law period have given way to disorder and uncertainty.

Although Buddhists leaders do not publicly criticize the process of democratization, their speeches on the "purification of minds" and their ban on political participation do not support it.

The limited evidence available on their political ideas suggests that Buddhist leaders, while not opposed to democracy per se, hold political views that are more germane to neocorporatist regimes and other forms of minimal democracies. Although the term, corporatism, has been abandoned in the political science literature to describe political developments in postindustrial societies,[69] it seems more relevant to understanding the politics of Taiwan, where the state has long licensed specific organizations with a monopoly over representation of their constituencies.[70] Although corporatist structures were undermined throughout the 1990s, organizations such as the BAROC have waged a rearguard campaign to maintain them. Because the BAROC benefited from the corporatist structure of representation of different sectors of society, which was enforced until the late 1980s, this should not be a surprise. Although Xingyun also has advocated some state intervention to regulate religion in Taiwan, Zhengyan has never expressed such a view. However, her own ideas on political participation suggest that she subscribes to a minimalist form of democracy: People have the right to vote, but they should not become involved in politics, which is considered unworthy activity.[71] Zhengyan's negative views on politics are derived from the teaching of her mentor, Yinshun, who derides it as a pursuit as condemnable as prostitution and drunkenness. This is a sentiment mirrored by many Buddhist individuals belonging to Ciji whom the author has met over the years, who admit that they see politics as a source of perplexity and confusion. Even Xingyun, who approved the candidacy of Chen Lü'an, justified his decision in purely religious terms. However, besides these similarities in the negative opinion held toward the confusion inherent to politics, important differences remain.

Although Xingyun and Zhengyan, like many other important contemporary Buddhist leaders in Taiwan, claim to uphold the legacy of Taixu, they differ in many respects from him and use his legacy as a rationale to justify a diversity of attitudes. The complex and controversial views of Taixu himself on politics, social justice, and nationalism, are no stranger to the inconsistent interpretations of his thought.[72] The most lasting legacies of Taixu's work are the reform of the monastic order, the development of the laity, and the creation of an international organization representing Buddhists,[73] objectives that Xingyun and

Zhengyan also approve in their own activities. Taixu, however, also took a keen interest in politics and was close to lay activists such as Ouyang Jianwu and Zhang Binglin.[74] The KMT suspected some of its followers—such as Xingyun and Yinshun—of communist sympathies after they escaped the turmoil of the civil war and relocated to Taiwan. Subsequent events would demonstrate that these concerns were misplaced. Nonetheless, this suspicion may explain why both Yinshun and Xingyun over the years have avoided any association with the most radical elements of Taixu's thinking, and substituted for his concept of "Buddhism for human life" (*rensheng fojiao*), the idea of "Buddhism for the human realm" (*renjian fojiao*). The result is that, while Xingyun is a liberal who reconciles "spreading the Dharma" (*hung fa*) with a wealthy sangha in his interpretation of renjian fojiao,[75] Yinshun, arguably one of the most respected heirs of Taixu still living in Taiwan, uses renjian fojiao in more restrictive terms,[76] advocating a frugal lifestyle and inspiring his most famous student, Zhengyan, to use charity work as a path to enlightenment.[77]

As we have seen before, however, an examination of the course of action undertaken during the first decade of democratization by the leaders of Foguangshan and Ciji shows important differences between them in terms of their political behavior. Foguangshan has supported Chen Lü'an, and Xingyun has endorsed other candidates in local elections over the years. Wu Boxiong, a prominent member of the KMT, is also president of the ROC branch of the BLIA, the satellite lay organization of Foguangshan. Xingyun himself, as discussed before, has been involved with the KMT as adviser for the OCAC. He has said of Buddhists that they should follow Taixu's motto: "participating in politics, but not governing" (*canzheng erbu ganzhi*).[78] Zhengyan, for her part, has consistently distanced herself from politics, and says that members of Ciji "care about but do not get involved in politics" (*guanxin dan bu jieru zhengzhi*).[79] During the presidential election of 1999, however, a convergence among the large Buddhist organizations emerged, with Xingyun not endorsing any candidate in particular, therefore moving closer to the position of noninterference chosen by Zhengyan.

The views of Xingyun and Zhengyan on wealth and poverty also differ significantly. Xingyun has received his fair share of criticism for his positive appreciation of wealth, a view seen by other Buddhists as contrary to the vows of frugality expected of monks. The radically different views of Zhengyan on poverty also deserve mention because they shed light on the possibility for Buddhists to develop their own version of a "social doctrine of the Church," or a "social gospel," which has been instrumental in developing Christian democracy in Western Europe. The analysis by Zhengyan of poverty is straightforward: It blames illness, and, therefore, offers health care to eradicate poverty. Zhengyan's simple diagnosis aside, other large Buddhist organizations have yet to develop a systematic reflection on the issue. In sum, while Xingyun reconciles "this-worldly Buddhism" with the pursuit of wealth, Zhengyan emphasizes selflessness. These irreconcilable differences illustrate that Buddhist élites have yet to elaborate from renjian fojiao a "social doctrine" that can offer to Taiwanese voters an alternative to the existing parties' established social policies. Besides these differences, however, the leaders of these mainstream Taiwanese Buddhist organizations share two fundamental premises, making their differences trivial: They do not criticize the principle of the market economy and they do not believe that the state has any role to play in the redistribution of wealth. To put it mildly, this consensus does not represent an ironclad endorsement of democratization: Laissez-faire economics and a minimal welfare state can thrive under authoritarian regimes as well.

A Comparative Perspective

The overwhelming body of evidence available on Taiwanese lay Buddhist organizations demonstrates unambiguously that none of these groups nurtures the kind of resentment against the modern state that brings about the extremist and antisecular politics of lay organizations such as the World Hindu Council (better known as the VHP, or Vishwa Hindu Parishad) and the Jana Sangh in India,[80] the Islamist movements from the Maghreb to the Mashrek,[81] or Buddhist radical movements such as the Sri Lankan Mavbima Surakime Vyaparaya,[82] or the Japanese Aum Shinrikyō. These cases of religious extremism are often the expression of a resistance to the secular state, which is considered highly problematic by these organizations and somehow alien to the native culture.[83] Taiwanese Buddhist organizations do not hold such views. They are also uninterested in the advocacy of alternative sources of authority or new modes of political identity, as is often the case in other societies in Southeast and Northeast Asia.[84] Even though Buddhist organizations in Taiwan may criticize the virtue of specific leaders or scorn politicians, they differ from these religious organizations in a significant way:

They shy away from criticizing the state's secular values and seek to join the mainstream rather than to subvert it and replace it with their own views. In sum, Taiwanese Buddhist organizations do not belong to the class of phenomena associated with contemporary communal violence in other regions of the world or in other periods of Chinese history, and they are not alienated from mainstream society. In fact, their growth and success have been closely related to the expansion of capitalism and democratization.

Taiwanese Buddhist organizations are satisfied enough with the current social and political order to eschew the temptation of mobilizing their adherents into political parties that could push for policies more germane to the development of their values. Policies calling for sustainable development, an increase in foreign aid to developing countries, and animal rights, along with an emphasis on more traditional values that are critical of hedonistic consumer society, could presumably constitute a plank for a Buddhist political party. Buddhist organizations' support for a market economy and a compassionate social policy that includes the alleviation of poverty, in addition to their advocacy of moderately conservative moral values, place Buddhist lay organizations in the mainstream of Taiwanese society. In that respect, their situation does not differ much from that of lay Catholic and Protestant organizations sponsoring Christian-Democratic parties in post–World War II Western Europe. These groups articulated a political philosophy critical of liberalism and socialism, voiced since the nineteenth century in the "social doctrine of the Church,"[85] that did not differ much from what most Taiwanese Buddhist leaders stand for today. Furthermore, Chinese and Taiwanese Buddhists, like their Christian counterparts in Europe, can also claim to inherit a centuries-old legacy of charitable work, intellectual achievements, and close relations with secular authorities, from which they can draw to develop well-organized political parties.[86] Yet, in one crucial respect, Buddhists find themselves in a situation that differs considerably from what Christians have experienced for centuries in Western Europe: They cannot claim to represent a faith that is embraced by the overwhelming majority of the population. With the exception of a brief period during the Sui dynasty, Buddhism never became a state religion. In 2000 Buddhists represented less than half of all declared religious believers in Taiwan, and, therefore, could not hope to build from their minority position the basis for a party that could attract the vote of a majority.[87]

In addition, any attempt to establish a successful Buddhist political party in Taiwan may come at too high a price: It may entail abandoning values that are deemed to constitute the core of a Buddhist political philosophy. Hence, at the center of most engaged Buddhist leaders' approach to international relations and foreign policy, from the Dalai Lama to Thich Nhat Hanh, stands the principle of pacifism. The Komeito—which over the years has promoted a program of Buddhist socialism, advocating a "third way" between unfettered capitalism and authoritarian socialism—has often been derided as opportunistic and not very different from the mainstream Liberal Democratic Party. Still, at least in the area of foreign policy, it has been consistently supportive of the constitutional ban on Japanese military intervention abroad.[88] However, as long as the situation across the Taiwan Strait remains unsettled, no political party in Taiwan could hope to achieve a significant status if it pledged to unilaterally abandon the use of force. Taiwan's situation as an island that is militarily threatened by the People's Liberation Army would make such a proposal unattractive to most voters, who support the need for a strong defense. This represents one of the few areas in which politicians from the "Blue Camp" and the "Green Camp" agree. The advocacy of a pacifist stand may appear tantamount to treason by the most ardent supporters of Taiwanese self-determination. Previous governments acted accordingly for years: The main ground for the persecution of the Mormons, the Jehovah's Witnesses, and the Ba'hais by Taiwan's provincial police authority in the 1980s was not subversion, but their support of pacifism.[89]

The absence of religious militancy and the reluctance to create a large, mainstream political party begs the question about the mechanisms that Taiwanese Buddhist organizations may have to use for the promotion or the protection of their interests. So far, organizations such as the BAROC and Foguangshan have acted like American evangelical and fundamentalist Protestant movements that compete for influence over the agenda of mainstream political parties, while Ciji has preferred to adopt a low profile and rely on its grass roots to continue its work at the local and transnational levels. Because Taiwan may evolve into a four-tiered party system, and because it experienced the first peaceful changeover of power between political parties at the beginning of the twenty-first century, Buddhist lay organizations now face daunting challenges in a much more complex environment. The failure of the BAROC to gain the approval of the KMT regime for a law on religion and the disappearance of Chen

Lü'an from the political scene signal the passing of a brief and short-lived "moment" during which some Buddhist organizations could hope to lobby the government, or even hope to propose a political alternative. The fragmented nature of the party system, in addition, prevents Taiwanese Buddhist organizations from launching a party that is comparable to the Komeito in scope and popularity. Doing so would probably undermine the chance to gain power of the two parties that are most likely to listen favorably to their concerns: the much reduced KMT, shed of its nativist elements, and the PFP. The presence of a lay Buddhist politician, such as Wu Boxiong, within the KMT's central executive committee, in fact, may have represented the best option for Buddhists close to the BLIA, who might have wanted to gain a hearing from government officials had the "pan-Blue" coalition been elected in 2004. Under a "pan-Green" coalition government uniting the DPP and the TSU, the relationship between the BLIA and government officials must proceed through different channels. Zhengyan does not have to adopt a new strategy to ensure a smooth cooperation between Ciji and any new government, having always maintained a safe distance from previous administrations.

Conclusion

The unwillingness of Taiwanese Buddhist organizations to become engaged in the island's politics can be explained by the prudence of leaderships committed to their organizational interests and their theological ideals more than any other cultural, political, or socioeconomic factor. This attitude is buttressed by the deference of lay persons to a clergy subscribing to a conservative theology that does not question the socioeconomic status quo nor support the dominant neoliberal economic policies. Leaders of these organizations, and presumably their followers, prefer to leave the alleviation of poverty in the hands of charitable organizations rather than in the care of public agencies, which they do not trust. In that respect, they represent a large constituency that is uneasy with the development of a welfare state in Taiwan. However, they are unlikely to oppose such development, as long as they continue to benefit from the generally promarket policies of the government. For Taiwanese Buddhist leaders, the lifting of martial law has ensured more freedom of speech, but has not changed much per se, since discretion was and remains the favorite way in which they seek to speak to the political élites. As long as a majority of lay persons agrees with its leaders, and as long as the process of democratization does not work against it, the need for Buddhist leaders to speak out on political issues is not self-evident. Furthermore, large organizations such as Foguangshan and Ciji stand to lose their effectiveness as charitable associations and as religious institutions with a universal claim, if they appear to be partisans. Finally, the adoption of a neutral stand in politics makes sense, once we consider the broad picture. As religious institutions, Foguangshan and Ciji aim to reach a larger audience than the Taiwanese polity. Ciji, in particular, harbors the hope of developing "great love" across the Taiwan Strait: The fact that it appears "untainted" by collaboration with the KMT or the DPP must serve it very well.

Notes

1. See Murray A. Rubinstein, *The Protestant Community on Modern Taiwan: Mission, Seminary, and Church* (Armonk, NY: M.E. Sharpe, 1991), and Michael Stainton, "'Through Love and Suffering': The Role of the Presbyterian Church in Taiwan's Democratization," paper presented to the Joint Center for Asia-Pacific Studies Annual Conference on Democracy and Identity Politics, Toronto, December 4, 2000. The exception remains valid for other traditions.
2. Among the exceptions, see Ye Yongwen, *Taiwan Zhengjiao Guanxi* [Relations between politics and religion in Taiwan] (Taipei: Fengyuan Luntan, 2000); Qu Haiyuan, ed., *Taiwan Zongjiao Bianqian de Shehui Zhengzhi Fenxi* [A sociopolitical analysis of religious change in Taiwan] (Taipei: Guiguan, 1997); Song Guangyu, *Zongjiao yu Shehui* [Religion and society] (Taipei: Dongta, 1995); Lin Benxuan, *Taiwan de Zhengjiao Chongtu* [The conflict between politics and religion in Taiwan] (Panchiao, Taipei County: Daoxiang chubanshe, 1994).
3. Charles B. Jones, *Buddhism in Taiwan: Religion and the State: 1660–1990* (Honolulu: University of Hawaii Press, 1999).
4. Stuart Chandler, "Establishing a Pureland on Earth: The Foguang Buddhist Perspectives on Modernization and Globalization" (Ph.D. diss., Harvard University, 2000); André Laliberté, "The Politics of Buddhist Organizations in Taiwan, 1987–1995" (Ph.D. diss., University of British Columbia, 1999); Julia Huang Chien-yu and Robert P. Weller, "Merit and Mothering: Women and Social Welfare in Taiwanese Buddhism," *Journal of Asian Studies* 57, no. 2 (May 1998): 379–96.
5. Jones, *Buddhism in Taiwan*, 322–23.
6. Shi Zhaohui, *"Renjian Fojiao" Shilianchang* [Examining "this-worldly Buddhism"] (Taipei: Fajie, 1998), 90–94.
7. Xie Jianping, *Chen Lü'an Zhenhan* [The Chen Lü'an effect] (Taipei: Yaxiya, 1995), 146–52.
8. It is the most important of the lay branches of the Buddha Light Mountain Monastic Order (better known by its Chinese name, Foguangshan).
9. Wang Shunmin, *Zongjiao Fuli* [Religious welfare] (Taipei: Yatai Tushu, 1999), 172–210.

10. Fu Zhiying, *Zhuan Deng: Xing Yun Dashi Zhuan* [Handing down the light: The biography of Venerable Master Hsing Yun] (Taipei: Tianxia Wenhua chuban, 1995), 377.

11. Kang Le and Jian Huimei, *Xinyang yu Shehui* [Belief and society] (Banqiao, Taipei County: Taipei County Cultural Center Publishing, 1995), 92.

12. Government Information Office (GIO), *Republic of China Yearbook, 2000* (Taipei: GIO, Executive Yuan of the ROC, 2000), 459.

13. Jiang Canteng, *Taiwan Fojiao Bainianshi zhi Yanjiu, 1895–1995* [Research on a century of Buddhism in Taiwan, 1895–1995] (Taipei: Nantian, 1996), 454.

14. "Xingyun Yong Chen Fan Li Yinfa Zongjiaojie Yao Yuanzheng Duozhan" [Xingyun's support for Chen triggers competition within religious circles], *Guohui Shuangzhoukan*, September 1, 1995, 12–15.

15. "Cibei aixin lieche: huandao jietou bujiao" (Caravan of love and mercy around the island, on the streets, spreads the religion), *Foguang Shiji*, July 16, 1997, 1.

16. Foreign Broadcast Information Service (FBIS), "Buddhist Master Named Commissioner of OCAC," FBIS-CHI-97-032 (February 16, 1997).

17. Chen ran for the presidency against the KMT candidate, Li Denghui, while Wu Boxiong supported the ruling party.

18. This term describes Taiwanese with a Chinese background, and differs from "aboriginal people" (Yuanzhumin).

19. Hence, in the Taipei area, women represent 75 percent of the core constituency of the organization, the commissioners (*weiyuan*), while 65 percent of the "honored patrons" (*rongdong*) are wealthy males with a high socioeconomic status, and 94 percent are over forty years old. In addition, figures about membership, in the case of Ciji, may be inflated: hence, the study by Ding has demonstrated that a majority of the members are individuals who make regular donations on a monthly or bimonthly basis, but who include all members of the household as members of the organization. See Ting Jen-chieh, "Helping Behavior in Social Contexts: A Case Study of the Tzu-Chi Association in Taiwan" (Ph.D. diss., University of Wisconsin-Madison, 1997), 128–29, 131, 144. See also Kang and Jian, *Xinyang yu Shehui*, 88–90.

20. No study has yet provided data on the ethnic background of each organization, but we can infer the importance of the Taiwanese Benshengren presence in both organizations by the number of speeches and documents produced in Fukienese (*Minnanhua*), their native language. Detailed descriptions of the temples affiliated with Foguangshan and of the branches of Ciji also indicate that both organizations have managed to attract followers in all counties on the island, and studies by Kang and Jian suggest further that the membership of both organizations is more important in large urban centers. For the localization of Foguangshan's affiliated temples in Taiwan, see Fu, *Zhuan Deng*, 363. For Ciji's branches in Taiwan, see Fojiao Ciji Cishan Shiye Jijinhui, *Ciji Zhiye Xunli* [An overview of Ciji's purpose] (Taipei: Ciji Wenhua chubanshe, n.d.), 121–22. For a breakdown of members in both organizations by counties and cities, see Kang and Jian, *Xinyang yu Shehui*, 89, 171–72.

21. Deng Zimei, "Taixu yu Mading Lude: Xiandaihua Shijiaoxiade Zhongxi Zongjiao Gaige Bijiao" [Taixu and Martin Luther: A comparison on the basis of religious reformation viewed from the perspective of modernization], *Shijie Zongjiao Yanjiu*, no. 1 (2000): 22–33.

22. Holmes Welch, *The Buddhist Revival in China* (Cambridge: Harvard University Press, 1968), 29–35, 71.

23. Chan Sin-wai, *Buddhism in Late Ch'ing Political Thought* (Boulder, CO: Westview Press, 1985).

24. Hao Chang, *Liang Ch'i-ch'ao and Intellectual Transition in China, 1890–1907* (Taipei: Rainbow Bridge, 1971).

25. Guy S. Alitto, *The Last Confucian: Liang Shu-ming and the Chinese Dilemma of Modernity* (Berkeley: University of California Press, 1979).

26. Charles B. Jones, "Buddhism and Marxism in Taiwan: Lin Qiuwu's Religious Socialism and Its Legacy in Modern Times," *Journal of Global Buddhism* 1 (2000): 82–115, www.globalbuddhism.org/toc.html.

27. Jiang Canteng, *Taiwan Fojiao yu Xiandai Shehui* [Taiwanese Buddhism and contemporary society] (Taipei: Dongda Tushu gonsi, 1992).

28. Ian Harris, ed., *Buddhism and Politics in Twentieth-Century Asia* (London: Pinter, 1999).

29. Donald K. Swearer, "Sulak Sivaraksa's Buddhist Vision for Renewing Society," in *Engaged Buddhism*, ed. Christopher S. Queen and Sallie B. King (Albany: State University of New York Press, 1996), 195–236.

30. Daniel A. Metraux, *The Soka Gakkai Revolution* (Lanham, MD: University Press of America, 1994).

31. Sallie B. King, "Thich Nhat Hanh and the Unified Church of Vietnam," in *Engaged Buddhism*, ed. Christopher S. Queen and Sallie B. King (Albany: State University of New York Press, 1996), 321–63.

32. Brian A. Victoria, *Zen at War* (New York: Weatherhill, 1996).

33. Stanley J. Tambiah, *Buddhism Betrayed? Religion, Politics and Violence in Sri Lanka* (Chicago: University of Chicago Press, 1992).

34. Don Baker, "World Religions and National States: Competing Claims in East Asia," in *Transnational Religion and Failed States*, ed. Susanne Hoeber Rudolph and James P. Piscatori (Boulder, CO: Westview Press, 1997), 144–72.

35. C.K. Yang, *Religion in Chinese Society: A Study of Contemporary Social Functions of Religion and Some of Their Historical Factors* (Taipei: SMC Publishing, 1994).

36. David K. Jordan and Daniel L. Overmyer, *The Flying Phoenix: Aspects of Chinese Sectarianism in Taiwan* (Taipei: Caves Books, 1986); Joseph Bosco, "Yiguan Dao: 'Heterodoxy' and Popular Religion in Taiwan," in *The Other Taiwan: 1945 to the Present*, ed. Murray A. Rubinstein (Armonk, NY: M.E. Sharpe, 1994), 423–44.

37. Lin, *Taiwan de Zhengjiao Chongtu.*

38. Lily Lee Tsai, "Cadres, Temple and Lineage Institutions, and Governance in Rural China," *China Journal* 48 (July 2002): 1–27; Stephan Feuchtwang, "Religion as Resistance," in *Chinese Society: Change, Conflict and Resistance*, ed. Elizabeth J. Perry and Mark Selden (London: Routledge, 2000), 161–77.

39. Jones, *Buddhism in Taiwan*, 179–80.

40. *Zhongfohui Kan* 122 (April 13, 1994), 3–4.

41. Ho Fang-jiau (He Fengjiao), *Taiwan Sheng Jingwu Dang'an Huibian: Minsu Zongjiao Pian* [Documentary collection of Taiwan's police administration: Folklore and religion] (Hsintien [Xindian],Taipei County: Academia Historica, 1996).

42. Chen Zailai, *Zongjiao yu Guanli* [Religion and administration], research report for the Management Science Research Institute (Hsinchu [Xinzhu]: Chiaotung [Jiaodong] University, 1994).

43. Kang and Jian, *Xinyang yu Shehui*, 57–59.

44. Jiang Canteng, *Taiwan Dangdai Fojiao* [Buddhism in contemporary Taiwan] (Taipei: Nantian, 1997), 27–28.
45. James R. Wood, *Leadership in Voluntary Organization: The Controversy over Social Action in Protestant Churches* (New Brunswick, NJ: Rutgers University Press, 1981).
46. Jiang, *Taiwan Fojiao Bainianshi zhi Yanjiu*, 251–320.
47. Song, *Zongjiao yu Shehui*, 179.
48. Robert P. Weller, "Markets, Margins, and the Growth of Religious Diversity: Taiwan in Comparative Perspective," paper presented to the Third International Conference on Sinology, Academia Sinica, June 29–July 1, 2000, Nankang (*Nangang*), Taiwan.
49. "Foguangshan de Haohua Lingwei: Kaijia Zai Sanshiwan Yuan Yishang" [The starting price for funerary tablets in Foguangshan: 30,000 New Taiwan dollars], *Xinxinwen*, October 26, 1996, 47–49.
50. Li Guangshen, "Shijimou, Shenfo Man Tianqi? Taiwan de Xinxing Zongjiaofeng" [Taiwan's New Age cults], *Sinorama* (October 2000): 6–19.
51. Qu Haiyuan, *Zongjiaofa Yanjiu* [Research on the legislation pertaining to religion] (Taipei: Neizhengbu Weituo Yanjiu, 1989).
52. "Zhonghua Foxiehui Fandui Chengli Fojiao Zonghui" [The CBTA opposes the establishment of the BFA], *Ziyou Shibao*, September 24, 1996; "Fojiaofa Cao'an: Zhonghua Foxiehui You Yiyi" [Draft law on Buddhism: The CBTA disagrees], *Zhongshi Wanbao*, September 23, 1996.
53. Charles B. Jones, "Relations between the Nationalist Government and the Buddhist Association of the Republic of China (BAROC) since 1945," *Journal of Chinese Religions* 24 (Fall 1996): 77–97.
54. Fu Zhiying (Fu Chi-ying), *Xinhuo: Foguangshan Chengxianqihou de Gushi* [The story of Foguangshan founders' spiritual heirs] (Taipei: Tianxia Wenhua chuban, 1997).
55. Neizhengbu (Ministry of the Interior), *Quanguoxing Zongjiao Tuanti Minglu* [Registry of religious organizations across the country], comp. Zhong Fushan (Taipei: Zhonghua Minguo Xingzhengyuan Neizhengbu, 1994).
56. This becomes clear when considering the various voices with which Buddhists express themselves, whether through respected scholarly journals, such as *Faguang* [Dharma monthly], or the periodicals published by established organizations, such as *Zhongfohui Kan* [Chinese Buddhism monthly], the BAROC mouthpiece; *Bumen Zazhi* [Universal gate], *Jueshi* [Awakening the world], *Renjian Fubao* [Merit times], and *Foguang Jikan*, all owned by Foguangshan and its affiliates; *Jingdian Zazhi* [Rhythm monthly], *Ciji Yuekan* [Tzu Chi monthly], *Tzu Chi Quarterly*, and *Ciji Daolu*; or *Fagu Zazhi* [Dharma drum magazine], *Foyin Shibao*, *Haichaoyin*, and so on.
57. "Sense and Sensibility: On Taiwan's Political Future," *China News Analysis* 1558 (April 15, 1996): 1.
58. This term designates Chinese immigrants who came to Taiwan after 1945, when the authority of the Republic of China assumed political control over the island.
59. Alan M. Wachman, "Competing Identities in Taiwan," in *The Other Taiwan: 1945 to the Present*, ed. Murray A. Rubinstein (Armonk, NY: M.E. Sharpe, 1994), 17–80.

60. Denny Roy, *Taiwan: A Political History* (Ithaca, NY: Cornell University Press, 2003), 242–43.

61. Fu, *Xinhuo*.

62. Surveys from the Mainland Affairs Commission (MAC, or *Dalou Weiyuanhui*) indicate that, since 1997, between 45 percent and 60 percent of the population prefers the current political status of Taiwan with regard to cross-Strait relations to the alternatives of independence or reunification with the PRC. During the same period of time, the proportion of people supporting independence has never exceeded 28 percent, while the proportion of people supporting reunification was halved by March 2003 from a high of 26.8 percent in August 1996. These surveys were conducted by the Center for Public Opinion and Election Studies at Sun Yat-sen University in Kaohsiung. MAC 2003, www.mac.gov.tw/english/english/foreign/15.gif (accessed January 9, 2005).

63. Holmes Welch, *Buddhism under Mao* (Cambridge, MA: Harvard University Press, 1972), 1–108, 231–66, 340–63.

64. With the legislative election of 2001, the DPP became the largest party in the Legislative Yuan, holding ninety of 225 seats, but even with the support of the thirteen seats held by the TSU, the party fell short of having a majority. The KMT, with sixty-six seats, and the PFP, with forty-five, needed only two votes from the eleven independent lawmakers to defeat the government's legislation.

65. Thomas A. Metzger, "Will China Democratize? Sources of Resistance," *Journal of Democracy* 9, no. 1 (January 1998): 18–26.

66. I use the definition of O'Sullivan and Scruton, who describe conservative ideology as a "philosophy of imperfection." See Noel O'Sullivan, *Conservatism* (New York: St. Martin's Press, 1976), 9, and Roger Scruton, *The Meaning of Conservatism*, 2d ed. (London: Macmillan, 1984), 16, 19, 31.

67. O'Sullivan, *Conservatism*, 22–27.

68. A third conservative trend that Sullivan identified, which is rooted in skepticism and prevalent in the United Kingdom, is not present in the ROC.

69. Peter J. Williamson, *Corporatism in Perspective: An Introductory Guide to Corporatist Theory* (London: Sage, 1989); Wyn Grant, ed., *The Political Economy of Corporatism* (London: Macmillan, 1985); and Gerhard Lehmbruch and Philippe C. Schmitter, eds., *Patterns of Corporatist Policy-Making* (London: Sage, 1982).

70. Jonathan Unger and Anita Chan, "China, Corporatism, and the East Asian Model," *Australian Journal of Chinese Affairs* 33 (January 1995): 29–53; Harmon Zeigler, *Pluralism, Corporatism, and Confucianism: Political Association and Conflict Regulation in the United States, Western Europe, and Taiwan* (Philadelphia: Temple University Press, 1988).

71. Other authors discussing this type of regime prefer to talk of "illiberal democracy." See Daniel Bell and Kanishka Jayasuriya, "Understanding Illiberal Democracy: A Framework," in *Towards Illiberal Democracy in Pacific Asia*, ed. Daniel A. Bell, David Brown, Kanishka Jayasuriya, and David Jones (London: Macmillan, 1995), 1–16; and Clark D. Neher, "Asian Style Democracy," *Asian Survey* 34, no. 11 (November 1994): 949–61.

72. Taixu Dashi, *Taixu Dashi Quanshu* [The complete work of Venerable Taixu] (Taipei: Taixu Dashi Quanshu Yingyin Weiuyuanhui Yinxing, n.d.), 1040–1212.

73. Jiang Canteng, *Taixu Dashi Qianzhuan* [Master Taixu: Biography of the early years] (Taipei: Xinwenfeng chuban, 1993).

74. Although the authority Holmes Welch described him as "close to socialists," Taixu was also critical of socialism in his writings. See Welch, *The Buddhist Revival in China*, 29, and Taixu, *Taixu Dashi Quanshu*, 1207–12.

75. Xingyun Dashi, *How I Practice Humanistic Buddhism* (Hacienda Heights, CA: Hsi Lai University Press, 1997), 3–4, 7–8.

76. Yinshun Dashi, *The Way to Buddhahood: Instructions from a Modern Chinese Master*, trans. Wing H. Yeung (Boston: Wisdom Publications, 1998).

77. Ting Jen-chieh, "Helping Behavior in Social Contexts: A Case Study of the Tzu-Chi Association in Taiwan" (Ph.D. diss., University of Wisconsin-Madison, 1997), 124.

78. Xingyun Dashi, *Foguang Yuan: Renjian Fojiao* [The purpose of the Buddha light: This-worldly Buddhism], ed. Ceng Fengling (Kaohsiung: Foguang, 1994), 178.

79. *Lianhebao*, August 21, 1995, 3.

80. See Lise McKean, *Divine Enterprise: Gurus and the Hindu Nationalist Movement* (Chicago: University of Chicago Press, 1996).

81. See Gilles Kepel, *Jihad: Expansion et declin de l'Islamisme* (Paris: Gallimard, 2000).

82. See Tambiah, *Buddhism Betrayed?* 80–94.

83. Mark Juergensmeyer, *The New Cold War? Religious Nationalism Confronts the Secular State* (Berkeley: University of California Press, 1993); Martin E. Marty and R. Scott Appleby, eds., *Fundamentalism Observed*, vol. 1 of The Fundamentalism Project, dir. Martin E. Marty and R. Scott Appleby (Chicago: University of Chicago Press, 1991).

84. Charles F. Keyes, Laurel Kendall, and Helen Hardacre, eds., *Asian Visions of Authority* (Honolulu: University of Hawaii Press, 1994).

85. Kees van Kersbergen, *Social Capitalism: A Study of Christian Democracy and the Welfare State* (London: Routledge, 1995); David Hanley, *Christian Democracy in Europe: A Comparative Perspective* (London: Pinter Publisher, 1994).

86. Regarding Buddhist social welfare, see Liang Qici, *Shishan yu Jiaohua: Ming Qing de Cishan Zuzhi* [Charity organizations of the Ming and Qing] (Taipei: Lianjing, 1997).

87. Sources from the Civil Affairs Department of the Ministry of the Interior indicate that, in 2000, among Taiwan's 10.8 million believers in a population of 22,276,672, there were 3,673,000 Buddhists. Government Information Office (GIO), *Republic of China Yearbook, 2002* (Taipei: GIO, Executive Yuan of the ROC, 2002), 23, 453.

88. Metraux, *The Soka Gakkai Revolution*.

89. Ho, *Taiwan Sheng Jingwu Dang'an Huibian*, 479–504, 550–79.

4

New Karma

Buddhism and Democratization in Thailand

David Ambuel

In Kugrit Pramoj's novel, *Pai Daeng* [Red bamboo], a rural temple abbot, the venerable Grang, is reluctantly forced to confront secular politics when his best friend from childhood becomes a communist rabble-rouser. The peaceful balance of his world is disturbed when a village elder comes to consult him, because this "ism" thing has found its way into their remote region. The distinct world of temple politics notwithstanding, the abbot prefers to keep religion separate and pure from the contaminations of the "world," and, in the end, is able to reestablish something of this order that has been violated by his friend's harmless idealism.

Kugrit, a former Thai prime minister, who held office for a brief year during a short period of liberalization in the 1970s, surely felt sympathy with his character. While making fun of the Thai Red Scare, the story also makes it clear that the abbot's naive categories are preferable to those of clergy playing politics, namely the politics of the monk Kittivuddo, who gained a spot in history for preaching that the Buddhist precept against killing any living being did not apply to the killing of communists.

Kugrit's government (1975–1976) came at an interlude of democratization, liberalization of press restrictions, and attempts to decentralize political power subsequent to the student protests of 1973, which culminated in the conflict of October 14, 1973. Student protests were violently overrun by the military, resulting in seventy-seven deaths and over eight hundred injuries. But public reaction was strong, which led to the brief exile of the military leader, Thanom, and the drafting of a new constitution. This period ended on October 6, 1976, with the violent overrun of Thammasat University by the military, aided by civilian paramilitary groups fighting to preserve the values of "nation, monarchy, and religion." Some one thousand students were killed, many more fled to the jungles, and the military resumed control of the government.

Twenty-five years later, some of those students—now long emerged from the jungles—sit in parliament. October 14, 1973, and October 6, 1976, are commemorated in a steady stream of publications and public ceremonies, alongside honors that are bestowed upon the memory of Pridi Panomyong, leader of the 1932 coup, organized by civil servants, that put an end to the absolute monarchy. School history books are being rewritten, and political maneuvering continues over enacting provisions of the constitution of 1997, the sixteenth since 1932, and by far the most significant democratic reform effort yet.

Amid the shifting political realities, the meaning of the social center of political legitimization—nation, monarchy, and religion—again faces redefinition. The role of religion in the secular world of politics is changing, together with political attitudes and institutions.

Throughout the events and turns of the past century, the attitudes of the venerable Grang, fictional abbot of the *Wat* Red Bamboo, typify the relation of religion to politics. Direct Buddhist political activism, when it has occurred, often has been at the periphery and kept outside the political mainstream—due both to the choice of Buddhist activists and to the efforts of political insiders. At the same time, Buddhist institutions as well as Buddhist attitudes have permeated and shaped political culture.

Despite the traditional distancing of religion from direct engagement with political affairs, religion has maintained its imprimatur on the political culture of a self-consciously Buddhist nation. Its cultural, social, and symbolic value has never been far from the political arena. This remains true in a time of increasing secularization, especially urban secularization, and of more explicitly avowed toleration in a society that has long known many strains of toleration.

Recent reforms received an impetus with the protests of 1992, led, not by students this time, but by the rising middle class. Popular demands culminated in the adoption of the 1997 "people's" constitution, enacted in the same year that the floating of the Thai baht marked the onset of the Asian financial crisis. These contemporary reforms have been undertaken in the name of eliminating corruption and developing civil society, transparency, decentralization, and democratization. In the East, "democratization" is a topic that has caught the attention of the public sphere as much as "democracy" has in the West. However, the very core concepts that warm the democratic passions of the West tend, more often than not, to leave the East cold and indifferent. So, for example, while bills of rights have become pro forma an indispensable part of constitutions around the world, the question of rights is often not received as an essential political issue, even by Asian activists. Societies that perceive themselves and are perceived by others to be undergoing historically significant democratic developments may themselves hold a very different understanding of the meaning and importance of that democratization.

In Europe and America, the contemporary discussion of democratic ideals is inevitably accompanied by themes of pluralism, diversity, and rights. Frequently, political theorists, while implicitly finding universal value and global importance in the ideals of democracy, paradoxically at the same time regard pluralism and diversity as a contingent, historical, post-enlightenment fact, descriptive of the contemporary West but not necessarily applicable to other cultures or times. The descriptive "fact" of pluralism asserts that different people and different groups in society hold irreconcilably different beliefs about what is good or bad, virtuous or vicious, worthy or unworthy. Therefore, to speak of the "good" of society as a whole is to appeal to an abstract fiction; the "good" of the diverse society is only the formula for guaranteeing the broadest possible liberty, subject to procedural conditions for fairness and impartiality, for individuals to make their own independent choices. This set of presuppositions—widely accepted and a part of much Western political culture—has shaped the development of and prioritization of "rights," as well as interpretations of democracy and the rule of law.

In Thailand, by contrast, calls for democratic reform are made in the name of the good of society as a whole, and as a political development that will promote the traditional Asian values of social cohesion and harmony. The modern political process in Thailand has been variably described as a "patronage system," a "semidemocracy,"[1] or a "Buddhist democracy." Within the popular values debate, the Asian repudiation of Western-style "individualism" and pluralism is accompanied by another kind of individualism that can be found in traditional Thai Buddhist values and that is reflected in the latest reforms. Much of traditional Buddhism provides a weak basis for social theory. One reason is a traditionally common, albeit often rejected, sharp distinction of Abbot Grang between spiritual seeking and worldly pursuits.[2] Another reason lies in the fundamentally individualistic Buddhist orientation. This does not mean that Buddhist dharma encourages people to ignore duties toward society; on the contrary, societal obligations form a central part of the teachings. Rather, the ultimate "goal" for human practice—the attainment of enlightenment—is an accomplishment that is fundamentally individual. Therefore, even while much of Buddhist teaching, such as basic moral tenets, is socially oriented, and even while many contemporary Buddhist social critics are concerned with the state of society and the lack of social justice, very often the remedies suggested are individual rather than structural. They speak in terms of reforming individual attitudes, with the hope that a society of virtuous individuals will turn into a virtuous society, and offer little with regard to how institutional structures and organization may shape individual attitudes and lives.

Furthermore, by setting ideals of accomplishment firmly in individual attainment, there arises both a concentration on admiration for the accomplished individual (the *arhat*, the accomplished monk or accomplished lay person), and with that, a devaluation of specific rules and procedures. This, too, is deeply rooted in the tradition. The dharma and the precepts, the rules for living well, are only means or instruments to help in the pursuit of final attainment; they are necessary prerequisites perhaps, but not the attainment itself. They are often compared to the boat that carries one across to the opposite shore on a one-way trip; once the individual is transported and has arrived, that person's boat can be jettisoned, because it has no further use.

Hierarchy and Democracy

During the first nationwide elections under the provisions of the 1997 constitution (1999–2000; Buddhist era, or B.E. 2542–2543), the Thai press reported a sharp rise in the sales of bullet-proof vests, and police reported an increased demand for the services of hired guns. This was attributed to decentralization, which has raised the stakes of local politics. For the first time in modern Thailand, many local officials (outside of Bangkok and Pattaya) were now elected, rather than appointed from Bangkok. Among the year's incidents, police arrested a suspected gunman for a politically motivated shooting. He confessed and, according to newspaper reports, stated that he, in fact, had not wanted to shoot the victim, understanding how very wrong it was. However, he could not refuse: He was indebted because the man who hired him had helped the gunman's mother when she was desperately ill. The excuse, virtually inconceivable in the West, has a shade of plausibility in a Thai context, such that one can even imagine a lawyer incorporating it into a defense, so strong is the sense of value attached to hierarchy and to personal indebtedness.

The value attached to personal authority is often classed by the scholar of society and politics as an aspect of a pervasive "patronage" system, a social order that many Thai social critics have attacked as opposed to democracy. Under a patronage system, the inferior owes allegiance and some degree of service to the superior. This allegiance consists in not questioning or opposing, but following the superior's wishes. The superior maintains the position of superiority as a result of this allegiance and, in return, is obliged to take care of the inferior, to look after the inferior's interests, and to deliver the goods. This, of course, absolves the inferiors from thinking much about their own interest or how to obtain it. In such a political culture, the market for votes is a strategically rational investment.[3]

Social critics contrast the patronage mentality with democracy, precisely because it absolves the citizen of any real participation in the political process and defeats aspirations for self-government. Restrictions on the extent and significance of participation are at the same time restrictions on responsibility. The average subject offers loyalty to the political superior in hope of (or in exchange for) a return, but the means and ends of the political sphere are not a matter of direct concern. Anek Laothamatas sums this up with the observation that, if democracy is understood as government by the people and for the people, then under the prevailing Thai conception, the emphasis would fall on government *for* the people, not on government *by* the people. Concern in public opinion so often involves why the government cannot do more, as if "the government" is some foreign entity apart from society.[4]

In the above context, the gunman's excuse can be understood as a rationale, poor and self-serving, perhaps, but nonetheless a rationale and not an absurdity. Written rules of conduct are less important than the rule of the moment issued by a superior.

Such a system, in which the politician-patron is elected with the support of the politically indifferent clientele might well be called in structure a representative democracy. To look only at the institutional framework, governing is clearly the task of elected representatives. However, a representative structure overlaid on a culture of patronage produces guardians, rather than representatives.[5]

There are signs that elements of the patron-client structures are waning in the contemporary social and political environment, which has features that can be called a "Buddhist democracy" in the sense that its distinguishing mark is not so much the popular election of representatives, but rather personal deference to superior authority. Or, to borrow from the above-cited comparison, if representative democracy is government by the people and for the people, in that order, then Thailand's Buddhist democracy aspires to be government for the people and by the people.

This deference to position and authority is not only deeply embedded in everyday custom and etiquette but also is part of the cultural symbolism of the wise legislator. The real source of justice is not the written law or institutions that apply it, but the wise and authoritative person. Every Thai schoolchild learns early the frequently retold stories of King Ramkhamhaeng's hearing, evaluating, and dispensing fair and wise decisions in response to any subject's least complaint. The current monarch, Bhumibol Adulyadej (Rama IX), whose educational background was in engineering, made a symbolic connection with the ancient kings by spending time early in his reign sitting as a judge in court.

The role of the superior person is also evident in the traditional relations of the clergy and politicians. Individual monks who have become prominent can gain a large popular following throughout the country. Many people not only hold a charismatic monk in reverence, but also see him as endowed with special or supernatural powers. Typically, the well-known monks will publicly respect the division between the worldly and the spiritual, and refrain from overly direct engagement in the world of politics. Political leaders, however, seek not the explicit endorsement of, but association with, charismatic monks. Politicians will visit a prominent monk to be seen and photographed in the monk's company, seeking, no doubt, benefits from the contact in the realms of both the supernatural and public opinion.

While contemporary reformers have been seeking to move the country away from the traditional patronage structures, this political culture persists and is illustrated by contemporary developments in the interconnections between Buddhism and political institutions in the age of reform.

The Old and the New: The Shifting Relation of Religion to Politics

Organized Buddhism has had, overall, little public direct involvement with political reforms, but this is not to say that it has little impact on the shaping of the political landscape. The Buddhist influence has not been expressed through the formation of political parties or coalitions, as religious movements might in Europe or America. Buddhism, however, has been a prominent indirect cultural influence on political reforms. These attitudes have persisted in Buddhism as a significant element in political culture, despite changes in the always complex connections between Buddhism and politics in Thailand. And, yet, the traditional conceptions of the old karmic Buddhism have come increasingly under attack as both secular and religious conceptions shape political changes.

The officially recognized Buddhist institutions have been content to remain, for the most part, at their assigned position at the periphery of politics. This is in some sense the case throughout the history of modern Thailand, despite the fact that religious affairs have long been centered squarely within the province of government. Both the monarchy and, later, elected governments have always sought to make use of the culturally central Buddhist institutions to political advantage, while attempting to keep the direct political influence of the monkhood to a minimum.

The two main traditions of organized Buddhism in Thailand—the Mahanikai and the Thammayut sects—trace back to the influence of King Mongkut (Rama IV), who founded the latter. An ordained monk in the 1820s before his eventual coronation in 1851 and an eager student of Western sciences, Mongkut promoted a rationalistic reform of Buddhism. This movement to suppress what he saw as the unscientific and superstitious elements of Thai Buddhism, which are as stubbornly persistent to the present among the urban educated as among the rural poor, also assigned the proper role for Buddhist teachings to spiritual matters exclusively as distinct from "worldly" affairs.[6] From Mongkut's time to the present, the Mahanikai has continued to claim the majority of clergy, while the Thammayut has remained firmly in control of Buddhist officialdom: the supreme patriarch, the head of the official Buddhist *sangha*, since King Mongkut has been selected from the Thammayut.

Just as governments have sought to keep Buddhism in the temples and out of the world, they have also closely guarded the institution of Buddhism for its symbolic importance and value in legitimizing the order of the state. Over the past forty to fifty years, the major political value of the Buddhist religion has been as a state symbol, promoting nationalism, unity, and loyalty to the state. It constitutes one part of the tripartite core values promulgated in schools and all other state-supported activities: the values of nation, monarchy, and religion. The currency and prominence of these three official state symbols are watched over by various government organs, especially the National Board of Identity.[7] The legitimizing symbols of nation, monarchy, and religion have reinforced the traditional primacy of personal authority over codified standards. Dutiful respect for the precepts of religion will promote individual well-being and gain merit for a better future existence. Collectively, the virtue of individuals contributes to the harmony and unity of the nation. This unity is embodied in the person of the king, who has the role of moral leader of the nation, and, as moral leader, occupies the revered pinnacle of the political and religious hierarchies.

The coalitions of established authorities, since the coronation of the present and longest-reigning king of the Cakri dynasty, have been astonishingly successful at advancing the political culture of the three core values. Bhumibol Adulyadej ascended the throne still a youth at a time when the institution of the monarchy was feeble and threatened by the political designs of a strong military; now, the monarchy enjoys prestige and an air of untouchability, beyond even the Thai kings of the early 1900s, before the 1932 revolution brought about the end of absolute monarchy.[8] Buddhism has had an important part in this. Writing in 1981, Morell and Chai-anan observed of the influences on political culture that "each supports the others in a blend of social freedom and social tyranny that makes it possible for a highly organized military establishment and its civilian allies to rule."[9]

Although nation, monarchy, and religion are no less celebrated today, the political situation of religion has undergone significant changes with the economic transformations and democratic reforms of the 1990s. Peter A. Jackson observed in the 1990s a shift in the relation of Buddhist institutions to the political order, arguing that Buddhism had in recent years increasingly lost its prior relevance to politics. He made the case that in earlier decades different socioeconomic groups embraced different directions of Buddhism that would legitimize their respective political interests: "Karmic Buddhism and Brahmanism constituted a religion of justification," while, on the other hand, "reformist Buddhism" sought a "rationalization of social life," where merit deserved by skill and accomplishment, not merit demonstrated by privilege and attributed to good karma, is the basis for social order.[10]

The tradition of karmic Buddhism is a conservative one that lends to justification of the status quo and existing social structures. If one person's wealth and high position just as another's poverty are accepted evidence of the fruits from the merits or demerits earned in past lives, then the existing hierarchy constitutes an argument that those in power both deserve their positions and are superior to those who remain beneath. Success and ill-fortune, alike, are both premise and proof of "old karma" (*gam gao*).

Now, after the turn of the millennium (B.E. 2544), the belief in "old karma" is as pervasive as ever. Despite the importance of rationalistic and reformist movements in Buddhism, such as those that may trace themselves to Pra Buddhadasa, or other Buddhist-inspired social movements not associated with ordained monkhood, such as the Buddhist Peace Fellowship of Sulak Sivaraksa, the attitudes shaped by karmic Buddhism remain deeply held among the educated and élite as well as the general populace.

But if the divergence between karmic and reformist Buddhism continues, their functions in political legitimization have altered. While the reformist Buddhism of Mongkut's Thammayut sect was designed in part to prevent the monkhood from becoming a political threat, modern reform movements that have grown up outside of orthodoxy have given rise to more direct political aspirations.

Jackson marks the 1990s as the point at which the state began to move away from Buddhism as an institution on which to base political legitimacy and power.[11] Furthermore, the secularization of the political sphere—the diminishing political relevance of the sangha and the formal institutions of official Buddhism—has not been accompanied by a corresponding secularization of society in general. Jackson offers as evidence the flourishing of movements at the periphery of officially accepted doctrine, and the increased tolerance for such movements, citing in particular the two most prominent recent examples, the Santi Asoke and Wat Phra Dhammakaya. The developments within these two groups are instructive examples for following the recent changes and underlying continuities in the relation of religion to politics.

Santi Asoke

The Santi Asoke movement was founded in the 1970s by the controversial monk Photirak, a former television entertainer, who abandoned life as a celebrity singer known as Rak Rakpong to follow austere practices as a monk. Disillusioned with both Thammayut and Mahanikai temples, he eventually left to establish the Santi Asoke ashram. He both criticized the established clergy for laxity and offended higher authorities through symbolic acts of defiance, such as not shaving his eyebrows and banishing Buddha images.

In 1975, Photirak publicly repudiated the authority of the Council of Elders, and established the independent movement, taking his followers, and reordaining them himself. The movement became the object of increasing public attention and government concern through the 1980s, as Photirak challenged the authority of the state sangha and laws of conduct for monks. The followers live austerely in a communal style of life on two largely self-sufficient ashrams, follow a vegetarian diet, and preach ecological awareness and anticonsumerism. They preach that living in accordance with the dharma will lead people to "work harder, consume less and share the rest of what one has with society."[12] The movement also attracted a number of prominent and influential politicians, including Major General Chamlong Srimuang. Pressures from the sangha eventually led to Photirak's arrest in June 1989, followed by the arrest of over one hundred monks and nuns among his followers a month later. At the time, the Thai government imposed a news blackout on the incident. There was pressure from the orthodoxy for him to defrock voluntarily, which Photirak resisted, and subsequently legal charges were pressed against him, leading to a trial that continued for several years. Eventually, as is common in many public controversies in Thailand when both of the opposing forces have significant support, the conflict faded from visibility and dwindled into a kind of status quo ante, allowing both sides to maintain their dignity. Though found guilty in 1995, the sentence was suspended and Photirak has continued the ascetic Santi Asoke movement, centered in a flourishing commune, with little interference or interest from the government, despite the ire of official Buddhism. He made the concession of changing the color of his robes to white, the color of a layman, allowing the sangha to look upon Photirak as one who is no longer pretending to the position of a monk, and permitting him to continue to assert that Santi Asoke represents authentic Buddhism and to label the mainstream sangha a corruption.

While Photirak appealed unsuccessfully to constitutional guarantees of religious freedom, the Santi Asoke movement represented a political threat to the state that the Muslim or Christian minorities never did, precisely because it is a Buddhist movement challenging the mainstream sangha and successfully attracting a large following. Photirak's challenge, despite his rejection of the supernatural, recalls the challenge of the peasant uprisings of a century past. The "religion" in "nation, monarchy, and religion" means the governmentally sanctioned version of Buddhism, and, consequently, the growing prominence of a splinter group signifies to many a danger to national identity and unity.

Furthermore, in spite of its isolated and communal form of existence, seemingly removed from the modern world, the message of Santi Asoke has been explicitly one calling for the reform of society as a whole. The movement and controversy was the first sign of weaknesses in established institutions, foreshadowing the reform movements of the 1990s.

Palang Dhamma

It has been noted that, for most of the past one hundred years, Thai politicians have sought to associate themselves with religious figures and religious merit, and both politicians and royalty have grounded the legitimacy of power partly in religion, while religion and clergy have remained apart and separate from party politics. This changed under influences from the Santi Asoke movement.

When he was governor of Bangkok, a prominent Santi Asoke disciple, Major General Chamlong Srimuang, who is celibate and eats a single vegetarian meal each day, founded the Palang Dhamma ("power of dharma") Party.[13] Like most Thai political parties, Palang Dhamma existed more through the personality of its leader than on the basis of any particular political platform. Nevertheless, Palang Dhamma actively pursued a political agenda explicitly based on Buddhist principles, and the party enjoyed a degree of success, especially among its urban supporters in the Bangkok region.

Chamlong was a strong, if doctrinaire, voice against the pervasive money and corruption of politics. The party itself, from its beginnings to the height of its popularity, was divided between its purists, Santi Asoke members like Chamlong who opposed any compromise of principle, even if politically disadvantageous, and its pragmatists, who sought to strategically advance their careers and the party's growth.[14]

Chamlong played an important role in the 1992 "middle-class" protests that led to the resignation of the unelected prime minister, Suchinda. Subsequently, Chamlong resigned from leadership of the party, but remained the party's behind-the-scenes de facto leader until 1995. Palang Dhamma joined the Democrat Party coalition from 1992 until leaving it in 1995. At this time, a number of supporters bolted from the party, and

Chamlong turned over party control to the tycoon Thaksin Shinawatra, Thailand's wealthiest businessman owing to his telecommunications monopoly. Thaksin, who had served as foreign minister under the democrat-led coalition, came from the Palang Dhamma's pragmatist faction. Moving away from the emphasis on religious principles, he presided for a year and a half over the declining party at a time when he joined the Banharn government as deputy prime minister for transportation.

The Palang Dhamma party is now defunct, while Thaksin went on to found the Thai Rak Thai party in 1998. The first in Thai politics to make full use of modern advertising, marketing, and polling, Thaksin also used his considerable personal financial resources to bring sitting members of parliament of other parties, and, indeed, entire parties, under the Thai Rak Thai fold. Thai Rak Thai secured a parliamentary majority in the 2000 elections, and, in early 2001, Thaksin became prime minister.

Chamlong departed from politics after 1996 and has headed the "leadership school" in rural Kanchanaburi Province. In July 2002, he was appointed by Thaksin as an adviser for human resources.

Wat Phra Dhammakaya

The new political tolerance for religious movements that threaten established religious hierarchies will hold as long as divergent Buddhist movements do not advance political claims too strongly. Wat Phra Dhammakaya had rapidly become an enormously successful new movement when its political hubris forced it into an extended public scandal.

The Dhammakaya movement was developed by the monk, Dhammajayo, who founded and became abbot of Wat Dhammakaya, and his associate and vice abbot, Dhammajivo. Both were Kasetsart University students, and both were followers of the renowned monk, Luang Po Sod (1884–1959), and his famous disciple, the nun, Khun Yay (1909–2000). Dhammakaya student followers aggressively took control of the Buddhist clubs at Bangkok universities, and funneled donations into construction of a world meditation center on the over eight-hundred-acre campus of Wat Dhammakaya, which was purchased in the 1980s in Patum Thani, north of Bangkok.

Though criticized from the inception for pandering "commercial Buddhism," the temple attracted an enormous following, especially among the rising urban classes. The Dhammakaya temple holds retreats that are attended by thousands of participants, with free shuttle buses taking followers to and from the temple. It also runs a successful enterprise purveying highly priced religious amulets and selling merit. The mass retreats are well orchestrated, and Dhammakaya advertises that the combined power of mass meditation will promote world peace. (Dhammakaya followers believe that, by meditation, Luang Po Sod and Khun Yay prevented Bangkok from being bombed during World War II.) The movement advertised on billboards, and simplified meditation practices to make retreats more accessible and appealing to people living in a modern urban setting. Further, the temple was effective at raising donations through a kind of merit pyramid: The faithful not only were told that their own donations to the temple would be repaid many times over in material prosperity in their personal lives, but also were taught that they could multiply their level of merit by soliciting donations from others. Wat Dhammakaya attracted its share of prominent supporters, including General Chavalit Yongchaiyudh, former prime minister and head of the New Aspiration Party, now merged with Thai Rak Thai.

Unlike Santi Asoke, Wat Dhammakaya never openly attacked the established authorities, yet its rising financial power and suspicion of its political designs brought charges both of distorting the Theravada teachings and of fraud. There were accusations of the forcible takeover by the temple of neighboring lands, extortion and misuse of funds, and sexual misconduct. Dhammajayo was accused of the heresy of claiming that he was an arhat, and the Buddha images at the temple bore an uncanny resemblance to his face. Nevertheless, the abbot became elevated to a revered and untouchable central figure.

As with the Santi Asoke movement, Dhammakaya drew sharp criticisms from the Buddhist establishment. The monk, Phra Dhammapitaka, a prolific and articulate scholar, wrote a book denouncing the movement, *The Dhammakaya Incident*, just as he had published a similar doctrinal attack, *The Santi Asoke Incident*, several years earlier. Both the sangha's council of elders and the parliament opened investigations. The government filed legal charges against the abbot and vice abbot, alike, and both appeared to be faced with being defrocked, and perhaps jailed. The controversy received a continuing stream of front-page coverage in the Thai media for over two years.

However, as in the case of the Santi Asoke movement, the public furor eventually faded into a kind of quiet and unspoken agreement among the conflicting powers. Wat Dhammakaya continues to function and attract followers, although its publicity is less aggressive and controversial. Abbot and vice abbot have resumed their positions, but have withdrawn from the public visibility they cultivated before.

In many respects, the Dhammakaya and Santi Asoke movements are poles apart. Dhammakaya consciously styled itself to a contemporary urban setting; Santi Asoke developed a rural and self-sufficient commune. Dhammakaya built upon the ambitions of a mass movement on a grand and imposing scale; Santi Asoke was content to remain modest and inconspicuous. The circumstances under which each came into controversy are equally contrasting. Wat Dhammakaya, apart from accusations of heresy, was accused of many of the same sorts of scandal that, in recent years, have plagued numerous individual monks from the establishment Mahanikai and Thammayut temples: failure to follow prescribed discipline and precepts, including financial and sex scandals. In contradistinction, Santi Asoke is austere, strict, and, while critical of mainstream practice and doctrine, has remained above suspicion of corruption.

For all the differences, both movements raised the ire of governmental and religious authorities, because each in its time drew a growing popular following away from the establishment that guaranteed the national identity and the role of religion in it. Accompanying the new popularity of religious movements at the periphery was an increasing public distrust of the monkhood, with its frequently publicized gambling and sex scandals, and public rejection of the sangha authorities who appeared unable and unwilling to enact reforms. Even the denouncements of Wat Dhammakaya often equally bespoke suspicion and rejection of the traditional seat of official Buddhist doctrine and policy. So, for example, the commentator Sanitsuda Ekachai writes, "The Religious Department has concluded that the teachings of Wat Dhammakaya violate Theravada Buddhism. The next question is how to deal with Dhammakaya without sacrificing the right to religious freedom. Should Dhammakaya be banished like the dissident Santi Asoke? Should new Buddhist groups, be they capitalistic or anti-consumerist, be suppressed just to protect the feudal and authoritarian Sangha?"[15]

Democratic Reforms and the 1997 Constitution

To the extent that religious orthodoxy is being pushed from the political center (and religious innovation socially accepted but politically marginalized) in an increasingly secularized political arena, "old karma" loses its leverage as a legitimizing basis for political power. This shift in the relation between religion and politics has occurred during the period of, arguably, the most significant democratic reforms in modern Thailand. Many Thai scholars and reformers have seen the traditional hierarchies with their patron-client relations as the major obstacle to democratization and genuine political participation. The increasingly secular and religiously pluralistic attitudes of the public reflect this mood toward a rejection of traditional justifications in the concurrent political reforms. And, yet, the reforms are far from the abandonment of traditional structures that a first glimpse might suggest.

The most striking element of recent democratization is the drafting of the new constitution of 1997. In considering its development and implementation, it will be seen that the old karma very likely is slowly being stripped from the institutionalized political sphere, while it reasserts itself in the prevailing political culture. The traditionally accepted justification of patron-client relationships is evaporating under the influences of modernization and reform, and practices previously considered normal are increasingly being seen as corrupt. At the same time, attitudes underpinning traditional hierarchies, attitudes informed, in part, by Buddhist individualism and its understanding of personal authority, shape the reforms. If democratization is accompanied by the departure of the old karma, it has made way for the new.

The sixteenth constitution of Thailand since the 1932 revolution, which put an end to the absolute monarchy, was born amid widespread calls for reform, construction of a civil society, and democratization. It was passed amid great hopes, and has been dubbed the "people's constitution."

The recent wave of public calls for greater democracy date from the early 1990s.[16] The last of previously frequent military coups, which has been followed now by an extended period of increased stability, occurred on February 23, 1991. In its wake, the fourteenth constitution was annulled and replaced. But the military-dominated government did not sit well with the increasingly affluent urban populace. In May 1992, middle-class democracy demonstrations followed dissatisfaction with elections. Troops opened fire, and there were some casualties. Public unrest was not quelled, however, and spread among a wider segment of society than during earlier movements, when activism had been confined almost entirely to the student population.

The next several years saw increasing calls for reform and demands that the government abolish article 211 of the 1991 constitution, which specified that the constitution could be amended only by an act of parliament. The coalition partners under Prime Minister Banharn finally agreed in November 1995 to amend article 211, opening the way for the drafting of a new constitution.

Extensive debates continued through 1996 over procedures for the selection and makeup of the constitutional drafting assembly (CDA). Discussion was difficult, in part because reformers were pushing to minimize the influence of parliament in the writing of the constitution.

On August 22, 1996, the parliament finally agreed to a structure for the CDA that would exclude from membership members of parliament and senators, but would reserve veto power. According to the formula for selection, candidates, who could not be members of any political party, could be nominated from across Thailand. The candidates in each of the seventy-six provinces then selected from among themselves ten nominees. This reduced the nineteen thousand candidates to a list of 760 that was forwarded to parliament. Parliament then cut this by a factor of ten, making the final selection of one member of the CDA from each province. The parliament then selected an additional twenty-three "expert" members, primarily from academic circles.

The CDA was given 240 days to draft the new constitution, which was passed on September 27, 1997, in parliament by a vote of 578 to 16, with 17 abstentions and 40 absent. The final document, in many ways an eclectic mix that reflects the strong input of academics' interest in European systems, especially France and Germany, nevertheless surprised many for the extent of its reform measures.

The changes are many and significant, and reflect an overriding concern with finding ways to end vote buying, corruption, and the role of money in politics, and to broaden participation in political processes. The reforms include, for example, an extensive section on human rights and the establishment of a human rights commission, even when—among the élites and the educated as much as among the general public—the topic of rights evokes either little interest or suspicion that rights are little more than a device to promote Western economic goals.

Other reforms are surely having far greater impact, though it will be years before their ultimate impact can be judged. Some of the changes include: giving greater power to the long-standing, but impotent, National Corruption Commission and making it independent of the prime minister's office and of the powerful Interior Ministry; establishing a new election commission to organize and oversee elections as well as investigate violations; authorizing an Administrative Court to handle disputes between agencies as well as complaints against agencies or bureaucrats for impropriety or failure to perform duties; founding a Constitutional Court to rule on constitutionality of legislation and interpret powers and duties of agencies and organizations under the constitution; requiring public hearings for public works projects and undertakings that affect the environment; instituting new measures to decentralize the government; effecting new restrictions on members of parliament and senators, including codes of ethics and minimum education requirements (members of parliament must now hold at least a bachelor's degree—this has been a windfall for many universities, which rapidly responded to market demand by setting up new correspondence courses specifically for politicians); organizing elections of local officials for offices that were previously appointed; and so on.

The constitutional reforms also include changes in the electoral process, both for the lower house and for the senate, which was previously appointed. The system for parliamentary elections was modified by adapting a party-list system, similar to that of Germany. Its main features are as follows:

1. Voters cast two ballots, one for a party list, and one for a constituency.
2. One hundred members of parliament are elected proportionally from party lists, with a 5 percent threshold.
3. The remaining four hundred members of parliament are elected from single-member constituencies.
4. Ministers must be drawn from elected party-list candidates, and they must forfeit their individual seats in parliament. (If a minister is selected from a constituency, the party must pay the costs for a new election to fill the open seat in parliament.)

The constitution also specifies that the senate, for the first time in Thai history, shall be elected by popular vote. Previously, the upper house was appointed by the king, and its membership was drawn primarily from the military, which was thus able to control the upper house and stay above the fray of party politics. The introduction of the elected senate was passed as part of the constitution over especially strenuous opposition. Under the new formula, the number of senators was set at two hundred. There are seventy-six senatorial constituencies (one per province), with the number of senators per constituency divided proportionally by population; each voter is given one vote. Thus, for example, Bangkok, the most densely populated constituency, elects eighteen senators; each Bangkok voter casts a ballot for one candidate, and the top eighteen vote-getters are seated.

The duties of the new senate were also redefined. The senate is officially an independent monitoring body that may debate and review legislation, which includes offering amendments, but its members may not introduce legislation. Senators also monitor appointments and conduct investigations as well as any impeachment processes.

This is a sampling, but indicates how far-reaching reforms have been. Constitutional reforms also touched religion. Increasingly over recent years, the popular calls for political reform have extended to calls for reform of religious institutions, attention to scandals involving monks, and skepticism about the role of the sangha. It is not surprising, then, that during the drafting of the constitution, an intense debate centered on whether Buddhism should be recognized as the state religion. While pressure was brought by the religious establishment, and thousands of monks and lay followers rallied in support, the proposal was rejected by the CDA in July 1997 on the grounds that it might be "divisive."

Old Karma and New

As the preceding indicates, many of the democratic political reforms have been designed to shift the basis for legitimacy away from traditional privilege and authority and center it in formal procedures, and to shift power away from its centralization in Bangkok and distribute it to the provinces. There remains, however, a very real tension between the rule of personal authority and the impersonal rule of law. The preeminence of the authoritative person—the ideal of the patron—continues to assert itself in different manifestations, even as its traditional forms lose prestige.

While the sangha has lost political standing, individual charismatic monks continue to command nationwide public attention and to be frequented by politicians. Beyond this, the ways in which constitutional reforms are being put into practice bear witness to that same tension between personal authority and impersonal rules.

This has been in evidence, for example, in issues of judicial discretion that have faced courts and commissions under the new constitution. While Americans may be accustomed to contrasts drawn in the media opposing judge-made law and strict constructionism, issues of discretion tend to have a very different focus in Thailand, concerning not gray areas in the range of possible interpretations, but rather gray areas in the exact role of the person passing judgment. Many of the first decisions of the Thai constitutional court subsequent to the 1997 constitution have been the subject of controversy, so much so that some groups have called for resignation of the entire court.[17]

In 1999 (B.E. 2542), under the provisions of the new constitution, Thailand held senatorial elections for the first time. The qualifications for office-seekers, as specified in the constitution, place a number of restrictions on would-be senators, among them one that forbids anyone who has held elected office, specifically as a member of parliament, from running for the senate for at least one year after leaving office. When the disaffected brought this issue before the constitutional court, the court decided that any current member of parliament could run for the senate, as long as that person resigned from parliament no later than the day before the deadline for filing as a senatorial candidate.

No matter how compelling an argument could be devised against the provision as written—that it is undemocratic, that it causes too much dissent, and so on—it is difficult to construe the decision as an interpretation, rather than a de facto amendment to the constitution.

In this respect, the court appeared to represent an institution acting more out of a sense of traditional authority than a sense of legality. As the highest interpreter of the law, it is the court's duty to decide what will be best, regardless of the law, and not to decide what is best under the given constraints of the law, taking legal procedure (not its human interpreter) as the highest condition that makes all applied justice possible.

In other instances, the court's own critics at times turn to it to act in a fashion similar to the criticized actions. The newly instituted and independent election commission was given broad powers under the constitution to investigate election fraud, and to annul the results in any district where the commission found evidence of corruption, thereby requiring a revote in such districts. The first elected senate was not able to meet until mid-2000 (B.E. 2543), as elections in some provinces went into a fourth or fifth round. Appeals were addressed to the court to "find a way out" of the mess. Many wanted the court to step in and override the actions of the election commission, although there would not have been any constitutional basis for the court to circumvent the legal process and dictate a solution from its wisdom alone.

The very existence of the difficulties in finalizing the senate elections have reflected the struggle to find a balance between the traditional superiority of personal authority and the development of a concept of the rule of law. Under the constitution, the election commission is vested with authority to withhold recognition of electoral results where there is evidence of vote fraud. It is a bold attempt to fight the corruption that so easily accompanies a system that prefers to find final and unquestionable decisions residing in personal authority. In fact, the current climate has also resulted in actual pursuit of corruption at levels higher than ever before.[18] However, in the case of the senatorial elections, the legal basis upon which the election commission was established shows preferences for the very structures that the election commission was intended to remedy. For example, the constitution gives the election commission extensive powers and a very wide range of discretion, but little guidance on how the commission members are to exercise that discretion. It has been largely entrusted to the commission members' own wisdom to make up the rules as they go along, with the result that election outcomes can be suspended on what the commission members accept as evidence, with no rules of evidence or legal proceedings needed. Rather than a shift away from the role of personal authority toward due process, the shift has merely moved the location and distribution of personal authority. Such looseness in following the rules and deference to those who are authorized to apply them has been widespread in other high government offices as well, according to watchdog groups.[19]

Reforms have begun to erode the authority of the traditional sources of political legitimacy. Within Thai political culture, this has led more to doubts about the legitimacy and competence of authority, than to rejection of personal authority and hierarchy. The traditional and very widespread understanding of karma,[20] karma as "old karma," provided a mechanism to intuitively answer the question about competence and legitimacy. Those individuals or families that are fortunate, and especially that are materially fortunate—having wealth, power, good health, and the like—are surely also good, and, therefore, competent. Good fortune is a sign of good karma, which is an indication of deserved reward and of moral authority. Yet, the growing rejection of the cultural assumptions that material success is evidence of deserved success and that occupying a position of leadership is evidence of qualified leadership does not lead to repudiation of the value placed on personal authority.

Instead, abandonment of previous cultural suppositions may cause disillusion, the hopeless muttering that often has been recorded in the Thai media and heard in the street, and from taxi drivers, vendors, and farmers, about how dirty politics is and how bad and corrupt the politicians are. This is a negative version of the hierarchical deference to authority. It is not a demand that citizens should no longer be willing simply to accept and follow authority, but rather the claim that the wrong people currently happened to hold the positions of authority.

The positive side of the negative disillusion is the shift to a call for "good" people to serve, for mechanisms to prevent people who are not "good" from running for office in the first place, and for all citizens to exercise their civic duties by voting only for the "good." This admonishment is an expression of the new karma replacing the old. Office, material success, position, or monks' robes are no longer sufficient indications of goodness and deserved authority.

The idealization of the "good" person and the search for new criteria of moral authority outside the traditional patron-client model play a role in reforms undertaken in the name of democratization, even if some reforms function contrary to the spirit of democratic process. A good example is the restrictions imposed on the newly instituted elected senate: Seekers of office cannot be members of political parties or currently hold political office, and they are forbidden from campaigning on issues, but instead may only "introduce" themselves as persons. That is, candidates are permitted, under the law, to present their resumes, their educational backgrounds, qualifications, honors, and awards, but they are not permitted to take a public political stand or advocate a platform. It is the wish to promote the "good person" who is clean of all "dirty politics." On the eve of the 1999 elections, the king addressed the nation, urging Thais to vote only for good people. It is a reform with which the Abbot Grang could feel comfortable.

This example is directly in line with traditional ideals of Buddhist democracy, but with a revised understanding of the mark of personal authority. Reform often ends in a new presentation of the same. The ideal of the good, wise, and authoritative person is not simply the outcome of traditional acceptance of hierarchies. There is more besides, and, in fact, a value not unique to any one society or cultural group.

Yet, if this new karma of a "Buddhist" democracy seems to fall short of the Western ideal of the rule of law, it is not without reason. Written law has traditionally been distrusted in Thailand and much of Asia not only because of its tendency to flatten the landscape of hierarchy. Beyond its conflict with certain cultural contexts, precisely the aspect of written law that is a source of justice—its generality and impartiality—is also a source of injustice. Insofar as law is written and general, it provides a fixed measure that helps to assure similar cases are treated in the same way. But it is not only a guarantee of fairness. By minimizing the unlimited discretion of the archaic ruler-legislator-judge, law provides a guideline by which individuals or groups can build expectations and plan actions.

In short, limitation on discretionary authority is a limitation on subjective influence in decisions that affect other people who are subject to that authority. Regardless of whether from malicious bias, unconscious prejudice, or simply the ignorance of incomplete understanding, when one person has powers to decide the affairs of others, but fails to correctly apply a legitimate standard, injustice arises.

Yet, the very blindness of the general law to discretion and differences can equally be a source of injustice. Consequently, while written law by its form is an instrument that limits human discretion and subjects its exercise to formal procedures, law cannot be successfully used to the ends for which it is designed without human discretion. Considering this, it is not hard to appreciate the sentiment that says the heart of justice lies in the wise and experienced person's exercise of legitimate authority, one case at a time. It is for reasons such as this, not only because of traditional hierarchical structures, that some societies, and notably many Asian societies, have long valued personal authority above impersonal statutes. In China, the need for written laws has been traditionally understood as evidence of the lack of social harmony, and, therefore, the very existence of law a failure of society. In Confucian traditions, rule was best exercised by the virtuous man, and law was viewed only as a derivative supplement to this.[21] In this respect, the Confucian tradition is very close to the Buddhist understanding.

Reformers in Thailand have been concerned to promote democratization and civic participation, but not at the expense of social balance and harmony. Rather, they have interpreted democratization as a process toward a truer social harmony, and the outcomes of that process are still in flux.

The Future of the Sangha

Among the traditional authorities that have lost standing are the Buddhist sangha and governmentally sanctioned religion. After much debate and vigorous lobbying by the clergy, the 1997 constitution did not, in the end, make Buddhism the state religion, on the grounds that such a move would prove divisive. Nevertheless, while guaranteeing freedom of religion, the authors retained the specification that the king must be "Buddhist and the upholder of religion."[22]

Even as the national identity board continues to promote the values of nation, monarchy, and religion, and to actively define what it means to be Thai, the sangha's loss of stature in politics has been accompanied by less favorable public opinion toward it. The scandals involving the breach of discipline and untoward behavior on the part of individual monks have been favorite first-page news for several years, and have fueled the demand for reforms.

The Department of Education, which oversees the Department of Religious Affairs, moved in 2001 to extend the secularization that was part of the constitution, and to reform the entrenched religious bureaucracy. There was a movement within the ministry to place the oversight of Buddhism under a newly proposed national commission that would consist of representatives from different faiths.

In response, the clergy hastily pressed for a new sangha act. The first sangha administration act was promulgated in 1903 by King Rama V (Mongkut). It centralized state control of religion and established the sangha supreme council as the highest religious governing body, directly advising the king. The act was revised in 1941, some nine years after the end of absolute monarchy, and again in 1962 under Sarit. The bill proposed in 2001 would have been the first reform of religious administration in forty years.

Although introduced in the name of a reform that would promise to bring errant monks under control, the bill represented, in fact, a conservative backlash against the declining status of official religion. It was reported to have been authored by Somdej Phra Buddhajarn, the most senior monk in the council after the ailing supreme patriarch. Under its provisions, a National Buddhism Office would be created directly under the prime minister. Ecclesiastical law and educational and other policy would be set by a newly established committee, to be called the Maha Khannisorn, whose thirty members, in turn, would be appointed to two-year terms by the council of elders. The bill also proposed criminalizing any press reports that could be seen as damaging Buddhism or Buddhist organizations, or that defamed monks.

The bill became the immediate object of intense controversy for failure to reform the governing structure of the sangha, and especially for its restrictions on freedom of the press. A group known as the Buddhism Protection Center of Thailand rallied to support the bill without amendments. While the central hierarchy pushed for the bill, there was significant dissent from within the clergy. The vice rector of Maha Chula Buddhist University, where monks received advanced training, spoke out in opposition, and a leading disciple of Luangta Maha Bua, a nationally known and influential monk, conducted a vigorous campaign against the bill.

The controversy came to a head with rallies in front of parliament in April 2002. Finally, sensing no easy resolution, Thaksin, the prime minister, intervened to table the bill, apparently killing for the time being efforts to advance or to repeal reforms.

Conclusions

Would Abbot Grang find solace and harmony in the world of new karma, some thirty years beyond the Red Scare? Reforms have continued in Thailand on their own indirect path, as tensions on the path resolve into quiet compromise. The outcomes and implications of the past decade's democratic reforms remain unpredictable. It is clear, however, that the traditional centers of the religious hierarchy have lost something of their former prestige and untouchability. Simultaneously, the old concentrations of political powers are under pressure to decentralize, and formerly accepted or tolerated uses of political power for personal gain are no longer self-justifying. The struggles over advancing or repealing reform are far from settled, but they never stray too far away from preserving an appearance of balance that, perhaps, would please the abbot. The old karma that afforded legitimacy to traditional political hierarchies has lost its footing; the new karma maintains a distinctly Buddhist imprint on the political culture of democratization.

Notes

1. Compare, for example, Chai-anan Samudavanija, "The New Military and Democracy in Thailand," in *Political Culture and Democracy in Developing Countries*, ed. Larry Diamond (Boulder and London: Lynn Rienner, 1994), 269–93.

2. It would be easy to draw up a list of those who have rejected this distinction, including Chamlong Srimuang, Pra Buddhadasa, Sulak Sirvraksa, Dr. Praves Wasi, and others. More on Thai Buddhist social activism is found in the pages ahead.

3. For a historical treatment, as well as a discussion of the accuracy of the patron-client model as a device to explain Thai society, see Barend J. Terwiel, "Formal Structures and Informal Rules: An Historical Perspective on Hierarchy, Bondage, and the Patron-Client Relationship," in *Strategies and Structures in Thai Society*, ed. H. ten Brummelhuis and J.H. Kemp (Amsterdam: University of Amsterdam, Department of South and Southeast Asian Studies, 1984), 19–38.

4. Cf. Anek Laothamatas, *Democratization in Southeast & East Asia* (New York: St. Martin's Press, 1997). Informal polling of university students in American and Thai classrooms tends to bear this out. Asked which is more important for a democracy, "by the people," or "for the people," American students answer overwhelmingly "by the people," and their Thai counterparts "for the people."

5. The "form" of government is never only the "form," that is, an actual form can never be understood just in terms of the formal structure, apart from how that structure is interpreted and lived: Mode of organization can guide action, but can never determine it mechanically. Therefore, one should not see a direct opposition between "representative" and "participatory" democracy. A formal representative structure may or may not be participatory. Consequently, if evidence of a lack of participation is found in pervasive public opinion demanding more from "them," "the government," it does not follow from that alone that a solution to social ills or to political apathy will be found in shifting responsibilities from the public to the private sector.

6. Cf. Tongchai Winichakul, *Siam Mapped. A History of the Geo-Body of a Nation* (Honolulu: University of Hawaii Press, 1994), 39–40.

7. Cf. Niels Mulder, *Thai Images: The Culture of the Public World* (Chiangmai: Silkworm Books, 1997).

8. Cf. Kevin Hewison, "The Monarchy and Democratization," in *Political Change in Thailand: Democracy and Participation*, ed. Kevin Hewison (London: Routledge, 1997).

9. David Morell and Chai-anan Samutwanit, *Political Conflict in Thailand: Reform, Reaction, Revolution* (Cambridge, MA: Oelgeschlager, Gunn & Hain, 1981). 17. Their list of "preeminent influences" goes beyond the official three, including: "family socialization patterns, the monarchy, the bureaucracy, the plentiful natural environment, and Buddhism."

10. Peter A. Jackson, "Withering Centre, Flourishing Margins: Buddhism's Changing Political Roles," in *Political Change in Thailand: Democracy and Participation*, ed. Kevin Hewison (London: Routledge, 1997), 76.

11. Ibid.

12. Cf. Marja-Leen Keikkila-Horn, "Two Paths to Revivalism in Thai Buddhism," *Temenos* 32 (1996): 93–111.

13. Chamlong, now out of politics, has gone on to found his own commune and model for an ideal society in Kanchanaburi Province. One of his former deputies is Taksin Shinawatra, whose telecommunications interests have made him among the richest men in Asia. Taksin went on to found the populist Thai Rak Thai Party ("Thais love Thais") and became prime minister in 2000 (B.E. 2543). In July 2001 (B.E. 2544), with a close vote of the constitutional court in his favor, he survived

corruption charges that threatened to force him from office under a five-year ban from politics.

14. Cf. Duncan J. McCargo, *Chamlong Srimuang and the New Thai Politics* (London and New York: Hurst and St. Martin's Press, 1997).

15. Sanitsuda Ekachai, "There's No Merit in False Claims," *Bangkok Post*, January 7, 1999, http://scoop.bangkokpost.co.th/bangkokpostnews/bp19990107/070199_news19.html.

16. A full accounting of democracy movements would have to go back to the student movements of the 1970s, mentioned above.

17. It should be added, discontent has existed not only over issues of legal controversy, but also concerning accusations of corruption.

18. Prior to the new constitution, any official of fairly high rank could not conceivably be touched by the countercorruption commission. Since the constitution, a corruption investigation resulted in the resignation of an interior minister. It also threatened to unseat Prime Minister Thaksin, although, in the end, he avoided conviction. How effective the new initiatives are over the long term remains to be seen.

19. Cf. "Guess Who Violates Constitution the Most?" *Nation*, October 11, 1999, http://www.nationmultimedia.com/page.arcview.php3?clid5&id=13262&date=1999-10-11&usrsess=1 (accessed January 9, 2005).

20. Widespread, but not the only interpretation.

21. Cf. David T. Hall and Roger Ames, *The Democracy of the Dead* (Honolulu: University of Hawaii Press, 1999), 214 ff.

22. Constitution of Thailand, chap. 2, sec. 8.

5

The Presbyterian Church in the Formation of Taiwan's Democratic Society, 1945–2004

Murray A. Rubinstein

The Presbyterian Church and Sociopolitical Activism in Taiwan

Let the present be prelude. In 1996 and again in 2001, theologians and activists within the Presbyterian Church of Taiwan (PCT) spelled out, in two key documents, the sociopolitical agendas for their independent Protestant church. In these documents, they also provided the theological rationales for their church's decades-long commitment to activism within the Taiwanese public sphere. Huang Poho's *A Theology for Self-Determination* and the PCT General Assembly's *21st Century New Taiwan Mission Movement*[1] are powerful statements that demonstrate just how deeply the Presbyterians have been involved in the life of the people of the complex island nation, or as some would have it, province of China, that is Taiwan. What these two documents also show is that the Presbyterian Church considers itself the vanguard of the multifaceted, multiclass movement for social change, political rights, and national identity that continues today.

The linkage of social action and political activism to mainline Christian Liberation Theology propelled the PCT into a position of leadership in the still-evolving struggle for Taiwanese selfhood. This chapter centers on the role of the Presbyterian Church in Taiwan's retrocession and ongoing postwar history. However, as it argues, taking a lead from Pastor Huang's powerful book and also from the General Assembly's mission statement, one cannot separate the political sphere from the domain of social action. It is in the realm of social policy and action—specifically, welfare and education—that the church has been dominant, at least among the island's Christian groups, and has been the model for other groups as well; it is in these functions that it has had the most dramatic and visible impact.

The Presbyterian Church on Taiwan spent the five decades of Kuomintang (KMT) control of Taiwan fighting difficult battles to win respect for the island's majority populations (Han Taiwanese, Han-Hakka immigrants, and tribal aborigine minority) and helping to transform the island's social and political systems. In order to do so, leaders and members defined new roles for their church. These included the functions of promoter of social and educational change, evangelist of an inclusive political practice, and advocate of ethnic selfhood for both the pre-1945 Han-Minnan and Hakka immigrants and the Australasian Yuanzhumin (aborigines). By assuming these roles, this independent, yet still Western-connected (or more accurately, World Council of Churches [WCC]-connected) church entered, almost inevitably, into conflict with the authoritarian Nationalist Party-dominated state. It was that regime's military forces that attacked the Presbyterian leadership, its institutions, and its members during the painful days and weeks of the tragic 2-28 Incident of 1947. It was also the regime's secret police who kept the church in check in its attempts to fight for political and social justice. Finally, in the early 1970s, the sociocultural and political atmosphere began to change. In that new atmosphere, fueled by a powerful and well-educated middle-class constituency, the PCT was able to launch and sustained a multileveled struggle against the hegemony of the state throughout the 1970s and 1980s. As it did so, it developed a close working alliance with the *dangwai* (the "nonparty" that became the Democratic Progressive Party, or DPP). The five sections of this chapter explore the discrete stages of the PCT's evolution as agent of social and political change.

The Presbyterian Church, 1945–1948

Presbyterian missionaries from Great Britain and Canada arrived in Taiwan in the 1860s and 1870s, and in the decades that followed, they established churches, school systems, hospitals, presses, and seminaries. Each group of missionaries evangelized and developed robust institutions that advanced both Christianization and Westernization. These Western-linked activities were examples of the church's benevolent and charitable undertakings.

Schools were at the core of the missionaries' efforts and the mission-run primary and middle schools, and later high schools, became an important part of the larger institutional landscape of both Tainan and Tamsui. The missionaries saw themselves as agents of social change, and Chinese, too, began to recognize them in this important capacity. Of great significance was the Presbyterians' desire to speak, teach, write, and pray in the language of Taiwan, the Minnan-Taiwanese dialect. Local residents north and south recognized the missionaries' efforts and began to pay some attention both to what they offered and to what they were saying about religion. Thus, it is not an accident that, over the years, these Presbyterian Church-run academies became important in the creation of Westernized Taiwanese élite. And, while not all of the élite became Christian, many did convert. By doing so, they contributed to the evangelical fervor of the ongoing process of Taiwan's transformation into a very Westernized part of China.[2]

The Presbyterians were able to continue their work after Japan took control of the island in 1895. They were permitted to provide medical and educational services. In addition, they became one of the few groups that could provide extensive Western-style education to the Taiwanese, a level of education that the Japanese were unwilling to provide to the public at large.

The end of World War II saw the dismantling of the Japanese empire. The island was handed to authorities of the Republic of China (ROC), and, thus, a new and painful period in the history of Taiwan began. The years from the fall of 1945 to the autumn of 1949 proved to be dramatic and traumatic for Taiwan and pivotal in the life of its Presbyterian Church. During these years, the leaders of the church were forced by events to define the role that their church would play on the now KMT-controlled island. At the core of this process of redefinition lay the intertwined themes of the church's ongoing establishment of its operational independence from missionary control and its identification with the cause of Taiwanese ethnic and national selfhood. The evolution of the PCT was connected to its leaders' ability to meet two related demands.

The first charge of the church's elders and laymen throughout the island was to reorganize and restructure the presbyteries and the synod and to make these, once again, the Taiwanese-controlled entities they had been early in the twentieth century. The decisions that church leaders throughout the island made in the years immediately before and after the Nationalists took control of Taiwan were seemingly simple but they had a host of complex implications. The process took years, but, in the end, a new and more independent church, free of missionary dominance, had evolved.[3]

Meetings were held in the northern and southern presbyteries. Those who attended these regional conferences focused upon basic problems of organization. The structures of local bodies now were designed and the relationships between local churches and the major councils and regional administrative bodies—Presbyterians had a history of operating both administrative and representative bodies as elements of their ecclesiology (or structure of church polity)—were defined and diagrammed. Thus, a flow chart of authority was established. The major church leaders also were chosen. Finally, control of the regional middle schools and high schools and each of the theological colleges was reaffirmed and steps were taken to reinvigorate each of these educational institutions. The thread that ran through the meetings was the demand for local and regional authority on the part of the Taiwanese Presbyterian lay leadership and pastorate. This demand reflected the recognition that tensions had developed between the northern and southern regions since the official union of the churches of these areas in 1912. There was also the recognition that, before one could recreate an effective national church, one had to restore the core churches to the earlier state of viability that they had enjoyed before the Japanese had instituted their own ultranationalistic program of reorganization.[4]

The second demand concerned the Western missionaries and their reintegration into the Presbyterian Church. The Western church leaders, and perhaps the Taiwanese laity, demanded that church leaders in Taiwan redevelop working relationships with the mother churches in England and Canada, and with the missionaries who served those churches. The missionaries had been forced from the island in 1940. Now, with the war over, they were returning and discovering that their status and roles in the newly reorganized regional churches were uncertain. They also found that the Taiwanese leaders and pastors had proved quite capable of running the churches and synods without their sometimes unwanted help.

However, the missionaries soon realized that, while the Taiwanese could run their own churches, they were willing to welcome their old friends and coworkers back. Thus, many of the "old Taiwan hands" were invited to serve the churches in which they previously had worked, sometimes for decades. These men and women returned and were warmly welcomed back to cities, villages, and congregations that they had known for years. Yet, both sides acknowledged that matters could not return to the ante bellum status quo, and that the relationships between the missionaries and their churches and the synods had to be renegotiated and redefined.[5]

Even as restructuring and reintegration were in process, both the northern and southern synods moved ahead with their efforts to evangelize among the populace, and, thus, to win converts and to indigenize the form of Christianity to which they were winning souls. As other evangelists, such as those missionaries representing the Southern Baptist Convention on the Chinese mainland between 1937 and 1945, had discovered, chaotic times produced a greater openness to the Christian message. The Presbyterian presence on Taiwan was able to expand during the years immediately following the war and the end of the Japanese occupation. Taiwanese and Hakka joined the church in ever greater numbers, as did the Yuanzhumin of the island's cordillera—the long north-to-south mountain range that occupies the center and the eastern coast of Taiwan.

A further comment about the Yuanzhumin is necessary, here. The Presbyterians had worked with the Yuanzhumin during the last decades of Manchu rule, and, as James Johnson and George Leslie MacKay showed at the end of the 1800s, were able to gain converts and prepare the ground for further proselytism.[6] However, the Japanese attempted to isolate the Yuanzhumin in reservations and constructed electrified fences to separate these lands from those of the Han Chinese who had settled the island. Even so, both Presbyterians and evangelists of the True Jesus Church made inroads and prepared the way for evangelism during the fifty years of Japanese rule. Thus, when the Nationalists arrived and made the mountain reserves more accessible (though only with special permits) to the Han Taiwanese, Hakka, the Western missionaries, the evangelists of the True Jesus Church, and the Roman Catholics representing the missionary orders, the mountain people responded and converted in great numbers.[7]

Within a few years, tens of thousands of mountain people were counted among the expanding Christian community, and the churches now faced the task of training ministers and lay leaders among this new population. Long involved in Taiwan, the Presbyterians, who stressed the development of an independent indigenous church, made the most notable gains. They were successful among the Yuanzhumin for the same reasons that they were successful among the Taiwanese and Hakka of the island's western coastal plains: They had developed useful romanizations of the local dialects and languages. Thus, they introduced a medium that would be used to maintain the regional dialects, such as Hokkien and the tribal tongues. The missionaries also worked to foster a sense of local cultural and ethnic identity, as they developed an indigenized and responsive form of reformed Protestantism. This stress on establishing a written language and fostering pride in the Han-Taiwanese, Hakka, and Yuanzhumin past would be used to confront the Nationalists' potent form of cultural imperialism—"Mandarinization"—from the 1940s through the late 1980s.

The Protestant efforts to preserve culture and heighten awareness of selfhood had a number of dimensions. One was the process of developing and making extensive use of the Hokkien romanization that the English Presbyterians first had developed in Amoy. Another was to rebuild the system of Presbyterian-run schools, such as those in Tainan and Taipei counties, which had long been the birthplace of the emerging Taiwanese middle class. Heroes of Taiwanese resistance to KMT repression, such as political scientist Peng Minming, had attended these schools, which provided access to a university education in Japan to him and thousands of others. Thus, these schools were the locus of training of the Taiwanese élite. While the Presbyterians had prepared at least two generations of Taiwanese leaders, they had not yet taken a next step, that of identifying their church with the Taiwanese people as a whole. Nor were they ready to bear witness to what many Taiwanese saw as KMT oppression. A crisis would unfold before this would take place and an unbreakable bond would be created between the members of the Presbyterian Church and the majority of Taiwan's non-Christian populace. The church's leaders and its members and thousands more Taiwanese who were believers in the "popular religion" (*minjian* tradition), Buddhism, Taoism, and in regional and China-wide sectarian movements, such as Yiguandao, would experience a baptism by fire and blood, the 2-28 Incident, before this enduring bond would be forged.

The 2-28 slaughter has been written about at length since the mid-1980s, and accounts in English, such as George Kerr's *Formosa Betrayed*,[8] are regarded as classics of a literature of martyrdom. Other works, such as the Myers, Lai, and Wei collaboration *Tragic Beginning*,[9] are more critical in tone and, thus, more controversial. Perhaps Steven Phillips's monograph for Stanford University has provided a necessary balance to the Western literature on the subject.[10] It is clear, however, that the traumatic set of events that began with a riot against the police of Taipei in late February 1947, to this day, remains a shattering episode in Taiwan's twentieth-century history. Members of the PCT also see the events associated with 2-28 as a defining period in their own history. During and after the 1970s, the circumstances of February 1947 took on an added significance. History, many believed, came near to repeating itself when, twice during the 1970s and again in the early 1980s, the KMT handled legitimate public protest—protest that erupted only after people were pushed to their limits—with an iron fist, and only later with a velvet glove. The open and very public role that the leaders of the Presbyterian Church played during the 2-28 Incident and the degree of suffering that they and other church members experienced during the event and its aftermath, led to defining moments of consciousness for Presbyterians. The PCT leaders determined then that they would continue to raise their voices, speaking for the population of Taiwan as a whole, while accepting as their burden any punishment that this public form of protest would engender. Developments of the 1970s and the 1980s would show that the PCT, once again confident of its path and mission, would rise to the new challenges posed by the KMT regime.

Lying Low and Defending Turf, 1949–1964

The next and most complex period in the history of the PCT and the Protestant community of which it is a part, spanned from 1949 to 1965. During this period, the Protestant missionary community on the island expanded dramatically, and, as it did, the pace of evangelism among Han Taiwanese, the newly arrived mainlanders, and the Yuanzhumin also increased. A new and more diverse Protestant community came into being. That community, with missionaries often in the lead, began to play an important role in the development of a social safety net for the people of the island. During this period more than in any other in the history of the Taiwanese Protestant community, benevolence and evangelism would go hand-in-hand.

The transformation of Taiwan from a Chinese province to the KMT-dominated and American-bankrolled nation-state created new challenges and opportunities for the Presbyterian Church in Taiwan. The years from 1949 to 1964 would see the church change in important ways as it responded to the new political, cultural, and spiritual climates created by the Nationalists' loss of the Chinese mainland and their leadership's retreat to the large and already populous island in the South China Sea. These years also would demonstrate the wisdom of the church leaders' decision to make their church the independent ecclesiastical body that it had become by 1949. Finally, these same years would demonstrate in subtle ways how intuitively correct it was for church elders and pastors to embrace the cause of Taiwanese selfhood and the Taiwanese population's striving for a sense of ethnic and provincial identity. Many of the PCT's benevolent activities, such as its medical and social welfare programs, stem from the church's vision of itself as the defender of Taiwanese rights and as the major benevolent actor in Taiwanese society.

The first challenge that the PCT faced arose from the KMT's decision to transform the province of Taiwan, with its own language dialects and unique history as a maritime frontier, into the ROC regime's vision of the one authentic China.

The KMT's program had a number of facets. The first was public security, implemented by the security forces commanded by Chiang Ching-kuo. Chiang, the first among equals of the newly formed Political Action Committee, demonstrated both his well-known administrative abilities and his ruthlessness, which had not been exhibited while carrying out his previous assignments, including the mayoralty of Shanghai.[11] He first placed under arrest and then had killed thousands of Taiwanese and newly arrived mainlanders in the process of implementing a wide-range purge of so-called corrupt elements.[12] The ballpark in downtown Taipei became an ROC version of a killing field.[13]

The reign of terror had its intended effect. No organized large-scale opposition to the regime was in evidence on the island, until the diplomatic and domestic crisis that came in the wake of the Nixon-Kissinger initiatives of the early 1970s. The lesson of the brutal intimidation was not lost on the Presbyterians. No matter how great their desire might have been to challenge the regime for its sins against the Taiwanese, they decided to adopt an expedient course of action and carefully watched their steps and measured their words.

The KMT's social and educational policies created different sorts of problems. The church had continued to use a romanized *Taiwanhua* (Hokkien) Bible that George Band had prepared in the 1930s and 1940s, and a romanized Taiwanhua hymnal. Furthermore, church leaders in the north and the south made it clear to all concerned that the language of prayer was Taiwanhua. The new KMT-led government opposed this use of the provincial dialect. It saw itself as the government of China in exile and mandated that Taiwan, as a province of China, was a *guoyu*-speaking nation. The state authorities ordered that guoyu must be the language of all public discourse and the language taught in school, no matter what language or dialect was used at home. During the first decades of KMT rule, children of mainlander, guoyu-speaking households had the upper hand, despite their minority status in the population. They passed the all-important examinations for the better middle schools, high schools, universities, and colleges. Their advantage was partially linguistic and partially political. The sons and daughters of the island's new rulers were given places of privilege, at least during the 1950s and 1960s.[14]

The linguistic imperialism went beyond the classroom into the printing house. Presbyterians found that their attempts to continue to use Taiwanhua as the language of instruction in their own church-run schools and seminaries was made difficult by the government's policy of preventing—or at least attempting to prevent—the preparation of romanized Taiwanhua texts and teaching materials. The government went even further, however, for it attacked the efforts of the Presbyterians and other Western churches and mission orders to prepare and publish useful romanized texts of the various Yuanzhumin tribal languages. Presbyterians were active in evangelism of the Yuanzhumin and resisted the government's efforts. Here, they were joined by seemingly unlikely allies, the members of the Catholic Missionary Society in America, who were known by most people as the priests and nuns of the Maryknoll Order. The Maryknollers had been active in both Guangdong and Fujian, and after being forced from the People's Republic of China (PRC), found that they could work among the Taiwanhua-speaking majority as well as among the Yuanzhumin.[15] The order was based in Taichung, but the missionaries—both Maryknoll fathers and sisters—also worked in the major cities of the western coastal plain and among the Yuanzhumin communities of Nanto County. Thus, their work paralleled that of the Presbyterians. The Maryknollers also took another important and perhaps provocative step and made their mission house an educational center, where they prepared texts in Taiwanhua and taught both their own missionaries and other Westerners, missionaries and nonmissionaries, Taiwanhua. The two groups—Catholic and Protestant—thus forged a private alliance to fight against their common enemy, the linguistically imperialistic KMT state.

Despite the repressive authoritarianism of the regime, there were opportunities for the PCT in the realm of social policy. The government's attempt to modernize as rapidly as possible meant that there were few funds available for social services and the creation of a modern health-care system. Here, the Presbyterians could and did act, and, as a result, had considerable impact. They had introduced Western-style medical knowledge and practice to the island, and, by the 1950s, had restored the hospital centers that they had built in earlier decades in the major regions of Taiwan to levels that equaled or exceeded pre–World War II efficiency. The reunited (and independent) Presbyterian Church of the 1950s stressed medical work.

To be sure, Presbyterians were not alone in their social-service efforts. Newly arrived Western missions, such as the Seventh-Day Adventists, established hospitals in Taipei and Taitung. Other evangelical bodies, such as the Southern Baptist Convention, organized clinics in the cities in which they worked. Maryknollers also operated eye clinics as part of their overall program of service to the Han-Taiwanese-speaking and Yuanzhumin populations with whom they were working. However, it is clear that the Presbyterians led the way and were certainly the most visible presence in this benevolent facet of Christian activity. Of equal importance was the fact that many of the doctors, nurses, and administrative staff who worked within the Presbyterians' health-service network were themselves Han-Taiwanese. Indigenization was a key element in health care as well as other aspects of the overall Presbyterian effort.

As the decade of the 1950s unfolded, there was yet another policy of the KMT regime that, on the surface, seemed to threaten Presbyterian evangelization efforts. This was the KMT's policy of opening Taiwan's doors to Western missionaries. Beginning in 1946, Western missionaries from various mainline, evangelical, and Holiness and Pentecostal denominations began moving into Taiwan. The leaders of these groups viewed the island as a potential place of refuge from the storm of revolution and civil war then engulfing mainland China.

At first glance, it would seem that the missionary invasion would work against the PCT by providing the church with numerous rivals in the struggle for Chinese souls. But the available evidence shows that the reverse was true and that the Presbyterian Church profited from this infiltration of Christian brethren in important and unexpected ways. First, when the Presbyterian Church was one of very few churches on the island, as was the case in 1947, it stood out as the only mainline Protestant body and could easily be persecuted by the government. Now, however, there were many witnesses to the government's treatment of Christian denominations. Furthermore, representatives of many of these denominations—the Southern Baptist Convention is one example—defended the Nationalist regime as a paragon of religious toleration and a bastion against the Red Chinese hordes who were driving the missionaries from their shores and restructuring the many Christian churches into two state-controlled patriotic churches, one Protestant and the other Catholic.[16] Thus, the Presbyterians retained their position as the defenders of the indigenous inhabitants and their culture.

Another important actor in the Protestant community came to Taiwan during the first years of the retrocession and then began making an impact over the years that followed. This was the YMCA. The Young Men's Christian Association had had a long history in China, going back before the turn of the century. It was a nondenominational organization and also was oriented toward education, outreach, and social organizations. In China and in Taiwan, it provided a wealth of services for the Christian and non-Christian publics. During the 1950s and 1960s, a period when the churches on the island were forced to play a major role in the organization of relief efforts as providers of social welfare programs, the YMCA was in the middle of the action.[17]

One final consideration is the nature of the role that the non-Presbyterian Protestant community played in Taiwanese society of the 1950s. One can see two facets of this role. The first is the churches' most familiar domain, the religious one. The churches and the missions did address the spiritual needs of many of the island's population. The newly arrived missionaries from the mainland-based non-Presbyterian denominations worked with the new immigrants and helped them to adjust to their life in "exile" to Taiwan. Missions and churches offered "shelters in the storm." As a result, links were forged between missionaries and mainlander immigrants that remain to this day. The irony is that these mainlander groups also took control of the country and imposed their political, social, and cultural systems upon Taiwan. In the end, their assistance to the mainlanders cost these missionaries dearly, for they were seen as supporting the KMT and as being mainlander Christians. Although mainlander churches began to grow, they soon came to a wall—for their leaders were dealing with a limited population that the Taiwanese and Hakka majority looked upon as conquerors, not liberators. The Presbyterians, on the other hand, were able to continue to build their strength and to develop their ties through the network of social service institutions that they had developed with the Taiwanese peoples, Hokklo, Hakka, and Yuanzhumin. This network and this sympathetic population would serve the Presbyterians well in the difficult years of struggle that were soon to follow.

The Years of Confrontation, 1965–1985

The centenary year of 1965 marked a turning point in the development of the Presbyterian Church of Taiwan. The church abandoned the gentleman's agreement it had with the neutral or more pro-KMT churches and it became both the defender of conciliar and reformed Christianity and the advocate for the Taiwanese people. It was forced, once again, to assume the "burden of witness." The leaders of the various Western missions and their client churches recognized that their hopes to create a Christian Taiwan were coming to naught and large-scale church growth virtually reached an end.

The churches that were oriented toward strong evangelism decided what would help remedy the situation was a vigorous evangelistic campaign. They invited the famous and fiery neo-evangelical preacher, Carl MacIntire, to conduct immense prayer meetings. MacIntire, who was a strict neo-evangelical, was also strongly anticommunist. These messages were anathema to the social gospel-oriented, avowedly ecumenical, World Council of Churches-connected Presbyterian Church of Taiwan. The tensions that were generated by the MacIntire campaign set the stage for the new and more serious conflicts that would pit the PCT against its sister churches and against the KMT-dominated state.

During 1966, a study committee of the World Council of Churches—which already was infamous in the eyes of many neo-evangelicals—recommended that the PRC should be permitted to enter the United Nations, replacing the Republic of China. President Chiang pressured the churches in Taiwan to protest against the announcement by withdrawing from the WCC. These churches did so in the face of the opposition of the largest and most important of the island's churches, the Presbyterian Church of Taiwan. The PCT did not make a loud public stir, but decided that it soon had to move to express the membership's antagonism toward the ROC government.

That moment arrived in 1971, when there began a turning point in the fortunes of the ruling party and its regime, one marked by a series of diplomatic disasters. Between 1971 and 1973, the government of the ROC sustained a series of diplomatic setbacks. First, there was disaster at the United Nations, with the United States withdrawing its usual veto, allowing the other members of the Security Council to replace the ROC with the PRC. Next were the Kissinger talks in Beijing, followed by Nixon's visit and the issuance of the Shanghai Communiqué in 1972.

Critics of the regime at home, students and intellectuals for the most part, took advantage of the situation that they saw as reflecting the KMT regime's vulnerability, and held a series of demonstrations calling for political reforms. This political ferment provided the PCT with its long-awaited window of opportunity. Late in 1971, PCT leaders on Taiwan, working in coordination with PCT leaders and activists in the West, began to issue a series of dramatic and forceful public statements that challenged the regime on a number of fronts.[18]

The first of these statements, issued by Gao Zhumin, the general secretary of the PCT, was entitled "Public Statement of Our National Faith" and was addressed to the international community and to the KMT regime of Taiwan. It said simply and quite forcefully that the fate of Taiwan should be left in Taiwanese hands and not in the hands of outsiders, such as the government of the PRC or the government of Taiwan's erstwhile ally, the Nixon-led United States. In the second section of the statement, the PCT leaders called upon the KMT regime to open up the political process and to hold elections for the National Assembly, a body that had been elected in 1947 and one that now was considered to be—given the ages of its members—a wheelchair assembly. Taiwanese church members in America rallied to the cause of the church in Taiwan and made statements, wrote letters to newspapers, and talked to all of the politicians and groups that they could in the name of their cause: political rights and *Self-Determination* for the people of Taiwan.[19]

The year 1975 brought further confrontation between the PCT and the KMT regime, and even fiercer rounds of battle began that resulted not only in the PCT's direct involvement in the dangwai, or *Meilidao* [Formosa magazine], movement of the late 1970s, but also in the arrests of members of the church leadership and central administration in early 1980. The conflict began with the Bible and the attempt to publish it. In late 1974 and early 1975, the PCT had prepared and begun to publish a new Taiwanese romanization of the Bible. It then began to place these new Bibles in church bookstores throughout the island and to package Bibles and mail them to Taiwanese communities throughout the world.

The government saw the steps taken by the PCT as direct disobedience of its policies, policies that mandated the use of guoyu. While it had repealed those statutes directly forbidding the use of many religious materials, the government still felt it had the power to stifle efforts to distribute Bibles, religious texts, hymnals in Taiwanese and in the languages of the Yuanzhumin, and the like. Thus, it took action. In January

1975, the government confiscated more than two thousand Bibles from the Presbyterian bookstores. The church protested against this action.[20]

The Western-based groups continued to monitor the situation, and at their meetings and conferences made public statements on the matters of *Self-Determination* and the publication of the Bibles. This level of backing was important for it demonstrated to the leaders of the PCT just how widespread the overseas support had now become. This would prove to be important when the PCT made another statement that attacked the KMT-dominated government and its various repressive policies.[21]

A new PCT statement was prepared and then voted upon at the meeting of the Executive Committee of the Presbyterian Church on November 18, 1975. It was entitled simply "Our Appeal," but it proved to be anything but an innocent document. Rather, it was a six-page brief against the government and its actions. The church leaders then moved beyond their political agenda and discussed issues directly related to the church and what it had to do for itself during these critical times. The leaders made bold statements, but these were seen as ones they had to make, given the political environment. In the statement, they laid out five basic proposals that they hoped would help the government confront a variety of basic problems.[22] They knew that, acting as they did, they had opened the way for greater pressure from the government. The year 1976 proved to be a quiet one in terms of church-state confrontation, but the same could not be said for 1977. By then, the Carter administration had taken command of U.S. foreign policy, and Cyrus Vance, the secretary of state, was following up on the Shanghai Communiqué and attempting to improve Sino-American relations. The ROC and the PCT were wary of the steps that the United States was taking, and each responded to what it perceived as danger to Taiwan's autonomy and to its relationship with its old friend and ally.

The Presbyterian Church made its own distinctive move on August 16, 1977. Its leaders issued a document entitled "A Declaration of Human Rights by the Presbyterian Church on Taiwan." It addressed President Carter and "all countries and . . . Christian Churches throughout the world." The PCT also addressed the leaders of the government and called upon the KMT-dominated regime to declare Taiwan a new and independent nation.[23]

The new declaration was a call to arms to which the KMT had to respond. One must note that 1977 was a troublesome year, in general, for the KMT. Events in the political realm provided context and subtext for the regime's reaction to the PCT's simply worded and quite powerful—and well-publicized—statement.[24]

The government soon took steps against the Presbyterian Church. On August 21, it confiscated copies of the *Taiwan Presbyterian Church News* that contained both the declaration and the newspaper's editorial support for it. Then, to cool the tensions, the Chiang Ching-kuo–led government initiated a series of talks with church officials that were held over the course of the next two months.

However, the talks did not mean that the government was assuming a benign posture toward the church, and it struck again early in 1978. The first step in the new campaign against the PCT came in mid-February, when four thousand copies of the *Taiwan Presbyterian Church News* disappeared.

On March 9, the Northern Synod met and discussed church policy. A number of critical issues were discussed by the General Assembly and key among them was the appeal that the Executive Committee had published. This issue was debated with considerable passion, and, in the end, a vote of support was taken that revealed 235 members were in favor, 49 against, and 10 had abstained by means of casting blank ballots.

A second debate centered on the reelection of Pastor Gao as the head of the church. The government had lobbied to defeat him and had threatened members of the church. The members of the General Assembly responded by voting 255 for Gao, 49 against him, and 8 for abstention by blank ballots. The vast majority of this key church body had spoken: They would not be intimidated.[25]

The government kept up its pressure during April by feeding the rumor mill with suggestions that the church leadership would be arrested in mid-April. The church members responded to the rumors by sending letters and appeals to the government, asking that this step not be taken. The government decided not to move at this time, but continued to watch the leaders of the church closely and let these men and women know that this was so. Intimidation was the card that authorities knew how to play best.[26] The state had created an additional weapon to use against the PCT and other religious organizations. This was the Law Regulating Temples, Shrines, Churches, and Mosques. It was designed to give the government the power to directly interfere with the operations of religious institutions. The law had been introduced in 1977 and was still on the drawing board as the confrontation with the PCT took place. However, all were aware that the government wished to promulgate the law and viewed even the discussions about the law as lightly veiled threats.[27]

The church leaders reacted to the assaults on its security in a most public way. They drafted yet another detailed public statement, one that they termed "A Clarification on 'The Declaration of Human Rights.'" They then had this piece published in the *Taiwan Presbyterian Church News*. The world church community and religious organizations based in the United States had watched the events on Taiwan, and, in the months that followed, sent letters of support.

The Presbyterian Church now stepped back a bit and the dangwai and its vanguard, the leaders of the Meilidao movement, took center stage. In late 1978, the United States declared its intention to officially recognize the PRC. This threw the Taiwanese political arena into turmoil. The government responded by suspending the elections that were to be held in the late fall of 1978. The opposition countered, in turn, by declaring that it would hold demonstrations and confront the state at any opportunity. The core of the dangwai leadership began to edit a magazine, *Meilidao*, and used this as the basis for its campaign of opposition. Over the course of 1979, tensions escalated as did the frequency and size of the demonstrations. Finally, a clash occurred at a large-scale demonstration held near the railroad station in Kaohsiung. Police and hired thugs confronted the dangwai activists and their followers. This event—this harsh confrontation—became known as the legendary Kaohsiung Incident.

The next day, most of the leaders of the Meilidao movement were arrested. Shi Mingde, the Lenin of the movement, escaped capture and managed to remain free for a few more months. The man who helped hide him was Pastor Gao. Shi was arrested and soon thereafter Pastor Gao and other members of his staff, a total of nine codefendants, also were taken into custody.[28]

The Meilidao leaders and the church leaders then underwent months of interrogation, followed by public trials. They were found guilty, even though most of the defendants recanted the confessions that had been forced from them. Thus, the core of leaders of the dangwai began long prison terms. Pastor Gao and the others arrested with him also were sentenced to years of imprisonment. The government finally had done what it had wanted to do at many moments over the course of the 1970s— it had apprehended the leaders of this troublesome and very publicity-oriented Presbyterian Church.[29]

The months and years immediately after the trials of the Kaohsiung defendants and the church leaders, from 1980 to 1986, proved to be difficult for the church in a number of ways. One aspect of this distress was a direct result of the earlier confrontations that had pitted the church against the state. The PCT and its members (and other religious institutions, as well) continued to find themselves besieged by the government that used proposed regulations to wear down the will of the now leaderless church. They also found themselves under attack by what might be termed extralegal arms of the state.

Let us examine the extralegal facet of the assault first. In February 1980, the mother-in-law and twin daughters of the lawyer and Meilidao leader, Lin I-hsiung, were brutally murdered. Those who committed the crime against the family of this lawyer and Kaohsiung Incident defendant remain unknown even today. The explanation that many observers provide is that the killers were working with the permission of the state, but this assertion has not been proved. The brutality notwithstanding, church leaders, such as John Tin, found that they could turn this tragedy to their advantage. Lin's wife gave the apartment, located in a street a few blocks from Xinyi Road and Xinsheng South Road, to the PCT, and its leaders founded a church on the site. This is the Gikong Church and it became a center for political and social activism over the course of the 1980s. This writer was given a tour of the apartment-church complex in 1984, conducted by the fiery theologian John Tin, who pointed out just where Lin's daughters had been cut down. The author also attended services there that year, in which church officials, such as Donal MacCall and other key figures, including Pastor Gao's wife, participated. The services were quietly powerful and the place of death became a place of hope and of religious life. The apartment had gone from serving as the home of an influential dissident leader to being the home of a socially and politically conscious congregation of Presbyterian leaders and activists. The services reflected what the church now was and how it would evolve over the course of the 1980s.

In the years ahead, the church and its members continued to honor the memory of those who had died. For example, on February 28, 1986, a memorial service was held at the church. The Reverend Xu Tianxian, pastor of Gikong Church and a former political prisoner like Lin Yixiong, officiated at the service. The sermon was delivered by the Reverend Wang Xianzhi of the Tainan Theological College. Once again, the power and the reach of the church were being demonstrated even as the tragic events that led to the founding of the church were recalled.[30]

The church also faced the problem of continued harassment when it tried to mail its publications to subscribers. Copies of the *Church News* never reached subscribers when certain issues were regarded by the authorities as too dangerous. Over the course of the 1980s, the author was a subscriber to the newspaper and became aware that, each year, certain issues of the biweekly publication never were received. Usually, these issues concerned 2-28. After the political thaw and end of much of the press censorship in the late 1980s, back issues were mailed and did reach subscribers as far away as Peekskill, New York. However, before political liberalization began, new government regulations had been developed in the earlier 1980s to control facets of the church's activities. The Tainan Theological College was marked for control or for closure because its teachers used Taiwanese as a medium of instruction and taught a socially conscious form of Protestantism. The college was the place where many of the most radical pastors were trained, and this, too, made it a marked institution. This author was given a clear idea of what the institution faced when he visited it in 1984 and met with its president and some key members of its faculty, including John Tin, a longtime and very articulate enemy of the KMT and all that it stood for.[31]

The local government in Tainan found multifarious ways to harass the Theological College and its staff and tried to stop its development and planned expansion. Officials went even further in 1984 and tried to find the means to close the college. The city government, under the mayor, Su Nanqeng, devised various strategies, going so far as to argue that the college was not under the Ministry of Education but under the Ministry of Interior, and, therefore, that the staff did not have the right to instruct students. These attacks were met by protests from churches throughout the world, and the local government consequently was forced to retreat.[32]

The government also returned to its idea of regulation of many of the religious institutions on the island at a fundamental level. While all types of institutions were mentioned in the draft regulations, it was clear that the PCT and the New Testament Church, a radical charismatic church, were singled out for control and harassment.[33]

The government attacked the church in a very direct way, as well, by making life exceedingly difficult for Pastor Gao, now serving his fourth year in prison, and for the other staff of the PCT who had been sentenced as a result of the Meilidao Incident. At times, Pastor Gao was held in a cell with no chair or bed, in what Marc Cohen saw as an attempt to break his spirit. Elder Lin Wen-cheng, who was also serving a prison sentence, was denied medical treatment and the authorities seized her property and the land that belonged to her relatives. Only after Gao staged a hunger strike in protest against this treatment was she given medical leave.[34]

Gao was seen as a martyr for his work for human rights and his personal intervention on behalf of the Meilidao leader (and Roman Catholic), Shi Mingde. Reports surfaced about how Gao was being treated and the worldwide Taiwanese network began to exert pressure on the government. Various organizations lobbied for his release, which was arranged in August 1984. Pastor Gao soon returned to his position as general secretary of the PCT. He took personal charge of the human rights-related work of the church, in which he had been deeply involved during the decade of the 1970s.[35]

In 1986, Gao was given permission to leave Taiwan and to speak to Western audiences about the PCT. He traveled for four months, from early May until August, visiting the offices of the United Reformed Church in London, the World Council of Churches in Geneva, the Presbyterian Church of the United States, the Presbyterian Church in Canada, and the Presbyterian Church in Korea. He spoke in his capacity as head of his church, but he also spoke as a man who had given of his life for his church and its people. He had traveled to distant places to give thanks to those who had supported him and lobbied on his behalf in the dark years of his struggles in the 1970s and his bitter years as a prisoner.[36]

The PCT and its allies in the WCC fought a battle for Taiwanese selfhood and social justice. By doing so, they helped to create a climate in which a variety of church-related programs could flourish. The other major Protestant churches took a different, safer, but perhaps more "fundamentalist" approach by deciding to "render unto Caesar." Thus, they continued to work as they normally did during these years and to avoid the hard decision to support the PCT. Some churches, such as the Southern Baptist Convention, closely supported and defended KMT-ROC leadership, and one of their most famous ministers, Zhou Lien-hua, served as pastor and religious counselor to the Chiang family. Zhou also presided over the funeral service of Chiang Kai-shek. His was a mainlander church and he was a friend of the regime. It was as simple as that.

Other churches, such as the True Jesus Church and the Assembly Hall Church, remained determinedly nonpolitical. They tailored their work to the spiritual needs of the *laobaixing* (the Old Hundred Names, or common people), and the Taiwanese community responded. Both of these independent churches expanded during the 1970s and 1980s. The other mission-linked churches reached a plateau and did not increase in size for much of this two-decade period. They met a powerful obstacle—the revival of the Chinese popular religious tradition. The economic miracle had brought people back to the local temples of the minjian (popular) tradition and to Buddhist temples as well. Modernization and Westernization were good, but Taiwanese still wanted to retain some sense of who they were as people, and this was one reason why they revived their interest in the local and regional gods and goddesses. Furthermore, many temples, including the major Mazu temples, had learned to appropriate Christian methods of linking religion to social services, and, thus, served their faithful more effectively than ever before. All of this meant that the mainlander-focused evangelical churches would lose ground.

The Protestant Community and the New Taiwan: Benevolent and Charitable Works and the Evolution of Democracy in the Republic of China, 1986–Present

By 1987, after twenty years of political turmoil, diplomatic isolation, and church-state conflict, a new and more open Taiwan was ready to come into existence. Most churches had avoided harm's way and the struggle of the previous two decades, but some, most notably the Presbyterian Church of Taiwan and the Maryknoll Order of the Roman Catholic Church, had not.

Even in the new era, the PCT remained committed to political change and proved willing to take risks for it. June 1990 saw yet another example of this and manifestation of the close relationship between the PCT and the Democratic Progressive Party that would take control of the executive branch of government in 2000. Shi Mingde, a DPP leader, was released from prison by Lee Teng-hui. Lee was, of course, the most famous member of the PCT, for he was now the president of Taiwan. Shi then began to give a series of speeches at meetings arranged by local DPP leaders for him and other Meilidao defendants and leaders. One such meeting was held at a Presbyterian church in the old part of Taipei, near the Longshan Temple. Here, Shi met with members of the church who had offered him help during his time of need.

Yet, even in seemingly more favorable political times, the church faced problems—problems created by the end of the large-scale conflict with the government. In the late 1980s and the early 1990s, the Presbyterian Church of Taiwan needed to redefine itself and to transform its former sociopolitical agenda. The wars for selfhood had largely been won as had the struggle for Taiwanese political participation. As a result, the church redirected its efforts and began to intensify its work among certain victimized communities. It took a greater active role in working with the Yuanzhumin and founded various organizations to help these minority peoples to cope with their plethora of social problems.[37]

The church also began to work with communities of fishermen who were often detained by other nations when their ships were blown off course or when those ships violated other nations' territorial waters. Church leaders and officials established a Fisherman's Service Center, designed to help these men and their families. The Presbyterians devoted additional time and energy to fighting the exploitation of teenaged prostitutes who worked near the infamous Snake Alley near the Longshan Temple.[38] Transforming itself even further, the church also began to preach an awareness of the need for environmental protection. As early as 1986, for example, an interfaith workshop addressing environmental concerns was held, designed to be the starting point for interfaith cooperation on environmental matters.[39]

While the 1980s and the early 1990s proved to be yet another turbulent period, with the church on the defensive as the state tried to take its revenge for church activities in the 1970s, the church survived the attacks. It also had redefined its agenda in the face of Taiwan's sociopolitical change and its implementation of genuine political reforms and a real expansion of opportunities for Taiwanese in the ROC's political and governmental systems.

Let us look at the work of the church in 1995, a dramatic year in the history of the Republic of China on Taiwan that saw the initial phase of the election campaign for the first freely elected president. We see the Presbyterian Church as the church saw itself, as reflected in its *1995 Annual Report*.[40]

That report gives us insight into a church looking back at 130 years of existence. The church celebrated its anniversary with large-scale festivities in various parts of the island, which were attended by some twenty thousand church members. President Lee, a man who considers himself a devout Presbyterian, sent words of congratulation and praised the church for its work in medicine, social-change activities, commitment to education, and promulgation of justice. The church members and leaders could look back with pride to what they had accomplished and contributed to the progress of their nation.

Yet, the church's leaders also recognized what still had to be done. They now decided that spiritual renewal was needed. Taiwan had become a modern and increasingly open and progressive society—but at a cost. There were now problems of crime, juvenile delinquency, the breakdown of the family, prostitution, and spousal abuse. The church saw that it must remain committed to social change but that it also had to develop a program for spiritual renewal and a deepening of the faith among church members. Thus, the PCT that had played the role of agent of social change and advocate of Taiwanese selfhood and *Self-Determination* was now returning to its own spiritual roots and rediscovering the act of Christian renewal as yet another means for helping its flock contend with old and also new problems that Taiwan faced.

Conclusions: Church, Society, and the State in Taiwan Today

Human beings seem to be at their best (and their worst) when disaster strikes. This hoary truism could certainly be seen as a reality in the days, months, and weeks that followed the February 21, 1999 earthquake on Taiwan. Most of the churches, whatever their formal stance on welfare and charity, were compelled to take action. Members of their own communities often were affected and the suffering was widespread among the larger Taiwanese community in towns near the epicenter and in major cities such as Taichung and Taipei. The PCT was the major Protestant actor in the relief work, and this can be seen in the rich media releases and published materials that the church produced to describe its efforts. These documents show that the church was able to pool its considerable resources to address the short- and long-range problems created by the February 21 earthquake.[41]

The PCT continues to have a deep commitment to providing a range of well-financed and well-run benevolent activities. It has built hospital complexes in the major cities of Taiwan. The chief hospital is the Mackay Hospital in Taipei, but there are others located in Changhua as well.[42] The church also recognizes that the AIDS crisis has come to Taiwan. There were three thousand recorded cases by the late 1990s, but estimates range to ten thousand cases not formally recorded. In 2000, the PCT established a center, Grace House, to help the segment of Taiwan's population that is affected by AIDS. It was formally opened on September 17, at a ceremony held at the Chinan Presbyterian Church in Taipei.[43]

Presbyterians also have been active in highly focused types of social welfare. There are Master of Social Work programs in the two major PCT seminaries, and annual conferences have been held to develop expansive programs and to discuss the impact and the result of PCT efforts in this area. Further, the PCT has designed special activities to meet the needs of different communities within the church and in society at large. Thus, there are groups that have been organized to help Taipei's teenage prostitutes. Others have been established to combat spousal abuse. Still others are designed to assist the members of the various Yuanzhumin tribes to manage the many social problems that they face.

By and large, it is only the Presbyterian Church of Taiwan among the island's religious institutions that devotes extensive resources to social-welfare work and to health care. There are simple explanations for this: The PCT is the largest church on the island and has had the longest continuous domestic history of any organization, including that of the present government. It identifies itself with the Taiwanese and the Yuanzhumin communities and is the only church in Taiwan to do so in such a total way. Its form of mainland Christianity has had a major focus on community building and society-wide benevolent work, as in the West; this heritage of public concern and activism was carried to the island by missionaries and the church's Western-trained (and also Taiwan-trained) Taiwanese pastors such as John Tin. Thus, the PCT is the very embodiment of a universal and liberal form of Christianity that does not recognize social barriers or confine itself to serving only persons within its own community when it decides to help those in need. It is, as we have seen, the major actor in the struggle for Taiwanese selfhood.

The political action that the PCT took over the course of the 1970s and 1980s was made possible because of the dedication of the church's leaders and workers to social service, medical assistance, secular and religious education, and the construction of large-scale structures that were designed to meet the needs of the Taiwanese public at large. There is an inexorable logic to the integration of social and political action. During much of the period of PCT history upon which this chapter is principally focused—the years from 1945 to 1986—the church could not act in the political realm without experiencing its own destruction as a religious body. Thus, its welfare-related activities and its educational and medical programs helped the church to gain public attention and to expand its pool of educated and well-trained sociopolitical activists. The sociopolitical agenda acted as a leitmotif underlying those programs and policies that the church developed, first by trial and error, and then by deliberate thought and praxis.

Notes

1. Huang Poho, *A Theology for Self-Determination: Responding to the Hope of the Chhut Thau Thi of the People of Taiwan* (Tainan: Chhut Thau Thi Theological Study Center, 1996); and The Presbyterian Church on Taiwan, General Assembly, *21st Century New Taiwan Mission Movement* (Tainan: Presbyterian Church on Taiwan Press, 2000).

2. On the development of the Presbyterian mission, see Murray A. Rubinstein, "Christianity and Democratization in Modern Taiwan: The Presbyterian Church and the Struggle for Minnan/Hakka Selfhood in the Republic of China," in *Religion in Postwar Taiwan*, ed. Philip Clart and Charles Jones (Honolulu: University of Hawaii Press, 2002). This chapter is derived, in part, from the essay in the volume edited by Clart and Jones. Another major work on the PCT is by a key Presbyterian missionary. See the Reverend W. Campbell, *Sketches from Formosa* (London: Marshall Brothers, 1915). Also see George Leslie Mackay, *From Far Formosa* (New York: Flemming H. Revell, 1896).

3. The leaders first took the simple but radical step of meeting separately to reconstitute, as best they could, their own presbyteries. Thus, the first step meant the destruction—or deconstruction—of the national church. Only then did they attempt to determine whether a national—and united—church should be restored and reconstructed. The first move that each side—one representing the northern churches and one representing the southern—took was to formalize a series of unofficial (and in Japanese eyes, illegal) steps taken during the final years of imperial Japanese control. The elders and pastors in the north (the Canadian-related branch of the church) held meetings in February 1943 and established their own synod. These meetings set an important precedent, for they established the principle that each church would now follow its own path of development. When the General Assembly of the now independent Northern Synod met again in October 1945, after the retrocession had formally begun, its members reaffirmed this basic decision. See *Historical Chronicle of the Presbyterian Church* (Tainan: Presbyterian Church Publishing House, 1965), 278.

4. Historical Commission Presbyterian Church (HCPC) on Taiwan, *Centenary History* (Taiwan: Presbyterian Church Press, 1965), 278–80.

5. Elizabeth J. Brown, "The Developing Maturity of the Presbyterian Church in Taiwan 1958–1985 as Reflected by Changes in the Organization, Functions and Nationalities of Missions Serving in It in Taiwan" (M.Div. thesis, Taiwan Theological College and Seminary, 1987), 2–5.

6. James Johnston, *China and Formosa: The Story of the Mission of the Presbyterian Church of England* (New York: Fleming H. Revell, 1896); and George Leslie MacKay, *From Far Formosa: The Island, Its People and Missions* (New York: Fleming H. Revell, 1896).

7. George Vicedom, *The Faith That Moves Mountains: A Study of the Tribal Church in Taiwan* (Taipei: China Post, 1967), 17–28.

8. George H. Kerr, *Formosa Betrayed* (Boston: Houghton Mifflin, 1965).

9. Tse-Han Lai, Ramon H. Myers, and Wei Wou, *A Tragic Beginning* (Stanford: Stanford University Press, 1991).

10. Steven E. Phillips, *Between Assimilation and Independence: The Taiwanese Encounter Nationalist China, 1945–1950* (Stanford: Stanford University Press, 2003).

11. On the younger Chiang, see Lloyd Eastman, *The Seeds of Destruction* (Stanford, CA: Stanford University Press, 1986).

12. See Thomas H. Gold, *State and Society in the Taiwan Miracle* (Armonk, NY: M.E. Sharpe, 1986), 54. See also the comments of the strongly pro-KMT journalist, H. Maclear Bate, in an interesting but neglected book, *Report from Formosa* (London: Eyre, and Spottiswoode, 1952).

13. This desire to present himself as a leader in touch with his people can be seen in the ROC Government Information Office's photobiography of its departed leader.

14. Some Presbyterians interviewed in the 1980s believed that the mainlanders continued to hold this advantage into the 1970s and 1980s, but other Taiwanese dispute that. And, here, the perception of advantage was more important than the reality, for it served as a subtext and as a basis for Taiwanese resentment. On the issue of "Mandarinization," see Robert L. Cheng, "Language Unification in Taiwan, Present and Future," in *The Other Taiwan*, ed. Murray A. Rubinstein (Armonk, NY: M.E. Sharpe, 1994), 357–91.

15. On the Maryknoll order in China, see Jean-Paul Wiest's magisterial study, *Maryknoll in China: A History, 1918–1955* (Armonk, NY: M.E. Sharpe, 1988).

16. The Southern Baptist Mission Board, based for many years in Richmond, Virginia, and now located in Nashville, Tennessee, had a sophisticated information and propaganda network. Its missionaries had been enemies of those they described as the Chinese Bolsheviks since the early 1920s, and were among the first Western groups in China to warn Americans at home about the communists during the Chinese Civil War of the 1940s. The Southern Baptist Convention and its perceptions of China have been examined in a number of articles. See Murray A. Rubinstein, "Witness to the Chinese Millennium: Southern Baptist Perceptions of the Chinese Revolution," in *United States Attitudes and Policies toward China: The Impact of American Missionaries*, ed. Patricia Neils (Armonk, NY: M.E. Sharpe, 1990), 149–51.

17. One of the most important books about the YMCA in China is John Hersey's lightly fictionalized account of his father, a key YMCA figure, entitled *The Call* (New York: Knopf, 1985).

18. The basic source of the section that follows is an important book edited by the PCT theologian and activist, C.S. Song. Song was the editor of a small journal, *Self-Determination*, that was published over the course of the 1970s and 1980s and that detailed the PCT's struggle with the KMT over questions of selfhood and Taiwanese rights. Many of the articles that appeared in the magazine were included in a book prepared by Song and published in 1986. See C.S. Song, ed., "Taiwan, Public Statement on National Fate, December 30, 1971," in *Self-Determination*, ed. Song (Tainan: Taiwan Church Press, 1986), 5–6. See also Robert Donal MacCall, "Political Theologizing in Taiwan Today" (unpublished ms., 1983), 20, Presbyterian Church of Taiwan Library, Taipei, Republic of China.

19. Song, ed., *Self-Determination*, 52–54; C.S. Song, "At Last Our Voice is Heard," in *Self-Determination*, ed. Song, 58–59. See also "The Future of Taiwan," New York Times, January 4, 1975, in *Self-Determination*, ed. Song, 60–61. See

Chiong-hua Hwang, "Taiwan: The Real Test," Letter to the Editor, *New York Times*, January 16, 1975, in *Self-Determination*, ed. Song, 61–62.

20. C.S. Song, "The Taiwanese Bible? An Unresolved Issue," in *Self-Determination*, ed. Song, 70–73.

21. See "Our Resolution Concerning Taiwan: East Coast Conference, Camp of the Woods, Speculator, New York, July 5, 1975," in *Self-Determination*, ed. Song, 75–76. Another example is "Declaration; The Second Annual Meeting, The World Taiwanese Club United, New York, July 12, 1975," in *Self-Determination*, ed. Song, 78–79.

22. See "Our Appeal," in *Self-Determination*, ed. Song, 83–88.

23. "A Declaration of Human Rights by the Presbyterian Church on Taiwan, August 16, 1977," in *Self-Determination*, ed. Song, 108–9.

24. The dangwai had run a slate of candidates throughout the island and had done well in the face of KMT opposition. They had seemed to have won the race in Chungli township in Taoyuan, but the vote count showed otherwise. As a result, the local citizens felt that there had been a miscount of the votes and responded by holding a mass demonstration. The demonstration turned violent and a police station was burned down in the city. While the government attempted to stifle the news of the confrontation, news of it was spread by word of mouth and soon many learned of this direct attack on governmental authority by an enraged populace. For a narrative of this period, see Murray A. Rubinstein, ed., *Taiwan: A New History* (Armonk, NY: M.E. Sharpe, 1999), 437–43. On these political events, also see "Chronology," in *Self-Determination*, ed. Song, 139–40.

25. "Chronology," in *Self-Determination*, ed. Song, 140–41.

26. Ibid., 142.

27. Marc Cohen, *Taiwan at the Crossroads* (Washington, DC: Asia Resource Center, 1988), 196. Cohen's book has an excellent chapter on religion and politics in Taiwan.

28. C.S. Song, "Government by the People," in *Self-Determination*, ed. Song, 156–62.

29. There is extensive literature on this period in the history of Taiwan in Chinese, and a growing number of accounts in English as well. The period is covered by the author in an as yet unpublished biography of Lu Hsiu-lien, the feminist activist and political leader, and now vice president of Taiwan. See also the author's chapter on the political development of modern Taiwan, in Rubinstein, *Taiwan: A New History*. Also refer to Cohen, *Taiwan at the Crossroads*, 197–98.

30. *Occasional Bulletin: Taiwan Church News* 3, no. 1 (1986): 6.

31. John Tin is an amazing figure and a true hero of the Presbyterian Church of Taiwan. The author has known him since 1984 and has met with him over the years. He is a man who inspires deep respect. Tin symbolizes the way the church has borne the burden of witness over the years.

32. Cohen, *Taiwan at the Crossroads*, 199.

33. Ibid., 198–99.

34. Ibid., 199–200.

35. Ibid., 200.

36. Ibid. See also "Dr. Kao Visits Overseas Churches," *Occasional Bulletin: Taiwan Church News* 3, no. 1 (1986): 4.

37. Cohen, *Taiwan at the Crossroads*, 200.

38. *Occasional Bulletin: Taiwan Church News* 3, no. 1 (1986): 3.
39. Ibid., 2.
40. *Presbyterian Church on Taiwan, Annual Report, 1995*. My thanks to Michael Stainton of York University for his help in keeping me up-to-date on the role of the PCT.
41. The key document is the *General Report of the Taiwan PCT General Assembly on the 921 Earthquake* (Taipei: Presbyterian Church of Taiwan, April 7, 2000).
42. The material on the PCT in present-day Taiwan is contained in *The Report of the 47th General Assembly Meeting of the Presbyterian Church on Taiwan* (Taipei: Presbyterian Church of Taiwan, April 25–28, 2000).
43. "Grace House Established for Aids Patients," www.pct.orgtw/english/newo928-2.htm. The material allows the observer to gain insight into the work of the PCT from afar.

6
Christian Churches and Democratization in South Korea

Hyug Baeg Im

Religious organizations, especially Christian churches, played key roles in the democratization of South Korea. Prominent transition scholars have paid attention to the contribution of Christian churches, both Protestant and Catholic, to the Korean democratic transition. Samuel P. Huntington noted in his *The Third Wave* that "by the early 1980s the churches had become 'the principal forum for opposition to the regime' ... and the Christian churches, their leaders and communicants, were a major force bringing about the transition to democracy in 1987 and 1988."[1] Bruce Cumings pointed out that "the circumstances in which the Park and Chun regimes fell, or entered into crisis, bear remarkable comparison to the Latin American cases.... O'Donnell and Schmitter's recent, eloquent description of 'the explosion of a highly repoliticized and angry society' fits the Korean case perfectly ... churches have been critical sanctuaries for dissidents ... often being the only institution relatively immune from regime intrusion."[2] A Korean political scientist, Jang Jip Choi, shared similar views with Huntington and Cumings that "churches played a central role in the political opposition movements and functioned as a kind of refuge for other dissident forces."[3]

With regard to the role of religious organizations in democratic transition in Korea, therefore, it is not questionable whether Korean Christian churches engaged in democratization. The researchable questions are why and how they were involved in the politics of democratic transition.

This chapter has three primary concerns: (1) Why did Korean Christian churches, previously known as accommodating and conforming to authorities, participate in the antigovernment democratization movement? (2) How did they participate and why did they gain success and contribute extensively to Korean democratic transition? (3) Who in the church communities participated, how did they achieve solidarity with nonparticipant church members, and how did they achieve hegemony in the whole church community, despite their minority status in numbers?

Korean Christian Churches Join the Democratic Opposition Movement

Until the mid-1960s, Korean churches, both Protestant and Catholic, had been apolitical, conservative, or "noted for their prudent accommodation to the authorities."[4] In the 1950s, the relationship between the Rhee Syng Man regime and Protestant churches was a very amicable one.[5] The persecution of Christians by the North Korean regime redounded to the Rhee regime's advantage. Many Christians fled from North Korea and these refugees supported Rhee's anticommunist ideology and policies. Church–government cooperation was not limited to the development of anticommunist ideology. The Korean Protestant leaders mobilized electoral resources for the Rhee regime.[6] Protestant churches systematically campaigned for Rhee and the Liberal Party through the networks of the Korean Church Committee for Election. In addition to organizational support, Protestant churches used their newspapers and religious gatherings to campaign for Rhee.

Catholics were not much different in their attitude toward and relationship with the Rhee regime. Archbishop Ro, the leader of the Korean Catholic Church, was pro-American, anticommunist, and pro-Rhee. Archbishop Ro sided with the U.S. Military Government rule over Korea and Rhee Syng Man in the turbulent years of the founding of a divided state beneath the 38th parallel, because he believed it was advantageous for the Catholic Church's position in liberated Korea and its social influence to do so. In the latter period of the Rhee regime, however, the relationship between the regime and Catholics soured because Archbishop Ro transferred political support to Vice President John Chang (Chang Myun), who was a Catholic, and persuaded forty Catholic laymen to join the Democratic Party of which John Chang was the leader. The transfer of support ended the close relationship between Ro and Rhee, and indirectly influenced the discontinuance of the Catholic-run *Kyunghyang Daily* by government authorities. In the 1950s, the Catholic Church maintained close relations, first with Rhee, and then with Chang, who came to power after the April 19, 1960, Student Revolution that toppled the Rhee regime. The Catholic Church failed to make any significant contribution to the Student Revolution, except by supporting one individual politician, John Chang.[7]

Why, then, did the relationship between Christian churches and the state, after General Park Chung Hee took control of power through a military coup, become frozen, and why did the churches transform themselves into the champion of democracy? In other words, what made Korean churches involve themselves in antigovernment activities and the democratization movement?

In the initial period of Park's reign, Korean churches did not oppose him actively, even though Korean churches, especially Protestant, were transformed from core organizations for the Rhee regime into organizations of less importance in the Park regime. Both the Protestant and Catholic churches took a noninterventionist position toward the military coup.[8] Most Christians supported Park until the late 1960s, and the majority of church members maintained the political stances of inaction and of separation of church and the state. Protestant leaders stressed St. Paul's teaching that all political powers are ordained of God and that one should obey civil authorities. In addition, anticommunist sentiments led church leaders to endorse the government that they believed combated communism.[9]

Until the late 1960s, most of the Christian opposition to the Park regime consisted of individual actions. The first organized opposition from the Protestant Church was the movement in 1965 against the normalization of relations between Korea and Japan. In 1969, Protestant Church leaders, such as the reverends Kim Chaejun and Park Hyungkyu, played a leading role in the "People's Council Fighting against the Revision of the Constitution to Allow Park Chung Hee the Third Term."

However, by the late 1960s and early 1970s, both Protestant and Catholic church leaders began acting in groups and in the name of their churches.[10] Why did Korean Christian church organizations participate in the democratization movements against the extremely powerful authoritarian state? According to Dohyup Shin, three forces drove Korean churches to participate in democratization movements: (1) religious organizations' pursuit of legitimacy from their constituencies; (2) invitations from social movements that sought legitimacy from religious organizations; and (3) competition among religious organizations for more followers in the religious market.[11]

First, religious organizations made efforts to set up new legitimacy formulas in a time of rapid socioeconomic change and political regime transformation. The pursuit of new spiritual and nonspiritual formulas for legitimacy to satisfy domestic and foreign constituencies motivated churches to participate in democratization. This is a typical push factor that drove churches to participate in social engagement. With rapid industrialization generating sharp socioeconomic inequality and dislocation of poor masses, church leaders felt the need to develop new religious doctrines. Armed with them, religious leaders fought for the human and political rights of the repressed, alienated, and exploited masses.

Second, a pull factor induced Christian churches to participate in antigovernment activities: the demand from other social movement forces. Religion is one of the most powerful sources of legitimization, and it is the most important derivation of legitimacy for political power. Both the incumbent and the challenger often seek the active and tacit support of religious organizations.[12] The Christian churches' role as legitimating democratization movements was recognized by Linz, who noted that "one of the most independent bases of all shades of dissidence can be a church. . . . Critics, dissidents, and opponents tolerated, supported, or sponsored by a church can represent a formidable resource in case of crisis in an authoritarian regime."[13]

Third, the churches' participation in democratization can be explained by the churches' efforts to find new niche markets for religion. Industrialization generated large masses of industrial proletariat and urban poor who migrated from the countryside into cities. Church leaders appealed to these new potential constituencies by participating in sociopolitical movements, including the democratization movement.

The Push Factor: Doctrinal Change and the Pursuit of Legitimacy

The "compressed industrialization" by the Park Chung Hee regime in the 1960s impoverished rural society, increased migration from rural areas, and resulted in the rapid growth of urban areas. In response to socioeconomic changes, church leaders felt the need to participate in social movements to gain legitimacy for themselves.[14] They found it necessary to build legitimacy for their pastoral activities by representing the interests of these groups of urban poor and the new industrial working class in the religious world. The catalytic event that drew attention to the new social phenomena of labor issues was the self-immolation of Chun Tae-Il. The self-burning of Chun Tae-Il, a garment worker, in the Chyunggye Peace Market on November 13, 1970, in protest against low wages, unbearable working conditions, and the government's repressive labor policies, was a watershed event that united broad antigovernment forces around labor issues. From that point forward, churches increasingly focused attention on social justice and the resolution of labor problems. The Urban Industrial Mission (UIM) of Protestant churches and the Jeunes Ouvriers Catholiques (JOC, or Young Catholic Workers) instituted programs to organize and to raise the consciousness of factory workers.[15]

The new "social missions," "special pastorates," or "Christian social actions" that targeted the industrial proletariat, urban poor, and university students needed a new religious doctrine that could legitimize their activities. In the case of the Protestant Church, a group of liberal Protestant ministers developed a militant theology called the "People's Theology" (*Minjung Sinhak*), which emphasized the "Koreanization" of Christian beliefs and ceremonies, social salvation rather than individual salvation, sociopolitical theology rather than religious-cosmic theology, and the liberation of the "People."[16] The Minjung Theology was deeply influenced by Liberation Theology, which was developed in Latin America. Liberation Theology provided theological bases and concrete models for social participation by religious organizations. The Minjung are defined as grass-roots members of society, such as workers, farmers, the lower and middle classes, owners of small- and medium-sized businesses, students, and progressive intellectuals. Doctrinal change to Minjung Theology influenced Protestant churches to act on behalf of social justice, human rights, and democratization.

Armed with the new religious doctrine of Minjung Theology, Protestant Church activists organized, first, social missions in urban industrial areas, and then antigovernment activities. The Protestant activists not only dared to criticize the Park regime but also assumed the leadership in an antigovernment coalition of students, intellectuals, workers, and farmers.[17] The Protestant churches were the most successful organizers of antigovernment forces.[18] They set up many affiliated organizations that played key roles in the struggle for democratization during the 1970s and 1980s, such as the Korean Student Christian Federation (KSCF), the Christian Professors' Conference, the Korean Christian Women's Association, the Urban Industrial Mission, and the Christian Academy. The Korean National Council of Churches (KNCC) was the umbrella organization for the antigovernment Protestant churches. It encompassed

12,700 ministers (about 30 percent of all Protestant ministers) and six progressive Protestant church denominations.[19]

The increased involvement of Korean Catholics in sociopolitical activities was attributed to the teachings of the Second Vatican Council and Liberation Theology.[20] The dominant theme of the Second Vatican Council was "transforming the world." In the Second Vatican Council, Pope John XXIII wanted the church to exert positive leadership in addressing world problems. His two major encyclicals were *Mater et Magistra* [Mother and teacher] on Christianity and social progress, and *Pacem in Terris* [Peace on earth]. *Mater et Magistra* examined trends and characteristics of modern society, and *Pacem in Terris* raised two issues, namely, the problems of rural peoples, and the problems of poor underdeveloped nations.[21] Liberation Theology emphasized: (1) violence and oppression by "unjust systems and structures"; (2) the failure of "development" policies; (3) an "international system of domination"; (4) "the obstacles social structures place in the way of conversion of domination"; (5) the need for self-determination by poor nations; (6) "the intervention of God's justice on behalf of the needy and the oppressed"; (7) a mission of preaching *and witnessing* to justice as proper to the church's mission; (8) the need for justice "within" the church itself; (9) education for justice (raising consciousness); and (10) hope in the coming Kingdom and "the radical transformation of the world."[22]

As Korean Catholics increasingly felt obliged to respond to the sociopolitical problems generated by Park's compressed industrialization and authoritarian rule, the teachings of Vatican II were an encouraging sign for Catholic activists. In May 1966, the Korean Bishops' Conference issued a pastoral letter urging the Catholic churches to accept and practice the Vatican II teachings. Following Vatican II, Catholic priests expressed their concerns about sociopolitical problems and participated in social movements, first, individually, and then gradually at the organizational level. The appointment of Cardinal Kim Su-Hwan as the Archdiocesan of the Seoul Archdiocese in 1969 was the turning point for the involvement of Catholic parishes in sociopolitical movements.[23] Cardinal Kim's progressive orientation encouraged the social participation of parishes and ignited subsequent democratization activities by Catholic activists.

Nonetheless, Korean Catholics had waited until 1974 to actively participate in democratization by groups, when Bishop Chi Hak-Soon was arrested and sentenced to fifteen years imprisonment on charges of supporting the members of the National League for Democratic Youth Students (Minchunghakryun). The arrest of Bishop Chi awakened the Catholic Church to the political repression of the Park regime. In reaction to the repression, young priests gathered at Bishop Chi's church and formed the Catholic Priests' Association for Justice (CPAJ, or Jungeuikuhyun Sajedan). Thereafter, the CPAJ served as the central organization for the South Korean Catholic Church's struggle for democratization.[24] The formation of the CPAJ was the Catholic Church's institutional reaction to the political repression of the Catholic Church itself. Another institutional response was the establishment of the Justice and Peace Committee (JPC) as an official organization of the Korean Catholic Church by the Korean Bishops' Conference in 1975.

The Pull Factor: The Invitation from Social Movements

Korean Christian churches not only were actively involved in democratization to seek legitimacy in the eyes of their constituencies, but also they passively accepted the invitation from social movements to join the struggle for democratization. Antigovernment social movements needed churches because they believed that churches could lend moral authority to their movements and provide shelter to them from the harsh repression of authoritarian officials.

Under authoritarian rule, the public perceived that Christian churches had an overriding moral authority and greater credibility and trustworthiness than other institutions, including the state.[25] This was evidenced by a remarkable increase in church membership during the 1970s and 1980s.[26] Having sensed the Korean churches' superior moral authority, both the state and the democratic opposition vied for support from churches. The state often sought legitimization from churches because it regarded them as the only institutions that could provide moral legitimacy to the government.[27] To occupy an advantageous position in the legitimacy war, social movements among students, intellectuals, workers, and farmers sought solidarity with progressive Protestant church leaders and invited them to join sociopolitical movements. Catholic parishes also protested against the state repression of the antigovernment social movements of workers, farmers, and students, and against the state's hiding and distorting the truth about its repressive activities.

The Catholic Church's moral pressure effectively forced the state to admit the truth because the public believed in the church's credibility.

Father Kim Seung Hun, as representative of the CPAJ and concurrently the vice chairman of Mintongryun (the United Minjung Movement for Democracy and Unification), revealed the cover-up of the torture and death of a student demonstrator, Park Chong Chul, by state repressive apparatuses, and the revelation ignited countrywide demonstrations for democratic transition in June 1987.

In addition, Christian churches willingly became the shelter for antigovernment activists in response to appeals for support from opposition social movements. Whenever faced with stern state repression, social activists took refuge in the sanctuary of churches or denominational offices. The Korean Christian Center in downtown Seoul was a famous Protestant place for sit-ins, hunger strikes, and news conferences of antigovernment activists. Myungdong Cathedral, the parish church of the Seoul Archdiocese, was the Catholic center for sit-in protests among the democratic opposition, striking workers, and the urban poor.

Competition for the Religious Market

Another factor contributing to the Christian churches' involvement in democratization was interest in expanding the Protestant and Catholic shares of the Korean religious market. Democratic engagement was the strategic choice of church leaders to maximize their market shares. To recruit new Christians in the wake of rapid social changes, such as industrialization, urbanization, and the expansion of higher education, Christian leaders adopted the strategy of participating in and leading the struggle for democracy.

The religious market experienced explosive growth during the authoritarian period of the Park Chung Hee and Chun Doo Hwan regimes. Many Koreans entered churches in order to seek spiritual security amid the disturbances and unrest, such as the national division, the Korean War, rapid industrialization, urbanization, and repressive authoritarian rule.[28] While Protestants at the time of Liberation in 1945 had only 2,793 churches, 5,923 clergymen, and 459,721 adherents, their ranks grew explosively during the 1960s, 1970s, and 1980s, but stopped growing rapidly following democratic transition in 1987. The Protestant Church had 5,011 churches, 10,954 clergymen, and 623,072 adherents in 1960, 12,866 churches, 16,982 clergymen, and 3,192,621 adherents in 1970, 21,243 churches, 31,740 clergymen, and 7,180,617 adherents in 1980, and 35,869 churches, 56,286 clergymen, and 12,091,837 believers in 1990.

The growth of Catholic parishes has been more explosive. While the number of Catholics was just 122,000 in 1945, their number grew phenomenally by twenty-six times to 3,200,000 by the mid-1990s. During the same period, the number of parish churches, dioceses, bishops, and priests increased 7.7 times, 3 times, 4.8 times, and 13.9 times, respectively. But not all religions grew rapidly. In fact, the memberships of Buddhism and Chundogyo (Religion of the Heavenly Way) declined during the same period.[29]

The statistics on Korean religions show that an overwhelming majority of new religious adherents chose Christianity over traditional religions such as Buddhism, Confucianism, and Chundogyo. Concern for young workers, farmers, urban poor, and students was one of the factors that attracted newcomers to Protestant and Catholic churches. Participation in democratization was a good marketing strategy to lure the young generation to join the progressive Christian community. This was evidenced by the fact that Protestant denominations under the umbrella of the KNCC grew faster than conservative Protestant denominations during the heyday of authoritarianism. KNCC members expanded from 34.9 percent of the entire Protestant community in 1969 to 37.4 percent in 1979.[30] In the case of the Catholic Church, two-thirds of the current Catholic community joined the Catholic Church since the 1970s. The proportion of Korean Catholics who lived in urban areas in 1992 was 86.2 percent, much higher than the national average of 74.4 percent.[31] Since the 1970s, Catholicism has become overwhelmingly the religion of urban residents. The prophetic and organic intellectual role of the Korean Catholic parishes in the democratic transition might have inspired young urban students, workers, and intellectuals to join the Catholic community.

The Contribution of Korean Churches to Democratic Transition

How, then, did Christian churches contribute to the democratic transition of Korea? First, they opened the space for transition to democracy. It was the Christian churches that broke the silence enforced by authoritarian regimes and provided shelter for democratic opposition activists from the regime's repression. Second, Christian churches played key roles in establishing broad antiauthoritarian networks.

The Church as Incubator and Shelter for Democratic Activists

The contribution of Christian churches to democratization started with serving the democratic opposition by becoming the incubator for it. Christian social movements in Korea developed quite differently from those in Latin America. The Christian social movements in Korea were formed "prior to" the antigovernment social movements and helped those movements to grow.[32] "Christian churches were the first to break the silence of the dark age of the Yushin system and they continued to resist Park Chung Hee more strongly than other groups."[33]

The incubator role of Christian churches was possible because Korean churches enjoyed a high degree of autonomy from the state. While the Korean state had a high degree of autonomy vis-à-vis domestic social forces, it had little external autonomy because of its great dependence on the United States. According to Hyun-Chin Lim, while the state secured an extensive autonomy from societal pressures, it had a low degree of autonomy vis-à-vis the structural pressures from abroad due to its peripheral status in the world system.[34] The state's dependence on a patron state, the United States, has been the center of external dependency since the beginning of the Cold War.

The external dependency of the state restricted the state's control over Christian denominations that had maintained a close network with the United States. Using the linkage with American Christian churches, Korean churches enjoyed relatively broad autonomy from the authoritarian state. Most Korean Protestant churches had networks with their counterparts in the United States through the mediation of missionaries. Korean Catholics also strengthened their ties with Catholic parishes in the United States after 1945 and were officially under the hierarchy of the Vatican.

Having made ties with American churches, Korean churches remained relatively immune from state intervention as, what Robbins called, "privileged enclaves." Consequently, a kind of "regulatory gap" emerged between secular and religious organizations.[35] Under the authoritarian peripheral state in Korea, a considerable "regulatory gap" existed between religious organizations and nonreligious organizations, and between Christian denominations and other religions.[36] The external dependency of the state restricted the regime's control over Christian denominations because Korean Christian churches had solid networks with their American counterparts, who had strong lobbying power in the U.S. Congress, the Vatican, and the World Council of Churches (WCC).

In-Chul Kang neatly describes the typical process by means of which Korean churches as "privileged enclaves" could work as incubators of the democratic protest movement. The process started with the authoritarian state's harsh repressive response to the protests from churches. Then high-level church leaders defied the state's infringement of their religious autonomy and made it a national issue. At the same time, the news about the repression of churches was spread internationally by missionaries who solicited churches in the United States and the world for support. American churches and international Christian organizations directly protested against the Korean government and appealed to the United States Congress, the United States government, and international organizations to exert pressure on the South Korean government. Faced with international criticism, the externally dependent Korean government withdrew repression against churches, which resulted in discrediting the state's authority and resurrecting democratic opposition within both religious and nonreligious civil society.[37]

In 1972, Park Chung Hee launched a repressive authoritarian *Yushin* (revitalizing reform) system and tightened harsher control over opposition politicians, journalists, intellectuals, workers, and students. The voices of antigovernment forces were finally silenced and their organizations were closed. But the government could not control churches as effectively as it controlled political parties and nonreligious organizations.

It was Christian churches that broke the forced silence and provided buildings where democratic opposition forces could meet and organizations through which they could spread their arguments.[38]

First, the Protestant activists tried to open the space for democratic transition. In December 1972, the Reverend Eun Myunggi criticized the Yushin authoritarian system in a night prayer meeting at his church in Chunju City and became the first clergyman to be arrested since Park Chung Hee had inaugurated the system on October 26, 1972. In February 1973, two clergymen of the Urban Industrial Mission were arrested for criticizing the Yushin system and repressive labor policy. On April 23, 1973, the Reverend Park Hyungkyu and members of the Korean Student Christian Federation passed out leaflets and demanded the repeal of the Yushin constitution. The arrest of Reverend Park and the students was followed by a series of petitions, prayer meetings, and public statements that demanded the release of the imprisoned church leader and students and the restoration of democracy.[39] The courageous acts of Christian leaders indeed opened the space for democratic opposition in the dangerous days of the authoritarian regime.

On the part of Catholics, it was Bishop Chi Hak-Soon who inspired protests. On July 6, 1974, Bishop Chi of Wonju Diocese was arrested and charged with supporting the National League for Democratic Youth and Students, which the government asserted was a procommunist organization. After being imprisoned, Bishop Chi made a "Declaration of Conscience," which denounced the Yushin system, and issued a "Message from Prison," professing solidarity with the poor and the oppressed.[40] After Bishop Chi was arrested, the Catholic Church immediately reacted with prayer meetings and masses. Bishop Chi's arrest motivated the formation of the Catholic Priests' Association for Justice on September 23, 1974, to facilitate the Catholic clergy's fight for democracy and human rights. The CPAJ announced "The First Declaration on the Times," followed by a street demonstration of some two thousand participants. It was the first street demonstration by a clergy group, including some twenty foreign priests.[41]

As Park's repression became harsher, Catholics and Protestants held joint protest meetings and rallies. On March 1, 1976, the fifty-seventh anniversary of the March 1, 1919, Independence Movement, a joint Catholic-Protestant prayer service was held at Myungdong Cathedral. Some seven hundred believers, including several Protestant clergymen and the opposition politicians, Yun Bo Sun and Kim Dae Jung, attended the mass, where twenty priests co-officiated. After the mass, the Declaration for Democratic National Salvation, calling for President Park's resignation, was made public. Afterward, twenty religious leaders were arrested, but they actually had broken Park's Emergency Decree No. 9, which enforced silence under Yushin authoritarianism.[42]

Second, Christian churches not only broke the enforced silence of the authoritarian age and helped to pave the way for the democratic opposition but also provided shelter. The most well-known shelters or sacred places for antigovernment forces were Myungdong Cathedral for Catholics and the Christian Center for Protestants. Myungdong Cathedral has been called the "holy place of democratization" since the 1970s. It was Myungdong Cathedral where the mass was held in protest against the arrest of Bishop Chi in 1974, the joint Catholic-Protestant Declaration demanding restoration of democracy was announced in 1976, and the cover-up of the torture and death of Park Chong Chul was revealed by the priest, Kim Seung Hun, in 1987, leading to the nationwide demonstrations for the restoration of democracy in June that year. Besides democratic opposition forces, workers, farmers, urban poor, and people of the ghettos took refuge at Myungdong Cathedral to avoid arrest by police.

The Christian Center at Jongro 5-ga, Seoul, is revered as the sacred place for the democratic opposition forces who were associated with Protestant churches. The KNCC and many Christian democratic opposition organizations led by students, workers, journalists, artists, and farmers had their offices at the Christian Center building. They used the building as the locus of hunger strikes and sit-ins, announcements of their positions, public criticisms of government repression, and meetings with other prodemocracy activists.

Church leaders not only provided shelter to opposition forces but also appealed to the national public and the international community to protest against the authoritarian government and to apply pressure on the regime in an effort to loosen its rigid control and speedily restore democracy in Korea.

Mobilization by Networking

The mobilization of students and young workers to join the democratic opposition through the establishment of networks was another contribution by Korean churches to the nation's democratic transition. Christian churches and their affiliated organizations mobilized people both at the micro level of schools and workplaces and at the macro level of the national protest movement.

The Protestant Christian Professors' Conference, Korean Students' Christian Federation, and Urban Industrial Mission, and the Korean Catholic Farmers' Movement (KCFM), Jeunes Ouvriers Catholiques, and the CPAJ, opened night schools to educate workers and shantytown dwellers in Liberation and Minjung theologies, and taught them to have greater concern about human rights, workers' rights, poverty, and democracy.[43]

These Christian organizations started mobilization at the micro level at workplaces and university campuses, and then expanded their mobilization efforts at the national level by creating broad networks for democratization. Church organizations played a key role in the June 1987 establishment of a nationwide coalition of democratic opposition called the National Council for Constitutional Reform. The newly formed united front of extrainstitutional groups and opposition parties jointly mobilized people to take to the streets and finally forced South Korea's military dictators to restore democratic competition on June 29, 1987.[44] During the nationwide mobilization for democracy, church and student networks were the most effective in organizing opposition to the government.

Who Participated and How Did Democratic Activists Acquire Hegemony?

Not all Korean Christians actively participated in the democratization movement. Most conservative Christians remained silent throughout the authoritarian period and some conservative Christians advocated and supported authoritarian regimes. In fact, churches that engaged in protest were the minority in both Protestant and Catholic communities. Then, how did protesting churches overcome their difficulties, owing to their minority status in their respective church communities, establish ideological hegemony in the Christian Church, and, finally, become the leaders of the democratic opposition in Korea?

According to Jong Chul Choi, Korean Christian church organizations during the authoritarian period can be classified into four groups regarding their stance toward authoritarian regimes: conformists, negotiators, adapters, and resisters.

With the inauguration of a repressive authoritarian regime called the Yushin system, Korean churches were faced with having to make a choice between conformity and resistance in their relationship with the government, since it was impossible to stand on both sides. Church organizations had to choose either conformity, thereby lending legitimacy to the authoritarian power holders, or resistance by means of actions that "delegitimized" the regime and helped to legitimize the democratic opposition.

The forerunner of resistance groups was the Reverend Kim Chaejun. Kim criticized the fundamentalism of the Korean Presbyterian churches, split from the Presbyterian mainstream, and organized the Korean Christian Presbyterian Church. In the 1970s, resistance groups gathered around the KNCC and its counterpart in the United States, the WCC. Six Korean Protestant denominations joined the KNCC.

But liberal ministers and the Minjung theologians were minorities within the Protestant Church. Most conservative Christians remained

Table 6.1

Christians' Attitude Toward Authoritarian Regimes

	Contesting against authoritarian regimes		
Passive	(*Zone of adaptation*) Korean Bishops' Conference Korean Gospel Council Christian Ethics Practice Movement Korean Association for Economic Justice	(*Zone of resistance*) (1) Protestant: KNCC, UIM, KSCF CFA, Minjung churches (2) Catholic: CPAJ, JPC, JOC, KCFM	Active
	(*Zone of conformism*) Korean Jesus Presbyterian Church (Haptong and Koshin denominations) Korean Baptist Korean Holy Church Evangelical Church	(*Zone of negotiation*) Christian Leaders' Council Christian Businessmen's Committee of Korea KCCC, KCAAC Unification Church	
	Legitimating authoritarian regime		

Note: See Jong Chul Choi, "Hankook Kidoggyo Gyohoedeuleui Jungchijuk Taedo" [The political attitudes of Korean Christian churches, 1972–1990], *Kyungjewa Sahoe* 15 (Autumn 1992): 215. Here, the abbreviation CFA stands for the Christian Farmers' Association; KCCC for the Korean Council of Christian Churches; and KCAAC for the Korean Christian Association for Anti-Communism.

silent or even supported and legitimized authoritarian rule. Even though conservative denominations declared political neutrality, in effect, they supported the authoritarian regime by emphasizing anticommunism, social stability, and patriotic Protestantism. Indeed, ministers of conservative denominations enraged democratic opposition forces by participating in the Presidential Breakfast Prayer Meeting (*Jochan Kidohoe*).

Conservative Christians further actively supported the authoritarian regime by holding progovernment mass rallies, including the World Pentecostal Campaign of 1973 and Explosion '74, for which Billy Graham was invited to conduct mass revivals during the year. Conservative rallies often were held after the government's reputation had suffered a serious setback owing to its repressive policies and its arrests of members of the democratic opposition. And whenever the KNCC criticized the government, the conservative members of the Korean Council of Christian Churches and the Korean Christian Association for Anti-Communism denounced the KNCC and defended the regime by claiming that "the Bible teaches Christians to pray for the secular power and to obey them," and that "there is religious freedom in Korea, contrary to the claim of KNCC."[45]

Catholic activist groups were a minority in the Catholic community, too. When the CPAJ performed a catalytic role for democracy and human rights in 1974 after Bishop Chi's arrest, mainstream Catholic organizations and the top body representing the entire Korean Catholic Church, the Korean Bishops' Conference, still did not give clear and concrete directions for coping with Bishop Chi's imprisonment. Throughout the 1970s and the 1980s, the Bishops' Conference displayed a conservative orientation, and among fourteen Catholic dioceses, only three were regarded to be favorably inclined toward the priests who supported democratization. Occasional statements by the Bishops' Conference concentrated mainly on nonpolitical issues, such as birth control and abortion. With regard to political issues, the Bishops' Conference emphasized gradual political change, separation of religion and politics, and the priority of anticommunism, all warmly welcomed by the government.[46]

How, then, did democratic activist groups in Protestant and Catholic churches gain hegemony in their respective religious communities, despite their minority status? They did so by different means. While Protestant activists acquired dominance through struggling with conservatives, Catholic activists' hegemony was transmitted from conservatives in amicable ways. And, while sharp bifurcation between conservative and progressive Protestants over the issue of democratization continued throughout the 1970s and the 1980s, Catholics maintained their internal solidarity during the same period.

Protestant activists exploited social pressures on religious organizations to persuade Protestant churches to be more responsive to nonreligious sociopolitical issues. In the 1970s, in contrast to rapid industrialization and social differentiation, interest groups and voluntary associations were nonexistent or weak and the political system was closed to their representation. Therefore, "popular masses" mounted pressure on religious organizations, which enjoyed relative autonomy vis-à-vis the state, to channel their discontent, to represent their interests, and to shield them from state repression.

Protestant church activists responded to pressures and demands from the popular masses. They opened channels to connect themselves with the masses through night schools, youth labor associations, small churches in poor urban districts, Christian student organizations, social and industrial missions, and the propagation of Minjung Theology. Protestant activists gained ideological hegemony also through martyrdom. They played a role similar to that performed by Korean nationalists early in the Japanese colonial period.[47] The progressive Protestant churches suffered more members' imprisonment in relation to the democratization movement than any other religious sector.[48] Through showing moral example by being incarcerated and representing "the voice for voiceless" people,[49] Protestant activists gained ideological hegemony over conservatives and could lead the democratization movement.

In contrast to Protestant activists, Catholic activists acquired hegemony in a relatively smooth way with the cooperation of the conservative mainstream of the church. Among Catholics, the CPAJ has served as the central organization for the Catholics' democratization opposition. In the initial period of Catholic involvement from the mid-1970s until the early 1980s, there had been exchanges of denouncements between the conservative Bishops' Conference and the progressive CPAJ. However, as the absolute majority of Koreans supported the democracy movement, the Bishops' Conference stopped denouncing the CPAJ and issuing conservative statements.[50] Several factors enabled a smooth transition of the leadership of the Catholic movement.

First, in contrast to the Protestant Church in which no dialogue between activists and conservatives existed, the membership of the CPAJ overlapped with that of the official Catholic Church, and participating CPAJ priests continued to communicate and interact with nonparticipating priests and lay persons in most organizational activities other than the democracy movement. There was no explicit distinction between in-group and out-group from either side.

Second, "The Principle of Church Unity" in the worldwide Roman Catholic Church prevented Catholics from being formally decoupled from each other in spite of serious differences and conflicts. Both bishops and priests were bound by the same Church Law. All the priests were individually under the formal supervision of bishops in ordinary organizational activities. Therefore, in spite of bitter disagreements over the democracy movement, the two groups maintained a cooperative relationship in routine operations of the church.[51]

Third, Catholic bishops acquiesced to church activists' involvement in social mission and democratization, and conceded the leadership role in democratization efforts to activist priests in a reaction to the harsh repression by the authoritarian state. When conservatives shared a sense of crisis that the state repression might have infringed on the institutional interests of the church, they united with progressive activists to resist the state. Despite internal differences and conflicts, the church's solidarity was strengthened in the face of external enemies.[52]

Fourth, under the prevailing circumstances, as the CPAJ priests and Cardinal Kim assumed a common stance, and as society as a whole came to believe that a consensus existed within the church and that prodemocracy activists represented the entire Catholic community, conservative bishops either tolerated the progressive stance of the activists or did not publicly voice their opposing views.[53] In this sense, Korean Catholic conservative bishops were good adapters.

Thus, the Catholic activists who were a minority within the church gained the upper hand, and society and the state came to believe that their progressive stance reflected the position held by the entire Korean Catholic Church. Indeed, division existed within the church, but the division never tore the church apart. On the contrary, the division actually inspired Catholic "unity amid diversity," and the Korean Catholic Church was able to present a united front to society and the state.[54]

The smooth convergence of the leadership with the activists in regard to the democratization movement in the case of Catholics, and the sharp decoupling within the Protestant Church between ministers who were resisters and those who were conformists, led Korean people to perceive that Catholics had contributed more to Korean democratization than Protestants, even though the Protestant Church actually had contributed more in terms of the frequency of prodemocracy activities, the proportion of activist clergymen, and the number of affiliated democracy movement organizations.[55] A survey conducted in the first half of the 1990s shows that 91 percent of the respondents believed that the Catholic Church had significantly contributed to South Korea's democratization; that is much higher than the 84 percent of respondents who said the same for Protestants. Sharp division within the Protestant ranks caused Korean people to believe that the democratization activities of Protestant clergymen were not supported by the entire Protestant Church, while they viewed the activities of the resistant priests in the CPAJ as being backed by the entire Catholic community. The influence that was gained by minority Catholic activists permeated the entire church through the contagion of legitimacy.[56]

Notes

1. Samuel P. Huntington, *The Third Wave: Democratization in the Late Twentieth Century* (Norman: University of Oklahoma Press, 1991), 74.
2. Bruce Cumings, "The Abortive *Abertura*: South Korea in the Light of Latin American Experience," *New Left Review*, no. 173 (1989): 7–8.
3. Jang Jip Choi, "Kwadae Sungjang Kukgaeui Hyungsunggwa Jungchi Kyunyuleui Jungae" [The formation of the overdeveloped state and the development of political cleavages], in *Hankook Hyundae Jungchieui kujowa Byunhwa* [The structure and change of contemporary Korean politics], ed. Jang Jip Choi (Seoul: Kkachi, 1989), 104.
4. Guillermo O'Donnell and Philippe C. Schmitter, *Transitions from Authoritarian Rule: Tentative Conclusions about Uncertain Democracies* (Baltimore, MD: Johns Hopkins University Press, 1986), 49.
5. Chung-Shin Park, *Protestantism and Politics in Korea* (Seattle: University of Washington Press, 2003), 174.
6. Ibid., 178.
7. Nyung Kim, "The Politics of Religion in South Korea, 1974–89: The Catholic Church's Political Opposition to the Authoritarian State" (Ph.D. diss., University of Washington, 1993), 221–27.
8. In-Chul Kang, "Religion and the Democratization Movement," *Korea Journal* 40, no. 2 (2000): 234.
9. Park, *Protestantism and Politics in Korea*, 183–84.
10. Ibid., 189.
11. Dohyup Shin, "The Effects of Organizational Coupling on the Legitimacy of Religious Organizations and Social Movements: An Organizational Analysis of Korean Religion in the Democratization Movement, 1972–1987," PONPO (Program on Non-Profit Organizations), Working Paper No. 203, and ISPS (Institution for Social and Policy Studies), Working Paper No. 2203 (New Haven, CT: Yale University, 1994), 4–7.
12. Ibid., 6.
13. Juan J. Linz, "Opposition to and under an Authoritarian Regime: The Case of Spain," in *Regimes and Opposition*, ed. Robert A. Dahl (New Haven, CT: Yale University Press, 1973), 200–201.
14. Shin, "The Effects of Organizational Coupling," 4.
15. Hyug Baeg Im, "The Rise of Bureaucratic Authoritarianism in South Korea," *World Politics* 34, no. 2 (1987): 254.
16. Dong-Sik Yu, *Hankook Sinhakeui Kwangmaek* [The veins of Korean theology] (Seoul: Junmangsa, 1982], 238. Prominent leaders of Minjung Theology included the reverends Moo Ik Hwan, Yu Dong Sik, Seo Nam Dong, Ahn Byung Moo, Park Hyug-Kyu, Moon Dong-Hwan, Kim Chan Kook, and Yoon Sung Bum.
17. Park, *Protestantism and Politics in Korea*, 189.
18. Shin, "The Effects of Organizational Coupling," 32.
19. The six denominations of the KNCC are the: Christ Presbyterian Assembly of Korea, Jesus Presbyterian Church of Korea, Salvation Army in Korea, Methodist Church, Anglican Church, and Christ Evangelical Church of Korea.
20. Kim, "The Politics of Religion in South Korea, 1974–89," 8.
21. Arthur F. McGovern, "Catholic Social Teachings: A Brief History," in

Catholicism and Politics in Communist Societies, ed. Pedro Ramet (Durham, NC: Duke University Press, 1990), 37.

22. Ibid., 40.
23. Shin, "The Effects of Organizational Coupling," 38.
24. Ibid., 39.
25. Mainwaring affirmed this view by noting that "the Church enjoys greater legitimacy in popular circles than do most politicians or political movements . . . because the Church does not worry about coming to power, it can remain more concerned with pedagogical issues than popular movements or political parties." See Scott Mainwaring, *The Catholic Church and Politics in Brazil, 1916–1985* (Stanford, CA: Stanford University Press, 1986), 241–42.
26. Kim, "The Politics of Religion in South Korea, 1974–89," 352.
27. Ibid., 353.
28. Park, *Protestantism and Politics in Korea*, 40–41.
29. Chi Jun Roh and In-Chul Kang, "Haebanghu Hankook Sahoe Byundonggwa Jonggyo" [Social changes and religion in Korea since liberation], in *Collection of Essays Commemorating the 50th Anniversary of National Liberation*, vol. 4, ed. Korea Research Foundation (Seoul: Korea Research Foundation, 1995), 195, 207.
30. Soo-In Lee, "Hankookeui Kukgawa Siminsahoe mit Gaesingyoeui Jungchisahoejuk Taedo Byundongeh Gwanhan Younku" [A study of the state and civil society and the changes of political attitudes of the Protestant church in Korea] (Ph.D. diss., Ewha Womans University, 2002), 142.
31. Roh and Kang, "Haebanghu Hankook Sahoe Byundonggwa Jonggyo," 216–17.
32. Kang, "Religion and the Democratization Movement," 226.
33. Park, *Protestantism and Politics in Korea*, 192.
34. Hyun Chin Lim, *Hyundae Hankoogwa Jongsok Iron* [Modern Korea and dependency theory] (Seoul: Seoul National University Press, 1987), 249–73.
35. Thomas Robbins, "Cults, Converts and Charisma: The Sociology of New Religious Movements," *Current Sociology* 36, no. 1 (1988): 164–68.
36. Kang, "Religion and the Democratization Movement," 229.
37. Ibid., 230–31.
38. Park, *Protestantism and Politics in Korea*, 192.
39. Ibid., 193.
40. Hak-Kyu Sohn, "Political Opposition and the Yushin System: Radicalization in South Korea, 1972–1979" (Ph.D. diss., University of Oxford, 1988), 133–34.
41. Kim, "The Politics of Religion in South Korea, 1974–89," 261.
42. Ibid., 267.
43. Chul Hee Chung, "Hankook Minjuhwa Undongeui Sahoejuk Kiwon" [Social origins of democracy movements in Korea], *Hankook Sahoehak* 29 (Autumn 1995): 501–32.
44. Hyug Baeg Im, "Politics of Democratic Transition from Authoritarian Rule in South Korea," in *Democracy in Korea: Its Ideals and Realities*, ed. Sang-Yong Choi (Seoul: Korean Political Science Association, 1997), 84–85.
45. Park, *Protestantism and Politics in Korea*, 186–87.
46. Shin, "The Effects of Organizational Coupling," 40–41.
47. Park, *Protestantism and Politics in Korea*, 192.
48. Shin, "The Effects of Organizational Coupling," 44.

49. Scott Mainwaring and Alexander Wilde, *The Progressive Church in Latin America* (Notre Dame, IN: University of Notre Dame Press, 1989), 26.
50. Shin, "The Effects of Organizational Coupling," 41.
51. Ibid., 42.
52. Kang, "Religion and the Democratization Movement," 243.
53. Kim, "The Politics of Religion in South Korea, 1974–89," 351.
54. Ibid., 352.
55. Shin, "The Effects of Organizational Coupling," 44. The number of Protestant ministers who participated in the democratization movement was 12,700 of 40,700 (about 30 percent) in 1983, while the number of participating Catholic priests was 200 of 1,200 (about 17 percent) in 1984.
56. Shin, "The Effects of Organizational Coupling," 45–46.

7
The Limits of Conservative Church Reformism in the Democratic Philippines

Coeli M. Barry

From the perspective of other countries in Southeast and East Asia, the Philippine Catholic Church is anomalous. In a region whose religious traditions are not Christian, the prominence of the church in the social and political life of the Philippines is notable. Throughout much of the Cold War era when militarized states restricted civil and political rights and brooked little opposition, the Philippine church was accorded a degree of freedom difficult to find in surrounding countries. Even at the height of martial law under the Marcos regime (1965–1986), the Philippine Catholic Church was able to maintain autonomy concerning its own institutional administration and with regard to the socioeconomic developmental projects in which it became increasingly engaged from the 1960s onward. Although the Marcos regime did not spare the church from attack during these years, religious personnel had more room to maneuver than their lay counterparts in the Philippines, and much more than political activists in other countries in Southeast Asia at the time.

With its highly visible role in the overthrow of Marcos in the People Power Revolution (or EDSA, an acronym for a major road called Epifano de los Santos Avenue, as it is referred to in the Philippines) in February 1986 and the restoration of democracy under the presidency of Corazon Aquino (1986–1992), the church confirmed for itself a place in the public sphere in the Philippines and in the popular memories of many from around the world as a crucial force in the overthrow of authoritarianism. In the postauthoritarian Philippines, the Catholic Church embraced its role as guardian of democracy, constitutionalism, and peaceful presidential succession and secured for itself a prominent place on the Philippine political landscape. After the church's eleventh-hour transformation, members of its hierarchy transitioned successfully from their

157

role as "critical collaborators" (the term coined by the Philippine bishops) to one of opponents of Marcos and from there to what appears from the outside to be part of a civil society–building institution. The church's tentacles reach in many directions with programs on such a wide range of social and economic issues that it has been likened, in the words of one observer, to "one big NGO [nongovernmental organization]."

On closer examination, this characterization of the church omits and obscures a great deal. For one example, this view is Manila-centric. Powerful though the cardinal archbishop Jaime Sin was, and effective though the Manila-based church networks were, the long fight by and against Marcos was principally conducted in the countryside and in urban centers in other parts of the Philippines. Much of the church's power stems not only from its voice at the national level but also from the everyday legitimacy it lends to the middle classes and élites spread throughout the Philippines. Second, though priests and nuns (especially the latter and especially when they wore their complete religious habits) lent symbolic weight to the demonstrations against Marcos, their presence did not necessarily mean they were in accord with the Manila hierarchy.

Last, although the end of the Marcos years was dramatic and history making, it did not reflect the long years of opposition by other groups in the Philippines, inside the church and out. The coalition of religious and political groups that formed in the mid-1980s included liberal reformers and social democrats. However, it was the conservative reformist group— dominated by the Catholic bishops to whom Corazon Aquino gravitated —that rose to prominence. Aquino democracy privileged certain church figures, notably Cardinal Sin and members of the Manila leadership, and they, in turn, lent legitimacy to her government.

Chapter Overview

This chapter will plot the rise of conservative reformism in the Philippine Catholic Church under the presidency of Aquino and identify the limits of its appeal among Filipino Catholics beginning in the early 1990s and lasting through the present. Conservative reformism can be characterized as the endorsement of elections and constitutionalism and the support of élite democracy. Conservative reformism is premised on the idea that the church has a role to play as moral guardian of the nation and that this role extends from the cultural and social spheres to the realm of formal politics. As such, there are commonalities between the postauthoritarian church and the conservative church of the 1930s, 1940s and 1950s.

But the contemporary church operates in a different climate in terms of the relations between clergy and laity and with regard to the wider domestic social and political landscape. The respect for clerical authority that bolstered the clerical conservatism of the 1930s, 1940s, and 1950s can no longer be taken for granted. Priestly authority does not carry the weight it once did. Nor can conservatism alone guide the contemporary church's actions. The experience of involvement with the poor and promotion of human rights that church groups accumulated from the 1960s through the 1980s left its mark inside the church and among the laity. The reformism of the 1990s rests uneasily on the memories of these experiences but they cannot be ignored entirely.

On one last front, conservative reformism can be better understood with reference to other forms of church conservatism. The concept of the church as defender of the faith against communism animated church policy from the 1930s on; church social involvement as well as its alliance with the Philippine state was guided by this principle. But contemporary conservative reformism was fashioned throughout the Aquino years, during which time communism had diminished in importance. The church was no longer challenged by a radical left. Instead, in the time after Marcos, the greatest challenges to the church have come from other forces, more likely religious than political. The spread of Christian fundamentalism and evangelicalism attests to the appeal of these groups for an increasing number of Filipino Catholics. While the new religious movements are no more likely than the church to offer long-term solutions to injustice and inequality, their popularity attests to the fact that many have lost faith in the Catholic Church.

The first section of this chapter gives a brief historical overview of church and state relations in the twentieth-century Philippines. The United States colonized the Philippines at the close of the nineteenth century and laid the foundations of Philippine democracy and post–Spanish-era Catholicism. While some observers argue the church is most likely to make its influence felt during times of social or political crisis, this section emphasizes its hegemonic role in less turbulent times as well. The interventionist role of the church in formal politics is juxtaposed to the longer battle against communism, which defined much of what the church did in the field of "social involvement."

The second section looks at the church from 1965 to 1986, the time frame corresponding not only to Marcos's tenure but also to the conclusion of the historical reforms in the worldwide Catholic Church known as Vatican II. In the name of transforming the lives of the poor, the church embarked on work that brought it into direct conflict with the Marcos state and work that prefigures much of what today is called NGO/civil society building. The church's importance politically and socially expanded under martial law when Marcos crushed or greatly limited other civil society forces (such as the press, universities, and opposition politicians) and created the vacuum into which the church moved, thus positioning the church to occupy center stage (quite literally in the case of the People Power demonstrations) in the succeeding years.

No government in modern Philippine history endorsed the church's public political role as clearly as Aquino's, and the third section of the chapter assesses the roots of this historic conjuncture. The contours of postauthoritarian democracy were drawn between 1986 and 1990 when the Catholic leadership's conservative reformism took root. A new constitution was drafted, elections were restored, the Communist Party of the Philippines (CPP) was brought close to collapse, and autonomy was introduced in the Muslim-dominated provinces in the south. The church emerged triumphant in the democratic landscape, displacing, if not ousting other groups. But it was primarily one group within the church, namely the conservative reformists such as Cardinal Sin and other bishops in the Catholic Bishops' Conference of the Philippines, who came to epitomize this victory.

Some of the latitude granted to the church stemmed not only from the particular domestic developments in the Philippines but also from the post–Cold War climate worldwide in which public religion gained in popularity and legitimacy. The prominence of religious forces in postauthoritarian democracy stems partly from the role that religious groups played in overthrowing dictatorships and partly from the increasing suspicion with which secularity is viewed more generally, especially in countries where it was imposed as part of a socialist or communist vision. In the Philippines and elsewhere, democracy in the post–Cold War wears a religious face more readily than in the past. The same forces that permitted the Catholic Church to impose itself on national politics so visibly also gave rise to the growth of other religious groups and more assertive Islamic communities.

The fourth and last section examines the ways in which the post-Marcos, post–Cold War climate has been conducive not only to a visible role for the Catholic Church in politics, but also to a host of new religious groups as well: Protestant fundamentalists, charismatic Catholics, and evangelicals of various persuasions. While these Christian groups are prepared to invoke the Bible and see divine sanction in their pursuit of good governance and poverty reduction, it is by no means a given that the type of government they support is democratic.

Historical Perspectives on Church, State, and Democracy

When the United States colonized the Philippines at the close of the nineteenth century, the confessional state through which the Spanish colonial powers ruled for three hundred years was dismantled in favor of a separation of church and state. In that transition period during the first two decades of the twentieth century, American military and civilian administrators laid the foundations for colonial democracy. This democracy in its genesis favored the landed élite and in its full flowering in the independent Philippines enshrined elections as the forum wherein rival clans and dynasts competed for the spoils of the state.

At the request of the Vatican, European and North American religious orders went to the Philippines in the early decades of American rule. After some 350 years of Christianization, the church there was headed by non-Filipinos. This curious multinational character of the Philippine Catholic Church added fuel to the charge that this was an anti-Filipino institution. Yet, the foreign character of the church added to its appeal where the education of the élites and expanding middle classes was concerned. And, while the Spanish monopoly over the church itself was broken, the Catholic symbols of social and cultural legitimacy retained their hold over the ruling classes. The church strengthened its hold over older élites, as well as laid claim to the newer middle classes by greatly expanding its secondary and tertiary educational institutions. In urban centers around the Philippines, but especially in Manila, lifelong friendships and networks were forged. Modern subjects and professional degrees offering possibilities of upward mobility (e.g., business, chemistry, and nursing) were offered in settings infused with Catholic traditions and a sense of membership in a Catholic world stretching beyond the Philippines borders.

While the church's direct involvement in formal politics was curtailed, church leaders cultivated an active, loyal laity that could be mobilized to defend the church in a climate it perceived to be anti-Catholic. Unlike in countries where the Catholic Church had to exert its interests on the state through church-influenced parties (notably Christian Democratic parties), in the Philippines there were no such parties. Instead, the hierarchy fashioned a form of "civic Catholicism" such that its laity (mostly urban-based middle and upper classes) could be relied on to rally and lobby for the Catholic position.[1]

When legislative battles brewed in the decades after independence, alumni and students of Catholic schools and lay organizations, such as the League of Mary or Catholic Women's League, could be called on to rally publicly. Beginning in the 1950s, the church intervened in electoral politics with election-watch movements, media campaigns, and mobilization of the parish networks and lay organizations. These interventions helped avert crises, and, as one study argues, were notable for containing the threat from "above" (in the form of excessive presidential power) as well as defusing radical pressure from "below."[2]

Although officially removed from the realm of formal politics, the church saw itself as integral to the survival of the Philippines as a religious-political entity. Until the 1960s at least, the church regarded the social and political fields as rife with anticlericalism and nationalism (often conflating the two), and this view only served to strengthen the church leaders in their conviction that the church alone could act as "moral guardian" or "custodian of the nation's values."[3] The presence of any non-Catholic populations in the Philippines undermines this claim, but because of their marginalized status at the time of American colonization and up until the 1960s, the church persisted in asserting that the "nation's values" were Catholic values. Minority populations, both non-Christian and Muslim, remained beyond the reach of the church, and even among the Christianized lowland population, popular religiosity embraced by ordinary Filipinos throughout the Spanish colonial period never abated. However, the most urgent challenge to the church's claim to guardianship was communism.

Beginning in the 1930s when communism first appeared in the Philippines, the church joined forces with the Philippine state to thwart it. Much of the attention to what some in the church (notably the Jesuits) called "the social question" was intended to hold onto the peasants and the workers who were most likely to fall under communist influence.

Fear of losing the peasant and the worker to communism informed the social action plans put in place after the Second Vatican Council (1962–1965). Throughout the Marcos years, this fear only grew as the Communist Party of the Philippines gained a following inside the church. The church became deeply divided on how to protect its own interests and continue to have the influence it thought it ought to over the country.

The next section will focus on the martial law years when the church assumed a significant role owing to the vacuum that was created when other social and civic groups were controlled by or subjugated to the Marcos state. The reformism that carried the day under Aquino—both in its conservative and more liberal guises—was nurtured throughout this period. The more the church's resources and networks were put into action, the greater the sense that this was the rightful place of the church in Philippine society. But the reformism emerged triumphant within the church only after radicalism was successfully suppressed, reined in, or transformed into forms more compatible with the reestablishment of élite democracy.

The Church Divided Under Marcos, United Under Democracy?

Much of what the Catholic hierarchy did both during the EDSA revolution and in the Aquino years was built on foundations that had been badly shaken during martial law. Throughout the church, from the highest levels in the hierarchy and heads of religious congregations, to parish priests and diocesan sisters, there were divisions about how to respond to the imposition of martial law in 1972. These divisions only grew with the expanding influence of the CPP and its affiliate organizations, especially among younger priests and nuns. For many in the church, the activism encouraged by the church's own reform movement, ushered in by the Second Vatican Council, gave way to radicalism as the Marcos government became more repressive. Mario Bolasco argues that a vocal minority of bishops took a critical stance and younger priests and nuns gradually became sympathetic to or outright supportive of the radical CPP. "The breakup in the early seventies of Church-backed student and professional groups advocating a Christian third way between leftists and rights . . . made alliance with the Communist Party of the Philippines and the New People's Army attractive to a good number of clerics and nuns."[4]

The contemporary NGO movement in the Philippines, in which church individuals and groups play an important role, owes much to the legacies of activism and radicalism inside the church and out. With exceptional resources at its disposal and with considerable experience honed in the 1970s and 1980s, the church entered the 1990s poised to adapt to the changing landscape both domestically and globally. For example, where once a religious congregation had specialized in homes for unwed mothers, it now focuses on migration and women's and children's health. When Marcos was removed and the Cold War ended, it was possible for many in the church to take up other issues and work. However, the aftershocks of deep ideological divisions in the church and the brutal way in which the CPP fell apart by the early 1990s, make it difficult to write about and discuss the history of the martial law years in the democratic present.

When Marcos declared martial law in September 1972, the church had only recently begun to put in place the drastic reforms introduced through the Second Vatican Council. Vatican II set in motion processes whereby most aspects of religious life were called into question and subsequently reformed or changed in some way, not the least of which concerned traditional notions of authority and obedience in the church. Above all else, Vatican II reforms sought to make the church more in tune with the modern world in order to strengthen its position in secular life. The premises on which religious life (i.e., the consecrated lives of priests and nuns) is based, however, are profoundly at odds with modern life. By practicing chastity and poverty, priests and nuns remove themselves from two of the primary channels through which modernity is experienced: consumption and sexuality. The church attempted to make religious life more in tune with the "modern world," while still insisting that consecrated life adhere to these vows.

To begin to reform vows was complicated, but the vow of obedience posed a special kind of a problem for the church. This vow is more immediately germane to the running of the church itself, both internally and in the public face it presents to the outside world. When Vatican II reforms were introduced in the midst of an increasingly politicized climate, the vow of obedience and the authority and discipline it represented were challenged; thus, efforts at some form of democratization inside the church were begun. These efforts were superseded by the political battles into which the Catholic Church of the Philippines was drawn during martial law in which the more radical goals of social and economic justice dwarfed concerns about democracy.

The Vatican II reforms called for the worldwide church to be more directly involved with the poor. The changes affected the training of religious, the sacraments, and prayer life of the community. Vatican II inspired the choice to direct more of the church's resources to socioeconomic developmental projects. Although all practicing Catholics were touched in some way by the changes from Vatican II, women's orders were more drastically affected because they lived under conditions at odds with modern life in almost every way. The women's congregations also responded to the call for the church to become more involved with the poor. Individual congregations made choices to leave their schools in order to free the sisters to be more involved in what was called the social apostolate. For some, this meant letting their sisters go on their own to start new programs or join the work of diocesan social action secretariats, under whose auspices many socioeconomic projects were carried out. Others adapted curriculum and programs in the schools to engage students and faculty in the lives of the poor.

For many priests and nuns, their decision to enter into the social apostolate or social action was transforming. Similarly, for many congregations centered in Manila or Cebu, the church in Mindanao, with its more innovative style (it was a much less-established area for the church as Christian settlements expanded rapidly after World War II), was appealing. It was in this kind of work that priests and nuns were most likely to become politicized and either directly involved or supportive of the Communist Party and its affiliate organizations. As Gaspar notes, this work inevitably led the church to the left. From this kind of work, it was a short step for many to a "working relationship" with the Communist Party of the Philippines. "It was common knowledge," Gaspar continues, "that the revolutionary movement, building its bases in the countryside, was the only other force that resisted the dictatorial government. Eventually some progressive church elements would enter into a dialogue and working relationship with the underground, if not actually join it."[5]

In the face of blatant human rights abuses at the hands of the Philippine military, especially in places such as Mindanao and Negros, the radicalization of the religious grew. The most dramatic instance of this was inside the Mindanao church. Here, on the large southern island, the church was a more progressive and less established one; here, also, the Philippine military was most heavily concentrated throughout the 1970s, fighting to obliterate the Muslim separatists and the increasingly capable

New People's Army. As fear of infiltration in the church by the CPP grew, the leadership became more vigilant over church personnel. By the early 1980s, an all-out split took place between the bishops and the more radicalized church workers, priests, and nuns.[6]

Nevertheless, church leaders themselves were forced to make choices, which made them vulnerable to the charge of supporting the insurgency. When individual bishops stood up to the Marcos government in defense of human rights, they became vulnerable to the charge of providing legitimization to a leftist-led rebellion.[7] The dilemma was resolved, "with Church conservatives adopting progressive idiom [sic] and with progressives renewing their vows to the institutional Church."[8] According to some scholars, notably the late Marlo Bolasco, this "hierarchical closing of ranks" is what made the church's intervention during the People Power Revolution possible. It also helped pave the way for the reformism that took hold under the Aquino years.

Aquino, the Church, and the Legacies of Martial Law

Following the ouster of the Marcos government in the historic People's Power Revolution of 1986, the Catholic Church assumed an increasingly vocal role in national politics. The hierarchy sought ways to translate the moral capital accumulated in EDSA into a permanent voice in public affairs. In certain church circles, it was believed that Aquino owed her continued rule in the face of repeated coup attempts to church support. The Aquino government, for its part, appeared comfortable with its closeness to the church; Aquino herself is an openly pious Catholic. The latitude granted to the church, however, and Aquino's reliance on its hierarchy and advisers from religious congregations, such as the Jesuits, was not a matter of personal sentiment alone. She owed her candidacy and presidency in part to church support. In August 1983, the Marcos government had assassinated Marcos's longtime rival (and Corazon's husband) Benigno Aquino. The assassination was the catalyst that forced hitherto reluctant groups among the middle class into more direct action and it galvanized the centrist and center-left opposition groups,[9] among whose numbers were many church personnel and church-linked associations.

By the early 1980s, the Philippine economy was in crisis and many felt that if Marcos were not removed, the economy would collapse. The business class, along with church figures sympathetic to them, such as the Jesuit Father Joaquin Bernas and the economist Bernie Villegas (a prominent member of the right-wing Catholic lay organization, Opus Dei), forged an alliance with liberal and social democratic groups opposed to Marcos. These groups came together in a coalition that began to search for a viable figure who could be pitted against Marcos. Aquino quickly became the chosen candidate, and this coalition held together well into the Aquino administration.

Early in her unofficial campaign, Aquino gave clear indications of how much she would rely on the church's moral leadership. Leading up to and through her campaign, she singled out the "moral leadership of the Catholic Church" as crucial to her vision of the Philippines under her rule. The widow Aquino began to associate herself publicly with the church, and this relationship helped set the tone for her own administration. Protesting together against the corruption of Marcos during the snap elections, the church and Aquino stood side-by-side during the demonstrations of February 1986.

The church and the Aquino government entered into an arrangement that benefited both of them. The new constitution, drafted in 1987, was a hallmark of the Aquino presidency and a vivid illustration of how much influence the church could wield. The constitution was significant for many reasons, not least because it signaled the restoration of the rule of law. Different faces of the church were represented in its drafting, notably that of Father Bernas, a lawyer by training, and that of Sister Christine Tan, former head of the Association of Major Religious Superiors (women) of the Philippines, who had earned a reputation as an outspoken critic of Marcos. It was the conservative prolife bloc within the church that left a very clear imprint on the 1987 constitution by successfully lobbying for a prolife amendment.

Land Reform and the Triumph of Élite Democracy

It was clear from the outset that Aquino was comfortable with church influence but not in all forms: She gave greater access to conservative reformists. On the issue of land reform, this reformism, in both its secular and religious guise, became enshrined, and Aquino-style democracy definitively came down on the side of the traditional élites and powerful newer agribusiness blocs.

From at least the 1930s onward, the issue of land reform has informed national politics in the Philippines. At that time, the worldwide economic depression exacerbated already unsustainable conditions of tenancy in what was then the rice bowl of the Philippines on the island of Luzon. Philippine communism first made inroads among the peasants of this region, and, on the heels of World War II, these same peasants launched a major rebellion. With the help of the U.S. government, the Philippine military put the rebellion down, but the specter of communism never disappeared. In the 1950s, the Philippine government initiated large-scale internal migration in the "frontier" province of Mindanao (setting in motion the conflicts between Muslims and Christians, which flared up in the 1960s and 1970s), but no government was prepared to undertake genuine land reform. Landlords and agribusiness only grew in strength over time. The church, for its part, was frightened of what peasant unrest indicated and much of its attention to what it called "the social question" was intended to thwart communist influence.

When Aquino assumed power, many in the Philippines hoped and even believed she might be able to do what other governments had not. The armed insurgency was in its eighteenth year at the time she became president, and, notwithstanding the fact that Aquino herself comes from a landlord family in Central Luzon, there was a sense that because she, too, had suffered during the Marcos years, her government might undertake meaningful reform. However, the Land Reform program languished until a protest in favor of it ended in a massacre in Manila in 1987. Even then, supported by the Catholic Bishops' Conference of the Philippines (CBCP), Aquino sanctioned the most watered-down version possible. Turning their backs on what might have been a historic opportunity to push for real reform, the bishops chose a course in sync with that of Aquino. The CBCP's view did not reflect that of the church at large. At the time, there were church groups and church-affiliated NGOs pushing for a more substantive reform program. And even as the bishops were preparing their statement, one of the auxiliary bishops of Manila gave encouragement to the protestors marching in the name of reform. In the end, though, the bishops collectively issued a statement in July 1987, endorsing the reform, which was destined to change little, and that, very slowly.[10]

Democratic Paradoxes and the Different Faces of the Church

Under Aquino's government, the new democracy was marked by the most undemocratic of features: Dictatorship was over, but forces inimical to the betterment of the lives of ordinary Filipinos grew in strength—

the counterinsurgency campaign against the Communist Party of the Philippines gathered momentum under the banner of Low Intensity Conflict.[11] A centerpiece of this campaign was the creation of armed civilian groups who were directed and supported by the Philippine military. At the hand of vigilantes (many of them were former members of the New People's Army), human rights abuses proliferated. The restoration of electoral politics brought with it a return of many of the older oligarchs,[12] and new rich legislators who grew richer still while in office.[13]

In the Philippines, postauthoritarian democracy brought about a restoration of civil and political rights, but many paid a large price for the privileges of democracy. Although the church mobilized at key moments in the postauthoritarian Philippines in ways that stabilized the redemocratization process, the apparent show of unity such involvement demonstrated masked differences among those who were participating. Cardinal Sin's leadership at the helm of the Archdiocese of Manila placed at his disposal a vast network of parish organizations, Catholic school students, and religious congregations headquartered there. But many appeared at meetings and demonstrations for reasons of their own, not because they had any great affection for Sin. In interviews with women religious, veterans of anti-Marcos marches, human rights activists, and teachers in theology schools, they lamented at times how powerful Sin had become; how he had come to overshadow others in the church.

In this way, the conservative reformist Catholic Church—which emerged so significantly under Aquino, or in tandem with Aquino—was nothing more or less than the religious face to the politics of the times. However, for each face that thrived under Aquino, there were many more persons out of the limelight who simply returned to the work they had been involved in since the Marcos years. The two church members of the constitutional committee mentioned above were Father Bernas, S.J., and Sister Christine Tan, Religious of the Good Shepherd. Bernas continues to have a voice in the public realm: He went on to become the president of the flagship Jesuit university, the Ateneo de Manila, and writes, speaks, and teaches on constitutional law. Christine Tan returned to the squatter community in a Manila slum from which she had come, and lived there until her death in 2003.

Tan had shown herself throughout martial law to be brave and outspoken; she was not an easy leader to accommodate but she was a leader nonetheless. Her style, politics, and voice were not the sort that was wanted or needed in the Aquino years. The same might be said for many of the other women religious who rose during martial law and then went their own ways to start their own NGOs, to begin women's studies programs, or to return to the classroom. They were, like many in the church and elsewhere, freer to choose from a range of options that martial law had kept from them. However, Aquino democracy and conservative reformist Catholicism did not encourage a public voice for them.

Democracy and the Church After Aquino

Throughout the Corazon Aquino administration, church and state seemed to work together more harmoniously than at any time in modern Philippine history. The Aquino–church alliance was in some way particular to the personalities involved, but it was also reflective of the democracy of the times that propelled them to the fore. During the presidencies that followed Aquino, those of Fidel Ramos (1992–1998) and Joseph Estrada (1998–2001), relations with the church were more strained, even downright hostile at times, especially at two important junctures. The first was when President Ramos tried to introduce a constitutional change that would have permitted him to run again for office. Term limits were and are an especially sensitive issue in the wake of Marcos's twenty-one years in power. The Manila church leadership under Sin helped to stage a large rally against Ramos. The second incident was in the days leading up to the ouster of Joseph Estrada in January 2001, in what is called People Power II.

Nevertheless, even as the church after Aquino showed itself capable of bringing large groups together and lending itself and its symbols to the service of political goals, its influence was not consistently brought to bear on other arenas, such as policy making. As Millard Lim wrote in his study of the Philippine bishops, the influence of the CBCP can neither be assumed nor generalized. Lim looked at the ability of the CBCP to influence national policy concerning two issues, acceptance of Vietnamese asylum seekers and abolition of the death penalty. While the bishops were successful in the former, their opposition to the death penalty was not successful in swaying the final vote. As Lim points out, "A case by case analysis of CBCP policy influence work shows that, like other policy stakeholders, the CBCP's policy influence is affected by other factors which may or may not be within its control or manipulation.... Socio-cultural and historical variables may give the *image* of a powerful and influential Church hierarchy but this notion cannot be readily translated to *actual* policy influence."[14]

When Aquino called on the church hierarchy, she did so claiming that its members could provide moral leadership. She placed her faith in the bishops and they supported her and legitimized her particular democratic vision. Yet, the church is suffering from what might be called a credibility gap at present. The archdiocese of Manila is in financial difficulties and two sex scandals involving prominent bishops (Bacani and Yalung) surfaced in 2003. The church's response has been heavy-handed toward the media, a point conceded by one priest publicly in an article for the national weekly magazine, *Newsbreak*.[15] While church officials remain focused on implementing procedures for reporting sexual abuse (here, they privately insist the problem is not abuse of minors in the Philippine church but relations with women), there are those laity and some religious who want a more thoroughgoing assessment of its root causes. When a group of women religious conducted a survey among church workers (lay men and women), their findings revealed extensive but unreported cases of harassment and abuse. The bishops refused to give credence to the report, insisting that the sisters involved had used standards of Western feminism to exaggerate the conditions in the Philippine church. The bishops argued that the sisters were, in effect, misinterpreting the incidences by relying on culturally inappropriate definitions and understandings of abuse and harassment.

An editorial in the June 23, 2003, edition of *Newsbreak*, entitled "Shadow over the Catholic Church," gives an indication of how seriously the Catholic laity view this issue and is worth quoting at length:

> Since we ran our story on Bishop Crisostomo Yalung [the highest ranking CC official to be forced to quit after fathering a child] in February our mail has almost always contained reactions to the whole affair. It's the single issue that has elicited the most feedback, ranging from disappointment that we printed details of the scandal to thoughtful calls for the Church to reexamine itself and confront similar problems with transparency.... For us the core issue is not the personal frailty of the priests but how the Church deals with them.... What we've seen, so far, makes us raise these questions: How can an institution demand accountability from the government and other sectors when it can't do so from those within its ranks? How can the Catholic Church uphold honesty when it doesn't admit its errors?... These are trying times for the Church. It can only emerge stronger—if it doesn't sweep this problem under a ton of verbiage.[16]

Fundamentalism and New Religious Movements: Is the Church Losing Its Hold?

Another significant measure of the loss of the Catholic Church's leadership is the inroads made by fundamentalists and evangelicals. As the end of the Cold War seemed to diminish the force of political ideologies and Marxist-inspired groups, so, too, did globalization bring an increase in Protestant fundamentalism and an upsurge in evangelical Catholic lay movements to the Philippines. The presence of the former is a challenge to the church's claim to a solid hold over the majority Christian population. One of the largest of the Philippine-grown Protestant groups is called Jesus is Lord. It is headed by Brother Eddie Villanueva, who mounted a bid for president in the 2004 elections and made a respectable showing, garnering some 6.2 percent of the vote.

Within the church itself, there has been a mushrooming of lay groups of many spiritual stripes. The largely middle-class lay association, Couples for Christ, has received official recognition from the Vatican and professes allegiance to traditional Catholic teachings. Members employ a curious mixture of profamily, nationalist, and civic-minded discourses to express the animating principles by which they work.[17] El Shaddai, on the other hand, is a very popular lay group that claims a following mostly of members of the working class, many of whom are poor. Officially affiliated with the Catholic Church, when, by the mid-1990s, tens of thousands of members began gathering every Sunday in downtown Manila (not inside any church), church leaders actively sought to keep them under clerical influence. Their charismatic leader, Brother Mike Vellarde, was "assigned" as a spiritual adviser from within the Manila hierarchy—by none other than Bishop Bacani, who was one of the bishops at the center of the sex scandals.

The roots of the new religious movements lay in the Marcos regime itself. By the mid-1980s, over one thousand religious groups had registered with the Philippine government.[18] Church leaders were well aware of this influx, and they began to address the issue of fundamentalism publicly in the late 1980s. In 1991, the Catholic Church of the Philippines met for the Second Plenary Council in order to draw up a plan for the church into the twenty-first century. While reiterating its commitment to the poor and embracing its role in formal politics, much of what truly concerned the church was revealed in its discussions of how to "evangelize" Filipinos. The term evangelize is generally associated with mission and conversion of non-Christians, but in this instance it was used to stress how much ordinary Filipino Catholics needed to be reeducated and brought back to the institutional church.

The Catholicism that led the day during Aquino's presidency seems today to be much less viable. From the late 1980s forward, Catholics flocked to fundamentalist groups (though not necessarily seeing their membership in the Catholic Church and Protestant sect as mutually exclusive), and those who remained in the evangelical groups exhibited the tell-tale signs of popular Christianity, which has been the bane of the institutional Church throughout most of Philippine history: spiritual zeal with heavy doses of individual interpretation on behalf of a charismatic leader outside the church's control.

Over the past fifteen years or so, the networks and infrastructure within the church for campaigns on behalf of good governance, voter education, and election-watch operations remain quite strong. Some have been strengthened with the rise of middle-class lay movements and newer civic associations openly allied with the church, some of which will be discussed below. However, the ground is shifting underfoot. Two of the longest standing election-watch groups organized in the name of free and fair elections, which the church has long supported, the Commission on Elections and the National Movement for Free Elections, have lost influence owing to internal conflicts and poor leadership. Although the Manila-based networks Cardinal Sin was so adept at calling on are still in place, Sin himself resigned in 2003. The massive Manila archdiocese has been divided into smaller dioceses and the new archbishop, Gaudencio Rosales, takes a view to politics that is very different from Sin's. Rosales's theology is more traditional and he advocates reaching out to the poor in ways that seem much closer to older ideas of charity.

Furthermore, even as the presence of church figures and public displays of Catholic symbols were so important in the People Power II demonstrations that helped secure the first term for the current president, Gloria Macapagal-Arroyo (referred to as GMA), the demonstration of support for the ousted Estrada some five months later was very different in tenor from protests preceding it. In the Poor People Power demonstration, as it is sometimes referred to, there were no middle-class representation, no church symbols in view, and no church personnel.[19] For some in the Manila church, Poor People's Power revealed the limits of church influence. Members of the Manila archdiocesan leadership (as well as urban NGOs) despair that Poor People Power demonstrations evidence the real fragility of the church's hold on the urban poor. Those who took to the streets in support of Estrada came from parishes and communities where church social and economic programs had long been established and the Manila church thought these parishioners could be counted on to follow Arroyo.

The defacement of the shrine built at EDSA during the People Power III demonstration angered some church leaders. In their anger, the distance between them and the poor is easy to see. Bishop Jose Oliveros, in a sermon at a recent meeting of religious leaders from the dioceses of Manila, highlighted this. He queried, "Why is it that when they [the poor] hold a rally like EDSA III at The Our Lady of Peace Shrine, where earlier Filipinos gathered to topple the dictatorship, they made it stinky and dirty?" Oliveros said that the people in the slums and squatters areas seem to be angry at the church, and asked, "Why is it so hard to make the people understand that the Church is their ally?"[20]

Conclusion

None of the governments that followed in the now nearly two decades of postauthoritarianism in the Philippines has made inroads into the profoundly unequal structures of Philippine society and politics. Elections were restored but elections in Philippine history have generally served the interests of a small number of business and political élites. Some headway in reforms, such as the decentralization initiatives and the shift from extralegal, underground politics to mostly legal, aboveground activities, has been beneficial to nongovernmental organizations. The grassroots performance of democratic groups in the Philippines over the past fifteen years has been impressive by many standards, but it has proved very hard to institutionalize these gains at the national or provincial levels. As Paul Hutchcroft and Joel Rocamora have written:

> No country in Asia has more experience with democratic institutions than the Philippines. . . . Filipinos know both the promise of democracy and the problems of making democratic structures work for the benefit of all. Some 100 years after the introduction of national-level democratic institutions to the Philippines, the sense of frustration over the character of the country's democracy is arguably more apparent than ever before.[21]

Aquino's ascendance brought with it the reentrenchment of pre-Marcos political groups. However, the memory of martial law also followed her into office and the demands for transparency, constitutionalism, a more restrained military, and some kind of justice were palpable during her presidency. The same standards were raised for the church. Though only one voice from within the church held Aquino's attention, elsewhere inside and outside the church, expectations were raised about what a more activist church *might* do. The case of a parish priest in the southern part of Cebu province gives weight to this reading. In the elections of 1998, members of the parish council decided to back a candidate who would challenge the politically dominant local clan there, the Abines family. Members of the clan had the ear of this priest's bishop who was based in Cebu City. The bishop warned the priest he should rein in his parishioners. In response, the local priest launched a public protest: He organized parish workers to take turns ringing the church bells twenty-four hours a day. This went on for a few days, and when word reached the bishop, he backed down. The Abines's candidate was defeated. This was by no means a typical scenario in Philippine political life after Marcos. Still, it does suggest that the triumph of conservative church reformism has not been complete.

The legacies of a church whose priests and nuns broke with decades of tradition and distanced themselves or openly criticized the élite families survived. Nevertheless, it has proved difficult to write the history of the Catholic Church during martial law, either from the standpoint of the radicalism that surfaced and thrived for a time, or from the standpoint of those within the church who were slow to oppose Marcos. The history of the radical roots of contemporary democracy is a difficult one to relate, owing in part to the brutal way the radical left came apart in the 1980s and 1990s in the Philippines;[22] nor has there been any effort on the part of the bishops to account for their own actions during martial law. In a publication commemorating the fiftieth anniversary of the Catholic Bishops' Conference, *Anamnesis*, the treatment of the Marcos years was exceptional in its tone: It was a lament in the most generalized terms, with no sense of anyone taking responsibility for either supporting Marcos or being very slow in moving to criticize him. This seems especially ironic given that one of the editors, Bishop Francisco Claver, did speak out against martial law, very forcefully and articulately, from the pulpit of his diocese of Malaybalay in Bukidnon, Mindanao, and in published essays.[23]

Subsequent to the end of authoritarianism in the Philippines, some of the worst of the Philippine Catholic Church's nightmares disappeared when the left crumbled. In the postauthoritarian context, the church has been spared the painful choice of legitimizing the élite or supporting the poor. In the Philippine's contemporary democracy, it is possible for clergy to baptize and marry the children of the landlord, while supporting an NGO that is dedicated to ameliorating the lives of the poor who work under him or her.

That the church would endorse this political arrangement is hardly surprising. Yet, how long it can continue to stand behind democracy without addressing its own undemocratic nature is hard to say. The Roman Catholic Church has shown itself capable of withstanding social and political change in the past, but the history of the Philippines has also demonstrated that, when the church advocates reform in society at large, there are many critics both in the church and outside who are quick to demand that the church reform itself.

For the Catholic Church worldwide, democracy is in favor. In many respects, democracy is the easiest form of modernity with which the church has been forced to reconcile. The great rupture between Catholicism and the modern world (the phrasing comes from the church) had many facets to it: intellectual, theological, cultural, and political. In the political realm, the rise of the nation-state in the eighteenth and nineteenth centuries in Europe and the nationalist revolutions in the Spanish colonies brought about a decline of the church's secular power. Nationalism, socialism, and communism in the twentieth century further undermined the influence of the church as a political and cultural force.

Democracy, by contrast, is the political form within which the church cannot merely survive but must have a significant role. Constitutional democracy offers the church the legal sanction it needs to control its own institution. However, more than providing the church with the mechanism through which it can participate formally in politics, democracy permits the church, in the Philippines and elsewhere, to reconcile with the modern world in the cultural realms as well. In the discussion above on Vatican II and the reconstruction of religious life, this chapter described the cultural divide that separates vowed life (poverty, chastity, and obedience) from the general experience of modernity insofar as modern subjectivity (here, the terms are being used in their most general sense) is derived from consumption, sexuality, and freedom. The church could never truly alter these vows without threatening its very survival; to do so would mean establishing another kind of church altogether. The reform efforts were, in any case, interrupted by the political battles into which church personnel were drawn on the heels of Vatican II and at the height of the Cold War.

In the wake of the Cold War, however, tending to democracy is a less fraught effort for the church. While still continuing with the most undemocratic of practices where its own institution is concerned, namely, asserting the sanctity of men as priests over women as nuns, outwardly the church can endorse the range of issues essential for any modern state: efficiency, constitutionalism, transparency, and elections.

The limits of democracy are apparent everywhere around the world, but the worldwide church, under the leadership of popes John Paul II and Benedict XVI, has continued to endorse it. In the Philippines, in the name of democracy, civil society groups take on the state, trying to force it to reform so that the most basic services can be delivered to its citizens. As long as these conditions persist, the church can use its resources to stand in where the Philippine state is unwilling or unable. As a national institution, the church will do little to redress the roots of the inequities in the Philippines because of its historic alliance with the Philippine state, stability, and important forces from the middle class. So long as reform efforts look possible, it will support them, but anything more radical than that seems unlikely at this juncture. In this way, the Philippine Catholic Church reflects the reformist temper of these democratic times, so succinctly depicted by Vicente Rafael as the call to consolidate authority and make it more transparent without questioning class divisions or the nature of the state itself.[24]

Democracy has become the means by which equality is advocated in principle but deferred in practice. For the poor who make up the majority of the Filipino population, it is hard to know how long this deferment can go on. In the face of frustrations and disappointments with the secular political realm, it is not surprising that religious forces would be appealing. But religious institutions such as the Philippine Catholic Church may not be the masters of these forces.

Notes

My thanks for assistance, editorial, technical, and otherwise, to P.N. Abinales, Benedict Anderson, Thanet Aphornsuvan, Jose Mario Francisco, S.J., Paul Hutchcroft, Audrey Kahin, and Nota Magno.

    1. Coeli Barry, "Polyglot Catholicism: Genealogies and Reinterpretations of

the Philippine Catholic Church," *Pilipinas*, special issue, *Philippine Post-War Nationalism*, no. 32 (Spring 1999): 59–81.

2. Eva-Lotta Hedman, "Constructing Civil Society: Election Watch Movements in the Philippines," in *Social Movements in Development: The Challenge of Globalization and Democratization*, ed. Staffan Lindberg and Arni Sverrisson (New York: St. Martin's Press, 1997), 210–33. See also Eva-Lotta Hedman and John T. Sidel, *Philippine Politics and Society in the Twentieth Century* (London: Routledge, 2000), 13–29.

3. I have never known women religious to use the terms, which is not to say they are less implicated in defending church interests in this realm; it is more a matter that influencing the nation-state as such was not a high priority for them. Women religious occupy a lower status in the institutional church and generally do not feel themselves responsible for the survival of the church as a whole. Additionally, their traditional work was in the less overtly political fields of teaching and social service.

4. Mario V. Bolasco, "The Problem of Philippine Church History: An Introduction," in *Points of Departure: Essays on Christianity, Power and Social Change* (Manila: St. Scholastica's College, 1994), 24.

5. Karl Gaspar, "Abante, Atras, Abante: Patterns of Mindanao Catholic Church's Involvement in Contemporary Social Issues," in *Civil Society Making Civil Society*, ed. Miriam Coronel Ferrer, vol. 3, Philippine Democracy Agenda (Quezon City: Third World Studies Center, 1997), 154.

6. Warren Kinne, *The Splintered Staff: Structural Deadlock in the Mindanao Church* (Quezon City: Claretian Publications, 1990).

7. Mario V. Bolasco, *Points of Departure: Essays on Christianity, Power and Social Change* (Manila: St. Scholastica's College, 1994).

8. Ibid., 24.

9. Mark R. Thompson, *The Anti-Marcos Struggle: Personalistic Rule and Democratic Transition in the Philippines* (New Haven: Yale University Press, 1995).

10. James Putzel, *A Captive Land: The Politics of Agrarian Reform in the Philippines* (Quezon City: Ateneo de Manila University Press, 1992).

11. Alfred W. McCoy, "Low Intensity Conflict in the Philippines," in *Low Intensity Conflict*, ed. Elaine McKay (Melbourne: Centre of Southeast Asian Studies, Monash University, 1989), 51–64.

12. Eric Gutierrez, *The Ties That Bind: A Guide to Family, Business, and Other Interests in the Ninth House of Representatives* (Metro Manila: Philippine Center for Investigative Journalism and Institute for Popular Democracy, 1994).

13. Sheila S. Coronel, Yvonne T. Chua, Luz Rimban, and Booma Cruz, *The Rulemakers: How the Wealthy and Well Born Dominate* (Quezon City: Philippine Center for Investigative Journalism, 2004), 118–71.

14. Millard O. Lim, "Policy Influence of the Catholic Bishops Conference of the Philippines: The Cases of the Vietnamese Asylum Seekers and the Death Penalty Law" (M.A. thesis, Ateneo de Manila University, 1999), 118.

15. Jose Mario C. Francisco, S.J., "An Imperfect Church," *Newsbreak*, February 17, 2003.

16. *Newsbreak*, June 23, 2003.

17. In the decree granted by the Pontifical Council for the Laity Couples for Christ, the organization was recognized on March 12, 2000, as a "private interna-

tional association of the faithful with a juridical personality" for their "apostolic works in more than seventy countries all over the world which serve the family based on the plan of God and which assist those who are struggling to be Christian in the modern world." Mimeograph, "Pontifical Council for the Laity."

18. Robert C. Salazar, "The Fundamentalist Evangelical Movement in the Philippines: An Overview," in *New Religious Movements in Asia and the Pacific Islands: Implications for Church and Society* (Manila: Social Development Research Center, De La Salle University, 1990), 190–210.

19. For a suggestive reading of this event, see Vicente Rafael, "The Cell Phone and the Crowd: Messianic Politics in the Contemporary Philippines," *Public Culture* 15, no. 3 (September 2003): 399–425.

20. *TODAY*, June 13, 2004.

21. Paul D. Hutchcroft and Joel Rocamora, "Strong Demands and Weak Institutions: The Origins and Evolution of the Democratic Deficit in the Philippines," *Journal of East Asian Studies* 3 (2003): 259–92.

22. Although its stronghold in the countryside was well established (Putzel estimated some 20 percent of barrios were fully under CPP control; see *A Captive Land*, 168). In the late 1980s, the CPP began to lose its standing with more moderate oppositionists. In a fateful decision, the CPP boycotted the protests which culminated in the People Power revolution in 1986 and lost more ground when it decided to boycott the constitutional referendum of 1987. In the early 1990s, there was a full-blown split in the party from which it never fully recovered. See also Patricio N. Abinales, ed., *The Revolution Falters: The Left in Philippine Politics after 1986* (Ithaca, NY: Southeast Asia Program, Cornell University, 1996), and Joel Rocamora, *Breaking Through: The Struggle within the Communist Party of the Philippines* (Manila: Anvil Publishing, 1994).

23. See, in particular, Francisco F. Claver, *The Stones Will Cry Out: Grassroots Pastorals* (Maryknoll, NY: Orbis Books, c.1978).

24. Rafael, "The Cell Phone and the Crowd," 399–425.

8

Hong Kong's Catholic Church and the Challenge of Democratization in the Special Administrative Region

Deborah A. Brown

The Roman Catholic Church is not a democratic institution. It is run by a hierarchy that refuses to allow women to be ordained as priests and forbids its male priests to marry. Compared to Protestant denominations, laity have a small role in church affairs, with the view that a patriarchal clerical order has better understanding of the correct interpretation of the articles of faith, and, of course, of the administration of sacraments. History does not always look favorably on acts—or nonacts—of the church. That is why Pope John Paul II asked for forgiveness at the turn of the millennium for the church's sins.

Yet, despite what some consider the church's shortcomings and the church's own confessed transgressions, a principle of the Catholic faith is belief in the primacy of the individual. This stands in sharp contrast to authoritarian governments, including the Central People's Government of the People's Republic of China (PRC), which insists on the primacy of the state. Thus, the contemporary Catholic Church advocates a government with limited power, while China's communist officials pursue an authoritarian state with all political power exclusively in the hands of the Chinese Communist Party (CCP) and its state apparatus. In the public arena, the Catholic Church works to give people the greatest leeway possible for individual action, while mindful that public safety and the rights of others also must be protected. In the 1980s, 1990s, and into the 2000s, the Catholic hierarchy in places around the globe, such as in Chile, Mexico, East Timor, Poland, Ukraine, and elsewhere, has encouraged freedom and the creative fulfillment of individuals. This advocacy of human rights and individual freedom places the church in tension with officials in Beijing who imprison—often without trial—and sometimes torture and kill religionists, democrats, and others who dare to exercise their own judgment, call for political reform, or criticize the party or the state.

The Catholic Church is headquartered in the Western world, which is admired most by persons globally for its freedom. The PRC, in sharp contrast, moves against the tide of political liberalism rising in much of the world, and remains steeped in tactics of political control, bureaucracy, and a growing aggressive nationalism, which suffocate individual initiative and freedom outside the economic sphere.

Many persons claim that Pope John Paul II was the most influential religious leader of the twentieth century, and his influence continued to hold sway—despite his weakened physical condition—until his death in April 2005. The outpouring of millions of persons to pay their last respects was a strong testimony to the power of his papacy among Catholics and non-Catholics around the world. (The Central People's Government was not represented at the funeral.) Few question that, in his dedication to spreading the Gospel, Pope John Paul II advanced democratic ideals internationally. It was not only his leadership of the worldwide Catholic Church that gave him stature, but also his determination to draw global attention to persons living in poverty and under oppression and to eradicate prejudices and intolerances that earned him respect. This sense of spirit and ideas is reflected in the Catholic Church leadership in Hong Kong, and sets this diocese in opposition to many governmental policies and practices in Beijing and in the Hong Kong Special Administrative Region (SAR). Commitment to protecting the sanctity of the individual and personal freedom enables the Hong Kong church to help the community search for liberties and integrity of life as its people adjust to living in a society that is contending with times that, since 1997, have changed politically, economically, and socially. The greatest strength of the Catholic Church is its ideas, against which officials in Beijing do not wish to compete. That is why Chinese officials pursue a harsh course to eradicate China's underground Catholic Church loyal to Rome, and have begun to interfere with the rights of the Catholic Church in Hong Kong since 1997.

Mainland communist leaders have viewed Christian churches as imperialist forces that disrupted the harmony of Chinese society. They generally lose sight that Catholics and Protestants were a major impetus for China's modernization until 1949, when the communists took control of power, and for Hong Kong's modernization, until the political transition of 1997. These contributions are principally owed to the churches' establishment and management of schools, hospitals, and social welfare programs and their calls for the end to practices that have diminished human dignity and life.

During British rule of Hong Kong, Christian and other religions were allowed to flourish. In helping to create a just society based on growing equality and freedoms, Hong Kong's Catholic Church challenged communist rulers in the PRC by advancing the standard of living for the territory's people through a vast educational program and improved care for the community's people. In the latter decades of the twentieth century, it was the Catholic Church, in particular, that extended great efforts to assist Hong Kong's unwanted Vietnamese refugees and to serve the region's large Filipino domestic worker population—who still live unenvied lives, although better ones than they have had in the Philippines. Since the 1800s, the church has worked to lighten the burdens of the urban underclass, the caged homeless, and the otherwise poor and disadvantaged, while also taking a lead in nurturing Hong Kong's business, professional, and civil service men and women who have stood behind the rise of Hong Kong to a world-class business, trade, and financial center. The church hierarchy acknowledged that Hong Kong did not measure up under the British to Western democratic ideals, specifically because Hong Kong was "executive-led," a benign way of describing British rule by means of an authoritarian—albeit benevolent—political structure. Yet, many critical elements of a democracy were in place in British Hong Kong, only a few of which were an independent judiciary and academic and press freedoms. The hope was that, over time, Hong Kong's systems would evolve and someday rectify inequalities in political participation and other areas of disadvantage, such as those from which the Filipinos, other minorities, and the poor still suffer. What the church tried to engender over the one and one-half centuries of British rule was a sense of compassion that was so eloquently demonstrated in 1989, when over one million residents poured into the streets in protest against the students who were massacred at Tiananmen Square, and thereafter, when tens of thousands attended annual candlelight vigils of commemoration for the deceased, in numbers reaching forty to sixty thousand. It is not accidental, then, that many of the leaders of the democratic movement in Hong Kong are Catholics—and other Christians.

The Catholic Church in Hong Kong measures progress largely by its success in spreading the Gospel and in providing educational and other services to the community. In contradistinction, the CCP measures progress by the escalation of China's military power and the people's commitment to the pursuit of material and financial gains. In keeping with *Document 19* of 1982—which remains the PRC's official policy on religion—secular, rationalistic, and scientific values are still expected to triumph over religious ones, and in so doing, bring about the advancement of the Chinese socialist state.[1] However, in the view of many students of China, the promise of the communists as a moral force during the pre-1950 civil-war period badly degenerated into great brutality during the 1950s and 1960s, and, later, into a political and economic selfishness marked by CCP excesses to maintain political control. This includes widespread corruption that is fanned by the conviction that materialism is the answer to personal happiness, better standards of living, national prestige, and continued CCP dominance.

As Hong Kong moves further along the path of its political, economic, and social integration into China, the Catholic Church is forthright in trying to help the SAR to value and also demand philosophical bearings in which freedom, justice, social equality, and political participation are important societal and political objectives. These aims often have set the church hierarchy at odds with leaders in Beijing. Further, they have set the Catholic Church apart from some of Hong Kong's other religious institutions.

Hong Kong's Roman Catholic Church distinguishes itself from the local Anglican Church and the Hong Kong Buddhist Association because the latter two institutions jeopardized their credibility by their leaders' involvement in partisan politics in the run-up to 1997. Both the Anglican bishop (now archbishop) and the headman of the Hong Kong Buddhist Association accepted a variety of appointments by officials in Beijing to what euphemistically became known as the "second stove," or governmental framework of appointed loyalist committees that Beijing established to undermine the administration of Governor Christopher Patten (1992–1997), as it struggled to democratize Hong Kong in the last half decade of British rule.

Alexis de Tocqueville made important observations on the dangers that arise when church leaders link themselves to leaders of a government. He wrote in *Democracy in America* in 1835:

> I know that, apart from influence proper to itself, religion can at times rely on the artificial strength of laws and the support of the material powers that direct society. There have been religions intimately linked to earthly governments, dominating men's souls both by terror and by faith; but when a religion makes such an alliance, I am not afraid to say that it makes the same mistake as any man might; it sacrifices the future for the present, and by gaining a power to which it has no claim, it risks its legitimate authority.
>
> Hence religion cannot share the material strength of the rulers without being burdened with some of the animosity roused against them.
>
> Hence any alliance with any political power whatsoever is bound to be burdensome for religion. It does not need their support in order to live, and in serving them it may die. . . .
>
> When governments seem so strong and laws so stable, men do not see the danger that religion may run by allying itself with power.
>
> The American clergy were the first to perceive this truth and to act in conformity with it. They saw that they would have to give up religious influence if they wanted to acquire political power, and they preferred to lose the support of authority rather than to share its vicissitudes.[2]

Unlike the Anglican and Buddhist leaderships in Hong Kong, the leaders of the SAR's Roman Catholic diocese, while not always as outspoken on important matters in past years as some would have liked, nevertheless have seen the dangers of befriending authority and intimately uniting with the governmental powers of Beijing and Hong Kong. Now that these very powers are making encroachments into the rights and influence of religious institutions in Hong Kong, because it has preserved a nonpartisan public stature,[3] the Catholic Church is able to stand essentially uncompromised, not only for the preservation of the Catholic Church's rights, but also for religious freedom for all religious communities in Hong Kong and for the rights and liberties of others.

The importance of the independence of religious groups and institutions in society cannot be underestimated. Turning again to Tocqueville, he observed that the sway Christian churches had over government in the United States came indirectly through their influence over mores and domestic life, not directly through mixing clergy with political parties. Viewing religion as "useful" and "natural" to mankind, Tocqueville maintained that individual conscience led a person to reflect on personal actions until they were checked against religious assumptions and practices. This, in turn, led to restraint in the political sector, which favored respect for law, peace among people, and the durability of institutions. Thus, religion indirectly led to restraint in the exercise of liberty, which is one reason Tocqueville viewed Christian churches as indispensable to the maintenance of republican institutions. Tocqueville saw that Americans linked patriotism and the hope of remaining free to strong influence of religion in civil society. He concluded that, "Despotism may be able to do without faith, but freedom cannot." Faith, said Tocqueville, was the only permanent state of mankind because through it came hope. Convinced that separation of church and state was essential to the survival of liberty, he counseled that, while remaining separate from politics and affairs of state it might seem that religions diminish their power, in fact, they increase their strength by gaining effectiveness as independent moral forces in society to be a bulwark against tyranny. The strength of religions, as Tocqueville saw it, rested in their ability—separated from the state—to maintain their precepts of faith and to command independent allegiance from their members. To him, Christian faiths were fertile ground for building and preserving democratic institutions, largely because they were independent forums for the evolution of new opinions that could affect the state.[4]

In the past, one way the Roman Catholic and other Christian churches fit into the politics of Hong Kong's preponderantly non-Christian society, governed by a foreign élite that was rooted in Christian tradition, was by sharing Christian heritage with the government's top officials. Nevertheless, more importantly, as previously noted, the churches supplied to the community essential services that were critical to the government in its efforts to provide to residents, first, the basic necessities of life, and later, an increasingly higher standard of living.

However, sovereignty over Hong Kong shifted in 1997 from believers in London to unbelievers in Beijing, and there are indicators that these leaders may have embarked on a course to reduce Christian, especially Roman Catholic, influence. In the past, Hong Kong did not, and today it does not, propound an official religion—or unbelief—and, formally speaking, no religion (e.g., Buddhism) is considered more "Chinese" or patriotic than others (e.g., Christianity). Regardless, the Roman Catholic Church now feels pressures from leaders in Beijing and Hong Kong on multiple fronts. Still, the church has chosen not to soften its positions on matters it deems critical in order to gain political acceptance. Rather, it has dug in its heels as a counterwitness against the governments' actions that are offensive to the church, with an eye toward persuading the faithful, general public, and SAR and Beijing officials that they must steer a steady course toward human rights, civil liberties, and other democratic values.

It is evident, then, that the Catholic Church has not removed itself from politics in Hong Kong. However, it has set limits with regard to the type of political involvement in which it engages, choosing to act as a voice in civil society that does not legitimize, by its leaders' acceptance of political appointments, governmental acts that violate either the laws of the region or fundamental Christian tenets and ethics. Otherwise said, the top leaders of the local church have not been seduced into active political engagement in concert with the SAR or central government, in the belief of the efficacy of their involvement to mold the attitudes of officials in Beijing or to gain power, prestige, and future influence for the Roman Catholic Church with them or their political appointees in Hong Kong.

The temptation for church leaders to form an "unholy alliance," as SAR legislator Emily Lau[5] has called it, with many business leaders and other pro-China supporters in Hong Kong to hinder the advancement of democracy, as mentioned, proved too strong for some religious leaders prior to 1997. By accepting Beijing appointments, the leaders of the Anglican and Buddhist institutions were at the center of important affairs and avoided finding themselves on the periphery in 1997 at the time of the change of sovereignty and heightened international attention. Thus, acceptance of Beijing's appointments to the Basic Law[6] Drafting Committee, Basic Law Consultative Committee, Preliminary Work Committee, Preparatory Committee, and as specially selected advisers to leaders in Beijing, meant that Anglican and Buddhist leaders were successfully courted by China's and the SAR's officials. Conversely, the Catholic Church, which among religious institutions runs the largest number of schools and social welfare units in Hong Kong, assumed the more hazardous role of prophet or counterwitness, denying itself the temporary comforts of an expedient relationship with Beijing. Today, it stands outside the corridors of power, urging authorities within and the people of Hong Kong to the pursuit of what is just and moral—thus, knowingly sacrificing any prospect of political advantage.

Despite successfully drawing some religious leaders in Hong Kong into a united front with the SAR and central governments, the prevailing mantra of China's leaders regarding religion is that religious belief is the stuff of uneducated, unsophisticated minds and is dangerous because it fosters injustice and oppression. Yet, freedom is an idea that is integral to Christianity, the passion for both it and justice having been learned first from the ancient Hebrew prophets, an exceptional moral force in human history, and then from Jesus and his disciples. It is from these ancient prophets and seers, and from their concept of a power that is prior to the state, that Jews and Christians finally came to understand that rulers are not divine, and, instead, are deserving of the criticism and sometimes the resistance of common citizens. What follows in the next two sections explains two of many areas in which Hong Kong's Roman Catholic Church, since 1997, has criticized the SAR government and resisted its acts, or in which it is experiencing governmental encroachments. These accounts demonstrate both erosion to religious freedom in Hong Kong and significant tensions between the Catholic Church and the SAR and Central People's governments over the governments' unwillingness to promote Hong Kong's democratization.

The Hong Kong Catholic Church's Fight for the Right *Not* to Engage in Electoral Affairs

When a church endorses candidates, links itself to one political faction or another, or serves authority in a partisan way, it takes one side against another, which a church can ill-afford to do.[7] Further, it risks association with the mistakes of politicians and can endanger its doctrine and missions by compromises made in order to be viewed as "politically correct," or to gain favor with authorities. The risks of political involvement are particularly acute when the political system is "stacked" and otherwise undemocratic. When a church sides with a government that does not have the public's confidence—or worse, denies the people advancement of their rights and freedoms—that church places its influence in jeopardy, and perhaps risks becoming irrelevant to existing or potential constituencies. Hong Kong's Catholic hierarchy appears to be keenly aware of this reality, although this does not mean that the church is not acting as a matter of conscience in the political arena, for example, in its objections to Hong Kong's electoral system.

When it provided by electoral law for the participation of forty representatives of six religions (Catholicism, Protestantism, Islam, Buddhism, Taoism, and Confucianism) in Hong Kong's electoral affairs, the SAR government hoped to gain the cooperation and active engagement of religious institutions in a political system that is designed to ensure that pro-Beijing forces retain control of power.[8] The SAR government touted this electoral law provision as a step in democratization that would allow certain religionists to have their voices heard in the selection of Hong Kong's top leadership.

In the spring of 1996, prior to the political transition, the Roman Catholic Diocese of Hong Kong held a series of consultations to determine whether the local church should nominate members to participate in a Selection Committee—appointed by Hong Kong's Preparatory Committee—whose responsibility was to "elect" the first chief-executive-designate of the future Hong Kong Special Administrative Region. The name of this nominee was to be forwarded to Beijing for official approval and appointment. The Selection Committee also was charged with the task of nominating the members of the Provisional Legislature, which would replace the elected legislature of 1995, determinedly abolished before the end of its four-year term as a hard-line demonstration that Beijing would not tolerate the steps in democratization made by Britain's last governor. Provisions for a Selection Committee had been made in 1990 in the *Decision of the National People's Congress* [NPC] *on the Method for the Formation of the First Government and the First Legislative Council of the Hong Kong Special Administrative Region*, which was adopted by the Preparatory Committee for the SAR, under the auspices of the NPC, at its fourth plenary session on August 10, 1996. The Preparatory Committee members, who included the local leaders of the Anglican Church and the Hong Kong Buddhist Association, all were appointed by Beijing.

Cardinal John B. Wu of Hong Kong's Roman Catholic diocese and the Board of Diocesan Consultors concluded that the Catholic diocese would nominate some church members to serve on the Selection Committee who would be lay persons, members of religious orders, or clerics—but not persons who were canonically appointed members of the Diocesan Curia. These representatives were permitted by the church to participate in the selection of the chief executive nominee, but not in the process of choosing legislators to remove legitimately elected legislators from their seats.[9]

On the advice of the Diocesan Pastoral Council, Cardinal Wu established an ad hoc committee to prepare regulations for church members who wished to join the Selection Committee. Each Catholic who desired to participate was required to obtain an application form from the Hong Kong Office of the Secretariat of the Preparatory Committee and to present to that office a personal identity card. A completed application form then was to be submitted to the church's Chancery Office, accompanied by duplicate copies of the applicant's identity card, birth certificate, and testimonials of profession and offices and positions held in the church and other public sectors. The Catholic Church stated emphatically that the Chancery Office would be responsible only for certifying that the applicant was a Catholic and for sending the completed application with attachments to the Secretariat of the Preparatory Committee. Applicants themselves were responsible for the truth of their representations, not the church.[10] Thus, diligent efforts were made to keep the church as an institution as remote as possible from the Selection Committee processes.

In 1997, the diocese publicly raised stronger concerns about Hong Kong's electoral system. In July of that year, the SAR government released a consultation document on the first election of Hong Kong's legislature under China's sovereignty. It revealed that the fully appointed Provisional Legislative Council would be replaced through elections held in May 1998 for a new legislature returned by a combination of disparate electoral methods. The church took note that the public was given only one week to respond to the consultation document, which ostensibly solicited public comment about which groups should fill nineteen seats, or virtually one-third of the sixty-seat legislature. The government's proposal recommended that nine seats be determined by nine new functional constituencies[11] and that the remaining ten seats should be chosen by an eight-hundred-member Election Committee. The government also called for believers from the six mentioned Hong Kong religions to vote as members of the Election Committee in representation of their respective religious communities.

The government's proposals prompted the Catholic Bishop's Office to express its views to the government, to Catholics, and to Hong Kong's citizens. At the time of consultations on the drafting of the Basic Law in the 1980s, the Bishop's Office had voiced concern about why it was necessary to include the religious sector in the Election Committee. It maintained that religions should promote "harmony and communion" among themselves and with society as a whole, implying that the church's involvement in politics would work against Catholic principles and missions. It also made known its displeasure with the government's reservation of "religious seats" on the Election Committee on the ground that this was an injustice against unbelievers. A third complaint vented by the church leadership was that representatives of only six religions would be permitted to participate in the Election Committee's deliberations, an unmistakable slight to Hong Kong's other faiths.[12]

The Bishop's Office made note that an official from the Constitutional Affairs Bureau of the Government Secretariat had consulted the leaders of the six designated religions with regard to the method for determining the electorate within the religious sector. In disapproval of the government's method, the Catholic hierarchy categorically stated, "The diocese has no intention of participating in a delineation for which it is impossible to have objective standards."[13] The church further disputed the government's method of returning all Election Committee members, pointing out its undemocratic nature that, in part, was owed to no alternatives ever having been offered. The hierarchy insisted that the method of returning Election Committee members was very important as it would "determine whether the whole arrangement [was] acceptable or not."[14]

In February 1998, the Catholic diocese formally expressed its disapproval regarding the government's arrangements for the Election Committee, noting it had done so on several previous occasions, and urged the government to amend its electoral methods. Nevertheless, to demonstrate its recognition of the Basic Law and its respect for the rights of Catholics as individuals, the diocese accepted a "provisional arrangement" and offered "passive cooperation." The church hierarchy was unequivocal, however, that diocesan authorities would not select or nominate candidates. Moreover, the leadership made it clear that candidates would not be official representatives of the church.[15]

Prior to the May 1998 Legislative Council elections, the Catholic Church's Chancery Office issued *Guidelines on Participation of Parishes and Church Organizations in Election Activities.* Originally promulgated on August 11, 1995, the guidelines had been amended to bring them abreast of the latest relevant civil legislation. The instructions were issued to ensure that Hong Kong's Catholics were in stride with the social teachings of the worldwide Catholic Church. Those teachings encourage Catholics to participate in elections "under the guidance of their Christian conscience and with the enlightenment of the Gospel."[16]

Individual Catholic voters were asked to consider issues facing local society and to weigh needs demanding attention for the common good. However, they also were advised to scrutinize the capabilities and integrity of candidates, including their philosophies and values. Thus, the Catholic Church provided lessons in civic obligations and conduct and told its parishes and church organizations to exhort the faithful to fulfill their civic responsibilities and to exercise their civil rights both by voting and standing for election. The church at large was counseled to organize talks and seminars on the teachings of the Catholic Church, Hong Kong's political system, and social analysis.[17] One may surmise that the church wished to pinpoint for its members discrepancies between church teachings and the many undemocratic aspects of Hong Kong's electoral system. The Bishop's Office permitted the premises of parishes, church organizations, and social centers and units to be used for political forums at the request of candidates, with the provisos that access be made available to all candidates and the premises never reserved for particular candidates or political parties or groups. While taking an active role in promoting civic responsibility, the church also took careful steps to stay removed from partisan politics. Thus, the hierarchy forbade parishes, church organizations, clergy, and other church professionals to exercise their religious authority in the political field. That included a ban on clergy and religious standing for election, or, in either their own names or as a group, lobbying for or endorsing a particular candidate or political party or group, either through support or opposition.[18]

In 1999, the displeasure of the diocese with electoral affairs in Hong Kong was disclosed again by its request to withdraw from participation in the Election Committee for the pending 2000 Legislative Council elections. Once more, Hong Kong's six major religious communities were expected to participate in the Election Committee of eight hundred mostly nonelected members, this time to select persons to fill six, or one-tenth, of the Legislative Council seats.[19]

In a letter to the head of the Constitutional Affairs Bureau, the Catholic diocese asserted that the Election Committee was unfair and undemocratic. Requesting to be excused from participation, the diocese reiterated that Catholic tradition did not embrace church bodies' direct involvement in politics. Although still acknowledging the right of Catholics as individuals to engage in political activity, the diocese charged that the Election Committee was "'against the principle of fairness and openness of an election,'" and said that the diocese, therefore, did not want to be associated with it.[20]

Some religious groups believed that the Basic Law *required* the six named religions to participate in the Election Committee, and consequently disagreed with the Catholic diocese's stance. However, the interpretation the Catholic Church chose to make of the Basic Law guidelines for selecting the legislature was that a right had been extended to the six religions to participate in the election process, but the religions were not under any obligation to do so. Thus, the Catholic Church determined, indeed, it had a choice.

The general secretary of the Hong Kong Christian Council, whose members are twenty-one Protestant churches, denominations, and organizations, reasoned that Protestant participation in the Election Committee was less controversial than in the case of Catholics because a democratic election would be held among the various Protestant churches to elect the Protestants' allotted seven representatives. A second rationale for Protestant involvement was that it would be unwise to withdraw from participation and leave religious representation in the Election Committee to non-Christians. It must be noted, however, that the general secretary did not view participation as a matter of choice, saying that if a choice were allowed, the council would have declined to take part in the Election Committee. The leader of the Evangelical Lutheran Church publicly concurred.[21]

The Reverend Kwok Nai Wang, then director of the Protestant Hong Kong Christian Institute, observed that most Protestant leaders endorsed participation in the rigged and undemocratic Election Committee in the belief it would help to preserve the status quo. Still, he noted that some Protestant leaders urged fellow religionists who viewed Election Committee participation favorably to reconsider and follow the lead of the Catholic Church. Kwok expressed his belief that non-Christian religions would support the government—right or wrong—absent the prophetic tradition of Protestants to be "'a critical voice in society.'" Indeed, the Taoist Association and the Chinese Muslim Cultural and Fraternal Association confirmed their intentions to participate in the Election Committee, maintaining there had been no debate within their religious constituencies over whether to do so. Buddhist and Confucian leaders participated without comment.[22]

In 2000, following discussions between the Catholic Diocese and the Constitutional Affairs Bureau of the SAR, an amendment to the provisions for the Religious Subsector under the Election Committee was approved by the Legislative Council. This permitted the Catholic diocese to limit itself to "a 'more passive' collaboration" in the 2000 Legislative Council elections than was the case in the elections of 1998. Now, the Diocesan Curia was required only to verify Catholic identity of church members wanting to join the Election Committee and to present the full name list to the competent returning officer.[23] Seven Catholics did join thirty-three other religionists from the five other sanctioned religions on the eight-hundred-member Election Committee, but their participation was in a purely private capacity. Thus, some religionists seated in the Election Committee were official representatives of their religious communities, while others participated solely on the basis of personal interest.

Observers sympathetic to the government have argued that the provision for six religions to participate in what democrats call undemocratic and manipulated "small-circle" elections, is a sign that the SAR administration has made an earnest effort to be inclusive in the electoral process by ensuring that a significant cross-section of Hong Kong's religious sector is represented. In sharp disagreement, critics maintain that the SAR government has co-opted and domesticated most of the SAR's major religions through electoral arrangements that draw them into participation in an undemocratic process, giving an impression to the public that SAR religious institutions sanction electoral arrangements that have been engineered to produce a government-favorable outcome.

The Catholic Church has sought fairness and equality in the electoral process and has asked the government to amend its system through a sense of justice and change of heart. However, this request and the church's refusal to participate in the undemocratic system places the church in opposition to the government, which has designed a complex "homegrown" electoral scheme that assures officials in Beijing and their appointed representatives in Hong Kong regarding who will be in charge. The church does not seek authority over the government. Rather, in the prophetic tradition, it has called upon the government to rise to a higher standard than it has set for itself. And in this, as in the case of the prophets of old, it risks being viewed by government leaders as playing a subversive role—and as unpatriotic.

Government Threats to the Influence of the Catholic Church in Hong Kong Through Its Schools

Although the Catholic Church has aired its concern regarding Hong Kong's electoral practices, skeptics reasonably question how genuine the church's voice can be as a counterwitness since the government heavily subsidizes Catholic schools, for generations the vital contact point for spreading Catholic influence in the community.[24] Because the Catholic Church runs more schools in Hong Kong than any other school-sponsoring body (SSB), it places a major lifeline to the church's influence in Hong Kong in jeopardy if its relationship with the government deteriorates. Indeed, some Christian critics of the local Catholic diocese have asserted the church is insufficiently prophetic because it and Protestant churches are financially beholden to the government for the survival of their educational and social welfare programs. Thus, detractors say the Christian mainline churches historically have been self-seeking in accepting patronage from the government, making it impossible for church leaders to press on the government ideas that their understanding of the Gospel demands.[25] In short, many democrats argue that the mainline churches' institution-building has come at the price of diminished power in prophetic politics. According to critics, once Christian churches accepted funding from the government, they no longer could truly stand as uncompromised voices in civil society to hold the government accountable.

But, assessing the political merits of the Catholic and other churches' acceptance of government subvention is beside the point at this historical juncture, because this was a long-established practice under British rule. Further, it is a practice that ostensibly is protected by the Basic Law. What matters is that, in terms of church leadership of schools and other outreach programs to the community, since 1997, the dependence of religious institutions on the government has had a clear downside in matters of control of religious missions.

History of Government-Subsidized Religious Education in Hong Kong

During Hong Kong's more than 150 years of British colonial history, a partnership developed between the community's churches and the British Hong Kong government to build Hong Kong's educational sector. Religionists' involvement in education began at the outset of British rule following the Treaty of Nanking, when Hong Kong Island was ceded to Great Britain in perpetuity by China at the conclusion of the Opium War of 1839–1842. The Morrison Education Society, begun in Macao in 1839, moved to Hong Kong in 1842, to become the colony's first mission school, with the goal of training Chinese minds for creative thinking in an age that demanded accommodation of progress.[26] Hong Kong's first resident missionary, the Reverend Issachar J. Roberts, a Baptist, opened a school in Stanley about the same time, although it was short-lived. The Reverend James Legge of the London Missionary Society relocated from Malacca to Hong Kong in 1843, bringing with him nine converts, of whom the younger formed the nucleus of a reorganized Anglo-Chinese college, originally founded in Malacca in 1819. The same year, the Reverend Elijah Bridgman of the American Board of Commissioners for Foreign Missions arrived from Macao to open a chapel, school, and dispensary. Roman Catholics, too, began educational activities in 1843 by establishing a school for Chinese boys. Anglicans entered the mix in a significant way in 1851, with funds brought to Hong Kong by the first Bishop of Victoria, the Right Reverend George Smith, when the school begun in 1847 by the Anglican colonial chaplain, the Reverend Vincent Stanton, was reorganized into St. Paul's College. St. Paul's was to become, and still is, one of Hong Kong's most prestigious boys' schools. Thus, missionaries of many Christian persuasions, who were the pioneers of education in Hong Kong, arrived to spread the Gospel and to convert those who were outside Christendom through evangelization. By means of their schools, missionaries hoped to convert and "civilize" the Chinese and otherwise improve their lives. Another significant educational goal was to nurture local Chinese as Christian catechists, evangelists, and pastors. Because of the urgent need, missionaries sought to develop among the Chinese skills that would allow them to translate and write Christian literature.[27] Although encouraged by the government, the missionaries received little financial support from it.

In sum, for almost two decades, education in Hong Kong was left principally in the hands of Protestant and Catholic foreign missionaries. However, a turn of events occurred in 1860, when the government's Education Committee, established in 1847 to oversee government aid to schools, was transformed into Hong Kong's first Board of Education. Legge, a missionary and also a board member, paradoxically was a strong proponent of secular education. As Carl T. Smith observed,

> As in all the missionary schools, the main objective was the conversion of the students, but for this the missionary had to wait for the evidence of "pious conviction" and the work of the Spirit. Therefore, they set out to "discipline the mind and give them [Chinese students] a knowledge of English, as the medium through which they should acquire knowledge."[28]

Under Legge's direction, Central School was opened in 1862 to advance the use of the English language and scientific understanding among Chinese students, and with time, secularized schools became the norm.

The government had a rude awakening in 1867, however, when a study it conducted revealed that 87 percent of Hong Kong's 12,400 school-aged children were unschooled. By 1873, a Grant-in-Aid program was in place to encourage missions, other organizations, and private individuals to open schools. As an inducement to missionaries, the government pledged not to interfere in the teaching of religious subjects.[29] Thus, missions reemerged in Hong Kong as a major force in education and their schools became highly regarded.

During the 1950s to 1970s, Hong Kong experienced rapid growth that was so fast-paced that the government found it expedient to rely on nongovernmental resources to meet the demands of an explosive population. Most churches in Hong Kong are indigenous Chinese parishes. Assisted by governmental subsidies, these Chinese ministries opened church schools at a rapid pace, which helped to fill the gap between growing educational demands and the limited resources of the government. Increased educational demands arose through three causes: a postwar baby boom, immigration of Chinese from the mainland fleeing the excesses of communist oppression, and the implementation of compulsory education in two phases in the 1970s, resulting in nine years of compulsory schooling. Thus, the expanding need for education led to the Christian churches' becoming a major influence in Hong Kong's educational system. Today, that influence remains profound, as shown by the data on secondary schools alone (see Table 8.1).

Of Hong Kong's 512 secondary day schools, 29 percent are operated by Protestants and 20 percent by Catholics. Together, Protestants and Catholics run 250, or 49 percent of Hong Kong's secondary day schools. Of these 250 schools, 212, or 85 percent, are heavily subsidized by the government. All non-Christian religions together operate only thirty-eight, or some 7 percent of the SAR's secondary day schools. Among Christians, Catholics run the largest number of schools in Hong Kong. Altogether, including kindergartens, primary, secondary, and other schools, Catholic sponsors, by themselves, run 323 schools, which serve 285,327 students.[30]

Sweeping Educational Reforms in the Hong Kong SAR

Early in 1998, the Education Commission of the newly formed SAR government, then chaired by Antony K.C. Leung (later, Hong Kong's chief financial secretary, who was forced by scandal to resign on July

Table 8.1

Number of Secondary Day School Locations by Sector by Religious Background of School (2000)

Sector	No religion	Catholic	Protestant	Buddhist	Taoist	Confucian	Muslim	Total
Government	36							36
Aided	119	85	127	22	11	1	1	366
Private	69	17	21	2		1		110
All Sectors	224	102	148	24	11	2	1	512

Source: Enrollment Statistics 2000, Statistics Section, Education Department (Hong Kong), 130.

16, 2003) started a review of Hong Kong's educational system to study in three phases: (1) the aims of education in the twenty-first century, (2) the direction and overall framework for reforming the educational system, and (3) proposals for the reform of the educational system.[31] The commission conducted three rounds of public consultation from January 22, 1999, to July 31, 2000, which entailed some three hundred sessions. Commission members claimed they had received over thirty thousand written suggestions and comments, showing both interest and concern. While Leung said the public agreed "to the principles and directions of the reform in general," he admitted that there were worries the reform scheme was too broad and that there would be too many drastic changes to which students, parents, teachers, and other parties would have difficulties adapting.[32] Nevertheless, the government decided to move forward on vast restructuring of Hong Kong's educational system. Some of the proposals have been realized; others are still under advisement regarding the modes to be adopted before implementation.[33] However, many religious SSBs adamantly oppose the government's views and the Tung Chee-hwa administration's Education (Amendment) Bill 2002, which was passed in July 2004 by a 29 to 21 vote in the Legislative Council[34] and will come into full effect in 2006. Indeed, the Catholic Church publicly indicated that it might sue the government on the grounds that the legislation infringes on the rights of religious organizations to manage their own affairs. The Parents' Alliance, an organization of parents with children in government-funded schools, has observed: "'The issue is the government wants to undermine the existing power of sponsoring bodies . . . it wants to increase its power by setting up incorporated management committees which are only answerable to the government for running schools.'"[35] William McGurn of the *Wall Street Journal* observed that the new laws are deliberately "designed to gain control over the Catholic schools, which educate a good chunk of the citizenry."[36]

The government's perspective is that there is an urgent need to reshape educational programs to meet the demands of a new society. Citing the transformation of industrial economies to knowledge-based ones in many areas of the world, the government underscores the necessity to create, update, and apply knowledge in ways that will maintain Hong Kong's prosperity. A fresh approach to education is considered essential to harnessing new technologies, developing new industries, adopting competitive business strategies and modes of operation, and nurturing creative people who are able to cope with the challenges of a transformed international environment.

The Education Commission has identified shortcomings that it insists must be overcome. One is that the people of Hong Kong lack historical awareness and contemporary appreciation of the motherland, the PRC. The commission gives the purported success of the "one country, two systems" formula and the closeness of the relationship between the SAR and the mainland as reasons that students and others should enhance their understanding of China and its culture and strengthen their sense of belonging and commitment to the nation.[37]

In addressing the new role and functions of education in Hong Kong, the commission points to what it perceives are the inadequacies of the British-established educational system. Although acknowledging that "many of [Hong Kong's] high quality schools have produced large numbers of outstanding students who have played key roles in both our society and at the national level," an underlying theme of the sweeping reform is that education under the British was driven by elitism and that it is time for a leveling among schools to "enable the majority of Hong Kong people to achieve lifelong learning and all-round education."[38] The commission expresses its dissatisfaction with Hong Kong's existing approach this way:

> All in all, despite the huge resources put into education and the heavy workload endured by teachers, learning effectiveness of students remains not very promising; learning is still examination-driven and scant attention is paid to "learning to learn." School life is usually monotonous, students are not given comprehensive learning experiences and have little room to think, explore and create. The pathways to lifelong learning are not as smooth as they should be. To make up for these weaknesses we need to uproot outdated ideology and develop a new education system that is student-focused.[39]

Reminiscent of zealous ideological campaigns in the PRC, the commission has called for society-wide mobilization, which includes the government, the education sector, various other segments of society, and learners, all of whom are "obliged to make contributions."[40] To the relief of those who are concerned that the reforms are geared exclusively toward advancing the materialistic aspects of society, the commission acknowledges, "It is the society's expectation that education should enrich our moral, emotional, spiritual and cultural life so that we can rise above the material world and lead a healthy life."[41]

Trouble Brews for Christian-Sponsored Education

Already fearful that the government's plan to reform the educational system was aimed at their schools, alarm among Christian school-sponsoring bodies was heightened when Secretary of Education and Manpower Fanny Law Fan fired off a letter of criticism to the chairman of the Grant Schools Council on January 30, 2001. She lambasted the twenty-two Grant Schools of Hong Kong for a variety of failures. The charges leveled at these "traditional élite schools," as they were labeled, all of which are run by Roman Catholics or Protestants, painted the schools as stultifying in their conservatism and reliance on past laurels. These schools, Law had claimed, produce dull students who lack spontaneity, creativity, and self-confidence. This state of affairs Law attributed to conventional and rote methods of teaching, which she asserted did not match the advanced methods of Hong Kong's international schools. She cited "a strong sense of dissatisfaction with traditional élite schools," causing a flood of irate and defensive letters from participants in these schools, conveying outrage for the perceived injustice and bias of Law's remarks. Students, parents, and teachers at the Roman Catholic St. Stephen's Girls' College, for instance, rushed to the barricades to defend their learning programs and activities, express their overwhelming satisfaction with the school, and ask: "What is wrong with a school's treasuring a good past, and building on prior successes?" Representing the sentiments of many, one teacher inquired: "How could these past and present successes suddenly become a burden to continued success?" Rebutting that the Grant Schools were out-of-date and unwilling to change, as Law had claimed, another teacher queried, "[Since] most of [the students'] parents are financially sound enough to send [their children] to international schools . . . why do these parents still go to great lengths to try to get a place in our school?"[42] Most participants in the twenty-two Grant Schools, some of which date to the 1800s, found Law's criticism ill-informed and disturbingly biased, and asserted that her designation, "traditional élite schools," was designed purposely to create public prejudice against the schools as "exclusive" and "specially privileged."

Defenders further argued that, through their long histories, the Grant Schools had witnessed many reforms, and, consequently, had found a model that suited the needs of students and the expectations of parents. If Grant Schools did not meekly follow the directives of the Education

Department, it was because the schools had well-established and time-honored systems that had produced many of Hong Kong's most prominent and productive citizens.

The conclusion of Grant School defenders was that, at the very least, Law had been careless and ill-advised in her attack. The final result of her barrage of criticism, the defenders said, was that Law had "implanted misconceptions and aroused confusion in the public toward Grant Schools," causing damage to the schools' public image.[43] Other defenders called the attack a tactless gesture from a high-ranking government officer, pointing out that the Grant Schools had been accorded a high status, not because of history and seniority, as Law had professed, but because generations of Hong Kong people had placed a high premium on sending their children to these schools as a result of the excellent caliber of their graduates.

Sea Change for Church-Run Schools

Comments made by two legislators during the February 21, 2000, meeting of the Legislative Council's Educational Affairs Subcommittee, added to the anxieties of Christian sponsors of schools. The legislators remarked that most of the government-subsidized schools were dominated by the management of a limited number of sponsoring bodies. Of the top ten sponsoring organizations, six are Christian.[44] Together, these six Christian SSBs manage more than 440 Hong Kong schools. Over 40 percent of Hong Kong's primary schools and 56 percent of its secondary schools are affiliated with religious organizations, mainly Christian.[45]

Yet, regardless of the long history and important role of church-run schools in Hong Kong, their critics are outspoken. Siding with Fanny Law, some well-respected residents, such as the former president of the American Chamber of Commerce in Hong Kong (a Roman Catholic), assert that, although society has changed with the times, church-run schools remain antiquated. In agreement with the government, secular detractors complain that, despite strong criticism by teachers and parents for years, religious sponsors of schools have not appropriately responded with revisions to policies and practices.[46]

Therefore, school-based management (SBM) is central to the reforms initiated by the government, ostensibly to advance openness, accountability, and democracy in Hong Kong's educational facilities. Many religionists, however, view SBM first and foremost as a direct challenge by the government to religious-based education, the aim of which is not only to equip students to contribute to the economic development of society, but also to instill in them an appreciation of truth, the commitment to love one's neighbor, and other values central to the Christian faith. In sum and substance, many Christians see SBM as serious governmental infringement of religious freedom, most especially for the following reasons.

Under the SBM system, no Christian or other school-sponsoring body can appoint more than 60 percent of the school managers (or the school governance council) in each school. A minority, or 40 percent of a school's managers, will be representatives of teachers, parents, alumni, or segments of the community who likely will not be Christian. These representatives are to be appointed by their respective constituencies. Given that a school sponsor can appoint the majority of positions, at first blush, it appears that the sponsor easily can maintain control of its schools. However, the reality is quite different. There are too few Catholic or other religious professionals in Hong Kong to fill the majority of management positions in the many schools that Christian denominations run.[47] In the past, a religionist could serve in a management capacity in more than one school that was sponsored by his or her denomination. But with the end of this practice, there will be too few religionists to fill the number of management slots.[48] In Catholic schools today, 99 percent of the teachers are lay persons. Priests, sisters, and brothers comprise only one percent of the teaching staffs. Of the lay teachers, the majority (72.63 percent) are non-Catholics.[49] Given such patterns in Christian-run schools, Catholics and Protestants look glumly toward the probability that, with changes to the school management committees, they will be overruled in their desire to have Christian-based education a priority in church-run schools.

As previously described, there is in Hong Kong a long history of government grants to churches to operate their schools. Religionists concur with the Education Commission that the public deserves accountability in return. Yet, in the view of church leaderships, accountability for conduct must extend beyond the minimum standards required by the government, to Christian teachings pertaining to morality and justice. In view of the changes to the educational system, many religionists are concerned that the government will introduce compulsory teaching requirements that contradict the tenets of Christianity, in general, or of their respective denominations, in particular. For example, Bishop

Joseph Zen Ze-Kiun, leader of the Roman Catholic Diocese of Hong Kong, contemplates that, at some point, the government will introduce on a compulsory-use basis texts that include positive views on matters held by the church to be offensive, possibly including teachings that diminish the sanctity and rights of individuals. This would include advocacy of abortion. In such instance, Bishop Zen explains, the church could not participate in propagating acceptance by students of practices that the church regards as displeasing to God. Under this circumstance, he says, the local church would have to reevaluate its role in education.[50] While the enforcement of an objectionable curriculum on religious-based schools might seem remote to casual observers, it is not inconceivable to Catholic clergy. Indeed, some believe that the SAR government is taking intentional steps to have mainland-produced texts at the core of all education in Hong Kong within the first decade of coming to power.[51]

A Hydra lurks in the Christian schools, each fearsome head a serious problem with which the Catholic and other Christian churches now must duel. Besides revised incorporated management committees held accountable to the government (about which more will be said) and the government's teaching requirements, both of which threaten religious influence in schools and the community, a third head could devour religious institutions. Hong Kong is known for its inflated land prices, which place the purchase of property beyond the capability of most churches. The majority own neither land nor structures. With scarce financial resources, an alternative for churches has been to use government-funded schools they operate for religious activities and services on weekends. However, because the government owns the properties, the churches are vulnerable to the will of the government to permit religious functions to occur on school sites. Two costly scenarios—each potentially ruinous in its own way—loom large. One is that the government will charge unaffordable rent for space used for religious functions; the other is that the government could disallow religious activities on publicly funded school properties altogether. A third possibility is that the government will permit the churches to carry on their religious activities as in the past, yet church leaders are mindful that the SAR government does not view Christian religions with the same eye as that of its British predecessor, which entered a partnership of sorts with them. Indeed, some Christians perceived a leaning of the government toward Buddhism under the Tung Chee-hwa administration, noting that Tung, Hong Kong's

Beijing-appointed chief executive from 1997 to 2005, is a Buddhist.[52] They conjecture that the slant toward Buddhism that they have sensed perhaps is a balancing measure against Christian influence in society, which was substantial, especially through schools, social welfare programs, and health care, under British rule.

Regardless, the current use of government-funded schools by Christian churches for religious purposes poses disquieting hazards. On Christmas Day 2000, a local Chinese newspaper *Tung Fong Yat Po* [Oriental daily news] charged that the Catholic diocese owed millions of dollars to the SAR government in rent for use of school buildings for "religious activities." Accusing the church of fraud for not paying rent, the paper said the church had failed in its moral leadership. Although within a few days the government assured diocesan officials that schools were acting within the law in their use of premises for such activities, concerns were raised that the attack represented the beginning of an initiative by Beijing to take control of the schools and remove Catholics from the educational sector.[53]

Because of the government's educational reform program and concerns about future infringements on religious education, Catholic and Protestant leaders now are asking themselves hard questions: Have changes occurred since 1997 in the relationship between the government and the Christian churches that threaten the latter's missions? In the future, will church leaders truly be decision makers in the schools they operate, or will they be marginalized by the government, non-Christian school managers, and a secular agenda? Despite Basic Law articles 137, 141, and others, which presumably protect the rights of churches to operate schools and provide religious-based education, including courses in religion, does the future bode well for religious supervision and instruction if the voices of non-Christian school managers and teachers build in opposition to the use of government funds for such purposes? As pioneers in Hong Kong's educational system at the invitation of the British Hong Kong government, will church SSBs soon sink into a subservient role and find lost to them their heavy investments of money, personnel, and other resources to provide universal and upgraded education to Hong Kong citizens?

Divide et Impera

Many religionists view the educational reform policy as a distinct power struggle between the government and the Christian churches, which pits the authoritarian power of the former against the persuasive authority of the latter. Some describe the reforms as a bold strategy of *divide et impera*, and as evidence that the government does not trust the Christian churches.[54] These Christians define the battle as one over the division of responsibility and power in schools. Specifically, they view the government as determined to restructure the relations between religious school-sponsoring bodies, such as the Roman Catholic Church and the Anglican Church, and the schools' management committees.

One complaint raised by religionists is that some of the Education Commission's consultations were bogus. A case in point is the school-based management advisory committee, which studied management committees and supervisory roles. This group claimed that its members consulted with sponsoring bodies. But it is unclear to at least some religious sponsors which advisory members discussed management committees with what sponsoring bodies. Furthermore, a leader of one chief religious sponsor of schools asserts that no minutes were available to church leaders of the alleged discussions. Thus, religionists have charged that the Education Commission launched a profound reform program on the basis of enhancing participation, accountability, and transparency, but has not adhered to these principles itself.

At the core of the church–state battle is the tension many religionists say the government is stirring between the managers and supervisors of schools. They maintain that, under the British system, there was an effective division of responsibilities and powers in government-subsidized schools. Those who fear deterioration of religious rights believe the government now has placed the position of school supervisor in jeopardy as a way to strip a religious SSB of responsibility, authority, and power.

Church leaders maintain that, in keeping with democratic principles, a school indeed should function with the participation of those involved. Students, parents, teachers, staff, and key members of the community who have a recognized interest in education should be consulted in a school's operation. What troubles Christian churches in the SAR, however, is that the government appears to be shrouding in democratic rhetoric the true intent of the reform of management committees, which they believe is to elevate non-Christian authority in them so that decisions can be made beyond the control of Christian SSBs.

The understanding of management committees held by religionists is that they are supervisory bodies responsible for personnel and financial matters. Under the British-established system, a school-sponsoring body, *in collaboration with* the school supervisor and management committee, has been accountable to the government for personnel policies and practices. This includes the hiring, management, promotion, and dismissal of principals and teachers. Because they are responsible and accountable for personnel, church SSBs have adhered to government requirements, but also they have been able to fulfill their Christian visions of education. This includes attention to moral education, the Golden Rule, and reverence to God.

However, the reform plans are not clear as to where the responsibility for personnel will reside in the future. To assist a school with human resource management, some churches have higher-level bodies from which administrators and management committees have been able to draw support. For example, Hong Kong's Catholic Church has a Central Management Committee and a Catholic Education Office to assist schools in the complex duty of personnel management. Nevertheless, an apprehension now raised among religious sponsors of schools is whether personnel management will become the exclusive domain of the new incorporated management committees, composed in part of parents and alumni whose judgments quite possibly will be compromised by conflicts of interest. Christian sponsors also argue it would be equally inappropriate for the responsibility for personnel to be passed to salaried principals and teachers, who themselves are the subjects of this management, and likely to have a biased approach to personnel policies. Church SSBs maintain that recommendations should continue to be made by the sponsoring body, based on consultation with the professional school supervisor and staff.

The government plan also is unclear regarding the role of the school supervisor, him- or herself, who, under the British system, was the important bridge between the school-sponsoring body and the frontline staff. The supervisor attended management committee meetings and was onsite with administrative and teaching staff daily. What religionists anticipate is that the power of the principal will expand under the new plan, perhaps in part by his or her being the chairman of the management committee. If this becomes reality, further question is raised about who, if not the government directly, is going to supervise the principal.

Religionists' concerns about supervision also are attached to financial matters. Sponsoring bodies generally are nonprofit organizations. In the years when the government lacked resources to meet the growing educational demands of Hong Kong, churches voluntarily lent vast support. They paid for many of the buildings in which current government-subsidized school programs run. And although the government itself started to build school structures, it continued to rely on sponsoring bodies for partial support. When finally the government built schools on its own, it entrusted not only the schools to the churches, but also the supervision of financial matters. Through local and foreign church membership, over the years, religious institutions have provided materials and resources to the schools to enhance the learning environment beyond the limited capabilities of government subvention. The advantage, as religionists see it, is that financial accountability has resided with a nonprofit religious organization that can draw on supporting structures. What religionists now question is whether the members of newly structured management committees, who are salaried or have other conflicts of interest, will manage finances as carefully and as selflessly as (they maintain) they have.

While the reform plan indicates that there will be decentralization of power to lower segments of the educational system, skeptics observe that this does not correspond to governmental trends in Hong Kong. Because in the run-up to 1997 officials in Beijing used harsh rhetoric and tough tactics to hinder democratization, Christian SSBs are dubious about the Education Department's promises. Many of them suspect the true government agenda is to eradicate the chance that religious SSBs can block the changes to Hong Kong's educational system that the government plans. Indeed, they are wary that the government is resolute in wresting power and influence in the educational sector from the Christian churches by instituting changes that make religious school-sponsoring bodies unconnected, unimportant, and unnecessary.

Even distrustful religionists agree that some educational reforms are needed.[55] But they sense that a conspiracy of the government against the Christian churches has been launched, and it is cloaked in terminology of democracy, participation, transparency, dynamism, and accountability. Who, they ask, will be opposed? Those who believe the government is determined to erode the Christian churches' important role in education, are equally convinced that many well-intentioned people in Hong Kong and abroad, taken unaware, will be drawn into a united front against the churches' rights to provide education, including religious instruction—rights presumably carried forward from colonial rule to PRC sovereignty and protected by the "one country, two systems" pledges of mainland officials and specific articles of Hong Kong's Basic Law.

The educational reforms initiated by the SAR government signal to many Catholics and Protestants in Hong Kong a developing political atmosphere they view as threatening. They fear that the government and the non-Christian culture of Hong Kong are beginning to undermine Christian missions. In Hong Kong's undemocratic political environment, Christians see no means to alter the direction of the changes being made. To some, Hong Kong is now mired in a cultural war—the old traditional mainline churches that have contributed vastly to China's and Hong Kong's modernization (but are viewed by pro-Beijing supporters as un-Chinese and imperialistic) pitted against the rising PRC culture that emanates from the mainland and is nationalistic, anticolonialist, and antireligion, most especially with regard to the Catholic Church that is loyal to Rome.

Christians are only some 9 percent of Hong Kong's population, but they have educated a huge percentage of Hong Kong's people for generations. However, the changes being made in Hong Kong's educational system may be a harbinger that the government will prevent the churches from having the vitality they possessed during the British colonial period. One can expect inroads into their influence to derive from a variety of sources, among them: reduced influence with the progovernment élite; the hostility of non-Christian progovernment Chinese who deride Christian training; and indifference or even opposition by most Chinese to the battles the churches wish to wage (examples are the Catholic Church's determination to celebrate, in October 2000, the canonization of 120 martyrs of China, regardless of official opposition from the mainland, and its struggle for the right of abode for certain mainland Chinese children to join their Hong Kong parents, although the SAR and central governments denied these family reunions that were thought by democrats to be protected by the Basic Law).

The cooperative partnership the Catholic and other Christian churches had in the field of education with the British Hong Kong government is now a relationship with a government that is less inclined to favor Christian churches because of their links to colonialism on the one hand, and to democratic tenets on the other. The dilemma for the Catholic and other Protestant churches is that, if they press the government on human rights and other democratic values that are fundamental to the Christian message, the government will view their influence in schools to be increasingly problematic. The tension between the Catholic Church (and Protestant churches) and the government over the educational policies and practices addressed in this chapter, could come to this: The price to the church of staying engaged in schools will be to sacrifice the teaching of its understanding of the world, which is the essential reason the church became involved in education in Hong Kong in the mid-1800s. Finally, this question must be posed: If Catholic schools provide the same content as the government schools, what special role will they be fulfilling if, under legislation, they are restricted from propagating Catholic moral views?

The Hong Kong Catholic Church's Commitment to the SAR's Democratization

In January 2004, Bishop Zen met with the United States Commission on International Religious Freedom. Xinhua, the mainland official's eyes and ears in Hong Kong, called the commission's visit to the SAR "inappropriate" and "improper" at the time. Originally scheduled to visit China in December 2002, the commission's plans were cancelled in August that year, and again in December 2003, because authorities in Beijing insisted that Hong Kong be excluded from the itinerary. Michael Young, chairperson of the commission, pressed that, "'As a commission concerned [about] religious and related rights, we cannot accede to such a condition.'" When in December 2003 the central government finally agreed to the Hong Kong stopover, it did so demanding that no meetings be held. Risking deepening the ire of mainland officials, Bishop Zen met with members of the commission on the grounds of his never refusing to talk to anyone and Hong Kong's being a city in which persons presumably are free to converse with whomever they want. In the customary fashion of Chinese official warnings, Liu Jianchao, spokesperson for China's Foreign Ministry, warned participants in the commission's visit not to jeopardize Hong Kong's stability and prosperity. Bishop Zen countered, "'The question is, what do they mean by "stability"? There is short-term stability, there is long-term stability. . . [.] Just caring about short-term stability is unwise. . . . Some would like to keep a "false peace". . . but as Holy Father has said, real peace requires justice and love.'" He went on to urge, "'What we really need . . . is a united, concerted effort by the Western powers to remind China that religious freedom belongs to all civilised societies.'"[56]

Bishop Michael Fu Tieshan, a central government appointee, member of the Chinese Catholic Patriotic Association, and a vice chair of the

Tenth National People's Congress, blames, in a not well-masked fashion, Bishop Zen not only for strained relations between the Hong Kong Catholic Church and the central government, but also for complicating relations between the PRC and the Holy See.[57] As described at the outset of this chapter, the Catholic Church has not removed itself from politics; rather, by campaigning for what it views as moral and just and acting as a counterwitness against the SAR and central governments, its leader has placed himself and the church in the vanguard of the region's prodemocracy movement. The conflict between Bishop Zen and the SAR and national governments centers not only on the rights of his and other churches as discussed but also on interpretations of the Basic Law in Beijing, and the governments' reluctance to democratize Hong Kong.

On April 6, 2004, the Standing Committee of the National People's Congress (NPCSC) issued a legally binding interpretation of the Basic Law that requires Hong Kong officials to obtain approval before changing the method of selecting the SAR's chief executive. Annex I.7 of the Basic Law stipulates:

> If there is a need to amend the method for selecting the Chief Executives for the terms subsequent to the year 2007, such amendments must be made with the endorsement of a two-thirds majority of all the members of the Legislative Council and the consent of the Chief Executive, and they shall be reported to the Standing Committee of the National People's Congress for approval.

Thus, the NPC, which promulgated the Basic Law, had crafted assurances that both the Beijing-appointed chief executive and members of the NPCSC would be able to block any changes of which they disapproved. Yet, the promise of the 1984 Sino-British Joint Declaration on the Question of Hong Kong, which professed that Hong Kong people would rule Hong Kong, and the prospect of eventually electing the chief executive and the Legislative Council by universal suffrage, dangled before the public by Basic Law articles 45 and 68, respectively, are thought by democrats to have been badly violated by the April 6 NPCSC interpretation. That the NPCSC mandated the unpopular curtailment of democratic development is widely held to have been in response to the large demonstrations by democrats in Hong Kong since December 2002 for direct elections for the chief executive in 2007 and the full Legislative Council in 2008.

Both the Hong Kong Catholic Bishop's Office and the leadership of the Protestant Hong Kong Christian Council vigorously objected to the NPCSC's having interfered in the constitutional development of the region, noting that its actions raised doubts that the central government would respect the policy of "one country, two systems" in the future. They maintained that the restrictions imposed on the advancement of universal suffrage badly fractured constitutional development in Hong Kong, which they insist should proceed according to public will. These religious leaders caution that discussions on constitutional development were not concluded with the NPCSC's interpretation, and they subsequently have encouraged Christians and other Hong Kong residents to take responsibility for their rights, in part by actively expressing their views. Further, they assert that dialogue concerning constitutional development not only must be genuine but also broadened beyond discussion of the methods for electing the chief executive and legislators, to include a review of the relationship between the executive and legislative branches of government, an evaluation of the Tung Chee-hwa administration's Principal Officials Accountability System (which made all top SAR officials directly responsible to the chief executive and diminished the role of the civil service), scrutiny of advisory and statutory bodies, and more.[58]

Control over government decisions in Hong Kong is vested in the chief executive and his cabinet, which is composed of fourteen Beijing-appointed principals. This tiny minority of unelected officials determines the policies of the SAR. Increasingly, the public has little hope that its voice will prevail unless it takes to the streets as it has been doing repetitively and in huge numbers.

Following July 2003, the Web site of the Hong Kong Catholic Diocese was blocked in the PRC, most likely in response to Bishop Zen's efforts to advance Hong Kong's democratization. The bishop spoke out forcefully against the national security law (which blatantly threatened Hong Kongers' rights and freedoms) that the Tung administration attempted to impose with a heavy hand by July 2003. Owing to a July 1 demonstration that year of some 500,000 persons, the administration, at least temporarily, had to retreat from the proposed legislation and two unpopular principal leaders of the government, the secretary for security and Antony Leung, then the chief financial secretary, were forced to resign. In March 2004, in advance of the NPCSC action, the bishop said that the interpretation, in fact, would be an amendment to the Basic

Law, and that the government could either tighten or relax the amended law, affecting the people's freedom and rights. He argued, "The only way to improve the present situation in the city is to elect a chief executive whom we can vote out of office if his performance is not up to standard."[59] He went on to pray with some three thousand protesters, who then gathered in a candlelight vigil before the Legislative Council building in opposition to the NPCSC's pending interpretation, which would erode electoral arrangements set forth in the Basic Law that had been carefully crafted prior to 1997 to give the illusion that there was a prospect for direct elections through universal suffrage in the first decade of the twenty-first century. Opposition to the interpretation led an estimated twenty thousand persons to join an Easter Sunday (April 11) protest march, at which an unfurled banner appealed to the community to "Fight for democratic elections in 2007 and 2008."

In May, while the government continued to shut out any demand for democracy, the bishop urged "the faithful to join the activities of June 4 and July 1 because they are standing for justice and human rights."[60] Thus, the bishop clarified that the June 4 and July 1 crowds that soon gathered in tens and then hundreds of thousands, did so in political protest, not simply to commemorate historical events. While the June 4 demonstration marked the fifteenth anniversary of the massacre of students at Tiananmen Square, it took place under the cloud of Hong Kongers' loss of hope for universal suffrage and the government's labeling persons who opposed the national security legislation and demanded universal suffrage "anti-China" and "unpatriotic." This included Bishop Zen. Bishop Zen explained, "We join demonstrations to protest against injustices. As Pope John Paul II has said many times: 'peace must be based on justice.'"[61] In sharp contrast, the *South China Morning Post* of May 17, 2004, quoted the headman of the Hong Kong Buddhist Association, the Venerable Sik Kok Kwong, as warning, "We all should not participate in thing[s] like demonstrations," in order to maintain social harmony.[62] Bishop Zen responds that protest is essential to the long-term stability and prosperity of Hong Kong and that the inviolability of the right of demonstration is necessary to show the world that, indeed, the principle of "one country, two systems" is honored by the government. While calling for no violence and only peaceful protests, he asks each member of the faithful to take a "combat position," as a parent, teacher, legal professional, member of the media, or party politician, to "sow seeds of democracy and hope."[63]

Conclusions

Hong Kong's Catholic hierarchy is well aware that the characters of both the SAR and central governments—not to mention that of Hong Kong's people—are crucial in determining the fate of the Catholic Church in the SAR and the prospects for the region's democratization. Catholic leaders, therefore, have been nurturing Catholic and other Hong Kongers to be better equipped spiritually, intellectually, socially, and politically in order to preserve the freedoms and choices they enjoyed under British rule and to dare to demand expanded rights and freedoms, rule of law, and justice in the future. But it is not an easy undertaking for a few wise people to shape the opinions and the will of the multitude, who through Chinese Confucian heritage and a century and a half of British colonial rule, are inclined to acquiesce to governmental preferences with the apology that it is necessary in order to preserve "stability," "social harmony," and "prosperity." What democrats both inside and outside the church fear is that it is far easier for even the wise to be silent and accept despair than to act as counterwitnesses against the government when necessary. Chinese character and customs, Hong Kong's laws and circumstances, a long colonial history, and the PRC's sovereignty are the varied and complicated factors that will determine whether there is hope for democratization of the SAR, and for the preservation of the integrity of its Roman Catholic and other Christian churches. Meanwhile, regardless of the historical answer that awaits, decision makers deliberate under the long shadow of Pope John Paul II, who called on Hong Kong and other Asian youth—the hope of Asia's future—to "be fearless witnesses to the Gospel and builders of the civilization of love and truth."[64]

Tocqueville anticipated that if Americans remained religiously strong and well educated, and maintained their commitment to freedom, rule of law, and responsible government held accountable by independent agents in civil society, the promise of the American democratic revolution would be realized in the benefits of prosperity, stability, peace, and liberal society.[65] In contrast, China's central government has distaste for strong religious leadership and influential communities, those who demand accountable governance, and independent counterwitnesses in civil society who rise to challenge political authority.

"Well educated," too, stands open to interpretation in Hong Kong, as shown in the tensions between Hong Kong's Catholic and other Christian churches and the Education Department of the SAR government. In particular, the churches sense a dangerous enervating taste for "equality," packaged in democratic terms, which threatens to compel religious school-sponsoring bodies to abandon their missions, expectations for students, and instructional content in order to conform to SAR secular norms. While the government asserts it is raising standards, many Christian leaders fear standards are being debased. In the changes to Hong Kong's educational system, which include a move to elevate non-Christians in Christian school management, many Catholics and Protestants sense the mistrust of the SAR and central governments. The two church–state conflicts presented in this chapter share two underlying themes: (1) governmental mistrust of the SAR's people, and (2) the assumption that Hong Kong's pro-Beijing political élite know what is best for the SAR. Further evidence of these governmental attitudes is found in frequent condescending or authoritarian statements of PRC and SAR governmental officials, in the pressures felt by journalists and academicians to engage in self-censorship or to conform, and in Hong Kong's electoral system and legislative voting procedures which are designed by SAR authorities to minimize the risk of voting outcomes.[66] Among pro-Beijing conservatives, the marketplace of political ideas must be closed to all but a select few, in the belief that Chinese people, whether in the mainland or in Hong Kong, are simply too immature to conduct themselves with propriety in a pluralistic, democratic society.

Recognizing the power of churches to be moral forces in society and to rally people to human rights and other democratic causes, the SAR government has tried through electoral modes to manipulate Catholics and Protestants (as well as believers of other faiths) into placing their stamp of approval on an undemocratic electoral system by means of their participation in it. Meanwhile, as many Christian leaders perceive it, officials have begun an effort to undermine Christian influence in Hong Kong. One way is through educational policy changes, described by governmental authorities as democratic and aimed at achieving equality in Hong Kong's educational system, but widely viewed by Christian school-sponsoring bodies as designed to ultimately erase Catholic and Protestant influence among hundreds of thousands of students and their families.

Democracy, of course, requires that paths of choice, including in electoral practices and educational policies, be kept open to all. And, here, Hong Kong's Catholic Church is filling a vital role. For at the foundation of Catholic theology is the belief that each person is a sacred individual, whom God commands must be allowed by the "city of man" to realize his or her full potential. Thus, the Catholic Church is struggling to ensure that freedom of choice is integral to Hong Kong's political system and its schools.

Notes

1. See People's Republic of China, State Council, Central Committee, "Document 19: The Basic Viewpoint and Policy on the Religious Question during Our Country's Socialist Period," in Donald E. MacInnis, *Religion in China Today: Policy & Practice* (Maryknoll, NY: Orbis Books, 1989), 10–26. See especially pp. 10, 15–17, 21, 24–26.

2. Alexis de Tocqueville, *Democracy in America*, ed. J. P. Mayer, trans. George Lawrence (New York: Harper and Row, 1969), 297–99.

3. Like other religious institutions in Hong Kong, the Roman Catholic Church receives substantial financial support from the government for its educational, health care, and social welfare programs, which, of course, compromises its ability to be a counterwitness in society against the government. More will be said about this in the pages ahead.

4. Tocqueville, *Democracy in America*, 269–75.

5. Emily Lau, former reporter for the *Far Eastern Economic Review*, is the leader of a prodemocracy political group, the Frontier, and an outspoken critic of the former Tung Chee-hwa administration. She fought a losing battle to see the records kept on her by Xinhua (now called the Liaison Office), the Chinese Communist Party's outpost in Hong Kong, despite a Personnel Data (Privacy) Ordinance that gives her the right to review data maintained in files that are kept on her. Xinhua claimed that it kept no such file. Lau's legal action against Xinhua failed in 1998, and she was forced to pay HK$1.6 million in legal costs to Jiang Enzhu, the head of the Liaison Office. Lau is one of the directly elected democrats whose seat was denied to her when the 1995 legislature was abolished. She was reelected in the geographical direct elections for the legislature in 1998, 2000, and 2004.

6. The Basic Law was promulgated by the Third Session of the Seventh National People's Congress on April 4, 1990, and became Hong Kong's constitutional document on July 1, 1997.

7. Steven Carter is one of many analysts of church–state relations who have stressed the importance of religious autonomy. See, for example, Stephen L. Carter, *The Culture of Disbelief: How American Law and Politics Trivialize Religious Devotion* (New York: Basic Books, HarperCollins, 1993), 33–43, 136–55, 146–47.

8. For a comprehensive analysis of Hong Kong elections from 1998 through 2000, see the following articles by Deborah A. Brown and James A. Robinson: "Hong Kong's 1998 Legislative Elections," *American Asian Review* 16, no. 4 (Winter 1998): 149–55; "Les Modes de Scrutin à Hong Kong," *Perspectives Chinoises*, no. 47 (May–June 1998): 12–17; "High Turnout in Hong Kong Poses Questions for Future," *Free China Journal*, June 5, 1998, 7; "Hong Kong Voters Send a Message to Beijing," *E-Notes*, Foreign Policy Research Institute, June 19, 1998; "How Hong Kong's Electoral System Works," *China Perspectives* (July–August 1998): 12–16; "Quelles Leçons pour le Processus de Démocratisation?" *Perspectives Chinoises*

(November–December 1998): 31–41; "Hong Kong's 1998 Legislative Council Elections: Appraising Steps in Democratization," *American Asian Review* 17, no. 2 (Summer 1999): 27–71; Deborah A. Brown, "Democracy in Hong Kong: Slow Steps along a Direct Path?" *American Asian Review* 18, no. 1 (Spring 2000): 69–120; and with James A. Robinson and Jermain T.M. Lam: "Voters without a Cause," *Asian Wall Street Journal*, September 12, 2000, 12; "The Second Legislative Council Election in the Hong Kong SAR: The Routinization of Pretended Self-Rule," *E-Notes*, Foreign Policy Research Institute, October 2000; "What Voters Said About Democracy," *China Perspectives*, no. 32 (December–November [sic] 2000): 57–61; "Democracy in the New Hong Kong: Is It a Reality or a Dangerous Fiction," *Taipei Journal*, December 29, 2001, 7; and "Hong Kong Democrats Must Stand United or Fall Alone," *Taipei Journal*, January 5, 2001, 7.

9. Democrats in Hong Kong had handily won the minority of legislative seats for which direct election in geographical constituencies had been allowed in 1991 and 1995. In the 1995 election, they gained enough seats to enable them sometimes, through coalition voting, to have enough votes in the legislature to occasionally shape voting outcomes. It is widely held that, for this reason, the 1995 Legislative Council was dissolved.

10. The Reverend Lawrence Lee, Chancellor, "Chancery Notice," August 16, 1996, in *Sunday Examiner* (Hong Kong), August 23, 1996, 2.

11. Functional constituencies are twenty-eight blocs of voters who are divided by occupational classification, or, in some cases, by political group affiliation, such as Hong Kong delegates to the National People's Congress. Unlike most voters who have one vote, the participants in functional constituencies, who are a very limited number of Hong Kong's people, enjoy two votes per voter in Legislative Council elections: one in the geographical direct election constituencies, and one in the functional constituencies. Different voting procedures apply among the twenty-eight functional constituency groups. Functional constituency voting, by which one-half of the legislature is determined, is undemocratic in effect. See Brown and Robinson, "Hong Kong's 1998 Legislative Council Elections," 35–37.

12. "Diocese Questions Church Role in Election Committee," *Sunday Examiner*, August 10, 1997, 1.

13. Ibid.

14. Ibid.

15. The Reverend Lawrence Lee, Chancellor, "Chancery Notice: Method for Filling the Seven Seats Assigned to the Catholic Diocese of Hong Kong in the Religious Subsector of the Election Committee for the First Legislative Council of the Hong Kong Special Administrative Region (SAR)," January 9, 1998, in *Sunday Examiner*, February 15, 1998, 2.

16. The Reverend Lawrence Lee, Chancellor, "Chancery Notice: Guidelines on Participation of Parishes and Church Organizations in Election Activities," Chancery Office, April 27, 1998, in *Sunday Examiner*, May 10, 1998, 2. The Hong Kong Catholic Church's guidelines were based on: John Paul II, *Pastoral Constitution on the Church in the Modern World*, no. 75; John Paul II, *Post-Synodal Apostolic Exhortation on the Vocation and the Mission of the Lay Faithful in the Church and in the World*, no. 42; and John Paul II, *Encyclical Letter on the Hundredth Anniversary of Rerum Novarum*, nos. 46–47.

17. Ibid.

18. Ibid.

19. The Election Committee was eliminated in the 2004 Legislative Council election, in keeping with the Basic Law annex on methods of selecting the legislature. Beginning in 2004, thirty legislators were returned by direct elections in geographical constituencies and thirty were returned by "small circle" elections in functional constituencies. The Basic Law makes no concrete provision for the majority of legislative seats or the full complement of sixty seats ever to be directly elected by universal suffrage.

20. "Diocese Request to Opt Out of Legco EC Draws Mixed Reaction," *Sunday Examiner*, April 25, 1999, 1.

21. Ibid.

22. Ibid.

23. The Reverend Lawrence Lee, Chancellor, "Chancery Notice: Arrangements for Catholics to Join the Election Committee Religious Subsector for the Second Legislative Council Elections (2000)," Chancery Office, May 15, 2000, in *Sunday Examiner*, May 21, 2000, 2.

24. At the General Meeting of the Diocesan Schools Council on December 12, 2003, Bishop Zen maintained that the Catholic Church would "never cease running schools, for schools were the basic ground for evangelisation." See "Thirty-Third Annual General Meeting of the Diocesan Schools Council" (amended title), *Sunday Examiner*, January 4, 2004, 2.

25. For commentary on the compromised nature of mainline churches, see, for example, Mariana Wan, "Pastor Attacks Church for Lack of Support in 1997 Run-Up," *Sunday Morning Post* (Hong Kong), October 20, 1991, 2; Kwok Nai Wang, "The Preparatory Committee Became Official," *Hong Kong Christian Institute Newsletter*, no. 87, January 2, 1995, 2; Fanny Wong, "Looking to the Church for Guidance," *South China Morning Post*, May 3, 1995; Kwok Nai Wang, "'Looking to the Church for Guidance,'" *Hong Kong Christian Institute Newsletter*, no. 79, May 3, 1995, 2; Kwok Nai Wang, "Speaking Up Does Bear Fruit," *Hong Kong Christian Institute Newsletter*, no. 89, March 4, 1996, 2; Kwok Nai Wang, "Religious Education in Hong Kong," *Hong Kong Christian Institute Newsletter*, no. 109, October 3, 1997, 1–2.

26. Carl T. Smith, *Chinese Christians: Élites, Middlemen, and the Church in Hong Kong* (Hong Kong: Oxford University Press, 1985), 13.

27. Ibid., 10.

28. Ibid., 65.

29. Ng Tze-ming Peter, "Education in Hong Kong: A History of the Churches' Involvement in Schools," *News and Views*, Hong Kong Christian Council (Spring 2000): 4–5.

30. *Hong Kong Catholic Church Directory 2001* (Hong Kong: Catholic Truth Society, December 2000), 592. The breakout of Catholic schools is as follows: 38 kindergartens, 151 primary, 79 secondary and middle, 9 prevocational, 3 vocational, 25 adult education, 5 evening, 11 special, and 2 post-secondary. Of all students in Catholic schools, only 7.21 percent are Catholic. Of the 11,724 teachers in Catholic schools, 11,564 are lay teachers. Of these, 27.37 percent are Catholic.

31. Hong Kong Special Administrative Region of the People's Republic of China, Education Commission, *Learning for Life, Learning through Life: Reform Proposals for the Education System in Hong Kong* (Hong Kong: Education Commission, September 2000), 1.

32. Antony K.C. Leung, chairman, Education Commission, foreword to Education Commission, *Learning for Life, Learning through Life*.

33. Chan Oi Wan, education officer, Education Department, Hong Kong Special Administrative Region of the People's Republic of China, e-mail to author, June 18, 2001. This situation is still the case.

34. Progovernment legislators voted for the Education (Amendment) Bill 2002, and prodemocracy legislators voted against it.

35. "Education Bill Still under Attack," *Sunday Examiner*, July 4, 2004, 1–2.

36. William McGurn, "China's Island of Discontent," *Wall Street Journal*, http://online.wsj.com/article_print/0,,SB108958336708360744,00.html, July 12, 2004. Additional criticism of the legislation is found in, Frank Ching, "If It Isn't Broken, Don't Fix It," *South China Morning Post*, http://archive.scmp.com/showarticles.php, June 29, 2004. Cf. Christopher Cheng, "A Step towards Higher-Quality Education," *South China Morning Post*, http://focus.scmp.com/cgi-bin/gx.cgi/AppLogic+FTContentServer?pagename=SCMP/Print..., July 13, 2004.

37. "Developments in Hong Kong," 3.9, in Education Commission, *Learning for Life, Learning through Life*, 28.

38. "The New Role and Functions of Education," 3.14, in Education Commission, *Learning for Life, Learning through Life*, 29.

39. Ibid.

40. "Principles of the Education Reform," 6.11, in Education Commission, *Learning for Life, Learning through Life*, 37.

41. Ibid., 6.18, 38.

42. Letter of Vivan Chan, teacher, St. Stephen's Girls' College, in response to the complaints of Fanny Law Fan, secretary of education and manpower, [n.d.], in *Parents' Newsletter*, Special Issue, no. 5, St. Stephen's Girls' College, March 2001.

43. Letter of Anna Lee, assistant principal, St. Stephen's Girls' College, in response to the complaints of Fanny Law Fan, secretary of education and manpower, [n.d.], in *Parents' Newsletter*, Special Issue, no. 5, St. Stephen's Girls' College, March 2001.

44. Eric So, "The Future of Christian Schools in Hong Kong: Challenges & Opportunities," *News and Views*, Hong Kong Christian Council (Spring 2000): 1. In China and often in Hong Kong, reference is made to Christians and Roman Catholics, as though Catholics were not Christians. In this chapter, references to Christians include both Protestants and Roman Catholics. Distinctions between Roman Catholics (often referred to simply as Catholics) and Protestants are made where necessary.

45. Ng Tze-min Peter, "Education in Hong Kong," 4.

46. Frank Martin, former president, American Chamber of Commerce in Hong Kong (retired, January 2005), interview by author, May 30, 2001. Martin served on the governing board of the American International School, which competes with the top religious-based schools for Hong Kong's most capable students.

47. Reliable statistics are not available, but it is said that there are approximately 355,000 (2002 data) Roman Catholics and 260,000 Protestants in Hong Kong. Thus, Catholics represent about 5.2 percent of Hong Kong's population and Protestants, about 3.8 percent.

48. The Reverend Stephen Chan, deputy director, Diocesan Liturgy Commission, and chaplain, Justice and Peace Commission, Roman Catholic Diocese of Hong Kong, interview by author, May 29, 2001.

49. Extrapolated from data provided in the *Hong Kong Catholic Church Directory 2001*, 592.

50. Coadjutor Bishop Joseph Zen Ze-kiun (now presiding bishop), Roman Catholic Diocese of Hong Kong, interview by author, May 28, 2001. At the time of the passage of the Education (Amendment) Bill 2002, the bishop noted that, under the new circumstances, it would be irresponsible for the church not to reduce the number of schools that it manages and speculated that the government might welcome a decline in church-run schools.

51. The Reverend Stephen Chan, interview by author, May 29, 2001.

52. On at least two occasions since taking control of Hong Kong, the atheistic central government has sent claimed relics of the Buddha to Hong Kong in a seeming effort to foster favor with the SAR's Buddhist community. It is noteworthy that the Venerable Sik Kok Kwong, headman of the Hong Kong Buddhist Association, led the first collective visit to the PRC by the Colloquium of Six Religious Leaders of Hong Kong (the delegation had seventy members) between March 28 and March 31, 2005. See "Historic Meeting of Religious Leaders in Guangzhou," *Sunday Examiner*, April 3, 2005, 1.

53. "HK Diocese Accused of Owing Millions in Rent," *Sunday Examiner*, January 21, 2001, 4.

54. As evidence that officials in Beijing do not trust Catholics in China, the Catholic Church in Hong Kong has taken note of the stepped-up control that has been exercised by the central government over the mainland's officially sanctioned Catholic Church. Specifically, it points to three new church management regulations that were issued in 2003: (1) the System for the Joint Conference of Chairpersons of the Chinese Catholic Patriotic Association (CCPA) and of the Bishops' Conference of the Catholic Church of China (BCCCC), forcing joint decision making on all important matters of the official church, therefore, infringing on the authority of the bishops; (2) the Work Regulations for the CCPA, affecting its operations; and (3) the Chinese Catholic Diocesan Management System, which gives the CCPA collective leadership with the local bishops on key matters, without defining what these matters are. See "Greater Control Exerted over the Mainland's Official Church in 2003," *Sunday Examiner*, January 11, 2004, 3.

55. For example, they find merit in recommendations that schools should place less emphasis on universal examinations than in the past, and that management committee members should advance transparency by sharing with the public relevant personal data, vested interests, and other information germane to the integrity of their positions.

56. See "Bishop Zen Says Recent Visit by US Religious Rights Commission Was 'More Than Reasonable,'" *Sunday Examiner*, January 11, 2004, 1.

57. "Greater Control Exerted over the Mainland Official Church in 2003," *Sunday Examiner*, January 11, 2004, 3.

58. See "HKCC's Response to the Constitutional Development of Hong Kong and the Interpretation of the Basic Law by NPCSC," *News and Views*, Hong Kong Christian Council (Summer 2004): 3. See also many issues of the *Sunday Examiner.*

59. "Bishop Zen Leads Prayer Prior to Protest Vigil," *Sunday Examiner*, April 11, 2004, 3.

60. "Bishop Zen Encourages the Faithful to Join in June 4 and July 1 Rallies," *Sunday Examiner*, May 30, 2004, 1.

61. Ibid.

62. Ibid.

63. "The People Demand Participation in Political Process," *Sunday Examiner,* July 11, 2004, 2.

64. "'Be Fearless Witnesses to Gospel,' Asian Youth Urged," *Sunday Examiner,* August 26, 2001, 1.

65. Neal Riemer, "Alexis de Tocqueville and the American Character: The Problem of Reconciling Excellence and Consent," *Journal of Federalism* 31, no. 1 (Winter 2001): 29.

66. For example, Tung Chee-hwa, when Hong Kong's chief executive, cautioned Hong Kong's people about the importance of Asian values and warned them not to be so focused on individual rights. Qian Qichen and other Chinese officials have warned journalists that they cannot violate national sovereignty by discussing certain sensitive issues, such as Taiwan's or Tibet's independence. It is widely held that self-censorship among journalists and academics is commonplace. The undemocratic nature of Hong Kong's electoral methods and legislative voting procedures has been the subject of many published political analyses.

9

Islam and Democratic Transition in Indonesia

Greg Barton

It is a sad reality of the age in which we live that Islam is much more likely to be regarded in the West as an obstacle to democratization than as a facilitator of liberal reform. This negative impression is the product of a vicious cycle: first, very few Muslim-majority nations have democratic governments, and second, Jihadi Islamist terrorism, itself a product of despair and anger caused in large part by domestic political oppression, argues forcefully that Western liberal democracy is the antithesis of Islam's ideals. That most Muslims reject the terrorists' interpretation of Islam, and welcome democracy and accountable government, does not stop some Western observers from adopting all or part of Samuel Huntington's "clash of civilizations" thesis. Huntington has correctly captured the spirit of radical Islamism in opposing Islam and liberal democracy, but his tragically self-fulfilling prophecy misunderstands the true nature of Islam.[1]

Radical Islamist rhetoric and Jihadi Islamist action reinforce the conviction of Huntington and other observers that the only form of state acceptable in Islam is one in which Islamic law, or Shari'a, narrowly interpreted, has preeminence over everything else and the government exercises power in the name of theocracy, punishing the sinner and disciplining the weak, regardless of whether it has majority support or not. The fact that the long history of Islamic civilization and the peaceful and moderate disposition of the vast majority of Muslims living today testify to a very different reality, is not sufficient to overturn this stereotype of endemic fundamentalism.

It is to be hoped that the coming decades will witness a deeper understanding of Islamic thought in the West, but for the moment, it is action, not theory, that determines how Islam is seen. This is one more reason why it is so vitally important that democratic Muslim nations such as

Turkey and Indonesia, where progressive Islamic thought supports vigorous civil society movements, succeed in demonstrating that Islam and liberal democracy are naturally compatible. It is true that, in the coffee shops of Cairo and Casablanca and among the political élites of Jordan, Lebanon, and Tunisia, the spirit of political liberalism is alive and well. But, generally, the political reality of the Arab world, and to a considerable extent of the rest of the Muslim world, is authoritarian and illiberal, leaving Muslims, and Islam itself, simultaneously denied the advantages of accountable government and blamed for its absence.

Indonesia has not yet arrived at its hoped-for destination in its transition to liberal democracy. The military has formally retreated from the political arena but remains largely unaccountable, is dependent upon criminal business interests, and is generally outside civilian control. Rule of law remains a cruelly distant fantasy for many Indonesians when it matters most. Corruption is endemic, and, even in recent years, there has been little sign of it being reined in. As a consequence of all of these factors, Indonesia leads the world in environmental degradation. At the same time, investment remains scarce and economic growth much too low to both meet the needs of a rapidly growing population and make up the ground lost in the 1997 Asian economic crisis. And yet for all this, Indonesia has made significant advances. In particular, the parliamentary elections of 1999 and 2004 were freer and fairer than anyone had thought possible less than a decade earlier. The end of the Suharto regime after thirty-two years of military-backed authoritarian rule came remarkably peacefully, and, although the period of transition that followed has seen more than ten thousand lives lost in bitter communal violence in Maluku and Sulawesi, it is easy to see how things could have been very much worse. Aceh remains a running sore kept from healing by continued violence on all sides and there are worrying signs of trouble brewing in Papua, but Indonesia has not "Balkanized," as some predicted that it would, nor is it likely to do so in the foreseeable future. Amid all of the sadness and disappointment of the post-Suharto years, ordinary Indonesians have shown uncommon good sense and remarkable grace, even where their leaders have shown neither. The movement toward liberal democracy has been bumpy and frustratingly slow, but it has by no means stalled.

If Indonesia and Turkey continue on their paths of nonsectarian democracy, valuable precedents will have been set for the Muslim world. But if it appears that Muslim leaders and organizations merely tolerate democracy, then the essentialist view of Islam as being antiliberal will remain unchallenged. Fortunately, there is strong evidence to suggest that, for many deeply religious Muslims, and, in particular, for many Islamic intellectuals, democracy and Islam are completely congruent. For them, democracy is seen as the best way to realize Islam's concern for social justice and social harmony.

If consideration is confined to a discussion of political parties and polling results, the contribution of Islam to democratization in Indonesia remains unclear. In the April 2004 parliamentary elections, the 42 percent of all parliamentary seats gained by Islamic parties was split between 23 percent of the seats won by Islamist parties (who want to see Shari'a law implemented and Islam recognized as the basis of the state) and 19 percent by "secular Islamic" parties (who are committed to Indonesia's current nonsectarian constitution but, nevertheless, draw their support from the membership of Islamic mass organizations). Looking at these numbers alone, Islamist politics appears to have more support in Indonesia than it does even in Pakistan. These numbers, however, tell but one part of the story—more of this later. In order to understand the contribution of Islam to democratization in Indonesia, we need to give attention to four different factors: (1) Islamic mass organizations; (2) individual Islamic leaders; (3) the development of Islamic thought in Indonesia; and (4) party politics.

Islamic Mass Organizations

Civil society throughout most of the Arab world has been severely restricted during the past forty years, as it has been through much of the Muslim world. Even in Indonesia, key elements of the civil sphere, such as nongovernmental organizations (NGOs) and the press, have faced decades of intimidation and occasionally violent repression.[2] Beginning with Sukarno's shift to "guided democracy" in 1957 up until the sudden collapse of the Suharto regime in 1998, Indonesians endured four decades of authoritarian rule. Even so, civil society in Indonesia never became as tightly constrained as has been the case in much of the Muslim world, where frustration with the lack of political freedoms has fueled semiunderground Islamist movements that, although illiberal and authoritarian in their own way, are nevertheless genuinely socially concerned and active in welfare delivery. As the Sukarno period approached its tragic denouement and then again as the optimism of the early Suharto period melted before increasingly overt militarism, the walls of the state inched inward on all sides of the courtyard of civil society, steadily narrowing the civil sphere, then retreating a little before repeating the cycle. To many of those who had the heroic resolve to stand up to it, or the simple misfortune to get in its way, the Suharto regime was absolutely crushing. But the claustrophobe's nightmare never did reach a zero point for civil society. Even at its harshest point, the authoritarianism of the Suharto regime always left a narrow little space for civil society. In part, this was because the regime's totalitarian ambitions, such as they were, were seldom matched by the surprisingly modest means of its badly underresourced military-security apparatus. But there was another reason why civil society was never completely crushed in Indonesia. For almost eighty years, the civil sphere has had two enormous girders buttressing its freedom from state pressure. As much as a third of the Indonesian population has been affiliated with Nahdlatul Ulama (NU) and Muhammadiyah, whose strength today is thought to number around forty million and thirty million members, respectively.[3] Support for these mass-based Islamic organizations, the largest of their kind anywhere in the world, is so extensive that, even in its most authoritarian phase, the Suharto regime dared not oppose them directly.

In the 1990s, one of the boldest and most influential critics of the Suharto regime was NU's executive chairman, Abdurrahman Wahid.[4] Toward the end of the decade, he was joined in his calls for democratic reforms by Muhammadiyah's chairman, Amien Rais. When Suharto eventually did resign in May 1998, as support for his rule dissolved in the face of the catastrophic economic collapse precipitated by the previous year's Asian economic crisis, it was these two leaders who were at the forefront of the push for free elections and democratic reform. The new political parties that they founded in June of that year, the National Awakening Party (PKB, or Partai Kebangkitan Bangsa) and the National Mandate Party (PAN, or Partai Amanat Bangsa) failed to achieve quite the success for which they had hoped; nevertheless, they were the most successful of the new parties. Significantly, although both parties were created to capture the votes of NU members and Muhammadiyah members, respectively, they were unambiguously committed to non-Islamist platforms.

The important role that Muhammadiyah and NU played in the peaceful transition to democracy post-Suharto was not simply the product of charismatic leadership nor was it an accident of history. From their early days, both Islamic organizations played a key role in politics and civil society.

Muhammadiyah was founded by Ahmad Dahlan in 1912, among petit-bourgeois traders living in Yogyakarta's *santri* (observant) Muslim quarter. Dahlan and his colleagues were inspired by the modernist ideas of Cairo's Muhammad Abduh, and his activist disciple, Rashid Rida, which were brought back to Indonesia by pilgrims and scholars returning from Egypt and Arabia. The modernist vision for combining spiritual and intellectual reform with practical innovations in education and health care struck a cord with the newly emerging urban middle class of santri traders and businessmen.

From the outset, the new organization threw itself into civil-sphere practical activism. And the more it succeeded in establishing schools and building health clinics and hospitals, the more it attracted earnest support. Although the intellectual vision of modernism centered around *ijtihad* (interpretation and exegesis) and the rethinking of Islamic thought, Muhammadiyah never gave concerted attention to theological scholarship, preferring instead to focus on modernism's other great concern with embracing rational, modern, scientific learning and using it to advance Muslim society.

Over time, Muhammadiyah's neglect of theological scholarship was institutionalized as it failed to train *ulama* (religious scholars) to replace men such as Dahlan. This was largely unintentional, but it did have a foundation in modernism's antipathy, or at least ambivalence, toward classical Islamic scholarship. Second-generation modernist leaders such as Rida were unable to replicate the breadth of vision that Abduh embodied. Abduh, who had lived and traveled in Europe and spoke its languages, was able to combine modern Western thought and classical Islamic scholarship in an enormously creative productive fashion and to synthesize a fresh approach to Islamic thought. The majority of Abduh's disciples, including Muhammadiyah's modernist pioneers, were unable to span the full range of his thought and instead focused on his call for practical social activism and the purification of Islam from superstition and syncretic accretion. For Muhammadiyah, this meant turning away from the traditional approach to education embodied in the *pesantren* (religious boarding schools) and embracing modern secular curricula in their new schools, which despite their Islamic title of *madrasah*, taught only the rudiments of religious knowledge. For the Muhammadiyah leaders, the pesantren were not merely old-fashioned but also dangerously unhealthy because most of them taught an acculturated approach to Sufism that was at odds with modernist reformism.

Modernist Islamic thought was well received when it was introduced to Indonesia, particularly among pious members of the emerging urban middle class. Modernism was forward-looking and positive; it offered a way of being a serious Muslim in the modern world, of being both religious and practical. Nevertheless, there were aspects of modernism that disturbed many pesantren-based ulama. The rapid growth of Muhammadiyah was admirable but it was also disturbing, for it threatened to become a dominant force in Muslim society and one that was antagonistic to traditional scholarship. Prior to the advent of modernism, social mobilization and networking had been ad hoc and informal. Ulama formed networks through the movement of students and through marriage but pesantren were, by their very nature, fiercely autonomous. The ulama typically commanded great charismatic authority and each scholar had his own specialist skills and knowledge such that students traveled from one to the other in pursuit of scholarship, spiritual discipline, and mystical insight. By the mid-1920s, a number of leader ulama in East Java decided that the only way to preserve Islamic traditionalism for generations to come was to take a leaf from the modernist's own book. They decided that they, too, would have to form a religious mass organization and modernize their networks, and so in 1926, Nahdlatul Ulama, the awakening of the ulama, was founded.

Predictably, a rivalry emerged between Muhammadiyah and NU as the Islamic community coalesced around the two poles of modernism and traditionalism. Muhammadiyah grew to become the world's largest modernist Islamic organization and NU grew to become even larger. Leaders from both organizations maintained cordial relations and some, rather more from Muhammadiyah than from NU, became key figures in the nationalist movement.

When the Japanese invaded and occupied Indonesia during World War II, it was obvious to them that the two organizations were too powerful and influential to lightly ignore or oppose. Instead, they sought to combine them under a general umbrella body, the Indonesian Supreme Islamic Council (MIAI), and to harness their support in "the war against European imperialism." And although the Muhammadiyah and NU leaders involved in MIAI became, as did most Indonesians, increasingly resentful of Japanese authoritarianism, they recognized that the occupation would likely be short-lived and that activism through MIAI afforded them the best opportunity to strengthen the nationalist movement in anticipation of declaring independence when the Japanese left.

In the wake of the four-year revolutionary struggle for independence, Muhammadiyah and NU turned to party politics. The wartime cooperation of the two organizations under the auspices of MIAI paved the way for their political partnership in Masyumi. Working together in Masyumi, the modernists, not all of whom were from Muhammadiyah, and the traditionalists, virtually all of whom were from NU, exercised considerable influence in the new Indonesian parliament and looked set to dominate the first general elections. Unfortunately for this vision, cultural differences between the urbane modernists and the rusticated traditionalists, and disputes over power sharing, saw NU exit from Muhammadiyah in 1952 and strike out on its own as a political party.[5] When elections were finally held in 1955, Islam did not prove to be quite the dominant force that the modernists and the traditionalists had expected it to be. Masyumi garnered 21 percent of the vote, and NU 18 percent—positioning both parties with a little more than the communist party (PKI) with 16 percent and a little less than the nationalist party (PNI) with 22 percent.

Clearly, if the modernists and traditionalists had been able to resolve their differences and work together within Masyumi, the single party would have had a very strong position indeed. But the obstacles to united action were not simply the division of political Islam into two parties, for even within the parties, significant divisions were emerging. A major division began to open up between those within both parties for whom the nonsectarian, secular but theistic state doctrine of *Pancasila*, or the Five Principles, represented a virtuous compromise and those for whom only an Islamist doctrine of state would suffice.

Sadly, after Muhammadiyah and NU had contributed so much to the achievement of independence and the establishment of parliamentary democracy, their division over the foundational philosophy of the state was instrumental in the early death of democracy in Indonesia. The 1955 elections led to the formation of a constitutional assembly, charged with developing a comprehensive, permanent constitution. However, after two years of disputation about many things, in particular whether Indonesia should be an Islamist state, Sukarno scuttled the whole process and declared that the vague and somewhat authoritarian interim constitution, hurriedly written in 1945, would become the permanent constitution. Under Sukarno's "guided democracy," no further elections were held.

NU made the best of the situation and reached a position of accommodation with Sukarno, but Masyumi, which had taken a lead role in pushing for an Islamist doctrine of state, continued to voice its disaffection. Regional uprisings, which erupted in West Sumatra and Southern Sulawesi the following year while Sukarno was on an overseas trip, and in which Masyumi leaders played prominent roles, gave Sukarno the excuse he was looking for to ban the "dissident" party.

In the decades that followed the banning of Masyumi, Islamist-inclined modernists, including some within Muhammadiyah, became obsessed with politics. The formation of the United Development Party (PPP, or Partai Persatuan Pembangunan) in 1973, when Suharto pushed for the consolidation of the ten opposition parties that had contested the 1971 election into two new parties, an Islamic party (PPP) and a nationalist party (PDI, or the Democratic Party of Indonesia), saw politicians from Muhammadiyah and NU once again working together within one party.

Many within the organizations did not, however, wish to be involved in party politics, and in the 1970s, Muhammadiyah and NU returned to their original concern with religious, social, and educational activities. In 1984, NU, under the leadership of Ahmad Siddiq and Abdurrahman Wahid, who had recently come to power on a reform ticket, announced that the organization was formally ending its association with the PPP.

From this point onward, NU under Abdurrahman Wahid became increasingly critical of the Suharto regime, although it was really not until the end of the decade that this oppositional stance was clearly seen. By 1989, Suharto was ready to embark on a new strategy. With most of his peers in the military retired and out of service, the president began to doubt the loyalty of the military. Seeking a way to counter the power of the military, Suharto decided to co-opt a key group of former critics and dissidents. Ever since he had come to power in the mid-1960s, Suharto had made it clear that he and his military-backed regime were suspicious of the sort of Islamist thinking that had been promoted by the right wing of Masyumi. In the late 1970s and early 1980s, the regime had tracked down and persecuted radical Islamists, including some who were later to lead the terrorist organization, Jemaah Islamiyah.[6] In 1990, Suharto had his protégé, B.J. Habibie, take the lead in the establishment of a new, government-sponsored Islamic organization, the Indonesian Association of Muslim Intellectuals (ICMI, or Ikatan Cendekiawan Muslimun se-Indonesia). While some of the key individuals associated with ICMI, including Amien Rais, were inclined toward Islamism, the majority of Muslim technocrats and academics who joined the association were Muhammadiyah moderates or social conservatives rather than radical Islamists.

Several NU figures did join ICMI but, essentially, NU was conspicuous by its absence.[7] This was due in no small measure to the stance taken by Abdurrahman Wahid, who warned that ICMI was a cynical political ploy by Suharto to consolidate his power (a view that many within ICMI also took), and, more important, that the inherently sectarian nature of this ploy represented a dangerous manipulation of religious sentiment that would likely have unforeseen consequences. This "vexatious" stance by Wahid annoyed many modernists, not least Muhammadiyah chairman and ICMI luminary Amien Rais, and even if it had not been Suharto's initial intention, it served his interests well by exacerbating divisions between NU and Muhammadiyah. It was only after Suharto, incensed by a series of critical comments from Rais, had ordered Habibie to expel Rais from ICMI, that Rais and Wahid, and Muhammadiyah and NU, began to work together.

Islamic Leaders

While it would be easy to overstate the importance of leaders such as Amien Rais and Abdurrahman Wahid within their organizations, there is no escaping the fact that strong, visionary leaders have made vitally important contributions to Muhammadiyah and NU at critical points in their histories. After all, the modernist movement would not have existed without individuals of genius such as Muhammad Abduh, and Muhammadiyah would not have become the world's most successful Islamic modernist organization without the leadership of Ahmad Dahlan. Similarly, NU was formed only after several of Java's leading ulama, including Abdurrahman's grandfathers, Hasyim Asyari and Bisri Syansuri, resolved to follow the example of Muhammadiyah. NU's contribution to the leadership of the nationalist movement in the late 1930s and the 1940s was dependent upon several dominant personalities, most especially Wahid Hasyim, Abdurrahman Wahid's father. The fact that Abdurrahman himself went on to play a vital role in leading NU for fifteen years and then became Indonesia's first democratically elected president, does not seem quite so surprising when one understands that, as a twelve-year-old and the oldest child, he witnessed his famous father mortally injured when the car in which they were traveling collided with a truck on a slippery mountain road. No doubt, Abdurrahman's indomitable mother, Solichah, who raised six children by herself and instilled in them a love of knowledge and curiosity about the world outside NU, should also be added to this list of remarkable leaders.

Much more could be said, here, about other leaders, such as NU's Ahmad Siddiq, or Masyumi's dynamic leader, Mohammad Natsir (who was not from Muhammadiyah but from the smaller Islamist-modernist group, Persatuan Islam, or Persis), or about Muhammadiyah's current chairman, Syafi'i Maarif, not to mention a host of younger men and women who are only now coming to the fore. Suffice it to say that, although the importance of organizations such as NU and Muhammadiyah lies very much in their mass bases and their ties to tens of millions of members, it is not possible to understand how these organizations work without an appreciation of the vitally important contributions of a surprisingly small number of outstanding leaders.

Islamic Thought in Indonesia

The contributions of many religious leaders are simply a product of charismatic authority and forceful personalities. But for others, and this includes most of those who have made the greatest contributions, it has been ideas rather than personalities that have been their source of lasting influence. The ideas that inspire and direct Muhammadiyah derive from the writings of seminal thinkers such as Egypt-based Muhammad Abduh and Rashid Rida, Pakistan's Abu'l 'Ala Maududi, and Indonesia's own Ahmad Dahlan and Mohammad Natsir, together with a host of contemporary writers.

Throughout its ninety-year history, Muhammadiyah has consistently remained a force for moderation and public good. Like any large organization, it has considerable diversity in ideas, attitudes, and orientations, some of which is due to personalities and organizational politics but the most important of which is due to intellectual conviction.

There are three main dichotomies defining the two hundred million-strong *umat*, or Islamic community in Indonesia. The first is the division between santri Muslims and nonsantri Muslims (sometimes referred to as *abangan*), which appears to divide the community into roughly equal halves. The second significant division, one that is obviously much more significant among santri than nonsantri Muslims, is between modernists and traditionalists (the mystical beliefs and practices of many nonsantri fit much better with the folk Islam of the traditionalists than they do with the Puritanism of the modernists). The vast majority of modernists are affiliated with Muhammadiyah, which is thought to have around thirty million members distributed widely across the archipelago, and enjoys strong support in Sumatra and Sulawesi as well as in Java. Similarly, the vast majority of traditionalists are affiliated with NU, but NU is much more Java-centered than is Muhammadiyah. It is not so much that there are many traditionalists outside Java that the forty-million-strong NU has not been able to enlist—there are significant communities in Aceh and Lombok, although their numbers are small in absolute terms—but rather that ninety years of discipline and industry have seen Muhammadiyah and Islamic modernism come to dominate outer-island Indonesia. The third major dichotomy, one that affects both modernists and traditionalists, but is of much greater consequence to the former than the latter, is the division between Islamists and non-Islamists.

Although a comprehensive consensus on definitions is yet to emerge, the term Islamist is increasingly used to denote Muslims who argue for the establishment of an Islamic state. Islamists believe not only that Islam provides the moral values and social ideals that should guide a nation, a view that most Muslims share, but also that it provides a detailed blueprint for building a truly Islamic state. When pressed for details, Islamists resort to asserting that the application of the Shari'a, or Islamic law, is the key to solving virtually all of society's problems, be they moral, legal, social, or economic. At the root of this belief are the twin convictions that a truly Islamic state should be a theocracy in which God's sovereign will is interpreted by the ulama, and that the "complete implementation" of the Shari'a will, of itself, produce moral virtue in the majority of citizens.

Islamists can be broadly divided into two groups. The first can best be called radical Islamists in that their aspiration is for nothing less than the complete, roots-up (hence, radical from the Latin for "roots," *radix*) transformation of Islamic society. For radical Islamists, an Iranian-style theocracy (albeit without the Shia elements that most radical Sunni Islamists find offensive) is the only acceptable long-term goal. The second group can be described as moderate Islamists. For them, it is important that the state recognizes Islam as being the religion of the state and gives a preeminent position to it. They, too, speak of the implementation of the Shari'a; yet, when examined, it is clear that this does not imply the radical reinvention of the state but rather the application of key areas of family and personal law and the symbolic recognition of Islam as representing the foundation of the state. For many moderate Islamists in Indonesia, it would be sufficient for the Indonesian state to become like the Malaysian or Pakistani state in these two key areas of personal law and official symbolism.

Symbolism is important to moderate Islamists in Indonesia because, at heart, many of them are essentially social conservatives. That is to say, they are fearful of rapid social change and the erosion of established values and mores, and they look to symbolic issues, such as the inclusion of Islam in the constitution, as a barometer of society's commitment to Islam. Their concern for such matters is analogous to the concern felt by social conservatives in the West for flag and anthem.

Most Islamists, whether radical or moderate, are quite prepared to work through the democratic system to achieve their desired outcomes, and most reject violence and militant revolutionary doctrine. Not only do most find violence abhorrent but also they recognize that it is by winning political power through the party system and then changing legislation that they can best achieve lasting reform. Many, particularly among the ranks of the radical Islamists, are sophisticated and politically savvy, and are prepared to distinguish between short-term goals and long-term goals. They are convinced that, by working through the democratic process and steadily changing legislation, they can effect the sort of incremental change that will eventually transform Indonesia's secular state into a properly Islamic one.

Sadly, there exists a smaller but even more determined group of radical Islamists for whom even short-term accommodation with secular democracy is unacceptable. Some of these, such as Indonesian followers of Jordan's Hizb ut-Tahrir, appear content to retreat from affairs of the state and maintain a quiescent approach to politics. But others, including many linked with Abu Bakar Ba'asyir's Indonesian Mujahidin Council (MMI, or Majelis Mujahidin Indonesia), are committed to achieving their ends through violent means. Many of the militant radical Islamists, who might best be called Jihadi Islamists, were radicalized either through the experience of fighting the Soviets as *mujahidin* in Afghanistan, or more recently through participating in communal conflict in Maluku and Sulawesi. Most of those who have spent time in training camps and radical madrasah in Afghanistan and the North Western Frontier Province of Pakistan have since become active within the al-Qaeda-affiliated Southeast Asian terrorist organization, Jemaah Islamiyah. Jihadi Islamism in Indonesia is a very large topic in itself and not really the concern of this chapter as it fortunately involves only a few thousand (with perhaps a few tens of thousand fellow-travelers) activists of Indonesia's two hundred million Muslims.

Of much greater concern, here, for reasons that will be elaborated below, is the influence of Islamism, in general, and of radical Islamism, in particular, in democratic politics in Indonesia.

Radical Islamists represent a small minority of all santri Muslims in Indonesia and occupy one end of a broad spectrum of Islamic thought.[8] Whether Indonesia has proportionately more or fewer radical Islamists than other Muslim countries is difficult to ascertain. Indonesians like to think of Indonesian Islam as being relaxed and tolerant, and there is no doubt that this is largely true. However, because few Muslim nations have free and fair elections, it is difficult to know how support for radical Islam in Indonesia compares with other nations. Pakistan, which for all its problems does have reasonably free and fair elections, makes for an interesting comparison with Indonesia. Radical Islamism is generally thought, and not without reason, to represent a greater problem in Pakistani society than in Indonesian society. Nevertheless, in Pakistan's 2002 general elections, which were characterized by a significant increase in support for radical Islamist parties, United Action Front (MMA, or Muttahida Majlis-e-Amal), a coalition of the country's six large Islamist parties, managed to garner only 11 percent of the vote. As we shall see below, in the 2004 Indonesian general elections, Indonesia's two radical Islamist parties, the Prosperous Justice Party (PKS, or Partai Keadilan Sejahtera) and the Crescent Moon and Star Party (PBB, or Partai Bulan Bintang) together achieved 10 percent of the vote, indicating that there exists a similar level of support in Indonesia for radical Islamist politics to that in Pakistan.[9] Moreover, the moderate Islamist PPP and its splinter party, the Reform Star Party (PBR, or Partai Bintang Reformasi), gained a further 11 percent of the vote, bringing the total share of the Islamist parties to 21 percent.

One way in which Indonesia clearly differs from Pakistan, however, is that Islamic thought in Indonesia is also very well represented at the other end of the spectrum. Indonesia also has a significant number of liberal, or progressive, Islamic intellectuals and activists, and they are free, and have been so for decades, to write, publish, and disseminate their ideas. This is the critical point of difference with Pakistan, and, indeed, with most Muslim countries, with the significant exception of Turkey (and the partial exception of Malaysia). Pakistan has produced outstanding progressive Islamic intellectuals, such as Fazlur Rahman (1919–1988), but they have not been free to disseminate their ideas in the country.[10] The Oxford-educated Fazlur Rahman was invited to return to Pakistan to lead the Central Institute of Islamic Research in Karachi but after several years was forced to leave the country because of opposition from radical Islamists. He moved to the University of Chicago, where he continued to teach and write for the remainder of his life. His doctoral students at Chicago included Nurcholish Madjid, Indonesia's leading liberal Islamic intellectual, and Syafi'i Ma'arif, leader of Muhammadiyah.

Nurcholish Madjid was very much influenced by Rahman's argument that Islamic modernism had tended to degenerate into revivalism, forgetting the movement's earlier commitment to ijtihad and the rethinking of Islamic thought, and that what was now required was a new movement, which he dubbed neomodernism, that would draw upon traditional Islamic scholarship and unite it with the spirit of modernism and the methods of modern Western thought. In fact, this was an approach already adopted by Nurcholish and other young Indonesian intellectuals, such as Abdurrahman Wahid and Djohan Effendi, independently of Rahman.[11]

This cohort of seminal liberal Islamic thinkers, all born around 1940, represented the first generation of santri Muslims in Indonesia to combine a basic education in traditional Islamic scholarship with modern Western studies. Over the past thirty years, their ideas have given birth to several new generations of liberal Islamic thinkers. This influence has been particularly felt among those who have a pesantren background, for it is those who have a theological education who are best equipped to engage in ijtihad and contribute to the development of Islamic thought. A natural outcome of this movement of thought has been the emergence of dozens of NGOs that are committed to liberal intellectual, social, and political reform. Many such Muslims have also made valuable contributions to "secular" NGOs and to journalism and education. Consequently, it can be said that liberal Islamic thought in Indonesia, sometimes called neomodernism, has made a significant contribution to the development of civil society as a whole, and has provided a way for Islam to play a leading role in the movement for democratic reform.

In Pakistan, and across the Arab world, the ideas of liberal Islamic intellectuals such as Rahman have not found broad support. Although many individuals are attracted to these ideas, there has been little scope for these concepts to be widely debated and disseminated, with governments generally succumbing to angry demands from radical Islamist minorities to silence public discussion about the progressive rethinking of Islamic thought. In Indonesia, however, the Suharto regime was not intimidated by the country's small groups of radical Islamists and was inclined to try do what it could to support this new movement of thought that advocated, in the words of Nurcholish Madjid, "Islam yes, Political Islam no!" Liberal Islamic thought in Indonesia was certainly not a product of the Suharto regime's policies, but it did benefit significantly from being given a degree of protection from hostile forces. The state itself did not produce the fertile soil that nurtured the seedling movement, for that was of society itself, but it did provide the windbreak necessary to allow it to become established.

It is a matter of no small importance that progressive Islamic intellectuals and NGOs played key roles in the Reformasi movement that helped end the Suharto regime in 1998 and pave the way for free and fair elections in 1999 and 2004. In the April 2004 parliamentary elections and the two rounds of the presidential elections in July and September 2004, for example, the largest network of independent observers was the People's Voter Education Network (JPPR , or Jaringan Pendidikan Pemilih Rakyat), composed of youth from Muhammadiyah and Nahdlatul Ulama. The involvement of such civil society groups and the overwhelmingly positive attitude of Indonesia's 125 million Muslim voters meant that the post-Suharto elections of 1999 and 2004 were remarkably peaceful and uneventful. In fact, after observing the July 5, 2004 direct presidential elections, former U.S. president Jimmy Carter declared them to be among the very best of all the fifty elections involving democratic transition that the Carter Center has observed.[12]

Not only did neomodernist liberal Islamic thought in Indonesia give rise to numerous progressive Islamic NGOs in virtually every large town and city in Java, and in many beyond, but also it helped to transform thinking and attitudes within the mass-based Islamic organizations, NU and Muhammadiyah. This transformation meant that, when the Suharto regime finally collapsed, the two large new Islamic parties that emerged in mid-1998 to channel support from NU and Muhammadiyah—PKB and PAN—were self-consciously nonsectarian and non-Islamist.

Party Politics

The results of both the 1999 and the 2004 elections make it clear that, in post-Suharto Indonesia, Islam will play at least as great a role as it did in parliamentary democracy during the 1950s.[13] (See Table 9.1.)

It was a little surprising that, after all the social changes that had occurred in Indonesia during the forty-four years following the nation's only free and fair election in 1955, the level of support achieved by Islamic parties in 1999 remained virtually identical to what it had been in 1955: 38 percent. This time, instead of there being two large parties representing the modernists of Muhammadiyah and the traditionalists of NU, there were three parties: PAN, drawing the support of the modernists; PKB, drawing the support of the traditionalists; and PPP, drawing support from both sides. After more than twenty-five years of political life, it was not surprising that the PPP should continue to maintain its established support base. Nor was it surprising, given the social-conservative nature of the PPP's mass base that, when it had the freedom to do so after the fall of the Suharto regime, the party chose to formally replace a commitment to Pancasila secularism with an Islamist agenda.

What is more significant is that the two new Islamic parties, formed in the wake of Suharto's departure—the NU-based PKB, led by Abdurrahman Wahid, and the Muhammadiyah-based PAN, led by Amien Rais, deliberately emphasized their pluralist orientation. Consequently, while Indonesia's "Islamic vote" has remained constant, support for Islamism is now more clearly delineated. And while, as has previously been noted, it is clear that radical Islamism is a significant political force in Indonesia, it seems possible that it has already reached its natural political ceiling. PKS achieved its remarkable 7.3 percent in April 2004, partly by consolidating the support for radical Islamism, spread across a multitude of small parties in the 1999 elections, and partly by appealing to urban santri who were looking for clean government and professionalism in political parties.

To the extent that cynical opportunism and lack of vigilance by other parties allow the PKS and the PBB, perhaps with the support of PPP and Golkar (Suharto's old party), to pass legislative changes in parliament that erode religious freedom, radical Islamism remains a significant political threat. Such incremental infringements on personal liberty as have occurred in other Muslim countries, for example, in Malaysia and Pakistan, produce a ratchet effect: once cast in legislation, they are

Table 9.1

The Performance of Major Parties in the 1999 and 2004 Elections

Big parties	Leader/key figure	Orientation	Notes	1999 % votes	1999 seats* 462 + 38	2004 % votes	2004 seats 550
Golkar	Wiranto/Tandjung	Secular nationalist	Indonesia-wide	22.4	118 (21.5%)	21.6	128 (23.3%)
Partai Demokrasi Indonesia Perjuangan	Megawati	Secular nationalist	Java/Bali strength	33.7	151 (30.2%)	18.5	109 (19.8%)
Partai Demokrat	Susilo B. Yudhoyono	Secular nationalist	Indonesia-wide	—	—	7.5	57 (10.4%)
Partai Damai Sejahtera		Secular nationalist	Christian party	—	—	2.1	12 (2.2%)
			Subtotal of secular nationalist parties	56.1	269 (53.8%)	49.7	306 (55.6%)
PKB	A. Wahid	Pluralist Islam NU masses	Dependent upon Wahid (Gus Dur)	12.6	51 (10.2%)	10.6	52 (9.5%)
PAN	Amien Rais	Pluralist Islam Muhammadiyah	Now arguably less liberal	7.1	34 (6.8%)	6.4	52 (9.5%)
			Subtotal of secular Muslim parties	19.7	85 (17.0%)	17.0	104 (18.9%)
PPP	Hamzah Haz	Moderate Islamist	Radical Islamist element	10.7	58 (11.6%)	8.2	58 (10.5%)
PBR	Zainuddin MZ	Moderate Islamist	Breakaway from PPP	—	—	2.8	13 (2.4%)

(continued)

Table 9.1 *(continued)*

Big parties	Leader/key figure	Orientation	Notes	1999 % votes	1999 seats* 462 + 38	2004 % votes	2004 seats 550
PBB	Yusril Mahendra	Radical Islamist	Yusril influential in cabinet 1999–2005	1.8	13 (2.6%)	2.6	11 (2.0%)
PKS	Hidayat Nur Wahid	Radical Islamist	Renamed; previously PK	1.3	7 (1.4%)	7.3	45 (8.2%)
			Subtotal of Islamist parties	13.8 / 18**	78 (15.6%)	20.9	127 (23.1%)
			Total of all Islamic parties	37.7**	163 (32.6%)	38.7	231 (42.0%)
			Grand total of all major parties***	89.6	432 (86.4%)	88.4	537 (97.6%)

Source: Greg Barton, *Indonesia's Struggle: Jemaah Islamiyah and the Soul of Islam* (Sydney: UNSW Press, 2004), 72–73. Reproduced with permission of the University of New South Wales Press.
*Elected representatives, 462, and TNI appointees, 38.
**Totals, including minor party organizations. See note below for further explanation.
***Grand totals do not add to 100 percent because, for the sake of clarity, minor parties have been left out of the table. See note below for further explanation.

Note: The subtotal for Islamist parties, 13.8 percent, is the sum of the votes gained in 1999 by the PBB, PK, and PPP (the major Islamist parties). However, in 1999, small parties captured a much larger share of the vote when forty-eight parties competed in the election, than they garnered in 2004 when parties that achieved less than 2 percent of the parliamentary seats in 1999 were excluded—hence, the PK was reinvented as the PKS. The subtotal for Islamist parties of 18 percent reflects the sum of the vote that was gained in 1999 by the PBB, PK, and PPP, and fifteen very small parties. This support appears to have been given to the PKS in 2004. This last point is important because it suggests that, while no doubt many voters in 2004 supported the PKS owing to the party's clean, professional image, most did so because of its radical Islamist agenda. Some of the 2004 backers of the PKS had voted for smaller radical Islamist parties in 1999. In 2004, a new Islamist party, the Indonesian United Awakening of the Islamic Community Party (PPNUI, or the Partai Persatuan Nahdlatul Ummah Indonesia), contested in the general elections. It achieved 0.78 percent of the vote, and, consequently, was not able to secure a parliamentary seat.

extraordinarily difficult to reverse. For this reason, it is encouraging that justice minister Yusril Izha Mahendra's attempts to engineer such changes during his 1999–2004 term of office failed and that his party, the PBB, lost two of its thirteen seats in the 2004 elections at the same time that PKS, which astutely downplayed its Islamist agenda, performed so spectacularly well in the polls. Even so, it is important to recognize that, had Mahendra succeeded in passing the new Criminal Code, which he acknowledges is an attempt to introduce elements of Shari'a law into Indonesia's penal code (criminalizing adultery, homosexuality, oral sex, and cohabitation), and the ironically named Religious Tolerance bill (outlawing proselytism, interreligious marriage, and "deviant teaching" and potentially requiring the state to police Ramadan fasting and observance of the *halal* dietary code), the nonsectarian secularism of the Indonesian state would have been fatally compromised. Given this, it is a matter for serious concern that Mahendra retains a senior post in President Yudhoyono's administration (as state secretary he is in charge of one of the most powerful elements of the state apparatus), and that he is joined in the cabinet by a dozen or so other Islamist sympathizers.

Conclusion

Islam is a vitally important political force in post-Suharto Indonesia. This includes, among other things, a vigorous radical Islamist element that has decidedly illiberal ambitions. Nevertheless, it needs to be recognized that, the very small number of Jihadi Islamists aside, even the radical Islamists are, for the foreseeable future, committed to the democratic process. Moreover, their contribution is overshadowed by the vital contribution to democratization made by progressive Islamic intellectuals and organizations. Individuals, such as former president Abdurrahman Wahid, may appear to have failed in their attempts at reform, but seen in a broader context, it is clear that such Muslim democrats in Indonesia have made a contribution to the development of a liberal society and a democratically accountable state in Indonesia that stands comparison with the contributions made by Jewish and Christian leaders, thinkers, and activists in Western democracies. This is not to say that Indonesia will not experience significant erosion of the civil liberties that it has achieved as a result of creeping Islamization. Clearly Islam, like the other great world religions, can both inspire liberal democratic reform and be used to justify the authoritarian repression of basic freedoms. But there can be no doubt that the efforts of progressive Islamic intellectuals and social movements will help determine the enduring character of Islam's overall contribution to democratization and liberal reform. They have already given ample evidence of just how positive a contribution than can be.

Notes

1. Huntington's thesis, borrowing the phrase "clash of civilizations" from Bernard Lewis, was first published in *Foreign Affairs* in 1993, and was further developed and published as a long study: Samuel P. Huntington, *The Clash of Civilizations and the Remaking of the World Order* (New York: Simon and Schuster, 1996).

2. For a comprehensive study of Islam and civil society, refer to Robert W. Hefner, *Civil Islam: Muslims and Democratization in Indonesia* (Princeton, NJ: Princeton University Press, 2000).

3. For information on NU, refer to, Greg Barton and Greg Fealy, eds., *Nahdlatul Ulama, Traditional Islam and Modernity in Indonesia* (Clayton, Australia: Monash Asia Institute, 1996); for information on Muhammadiyah and Islamic modernism, see, B.J. Boland, *The Struggle of Islam in Modern Indonesia* (The Hague: Martinus Nijhoff, 1971); Mitsuo Nakamura, *The Crescent Arises over the Banyan Tree: A Study of the Muhammadiyah Movement in a Central Javanese Town* (Yogyakarta: Gadjah Mada University Press, 1983); and Deliar Noer, *The Modernist Muslim Movement in Indonesia* (Kuala Lumpur: Oxford University Press, 1973).

4. For studies of Wahid's life, milieu, and thought, refer to Greg Barton, *Abdurrahman Wahid, Indonesian President, Muslim Democrat: A View from the Inside* (Sydney and Honolulu: UNSW Press and University of Hawaii Press, 2002), and to, Douglas E. Ramage, *Politics in Indonesia: Democracy, Islam and the Ideology of Tolerance* (London: Routledge, 1995).

5. Greg Fealy, "Rowing in a Typhoon: Nahdlatul Ulama and the Decline of Constitutional Democracy," in *Indonesian Democracy: 1950s and 1990s*, ed. David Bourchier and John Legge (Clayton, Australia: Monash University, 1994), 88–98.

6. For information on Jemaah Islamiyah, see Greg Barton, *Indonesia's Struggle: Jemaah Islamiyah and the Soul of Islam* (Sydney: UNSW Press, 2004). Refer also to the reports of pioneering research by International Crisis Group (ICG) Indonesia director, Sidney Jones, and staff: ICG Asia Briefing, *Al-Qaeda in Southeast Asia: The Case of the "Ngruki Network,"* in *Indonesia*, August 8, 2002; ICG Indonesia Backgrounder: *How the Jemaah Islamiyah Terrorist Network Operates*, December 11, 2002; ICG, *Jemaah Islamiyah in Southeast Asia: Damaged but Still Dangerous*, August 26, 2003. Copies of these ICG reports can be obtained from www.crisisweb.org. See also Maria Ressa, *Seeds of Terror: An Eyewitness Account of al-Qaeda's Newest Center of Operations in Southeast Asia* (New York: Free Press, 2003).

7. See Douglas E. Ramage, *Politics in Indonesia: Democracy, Islam and the Ideology of Tolerance* (London: Routledge, 1995).

8. For discussions of radical Islamism in Indonesia, refer to Robert Hefner, "Civic Pluralism Denied? The New Media and Jihadi Violence in Indonesia," in

New Media in the Muslim World: The Emerging Public Sphere, ed. Dale F. Eickelman and Jon W. Anderson (Bloomington: Indiana University Press, 2003), 158–79, and Martin Van Bruinessen, "Genealogies of Islamic Radicalism in Post-Suharto Indonesia," *South East Asia Research* 10, no. 2 (2002): 117–24.

9. For a study of the PKS in its earlier incarnation as the Justice Party (PK), see Mathias Diederich, "A Closer Look at *Dakwah* and Politics in Indonesia: The *Partai Keadilan*," *Archipel* 64 (2002): 101–15.

10. See Fazlur Rahman, *Islam and Modernity: Transformation of an Intellectual Tradition* (Chicago: University of Chicago Press, 1982), and Fazlur Rahman "Islam: Past Influence and Present Challenge," in *Islam: Challenges and Opportunities*, ed. A.T. Welch and P. Cachia (Edinburgh: Edinburgh University Press, 1979), 315–30.

11. See Greg Barton, "Indonesia's Nurcholish Madjid and Abdurrahman Wahid as Intellectual Ulama: The Meeting of Islamic Traditionalism and Modernism in Neo-Modernist Thought," *Islam and Christian-Muslim Relations* 8, no. 3 (October 1997): 323–50, and Greg Barton, "Neo-Modernism: A Vital Synthesis of Traditionalism and Modernism in Indonesian Islam," *Studia Islamika* 2, no. 3 (1995): 1–75.

12. Speaking at a Carter Center press conference in Jakarta on July 7, 2004, Carter declared the peaceful, positive conduct of Indonesia's first-ever direct presidential elections, despite minor hiccups, to be second only to the conduct of Mexico's last election. Having observed the election at a series of voting stations two days earlier before watching him speak, it was clear to me that Carter's comments were not mere platitudes.

13. For a discussion of Islam and politics in Indonesia, see Greg Barton, "Islam, Islamism and Politics in Post-Soeharto Indonesia," in *Islam and Politics in Indonesia*, ed. Damien Kingsbury (Melbourne: Monash University Press, 2004).

10

Democracy, the "Islamic State," and Embedded Realities in Malaysia

Patricia Martinez

This chapter explores Islam, democracy, and notions of an Islamic state as these entities have evolved in the Malaysian context—especially in terms of subsequent recourse to the bastion of democracy, the constitution. Whether the Islamic state is coherent or cohesive with democracy became an important consideration after the prime minister's declaration in September 2001 that Malaysia is an Islamic state, and focus on the issue continues until the present. During its annual convention in August 2004, the Islamist opposition political party, Parti Islam SeMalaysia (PAS), reiterated its primary objective of establishing an Islamic state. In varying degrees of intensity, the vision of an Islamic polity where the Shari'a (Islamic law) is supreme continues to resonate throughout the Muslim world, including in neighboring Indonesia.

This chapter also explores the complex tensions, negotiations, abrogation of constitutional guarantees, and the continuing evolution of the debate about the compatibility of configuring Malaysia as Islamic, with both the Shari'a and Common Law in operation as equally supreme and independent of each other. It also features a case study that exemplifies a challenge to freedom of religion—a definitive marker of a democracy.

The debate about whether Islam is coherent or contiguous with democracy is often delineated in the struggle over Islamic law and secular constitutions. For democracy to be an ongoing system rather than merely episodic elections, it must be instituted as a constitutional framework. Religion and politics coexist as nonoverlapping *magisteria*, but they conflict in their two overlapping visions that establish rules for the correct practice of their domains so as to defend their integrity and fend off false prophets. The conflict between the two overlapping visions of the competing monoliths is obvious, but the question is how the introduction of a particular form of politics—democracy—changes the relationship. Describing one of the Achilles' heels of democracy as its vulnerability to challengers who would use the opportunity offered by its own rules to annul it, many conclude that reconciling political religion and secular democracy is impossible. This is because each seeks a different sort of validation that excludes the other. I. William Zartman writes in a chapter, "Islam, the State and Democracy,"

> To the political religionist, religion excludes politics, those who do not acknowledge that fact or interpretation should be excluded from politics. ... To the secular democrat, politics excludes religion as a political principle (although not necessarily as an individual belief); yet, troublingly, the principles of democracy may be used by political religionists to win democratically and end democracy.[1]

It is against this symbiosis of state, society, and religion—each defining, limiting, and enabling the other in democratic processes—that this chapter analyzes reactions by political parties and civil society groups and individuals who use recourse to the constitution in their reactions to the pronouncement by the prime minister in 2001 that Malaysia is an Islamic state. This chapter then examines briefly a fundamental of democracy—freedom of religion—in a nation that enshrines such a right in article 11 of its constitution; yet, there are Shari'a enactments in individual states in Malaysia that detract from this fundamental right in significant ways. Lacunae (loopholes in a rule or set of rules) in the Shari'a and Common Law as well as the inability or unwillingness of some of the Malaysian judiciary to provide both remedy and relief to litigants because of the way Islam is both politicized and polemicized (so that any action outside what is prescribed and proscribed as appropriately "Islamic" risks an avalanche of critique and condemnation) is explored as the embedded reality of trying to configure both democracy and "Islamic statehood" as compatible systems in Malaysia.

The Islam and Democracy Debate

A brief excursion into debates about Islam and democracy is useful in providing a wider framework with which to understand the reflections on Malaysia in this chapter. Exploring the Islam and democracy debate elsewhere in the Muslim world enables a focus on the heterogeneity of resources, and especially on the many manifestations of Islam that exist because the world religion has evolved in various contexts. With a self-consciousness about the "essentializing" that summary and brevity engender, the debate about whether Islam is compatible with democracy or even inherently democratic, is in two camps. The first group finds structures, terminology, concepts, and principles in the Qur'an and/or the history of Islam that can be understood as fundamentally democratic, with a particular focus on *shura*, or consultation. The second group finds resonance with democracy in Islamic text and history. However, its members argue that any privileging of a religion or religiosity is not in consonance with the concept of a modern democratic state that is predicated on the principle of equality of all its citizens before the law, without discrimination on the grounds of race, color, gender, language, religion, politics, or opinion.

One of the leading proponents of the first group that finds elements of democracy inherent in Islam is Ahmad S. Moussalli, who argues that, by linking classical and medieval Islamic thought with current political and religious debates, "modern Islamic thought in general and current moderate Islamism in particular, has absorbed and 'Islamized' the notions of democracy and pluralism."[2] Moussalli states that, while the history of the highest Islamic political institution, the caliphate, is mostly a history of authoritarian governments, the economic, social, political, and intellectual histories of Islam abound with liberal doctrines and institutions.

Likewise, Fathi Osman finds democratic structures in Islam, arguing that the religious dimension in Islamic ideology does not mean the establishment of a theocracy, and that, because there are no clergy in Islam, "any intelligent human being who knows the language and style can understand and interpret God's message."[3] He argues that the principle of shura, or consultation, is binding, and finds that, "The modern democratic process is a practical mechanism for securing human rights and dignity for all the children of Adam. It allows for the implementation of the concept of shura and assists in achieving the goals of Shari'a in a modern Islamic state."[4]

Khalid Duran is in the group that finds resonances but not democratic structures in Islamic text and tradition. In a chapter entitled "How Democratic is Islam?" he writes that shura is significant as a democratic principle, but that it is "vastly exaggerated" and "overstating the case" when a Muslim refers to it as being nothing short of fully developed democracy. Duran states that a majority decision is not binding on a ruler, and offers as an example the Islamic Republic of Iran, where the Supreme Guide frequently makes decisions that run counter to the consensus of the assembly. He argues that "democracy is compromised in a double and triple sense. First, only people who subscribe to the state ideology can be elected. Second, their majority decisions are not binding upon the country's Supreme Guide. In other words, the assembly is not the highest authority, neither is the president."[5] Duran concludes that Islamic norms of society may not be innately democratic, but also that they certainly are not irreconcilable with democracy. His perspective on political Islam and its agendas (which would include the Islamic state) are his final words in the chapter: "I can state without hesitation that Islamism can never be democratic, because the moment that Islamists turn into democrats, they are Islamists no more but merely Muslims."[6]

In *Democracy without Democrats? The Renewal of Politics in the Muslim World*, others such as Ghassan Salame argue for a more nuanced understanding of democracy. He first agrees that often there are no compelling unifying factors triggering a unilateral political evolution toward democracy, and that calls for democratization may indeed be muted. Salame states, however, that, while the political discourse dealing with democratization may be only partly convincing, forms of political opening are increasingly viewed by the leaders themselves, if not by society, as precious instruments through which a rapid deterioration of law and order, if not the collapse of the whole state apparatus, might be avoided or at least delayed. "Pacts" on limited forms of political participation are, in these situations, negotiated between the ruling group and significant sectors of the civil society.[7]

Salame and his co-authors argue that such pacts could prove to be crucial not only to the survival of nascent experimentations with democracy but also to the survival of the state itself. They argue that, in this sense, democracy can be judged less by the attachment to its principles by some actor or another, and more by its common use as a means to avoid civil war or institutional chaos. Thus, forms of political participation are being sought by regimes that have come to believe that their old-style authoritarianism may be difficult to maintain or is becoming counterproductive. Other states have arrived at the same conclusion because of their inability to adopt an International Monetary Fund-inspired austerity program without help from representative sectors of civil society. Still others have concluded that greater liberalism is, after all, the only way to make a segmented society live together. Yet, those who have engaged in the process of democratization may well be intolerant, repressive, and dictatorial. The programs of some opposition groups perhaps are meant to replace an existing authoritarianism with one of their own. In all such cases, forms of democracy are better defined and judged less by the identity of those who initiate them and more by their efficacy in phases of democratic transition.

Democrats may not exist at all, or they may not exist in great numbers. However, democracy can still be sought as an instrument of civil peace and—it is hoped—gradually, inadvertently, produce its own defenders. Saad Eddin Ibrahim describes a three-way race to maintain or seize power among autocratic regimes, Islamic activists, and organizations in civil society. In some Arab countries, one variant of the race has been the squeezing of civil society out of the public arena by autocratic regimes on the one hand, and by Islamic activists on the other. In another variant, both the autocratic regimes and Islamic activists have attempted to win over or appropriate organizations in civil society. Ibrahim sees the second variant as containing the greatest promise for civil society and the democratization process. Notably, it has provided ample bargaining power for civil society organizations when they deal with the state in attempts to gain concessions of a sociopolitical reformative nature. It also has had a moderating effect on several Islamic activists groups: in Jordan, Kuwait, Yemen, and Lebanon, this promise actually has been unfolding, Ibrahim claims. In each, Islamists have accepted the principle of political pluralism, participating alongside other secular forces in national elections, and they are currently represented in those countries' parliaments.

Ibrahim proposes that, as long as religious-based parties and associations accept the principle of pluralism and observe a modicum of civility in behavior toward the different Other, then they can expect to be integral parts of civil society.[8] He suggests that, in this respect, even Islamists may evolve into something akin to Christian Democrats in the West. Ibrahim is emphatic that there is nothing intrinsically Islamic that contradicts the codes of civil society or democratic principles, and warns "that when the middle classes and other socio-economic formations that have a legitimate quest for participation in the public affairs of their societies are not allowed to do so peacefully, they force their way into the system, or against it—violently. Islam, in this case, provides a mere culturally legitimate idiom permitting this."[9]

This is too simplistic a conjecture. Social and political Islam are the most active and vital forces in the modern societies of the Middle East: Any account of civil society that ignores or even diminishes this fact is unrealistic. The strongest and most durable associations outside the government are precisely the "neotraditional" and "primordial" groupings excluded from civil society by most definitions. Patriarchal (and paternal)[10] associations and attitudes have persisted, or been reconstituted under modern conditions, argues Sami Zubaida. New Islamic and Islamist social and political forces have a special affinity with these social formations, and have sought in many places to control and colonize them, which is why the status of these formations as civil society has become an issue.[11]

The configurations of democracy and Islam in the Middle East provide vital insights into other Muslim nations, because it is Islam that defines the configurations. However, the cultural and historical contexts into which Islam is embedded elsewhere in the world differ considerably and provide new understandings of whether Islam is part of or enables democracy.

Malaysia as an Islamic State

Islam is described as the official religion of Malaysia, and there is a 60 percent Muslim majority in the population. Malaysia also describes itself as a constitutional democracy, with an election of representatives to the parliament as well as to state legislative assemblies every five years. Islam and democracy are both definitive of Malaysia, but the tension, engagement, and accommodation between both came to a head recently over issues of conversion of minors, custody, and freedom of religion.

The most important phase of the furor over Malaysia as an Islamic state was precipitated by the announcement by the then-prime minister on September 29, 2001, at the annual general assembly of a member party of the ruling coalition, that Malaysia was, in fact, an Islamic state. A week later on October 6, Dr. Mahathir Mohamad said that there was no need for a debate over whether Malaysia was an Islamic state, announcing that the leaders of the Barisan Nasional (BN, the ruling coalition) component parties were "comfortable" with the concept.[12] Subsequently, there were many statements in the English, Chinese, and Malay media by leaders of the component parties of the ruling coalition, that they had no problems with the announcement, were accepting it with an open heart, and were more concerned about the Islamist opposition's (PAS's, or Parti Islam

SeMalaysia's) version of an Islamic state, which PAS announced it would present at the end of 2001, but which materialized in very general terms, only in late 2003.

In the subsequent months after the September 2001 announcement by Mahathir that Malaysia was an Islamic state, assurances and explanations from the deputy prime minister included reiterating that the Federal Constitution would not be amended to turn Malaysia into an Islamic state, and that the government decree was for the benefit of the Malays and should not trouble the ethnic Chinese. "We just want the Malays to understand that we are an Islamic state and therefore they need not look for other agendas," he said in the Chinese newspaper *Sin Chew Jit Poh*.[13]

An example of the semantic gymnastics from the ruling coalition to explain how the democratic multiethnic and multireligious nation was now an Islamic state included, "Malaysia, under the present constitution, is not a theocratic state and therefore, can also be called a secular state . . . all races and religions will continue to enjoy the freedom which currently exists."[14] The statement was made by the president of the Malaysian Chinese Association (MCA), Dr. Ling Liong Sik, after an MCA-convened forum on the Islamic state, at which the adviser for Islamic Affairs to the prime minister, Tan Sri Abdul Hamid Othman (among others), gave a briefing. The press was not allowed to attend the session and did not report on the fact that all the members present from the Malaysian Consultative Council on Buddhism, Christianity, Hinduism, and Sikhism (MCCBCHS), as well as a representative from the Federation of the Evangelical Christians of Malaysia and some members of the MCA, expressed either concern about or outright rejection of the Islamic state and the statement that there was nothing about which non-Muslims had to worry. The uproar over the significance of the existing government and ruling coalition's proclaiming Malaysia as an Islamic state was and is not reflected by the mainstream media; rather, the concern appears in alternate venues, and this perhaps is the starkest example of the disjuncture between perceptions in public transcripts and discourse and realities on the ground.

A booklet was subsequently published and distributed at various briefings on the Islamic state beginning in early October 2001. The first edition of the booklet, by Dato Wan Zahidi Wan Teh, was published by the Ministry of Information and is entitled *Malaysia adalah sebuah negara Islam* [Malaysia is an Islamic nation]. The English version of the booklet has since been withdrawn, but it merits analysis because the Malay version was reprinted and remains in circulation, and because it is the most concrete explanation or envisioning of the Islamic state that the government has proclaimed. This first edition of the booklet has on its cover the seal of the government of Malaysia, slashes of lightning, and an airplane, which evokes the specter of the September 11, 2001, attacks on the Pentagon in Washington, DC, and the World Trade Center in New York.

The preface states that, in order to ascertain whether Malaysia is an Islamic nation, reference first must be made to the opinions of the *ulama* (literally, those knowledgeable about religion, meaning those trained in the study of religion) about their definitions of an Islamic state. The first definition given is that the nation must be under Muslim governance, its defense must be in the hands of Muslims, and that it is the responsibility of every Muslim to defend it. The second definition is that the nation is controlled by Muslims, in which they attain peace within it. The third definition is that the laws of an Islamic ruler are enforced. The fourth definition is that, whichever country has become a Muslim nation, even if has been defeated, it maintains its status as an Islamic state by adherence to *hukum fiqh* (the laws of Muslim jurisprudence); examples are given such as nations in which Muslims have been under communist or colonial rule.

The text then states that, based on these definitions by ulama and intellectuals, it is obvious that Malaysia is an Islamic state without any further debate or controversy. The chapters that follow are entitled "To What Extent Has the Government Fulfilled Its Responsibility as an Islamic Nation?" "The Legitimacy of the Government According to Islamic Jurisprudence," "The Responsibility of the Faithful towards Their Rulers," "The Boundaries of Loyalty towards Rulers," "The Obligation and the Way to Critique Rulers," and "Islam and Muslim Unity." The chapters provide legitimacy from traditional sources for the government's describing itself in its present form as Islamic, and are patterned on the rhetoric of the United Malays National Organization (UMNO) since at least the elections of 1999: that the government knows best how to lead Muslims, that Muslims should be grateful, that critique should be gentle, and that Muslim unity is paramount.

It is instructive to check the booklet issued in 2001 against one of the primary sources in the text, the Shafi'i Jurist Al-Mawardi (died 1058 C.E.), especially regarding the status of *al-dhimma*, or non-Muslims, since *Malaysia adalah sebuah negara Islam* uses the word "dhimmi" to describe *orang kafir*, or unbelievers. The paradigm of cross-checking contemporary context against another from a few centuries ago is problematic because the chasms of time, evolution, and context are summarily collapsed in a comparative analysis. However, since this was the route chosen by the booklet that explains Malaysia as an Islamic state (and it is a dynamic common to the use of traditional sources in Islam), it is best to maintain this logic in an analysis.

Al-Mawardi, indeed, does write that the second type of ministry—executive ministry—is open to members of *ahl al-dhimma*. But he makes it clear that the dhimmi should be watched closely, and cautions that if a dhimmi minister arrogates to himself a higher rank, he should be stopped.[15] However, it is Al-Mawardi's views on non-Muslims in an Islamic state that are especially troubling.

According to Al-Mawardi, the term *jizya* is derived from *jaza*, which means recompense, and non-Muslim subjects who live in the abode of Islam are required to pay it either as dues or as punishment for their unbelief.[16] The jizya is to be exacted from them either in the form of an action of humiliation (*sagharan*) or as remuneration to the Muslim community in return for a guarantee that security will be provided to the subject people.

In citing the qur'anic authority for jizya, Al-Mawardi quotes Surah 9:29, a verse that has caused considerable consternation, especially among dhimmi:

> Fight against such of those who have been given the Scripture as believe not in God or the Last Day, and forbid not that which God has forbidden by His messenger, and follow not the religion of truth, until they pay the tribute readily, being brought low (*an yadin wa-hum saghirun*).[17]

In the phrase that points to those who "believe not in God or the Last Day," Al-Mawardi argues that, while the *ahl al-kitab*, Christians and Jews, do acknowledge that God is one, their faith in God may be rejected or denied on the basis of two interpretations: that they do not believe in God's Scripture, the Qur'an, or that they do not believe in Muhammad, God's Messenger, for acknowledging the veracity of God's messengers is paramount to believing in them. As to the enigmatic words at the end of the verse, "an yadin," Al-Mawardi again provides two possibilities for interpretation. The first is to pay the jizya "out of sufficiency and ability"; the other is for ahl al-dhimma to become subservient and humbled by the conviction that Muslims have dominance and power over them. Finally, the phrase "wa-hum saghirun" is interpreted to mean either that ahl al-dhimma will be servile and submissive, or that the laws of Islam are applicable to them.[18] Al-Mawardi makes it incumbent upon the ruler to exact the jizya from Jews and Christians so that they will be entitled to dwell in *dar al-islam* (the house of Islam). Furthermore, by paying, or agreeing to pay the jizya, no harm will come to them and protection will be provided for them so that they may be secure and well guarded. In this, al-Mawardi seems to be advocating the more conciliatory interpretation as a standard for the caliph to follow, perhaps out of his desire to recapture the ideals of early Islam, since he goes on to quote the *hadith* (tradition or sayings of the Prophet Muhammad) reported by Nafi, on the authority of Umar, that the last words the Prophet spoke were, "Protect me in regard to my covenant (*dhimmati*).[19]

However, while al-Mawardi quotes Abu Hanifa's saying, "I will not take it [the jizya] from the Christian Arabs lest they be exposed to humiliation,"[20] and alludes to the caliph Umar's acceptance of a double *zakah* (tithe) from the Arab Christians in lieu of jizya, he goes out of his way to affirm that "the Arabs [i.e., Arab Christians] are liable to pay the *jizya* as do others."[21] He also classifies other conditions for the ahl al-dhimma in an Islamic state: requisite (*mustahaqqa*) and recommended or desirable (*mustahabba*), listing six items under each category.

Under the category of what is requisite or mandatory (mustahaqqa), are the requirements that the ahl al-dhimma:

1. Not denigrate or misquote the Book of Allah, exalted is He, nor alter it;
2. Not attribute lies to the Apostle of God, nor speak of him disparagingly;
3. Not speak of the religion of Islam with slander or calumny;
4. Not commit adultery with a Muslim woman, even in the name of marriage;
5. Not undermine a Muslim's faith or cause harm to his financial affairs or his religion;
6. Not aid the people of war, nor befriend (*yawuddu*) the rich among them.[22]

The six recommended (mustahabba) conditions are designed specifically to underscore the subservient status of the dhimmi. These conditions recommend that ahl al-dhimma:

1. Identify their appearance by wearing the distinguishing badge, and tightened belt;
2. Not build structures that are higher than the Muslims', but at the same level or lower;
3. Not allow their bell-ringing, the chanting of their scriptures, or their sayings (doctrines) concerning Uzayr or Christ, to reach Muslim ears;
4. Not display in public their wine-drinking, crosses, and swine;
5. Conceal the burying of their dead, and not publicly voice their wailing and mourning;
6. Be prohibited from riding horses, whether thoroughbred or crossbred, but not from riding mules and donkeys.[23]

Some of the above will seem familiar to non-Muslim Malaysians as reasons cited over the years by various local authorities for why it has been so difficult to obtain burial sites, or for the stipulations placed upon more recent applications for church-building plans in the states under the BN government. Al-Mawardi has been the authoritative text for many of the ulama of the Jabatan Agama Islam of the various states and for other issues described earlier.

In other words, there already are practices if not policies and laws under which non-Muslim Malaysians are treated as dhimmi and by means of which privileged favor is extended to Islam and Muslims by some state governments, especially those of the BN. If Al-Mawardi's text continues to define the Islamic state as envisaged by the BN government, and if at a later stage more of his positions about non-Muslims are invoked and implemented, resulting in non-Muslim Malaysians becoming official second-class citizens, these measures would be in conflict with the notion of egalitarian rights of citizenship that ostensibly are bestowed upon all Malaysians and are stipulated in Malaysia's constitution. What is more pertinent is that any implementation, whether by PAS or UMNO, of Al-Mawardi's edicts on non-Muslims would render them second-class citizens and abrogate their rights as defined for all Malaysians in the constitution of the nation.

In 1856, or 148 years ago, the Sultan-cum-Caliph Abd al-Majid brought to an end the status of dhimmi in the Ottoman Empire. In a proclamation known as *Hatt-i-Humayun*, he declared all inhabitants of the Ottoman Empire to be equal citizens under the law. Until recently, the issue of ahl al-dhimma and their status had disappeared from the area of public policy in the nation-state and was relegated to historical documents for historians to ponder. Now, the debate between Muslims and non-Muslims concerning the role and status of minorities in an Islamic state appears to have gathered momentum with the rise of political Islam and its advocacy of the reinstitution of the Shari'a.

The "Islamic state" is an ideological state based on the concepts and fundamental principles embodied in the Shari'a. It is important to recognize that, in the Qur'an, which contains about 6,236 verses, only about thirty-five verses implicitly or explicitly contain what can be construed as a system of politics and administration. There is no qur'anic term for "state"—in the text of the Qur'an, the term *dawla* occurs, but it is not used in the same meaning of state as is its current etymology; instead the term means wealth. Therefore, in the primary source of Islam—the Qur'an—an Islamic state is neither described nor mandated.

Historically, most jurists were more concerned to cultivate a habit of passive obedience to the ruler, and any attempt of the people to rise against the reigning Muslim ruler was always looked upon as apostasy or rebellion. "Therefore the traditional theory, under the pressure of political exigencies, is willing to tolerate even a bad ruler or a tyrant as long as he does not act against the Shari'a."[24] While Private Law in all its main branches was fairly well-developed on the basis of rulings laid down by Muslim jurists in the first two centuries, Public Law had mixed progress. The Law of Peace and War received much attention, as was natural in view of the fighting career of a new nation. Financial Law was likewise well developed since its basic elements, state revenue and state expenditure, were well defined in the Qur'an and in the Prophet's practice. However,

> Constitutional Law was not so fortunate. The unique role of the Prophet, both as interpreter and giver of laws and as supreme civil leader and commander, precluded any generalization as to the nature, distribution, limits, and proper assumption of state power, except for a single qur'anic text recommending consultative deliberation. In particular, there was neither text nor precedent indicating how state power should pass from one leader, or leading group, to another.[25]

The Islamic State and the Constitution in Malaysia

Four years after Mahathir's declaration of Malaysia as an Islamic state, the issue continues to dominate public political discourse. It has evolved beyond a strategy by the ruling party to contain PAS and the legitimacy

PAS appropriates because of the "true" or generic Islam to which it claims adherence. Increasing numbers of Malaysians have entered the public discussion, especially non-Muslims who seek recourse in the constitution of Malaysia.

However, constitutions are not ends in themselves. They exist to secure some purposes and to promote some ideals and values, one of which is "constitutionalism." Constitutionalism can be said to refer to a number of separate but related features of a democratic political system. Why should constitutionalism be an essential dimension of democracy? And should the concept of constitutional government be used as a synonym for plural democracy? In an article on democratization in the Arab world, Jean Leca writes,

> The usual answer is first, that democracy requires governmental accountability, and that accountability requires the rulers to be accountable not on their own terms but according to rules they are not at liberty to change at will; and, second, that democracy requires free, non-violent and regularly repeated competition between groups organized to gain power, as well as participation of all citizens in the choice of leaders and policies.[26]

Essentially, constitutionalism implies loyalty to the various provisions in the constitution by citizens and officials of the state. What this entails is that citizens accept limits on their freedoms, while officials on their part observe the limits on their powers. As Malaysian constitutional law expert, Shad Saleem Faruqi, writes, "The functionaries of the State should hold and derive their powers from specific laws and should act with respect for legality and constitutionality. There must be harmony between official action and the stated rule."[27] In this sense also, respect for the legality of the constitution is similar to the doctrine of the rule of law, the central claim of which is that public authorities must derive and hold their powers from specific laws and must act according to them. Constitutionalism also implies loyalty not only to the letter of the law but also to the spirit of the constitution. It requires a commitment to and an internalization of the values and ideals that inspired the basic law. Further, it demands observance of enacted rules as well as respect for the unwritten and informal practices, conventions, usages, and understandings with which the constitution has become inlaid over the course of time. These include a respect for the law. Constitutionalism refers to the "rule of law" protecting specific spheres of life against arbitrary power, making possible a competition between plurality of values and interests, and effecting compromise between strategic élites more or less representative of important social demands.

It is the element of the observance of the agreements, understandings, and practices beyond the actual stipulations of the constitution that non-Muslims have invoked in their protests over the declaration of Malaysia as an Islamic state. The "social contract" between Malays and non-Malays during the formulation of independence was the underlying and overarching argument of the Malaysian Consultative Council for Buddhism, Christianity, Hinduism, and Sikhism (MCCBCHS), the Council of Churches Malaysia (CCM, or umbrella for the mainstream Protestant churches), the Catholic Church, and the Christian Federation of Malaysia (CFM, which includes the CCM, the Catholic Church, and Evangelical churches), and the Democratic Action Party (DAP, an opposition political party that is multiethnic but that has a large Chinese base).

The social contract is described in the preface to the widely distributed statement entitled *A Declaration on Freedom of Religion or Belief and Elimination of Intolerance and of Discrimination Based on Religion or Belief* that was published by the MCCBCHS. In the press conference at which it was first distributed, it was announced that the Declaration, which was first issued in 1998, was being reissued in January 2002 as the response of the MCCBCHS to the declaration of Malaysia as an Islamic state. The statement's preface refers to "the social covenant" which was and is,

> ... based on due recognition to the pluralistic nature of our Malaysian community that has been threatened by extreme ideological forces based either on arrogance of race or religious dogmatism. The dangers of political religion cannot be over-emphasised as it threatens the delicate social fabric of our nationhood.[28]

The DAP describes this implicit agreement between the various races that came together to forge the Malayan nation as "the 44-year-old Social Contract." This argument was the most consistent statement from the DAP throughout 2002, and is prominent in alternative public discourse; as such, it bears quoting:

> Mahathir's declaration that Malaysia is an Islamic state is a fundamental breach of the 44-year-old Social Contract reached by our forefathers from the three communities in the 1957 Merdeka Constitution and reaffirmed

by the peoples of Sabah and Sarawak in 1962 on the formation of Malaysia, founding the nation as a democratic, secular, multi-religious, tolerant and progressive state with Islam as the official religion and not as an Islamic state. For 44 years, the mainstream nation-building agenda was to develop and sustain the democratic, secular and multi-religious nature of the Malaysian Constitution and voices calling for an Islamic state were at the periphery; but overnight, with Mahathir's declaration, the controversy over what type of an Islamic state Malaysia should become has hijacked the mainstream nation-building agenda.[29]

The CFM issued a booklet and the statement:

> The assurances by the Prime Minister and Barisan Nasional leaders that the Constitution will not be tampered with do not offer sufficient guarantee that Malaysia will not degenerate into something of the Islamic model which PAS is promoting. Rhetoric may lead to reality.[30]

The CFM stand describes how the impact of administrative Islamization policies and programs have undermined the secular and multicultural pluralistic basis of Malaysia, asserts that it has resulted in the marginalization of non-Islamic religions, and warns that there are fundamental signs of intolerance of non-Muslims and their beliefs and practices. It views these practices as having an uncomfortable parallel with orthodox Islamic theory and the ideology of an Islamic state and practice in dealing with dhimmis. The CFM document states that "there is justified concern that the Prime Minister's announcement might be taken to be 'freedom of action' authority to embark on policies and programmes to turn Malaysia into an orthodox Islamic state."[31]

The various statements that have been issued in opposition to the declaration of Malaysia as an Islamic state all refer to "guarantees" of freedom of religion in the constitution, and invoke precedents of the United Nations "reflecting the heritage of our common humanity with the global community" as a "source for reflection, [and] resource for law-making and administrative policy making and decisions,"[32] in order to stress recourse to the rule of law.

The guarantees entrenched in the constitution were first raised by Shad Saleem Faruqi in his presentation at the MCA forum in October 2001 to explain the Islamic state, and in the paper he distributed, entitled "Constitutional Perspectives on Freedom of Religion, Secularism and Theocracy." The paper outlined the various laws and articles in the constitution on religion, and described which were problematic even as his overall theme was one of reassurance. At the forum, Faruqui gave verbal reassurance that article 3, which provides for freedom of religion, could not be amended easily.[33]

In the paper that he distributed, Faruqui wrote extensively about conversion out of Islam and how any laws to legislate *aqidah* (belief) "will trigger a massive constitutional debate that will humiliate Malaysia internationally, cause divisions within the *ummah* [the community of Muslims] and embarrass the judiciary."[34] He concluded that "Malaysia is neither a full-fledged Islamic state nor wholly secular," but that "in view of the fact that Muslims constitute the majority of the population, and Islamisation is being vigorously enforced, Malaysia can indeed be described as an Islamic or Muslim country."[35] His regular feature article in the *Star* on October 28, 2001, concerning the Islamic state debate is entitled "Facing a Problem of Semantics." In it, he attributes the clash of opinions simply to the fact that there is no litmus test or list of criteria on which there is universal agreement that typifies a social or legal system as theocratic or temporal.

These reassurances notwithstanding from someone who is an expert and who struggled with integrity in his paper, the fact remains that the Malaysian constitution has been amended extensively since independence in 1957,[36] a reality that caused Mahathir himself to write, "The manner, the frequency and the trivial reasons for altering the Constitution reduced this supreme law of the nation to a useless scrap of paper"[37]—although in the past twenty years, his administration also enacted a considerable number of amendments to the constitution. Consequently, many participants at forums on the Islamic state have expressed concern about the possibility that, at any stage in the future, the constitution could be amended to enhance the claim that Malaysia is an Islamic state.

The most often cited provisions in Malaysia's constitution that support arguments against Malaysia as a religious (or Islamic) state are article 3, clauses (1) and (4), which state that Islam is the religion of the Federation but also that other religions may be practiced in peace and harmony, and that nothing in this article derogates from any other provision of the constitution. Article 11 specifies that every person has the right to profess and practice his or her religion and, subject to clause 4, to propagate it (however, clause 4 restricts the propagation of any non-Islamic religious doctrine or belief among Muslims). Clause 11 declares that every religious group has the right to manage its own affairs, establish and maintain institutions, and acquire and own property. Article 12 (1) stipulates that there shall be no discrimination against any citizen on the grounds of only religion, race, descent, place of birth, or gender. Clause (2) of article 12 provides for the right of every religious group to establish and maintain institutions for the education of children in its own religion. Clause (3) asserts that no person shall be required to receive instruction or take part in any ceremony or act of worship of a religion other than one's own.

In addition, historical documents often are cited to bolster Malaysia's constitutional guarantees. The Reid Commission, which was convened in 1956 through 1957 to draw up a constitution for Malaya, states in paragraph 169, article 4.2 on state religion that the commission considered the question of whether there should be any statement in the constitution to the effect that the state should adopt Islam as the state religion. The report by the commission then invokes the view of the rulers that it would not be desirable to insert a declaration that the Muslim Faith or Islamic Faith be the established religion of the Federation. The Reid Commission document quotes the statement of the Counsel for the Rulers, which said,

> It is Their Highnesses' considered view that it would not be desirable to insert some declaration such as has been suggested that the Muslim Faith or Islamic Faith be the established religion of the Federation. Their Highnesses are not in favour of such a declaration being inserted and that is a matter of specified instruction in which I myself have played very little part.[38]

The Reid Commission document's clause 4.3, paragraph 11, describes the note of dissent by commission member Justice Abdul Hamid. Justice Abdul Hamid wanted a provision declaring Islam to be the religion of the state, while making clear in that same provision that such a declaration would not be a disability "on non-Muslim citizens professing, propagating and practicing their religions, and *[would] not prevent the State from being a secular State*" (emphasis added).[39]

Years later and even before Mahathir's declaration of Malaysia as an Islamic state, there were jurists who wished that Justice Abdul Hamid's provision had held sway. Malaysia's most distinguished Dean of Law at the University of Malaya and the International Islamic University, the late Professor Ahmad Ibrahim, both defended the constitution and found it lacking in terms of the status of Islam. He came to the conclusion that it was easy to adopt a negative attitude and to say that the Federal Constitution was not in accordance with Islam. He suggested a "remedy" by accepting the constitution and trying the best to uphold the principles of Islamic government. In his argument, he wrote about the social contract between all Malayans at the birth of the nation:

> The acceptance of the Federal Constitution was made possible by the negotiations and compromise arrived at by all the communities in Malaysia. We should respect the agreement based on the understanding and friendship between the various communities. At the same time we should try to think and act positively and work the Constitution in such a way as to uphold the principles of Islamic government and have regard to the interests of all the communities in Malaysia.[40]

However, later in the same article, Ahmad Ibrahim also wrote that Muslims should argue that they are entitled under article 3(1) to lead their way of life according to the teachings of Islam, and that, if they wish to follow Islamic Law and not the English Common Law, they should be allowed to do so. He suggested that article 4, which states that the constitution is the supreme law of the land and that any law passed after independence that was inconsistent with it would be void, should be read in a practical manner. He further argued that article 4 refers only to written law and that there is a special status for pre-Merdeka laws that are not rendered invalid by inconsistency with the constitution, and maintained that Islamic law falls within such ambit. He continued by arguing that, in Islam, the rule of law is to be implemented to the fullest, and in conclusion suggested a way to amend the Federal Constitution: If Muslims want to make the constitution more in line with Islam, they must ensure that they are in a position to amend it. That is, they must register as voters and elect representatives who gain a two-thirds majority in the Houses of Parliament, thus ensuring that Islam-friendly amendments are adopted. "For this purpose we must strive to be united so that we can better serve the course of our people, our religion and our country,"[41] he counseled.

It can be argued that, although he recognized the social contract with non-Muslims, ultimately, Ahmad Ibrahim's definition of "our people, our religion and our country" in his widely cited treatise on the status of

Islam in Malaysia, was limited only to Muslims. This can be construed as a virtual abrogation of the social contract upon which the nation was founded, and it is this argument that is at the heart of the debate that has raged since PAS announced its intention to establish an Islamic state and Mahathir declared in 2001 that Malaysia already was an Islamic state.

In arguments resonant with Ahmad Ibrahim's, Abdul Aziz Bari, who is course coordinator for Constitutional Law at the International Islamic University, also states about the constitution that "it is not quite true to say that everything in the document—in this respect, Islam and matters related to the religion—was conceived at that particular point of time."[42] He argues that, consequently, we need to go beyond the point of time when the constitution was promulgated in order to understand fully the nature and extent of the provisions concerned. He insists that Muslims must be guided by the Shari'a and that the substance of such a state must also be guided by its spirit, going so far as to claim that *adat* (traditional native law) and secular law "may be called Islamic if they are put in place to regulate matters that are not dealt with by the texts."[43] He further states, "We may have an Islamic state while at the same time retain the existing constitution,"[44] but he relegates non-Muslims to participating "in the debate and contribut[ing] to it by pointing out the values that are universal in their application."[45]

Writing about the social contract as being more about race than about all religions being of equal status in Malaysia, but reminding us also about those who hold that the present constitution should be replaced with an Islamic state, constitutional law expert Andrew Harding states, "The choice depends on whether the social contract is regarded as fundamental to the Malaysian approach to government, or as a phase of national development."[46] He provides a prelude to this statement by describing the gradual erosion of the fundamental principles of liberty that the Malaysian constitution once embodied. He then states that the conclusion drawn from his survey of the Malaysian constitution is that "the principles of the Constitution have been eroded and limited to an extent where no further erosion or limitation can occur without affecting the very bone marrow and life-blood of the Constitution itself."[47] He offers two solutions: If further constitutional development is seen as taking Malaysia further away from the basic principles of the post-Merdeka period, "it would be best if the Constitution spelled out more frankly what the basic tenets of the Malaysian polity actually are,"[48] and second, that a Royal Commission on the Constitution should investigate constitutional reform, taking evidence from the public and making recommendations.

There have been few Muslims who have articulated positions on the Islamic state; as stated earlier, public discourse has been overwhelmed by protagonists from UMNO and PAS, all of whom propose courses of action or argue the issue largely on the premise of political promise, legitimacy, and expedience. However, research conducted by the author reveals that most ordinary Muslim Malaysians do not know what constitutes an Islamic state, nor do they particularly desire one. Nevertheless, it is significant that more than 70 percent of those interviewed by the author also expressed how they could not oppose an Islamic state, stating that it was probably incumbent upon them as Muslims not to oppose or reject one. Likewise, the high-profile women's activist group, Sisters in Islam (SIS), while strenuously opposing the enactment of the *hudud* legislation in Kelantan and Terengganu, has never taken an open position rejecting the notion of an Islamic state. In a personal communication of December 5, 2002, to the author from Zainah Anwar, executive director of Sisters in Islam, she wrote that SIS does, in fact, oppose the formation of an Islamic state, but she did not respond to a further question about why SIS has not taken a public position. The majority of middle-class Malay Muslims can be described as muted by varying degrees of such silence (although in fairness to SIS, its members can hardly be described as "silent" on many issues that affect Muslim women), and as unwilling to be chastised as being against Islam or being an infidel, or even as being "less Islamic" or an "insulter of Islam." It is the silence of the majority that enables public discourse to be dominated, by default, by the minority who want an Islamic state. This minority's stridence causes their definition of Islam and Islamization in Malaysia to hold sway beyond what their number in proportion to the total population of the country's Muslims justifies. The level of misrepresentation becomes obvious in a survey conducted in January 2004, in which only 2 percent of Muslims responded that religion was the most important issue in the country![49]

The issue of the Islamic state became intensified when it was conflated with the enactment of *hudud* legislation in July 2002 in the state of Terengganu (that is controlled by PAS). The contention as it has evolved is too complex to deal with in the limitations of this chapter, but it is significant that the hardening of PAS's position, irrespective of the resistance to the ramifications of the *hudud* legislation, has made some

Malaysian Muslims rethink the viability of an Islamic state. In an article published in December 2002, a regular columnist for the on-line newspaper *Malaysiakini* came out against the notion of an Islamic state. Mazeni Alwi, who in the past displayed obvious leanings toward PAS, wrote about the Iranian academic, Hashem Aghajari, and the death penalty meted out to him for his speech commemorating Ali Shariati's death, in which he argued that the clergy themselves are not intrinsic to Islam and that they have no divine right to rule. Mazeni Alwi asserted, "With the Hashem case, the notion of the Islamic state led by religious elite as a late twentieth century phenomenon seemed to have come full circle in a very short space of two decades . . . nobody can say now that we have not performed the experiment."[50] He concluded that, although Iran has had an adventure with the leadership of the ulama and the hope that through them an earthly paradise would be possible, it did not take long for that fanciful, simplistic hope to turn to disillusionment when a new, religious totalitarianism took over from the old. He states that Hashem's case "should lead us to reexamine the Islamic state project. Maybe it's time to restore the notion of leadership of the ulama to its traditional role of moral and spiritual leadership . . . political leadership by the religious elite is perhaps a late twentieth century aberration that will sooner or later run its course."[51]

In late 2004, there was an uproar in Malaysia over the conversion to Islam of two minors who were in the custody of their non-Muslim mother. Shamala Sathijaseelan had applied to the High Court of Malaysia for an interim order and custody was given to her, with visitation rights to her ex-husband, Jeyaganesh Morgarajah, who had converted to Islam. Without the consent or knowledge of Shamala, Jeyaganesh converted their two children and obtained an ex parte order for custody from the Shari'a Court. He took the children away, but when threatened with a contempt order by the High Court, he returned the children to their mother. Shamala applied to the High Court of Malaysia for a declaration that the conversion of her two children was null and void, but her application was dismissed on the ground that the High Court had no jurisdiction to grant her relief as the matter was within the jurisdiction of the Shari'a Court. However, as a non-Muslim, she is unable to apply to the Shari'a Court for relief or remedy because its jurisdiction is only Muslims.

At issue here are two parallel and equally supreme sets of laws and their courts: Common Law for non-Muslims and the Shari'a for Muslim personal law, concerning matters such as marriage, divorce, custody, and wills. The Common Law system has shown a growing unwillingness to defend its jurisdiction in areas where it could run into conflicts with the Shari'a system. At stake is Islamic identity, which is conflated with Malay ethnicity to define special privileges for Malays in the constitution, and the struggle over whether Malaysia is, in fact, an Islamic nation, in which case the Shari'a should have primacy. Women's nongovernmental organizations (NGOs) weighed in, and together with human rights groups and other NGOs, organized a half-day seminar entitled "Article 11" (the reference is to article 11 of the constitution of Malaysia, which guarantees freedom of religion). In response to a question on the Shamala case, the prime minister stated in parliament that, "This case does not alter law on custodial rights of non-Muslim parents,"[52] but skipped the fundamental problem and assured the body that provisions under existing regulations were sufficient to protect the rights of non-Muslim parents. Various representatives of religious minorities in Malaysia also issued statements expressing concern, and the Catholic Archbishop of Malaysia, Murphy Pakiam, protested against the High Court's unwillingness to give real relief or remedy. He said that authorities should ensure that the social contract forged at the time of independence is maintained with Islam as the official religion and freedom of religion of non-Muslims guaranteed. "Hence, just because Islam is the religion of the federation, the application of Syariah law cannot be extended to the sphere of public law. This social contract and constitutional guarantee is meaningless without the protection of the High Court," he added.[53]

Conclusion

Perhaps the time has come when the conflict of laws, Civil and Shari'a, should be resolved by legislation—the setting up of a Constitutional Court, if it is the constitution that is supreme. But that the constitution is supreme becomes less clear as matters evolve in Malaysia, with the "Islamic state" as symbol and metaphor for political and theocratic agendas.

It grows increasingly obvious from the interviews conducted for the author's research project that the turn to Islam and the willingness to consider the possibilities of an Islamic state are rooted not only in a sense that this might be required to demonstrate a fidelity to Islam. The cleaving to Islam is also a recourse against the corruption, cronyism, and nepotism that many feel plague public life in Malaysia. Many

Muslims believe that a return to religious fundamentals and ethics—in this instance, Islamic—will restore moral rectitude. For many Muslims in Malaysia, Islam is also enabling as a compass for negotiating the (sometimes debilitating) maze of modernity and hegemonic Western-oriented globalization that are often described as an anathema to Islam. Indeed, many are swayed by the PAS argument that it is only through the legislation and severe punishments that an Islamic state enjoins that transparency, good governance, and justice will prevail.

Few consider the grave problem that the concept of an Islamic state as it is articulated in classical text and tradition, no matter how altruistic, privileges fidelity to the ruler and religious strictures, pays little heed to the rights of the people, and is not contiguous with the modern nation-state that is founded on the emancipation of the human being through the right to vote, and on notions of individual rights and fundamental freedoms.[54]

Notes

1. I. William Zartman, "Islam, the State and Democracy," in *Between the State and Islam*, ed. Charles E. Butterworth and I. William Zartman (Cambridge, UK: Woodrow Wilson Center Press and Cambridge University Press, 2001), 243.

2. Ahmad S. Moussalli, "Islamic Democracy and Pluralism," in *Progressive Muslims: On Justice, Gender and Pluralism*, ed. Omid Safi (Oxford: Oneworld Publications, 2003), 287.

3. Fathi Osman, "Democracy and the Concept of Shura," in *Religions in Dialogue: From Theocracy to Democracy*, ed. Alan Race and Ingrid Shafer (Aldershot, UK: Ashgate, 2002), 88.

4. Ibid., 96.

5. Khalid Duran, "How Democratic Is Islam?" in *Religions in Dialogue: From Theocracy to Democracy*, ed. Alan Race and Ingrid Shafer (Aldershot, UK: Ashgate, 2002), 112.

6. Ibid., 116.

7. Ghassan Salame, introduction to *Democracy without Democrats?: The Renewal of Politics in the Muslim World*, ed. Ghassan Salame (London: I.B. Taurus, 1996), 2.

8. Nazih Ayoubi makes a similar argument in "Rethinking the Public/Private Dichotomy: Radical Islam and Civil Society in the Middle East," *Contention* 4, no. 3 (Spring 1995): 79–105.

9. Saad Eddin Ibrahim, "The Troubled Triangle: Populism, Islam and Civil Society in the Arab World," in *Islam in a Changing World: Europe and the Middle East*, ed. Anders Jerichow and Jorgen Baek Simonsen (London: Curzon Press, 1997), 26.

10. I differentiate between "patriarchal," which is andocentric, and "paternal," which intimates the paternalism of a dominant and/or authoritarian state, and choose to add in this distinction, although Zubaida uses only "patriarchal" to intimate both concepts.

11. Sami Zubaida, "Community and Democracy in the Middle East," 234–35; and "Islam, the State and Democracy: Contrasting Conceptions of Civil Society in Egypt," *Middle East Report* (1992): 979.

12. *Sun*, October 6, 2001, 1; *Star*, October 6, 2001, 1.

13. Tong Yee Siong, "Islamic State Declaration for Malay Ears Only: DPM," *Malaysiakini*, December 11, 2001, www.malaysiakini.com/News/2001/12/200121107.php3.

14. *New Sunday Times*, October 21, 2001.

15. Al-Mawardi, Abu'l-Hasan 'Ali ibn Muhammad ibn Habib al-Basri al-Baghdad (d. 450 A.H.), *Al-Ahkam al-Sultaniyyah* (London: Ta-Ha Publishers, 1987), 44.

16. Ibid., 207.

17. Ibid., 208.

18. Ibid.

19. Ibid.

20. Ibid.

21. Ibid.

22. Ibid., 210–11.

23. Ibid., 211.

24. Lukman Thaib, *The Notion of State in Islam* (Kuala Lumpur: Quill, 1990), 5.

25. Fawzy Mansour, *The Arab World: Nation, State and Democracy* (London: Zed Books, and Tokyo, United Nations University, 1992), 51–52.

26. Jean Leca, "Democratization in the Arab World: Uncertainty, Vulnerability and Legitimacy: A Tentative Conceptualization and Some Hypotheses," in *Democracy without Democrats?* ed. Ghassam Salame (New York: St. Martin's Press, 1994), 57.

27. Shad Saleem Faruqui, "Balancing Mights with Rights," *Star*, June 9, 2002.

28. The Malaysian Consultative Council of Buddhism, Christianity, Hinduism, and Sikhism, *A Declaration on Freedom of Religion or Belief and Elimination of Intolerance and of Discrimination Based on Religion or Belief* (Kuala Lumpur: Malaysian Consultative Council of Buddhism, Christianity, Hinduism, and Sikhism, January 2002), 1.

29. Lim Kit Siang, DAP national chairman, "Should Malaysia be an Islamic State," speech at the Penang Democratic Action Party (DAP) forum, February 28, 2002, available at http://dapmalaysia.org (accessed January 9, 2005).

30. Christian Federation of Malaysia, *Malaysia as an Islamic State: An Analysis* (Kuala Lumpur: Christian Federation of Malaysia, January 2002), 14.

31. Ibid.

32. The Malaysian Consultative Council of Buddhism, Christianity, Hinduism, and Sikhism, *A Declaration on Freedom of Religion or Belief and Elimination of Intolerance and of Discrimination Based on Religion or Belief*, 1.

33. At other forums, additional memoranda and papers were distributed by individuals, especially on the Federal Constitution, religion, and the secular state in terms of legal implications, safeguards, precedents, and problems. All these papers and information sheets repudiated the viability of Malaysia as an Islamic state.

34. Shad Saleem Faruqui, "Constitutional Perspectives on Freedom of Religion, Secularism and Theocracy," paper presented at the MCA Forum on the Islamic State, Kuala Lumpur, Malaysia, October 2001, 11.

35. Ibid., 18–19.

36. See Tun Salleh Abas, "Amendment of the Malaysian Constitution," *MLJ* 2: XXXIV, 1977, and H.P. Lee, "Constitutional Amendments in Malaysia," *Malaya Law Review* 18 (1976): 44–70.

37. Mahathir bin Mohamed, *The Malay Dilemma* (Kuala Lumpur: Federal Publications, 1981), 11.

38. Federation of Malaya Constitutional Commission, *Report of the Federation of Malaya Constitutional Commission, 1957* (London: Colonial Office, 1957), 73, para. 169.

39. Ibid., 99.

40. Ahmad Ibrahim, "The Principles of an Islamic Constitution and the Constitution of Malaya: A Comparative Analysis," *Law Journal of the International Islamic University* 1 (1989): 6.

41. Ibid., 10.

42. Abdul Aziz Bari, "Secularism or Theocracy: A Study of the Malaysian Constitution," a commentary on the paper of the same title prepared by Shad Saleem Faruqui for the MSRC-KAF Intercultural Discourse Series, September 5, 2002, 1.

43. Ibid.

44. Ibid., 2.

45. Ibid., 3.

46. Andrew Harding, *Law, Government and the Constitution in Malaysia* (The Hague and London: The London-Leiden Series on Law, Administration and Development, 1996), 273.

47. Ibid.

48. Ibid.

49. *National Electorate Survey Highlights: Voter Perceptions on National Issues, Economic Optimism, Crime and Public Safety, Islam and Political Participation* (Kuala Lumpur: MERDEKA Centre, February 2004).

50. Mazeni Alwi, "The Case of Hashim Aghajari: Islamic State Vision Comes Full Circle," *Malaysiakini*, November 30, 2002, www.malaysiakini.com/columns/20021130013683.php.

51. Ibid.

52. "Non-Muslim Parents' Custodial Rights Safeguarded by Law," July 14, 2004, www.bernama.com/bernama/v3/news.php?id=79673 (accessed January 9, 2005).

53. "Conversion: Let Court Hear Cases, Say Bishops," *New Straits Times*, July 13, 2004, 12.

54. An earlier version of this chapter's section, "Malaysia as an Islamic State," was published in *Contemporary Southeast Asia: A Journal of International and Strategic Affairs* 23, no. 3, Institute of Southeast Asian Studies (ISEAS), Singapore (December 2002): 474–503. Also, a more comprehensive version of the section, "The Islamic State and the Constitution in Malaysia," is available in Patricia Martinez, "Islam, Constitutional Democracy and the Islamic State in Malaysia," in *Islam and Civil Society in Southeast Asia*, ed. Lee Hock Guan (Singapore: Institute for Southeast Asian Studies, 2004).

11

The Soka Gakkai's Critical Role in the Rapidly Changing World of Postwar Japanese Politics

Daniel A. Metraux

Several religious organizations in Japan have emerged as key political forces in the postwar era. Many of Japan's "New Religions" have played an active role either in support of a specific party or group of candidates or by running candidates of their own. Seicho-no-Ie has had an active conservative political agenda, the Union of New Religious Organizations in Japan (UNROJ) has successfully run a number of candidates in the House of Councilors and has cooperated closely with the ruling conservative Liberal Democratic Party (LDP), and the now infamous Aum Shinrikyō ran twenty-five candidates in the 1990 general election. But it is the Soka Gakkai that has had the greatest impact on Japanese politics.

Japan's Soka Gakkai, a massive, modern, lay Buddhist movement with perhaps eight million members in Japan and another two million worldwide, has played a decisive but controversial role in the postwar maturation of Japanese democracy.[1] The Soka Gakkai, through its party, the Komeito,[2] has provided a voice for millions of alienated Japanese who otherwise might have become estranged from the country's postwar political system. For decades, the Soka Gakkai and Komeito, together with other progressive parties, prevented the conservative ruling Liberal Democratic Party (LDP) from amending Japan's liberal Occupation-era constitution. And, since 1999, the Soka Gakkai and Komeito have helped to bring political stability to Japan by forming a close working coalition with the LDP. There is every indication that the Soka Gakkai will continue to be a key political force in Japan for years to come. Table 11.1 indicates the important role of the Soka Gakkai and Komeito as a major force in Japanese politics.

The Soka Gakkai's participation in politics is by no means an anomaly in Japanese history. The fact that the Soka Gakkai is actively engaged in

Table 11.1

Komeito Seats in the Lower House Since 1967

Election year	Seats won
1967	25
1969	47
1972	29
1976	55
1980	33
1983	59
1986	56
1990	45
1993	51
1996	— (allied with Shinshinto)
2000	31
2003	34
Upper House elections, 1998 and 2001	
1998	22
2001	23

Sources: www.electionworld.org/japan.htm, and Daniel A. Metraux, *The Soka Gakkai Revolution* (New York and London: University Press of America, 1994), 67–69.

Japanese politics stems largely from a tradition in Japan that strongly links religion and other aspects of society. Americans have a long tradition of the separation of church and state, but such an idea did not exist in traditional Japan. Indeed, Japan has a long history that links politics and religion under the divine authority of the emperor.

The pre–World War II imperial state system in Japan was "a kind of patriarchal absolutism based on the absolute divinity of the Emperor from which all legitimate authority emanated."[3] Late in the Meiji era (1868–1912), the Japanese government fostered both State Shinto and Shinto theologians as a source by which to legitimize the newly built government and to unite the people under its authority. The government encouraged the spread of Shinto rituals and demanded that all citizens adopt them, thus utilizing the Shinto ceremonial events to enhance nationalism. "State Shinto was a sort of new national religion introduced by the government after the Meiji period, but the government regarded it not as a religion, but as the national ideology which dominated other general religions."[4]

The New Religions that flourished in the prewar era (such as Omotokyo) often displayed a concern with politics and with national political issues. Sociologist Nakano Tsuyoshi orders prewar New Religions into three groups in terms of their response to the government's policy of sponsoring National Shintoism. The first consists of movements like Omotokyo, which openly criticized the government for its alleged tampering with the "authentic" and "original" spirit of Shinto and called for a reconstruction of society based on a "true unity" of Shinto and the Imperial Way. The government eventually suppressed Omotokyo. A second group of New Religions, such as Tenrikyo and Reiyukai, supported the government's ideology of the emperor system and the national polity and thus were permitted some degree of spiritual independence in exchange for their support of the government. A third rather insignificant group denied the ideology of the emperor system and national polity. One of the leading organizations in this category was the Soka Kyoiku Gakkai (SKG), the forerunner of today's Soka Gakkai.

Makiguchi Tsunesaburo (1871–1944), the founder of SKG, strongly opposed the measures incorporated in the Religious Organizations Law of 1939, which sought to impose government control over religions by forcing the amalgamation of denominations. The SKG leadership also refused to worship and enshrine replicas of the sacred tablets of Ise Grand Shrine, stating that this ran contrary to its religious teachings. As a result, Makiguchi, his chief disciple, Toda Josei (1900–1958), and other SKG leaders were imprisoned in 1943 and the organization was itself dissolved. Makiguchi died in prison in 1944, and Toda, who resuscitated the Soka Gakkai after the war, was not released until July 1945.

This threefold political division of New Religions reemerged after World War II when the Occupation abolished most laws suppressing religious activity. The most radically conservative sect was Seicho-no-Ie, which sought to abolish many of the more liberal reforms of the Allied Occupation that it said were alien to Japanese cultural traditions. It wanted to reconstruct the state in accordance with the traditional ideals of the Japanese nation, including the revision of the Japanese constitution and the creation of a new educational system not dominated by left-wing teachers. A second grouping of New Religions, including Rissho Koseikai, Perfect Liberty (PL) Kyodan, and Sekai Kyuseikai, formed the Union of New Religious Organizations in Japan. UNROJ has successfully run a number of candidates in the House of Councilors and has cooperated closely with the ruling conservative LDP. The third grouping consists of the Soka Gakkai, which created its own opposition party, the Komeito, in 1964. The Komeito retained its opposition status, except for a few months in 1993–1994, when it joined a number of opposition parties in a brief anti-LDP coalition government. The Komeito entered a three-party coalition with the LDP in 1999.

The Soka Gakkai's interest in politics stems, in part, from the Nichiren tradition of political activism in Japanese history. Nichiren (1222–1282), founder of the only native school of Japanese Buddhism and patron saint of the many Nichiren sects, including the Soka Gakkai, is one of the great anti-establishment figures of Japanese history. His defiant stance against the political establishment won him the support of some ordinary Japanese, but also led to his arrest, exile, and near execution. Various segments of the Nichiren school have retained this anti-establishment stance ever since. Tokyo University Professor Nariyoshi Tamaru notes:

> In the history of Japanese Buddhism Nichiren's teachings occupy a unique position. They are distinguished from other schools by their pre-eminently political orientation, bringing Buddhism into the realities of social life, and the firm sense of mission to achieve this goal by any means. It is a mentality rarely found elsewhere in the Buddhist world and may be called "prophetic" in the proper sense of the word. Indeed, in the latter half of his life Nichiren came to regard himself as a prophet of the Lotus Sutra, a bodhisattva who had been commissioned by the Buddha to propagate the true teaching. These convictions seem to have been strengthened by the repeated persecution that he suffered. This activist spirit is clearly an integral portion of his legacy and can be found in a number of his followers, including the founders of the Soka Gakkai.[5]

Nichiren was himself an inherently anti-establishment figure who sought to reform society through the eradication of what he felt were false religions and doctrines that were supported by the Japanese government. He called for the establishment of his own form of Buddhism as the official religion "of Japan and the construction of a national high sanctuary (kaidan) to symbolize the centrality of this Buddhism and to support a class of priests charged with maintaining the tradition on behalf of the government. Only when this was accomplished would Japan experience an end to poverty, crime, disease and war."[6]

The Soka Gakkai today has rejected such an absolutist view of religion, although it remains true to Nichiren's view of a truly just, nurturing, and affluent society. Contemporary Soka Gakkai leaders champion freedom of religion, by means of which they can proselytize their doctrines without fear of interference by the government or any other social or political force in Japan.

The Soka Gakkai, like Nichiren, is a "world-reforming" sect that advocates the necessity of broad social and political change to bring about a kinder, more peaceful world. Because Nichiren and Soka Gakkai have always challenged the status quo, they are inherently anti-establishment in their nature[7] and have been feared and loathed by members of the ruling "establishment." As a result, Nichiren Buddhism traditionally has also gained a broad following among the less-advantaged segments of Japanese society, and the Soka Gakkai, in reality, a modern lay sect of Nichiren Buddhism, has attracted a huge following among lower-class and lower-middle-class Japanese.

The Soka Gakkai's interest in politics is part of the Nichiren tradition of political activism in Japanese history. Nichiren himself remonstrated against the government's support of other sects of Buddhism, blaming catastrophes afflicting Japan in the late 1200s on the government's neglect of the true laws and saving powers of the *Lotus Sutra*. The Soka Gakkai likes to think that it has inherited Nichiren's sense of determination and ardor.

The Soka Gakkai developed a strong power base, after launching a highly successful "Great Propagation Campaign" that appealed directly to urban-based Japanese in the lower economic echelons of society who were largely excluded from the benefits of the major economic expansion of the immediate post-Occupation period. Tamaru Nariyoshi notes that, when the Allied Occupation removed the many restraints on religious freedom, there was also a growing segment of the population that became dislocated by "the accelerated process of industrialization and urbanization—fertile soil for new religious movements."[8] A great many of these people found solace both in the religious doctrines and socialization practices of the Toda Josei-led Soka Gakkai.

The Origins of Soka Gakkai as a Sociopolitical Movement

Japanese sociologist Shiobara Tsutomu has distinguished four major stages in the sociopolitical development of the Soka Gakkai:

1. An initial stage of the ideological movement in a small circle that was led by Makiguchi (the 1930s to World War II);
2. The stage of a militant socioreligious movement, mainly under Toda's leadership (the late 1940s to 1958);

3. The stage of a religiopolitical campaign, aimed at the realization of *obutsumyogo*[9] by means of a dual organization—religious and political (1958 to the mid-1970s);
4. The stage of institutionalized movement trying to adapt to the existing social milieu (the late 1970s to the present).[10]

The Soka Gakkai's premise under Toda was that Japan had entered the darkest days of what Nichiren and other medieval Buddhist scholars in Japan had termed "the age of *mappo*,"[11] an eschatological view of Buddhist history. They suggested that the world would enter a state of complete turbulence and death as mankind became dangerously separated from the sacred teachings of the Buddha. People would become so ignorant of Buddhist doctrines that they would embrace false religions and become so dominated by greed and hate that the world would be convulsed in violent mayhem. Ultimately, however, some strong leaders would emerge who had discovered the essence of the Buddha's doctrines. These people would create a peaceful and prosperous society by directing mankind to the saving powers of the Buddha.

Nichiren was a major proponent of the concept of mappo. He declared that the root cause of the many political calamities and natural disasters that Japan encountered in the 1200s stemmed from a religious base—the failure of the people to follow the true teachings of the Buddha as espoused in the *Lotus Sutra* and the government's willingness to give alms to priests of sects that did not adhere to the *Lotus Sutra*.[12] Nichiren wrote a lengthy polemic, *Rissho Ankokuron* [The establishment of righteousness and security of the country, 1260], in which he concluded that a stable, peaceful society could exist only if the people had come to accept the correct teachings of the Buddha. Nichiren felt that redemption could be gained only here and now and that the sentient world could become a Buddhist paradise if people would turn to the correct form of Buddhism.

Toda and the Soka Gakkai theorized that Japan's total destruction during World War II and the misery of its people had occurred because the Japanese government had rejected Buddhism in favor of State Shinto and had tried to force Soka Gakkai leaders and other true adherents of Nichiren Buddhism to forsake their practice. Toda and the Soka Gakkai, however, had miraculously survived the inferno and now were set to guide Japan and the rest of humanity to a new age of peace and prosperity.

The Soka Gakkai's doctrines combined the salvation of both the individual and society. Each person would undergo a personal transformation for the better (*ningen kakumei*, "human revolution"), and as more and more people experienced this change, society itself would improve. A happy and more productive milieu would also be a wealthier society, so there was every reason for the believer to connect Buddhist practices with the pursuit of secular gain.[13]

The membership of the Soka Gakkai grew rapidly in the 1950s and 1960s mainly among those people comprising the "downtrodden classes in large urban areas who were excluded from the benefits of the early postwar boom."[14] Hiroshi Aruga provides the following sociological profile of the early postwar Gakkai members who came from the "lower to lower-middle stratum of large urban centers":

> To be more specific, one might say that these were employees, managers, or owners of small and medium-sized business that included the manufacturing and service industries. If one were to situate these individuals in postwar Japanese society, one could probably identify two distinct groups. The first consisted of those who, upon observing their circumstances amid the postwar chaos, found a living environment almost identical to that before the war. For these individuals, a decisive difference between their prewar and postwar experiences lay in the fact that they had been firmly rooted in their surroundings before the war—previously, there had existed communities in which they had even served as "district commissioners" (a prominent position in a local community). As the turmoil of democratization set in, these communities were destroyed, at least to all appearances. Hence, a strong sense of estrangement from postwar society developed. The second group . . . consisted of young working class laborers who flocked to the city in droves during the revitalization of postwar capitalism. Since these were individuals who had no stable base in their daily lives and tended to be mobile, they differed fundamentally from the first group. However, one could discern a number of commonalities as well. For instance, people in both groups had difficulty adjusting to the "isolating individuation" of the urban centers, and in many cases they felt what might be called a kind of nostalgia toward the community. Above all, they were among those who were excluded from the prosperity that was generated by economic development.[15]

The Soka Gakkai responded by providing to these people a sense of community, that is, a communal order that fostered a sense of satisfaction of a believer as a member of a group. Followers could rise rapidly in the Gakkai hierarchy through their mastery of Buddhist concepts and their realized leadership abilities, knowing full well that there was much to gain in the secular world through their religious practice. The next logical step was to use their power of numbers at the ballot box.

While other Japanese religious groups can be relatively inwardly directed, avoiding involvement in social problems as much as possible, the Soka Gakkai began its own political crusade, following the activist Nichiren tradition where it is believed that man can and must save the world in its present state, here and now. The driving force was a commitment to obutsumyogo, building a new ethical and moral foundation to counter the corruption of Japanese politics.

Komeito deputy leader Hamayotsu Toshiko expressed the Buddhist-based goals of her party in an interview in late 1998:

> One important aim of the Komeito is to bring about a fundamental shift in values, from a system that is overly materialistic to one that is more humanistic. The politics of humanism aim to establish various social programs (including governmental and economic systems) that will serve and benefit ordinary people rather than power holders. This shift should include national policies designed to tackle the "iron triangle" of the political, bureaucratic and business establishments. While superfluous government funds have been spent on public investment including construction, serving the interests of that particular industry, other areas such as social welfare, culture or education have been underfinanced....
>
> Komeito leaders have proposed a number of policies to revive the Japanese economy including structural reform and deregulation to create more open markets, and various measures to create employment opportunities. Komeito has suggested that the national budget allocation be changed from the current overemphasis on construction to a more meaningful allocation in favor of such areas as telecommunication, environment, social welfare and culture.[16]

Whatever one may say about the Soka Gakkai and the Komeito—and much of the criticism that they receive is quite justified and necessary—they did produce a new breed of politician who had few of the ties to select and often corrupt special interests of more seasoned political leaders. Aruga Hiroshi, Professor of Law emeritus at Tokyo University, presents the following rather convincing argument concerning the contribution to democracy made by the Soka Gakkai's involvement in politics and its politicians:

Once elected, the numerous representatives from the Soka Gakkai succeeded in presenting a layman's critique of politics, which was an expression of their impartial position based on a non-ideological stance. One such Diet member professed, "Because I am not fully versed in the intricacies of politics, I will study seriously from now on." Such expressions of sincerity, untainted by stale, business-as-usual "professionalism," were completely incompatible with previous images of politicians in Japan. Indeed, the reality of Japanese politics is that everything is limited to a question of political maneuvering, and the act of becoming a politician is itself supposed to guarantee expertise and know-how in politics. In fact, the job of a politician, far from requiring dedication or lofty ideals, is generally perceived simply as a job like any other, as long as it offers money, power and prestige. Therefore, one cannot deny that this kind of sincere and serious attitude on the part of Soka Gakkai-backed politicians shattered the way politics were conducted in Japan, serving as a catalyst for "cleaning up" the current situation. This layman's approach certainly made an impact that debilitated [the] state of postwar Japanese democracy, while having a positive effect on the development of the Soka Gakkai. However, because they voiced no fundamental criticisms against the existing system, representatives supported by the Soka Gakkai were faced with numerous dilemmas when they had to go beyond simple advocacy of clean politics to deliberating more concretely on various policy issues.[17]

The Movement of the Soka Gakkai into the Japanese Mainstream

Although Japanese political history is extraordinarily complicated, there is some truth to the perhaps oversimplistic assertion that one of the major aspects of Japanese politics has been a struggle for power between a potent and wealthy establishment and a large amorphous group, consisting of ordinary Japanese who work extraordinarily hard but have little or no power or voice in the nation's decision-making process. This situation was evident in the very stable "1955 political system," wherein the conservative Liberal Democratic Party controlled the Diet with sizable majorities over the perpetually weak Japan Socialist Party (JSP) and a host of smaller parties, including the Komeito. The LDP represented a very broad base of political interests, ranging from powerful businesses in Tokyo to small rural rice farmers and shopkeepers, but it was above all the party of the ruling establishment. The JSP represented the interests of various labor unions, while the Komeito worked in conjunction with its political patron, the Soka Gakkai, a massive self-proclaimed Buddhist social-reform movement that purported to represent the disadvantaged and underprivileged in Japanese society.

The "1955 system" does not exist today because the cliché that contemporary Japan is a very middle-class country has some merit. While there is tremendous breadth to this predominant middle class, Japan's surging economic growth in the first four decades of the postwar era reached virtually every sector of society and there were far fewer "deprived groups" in 1989 than there were in 1949. There was far less compulsion to support "laboring" class or union parties, such as the JSP, and more interest in non-LDP conservative or more moderate parties, such as the present main opposition party, the Minshuto.

Soka Gakkai members climbed up the economic "escalator" just as fast as other Japanese. I conducted a survey of the educational backgrounds of Komeito dietmen in the late 1960s and mid-1990s, and found a profound difference between them. Komeito dietmen in the 1960s had reasonably humble careers and most had only a high school education, but their counterparts in the 1990s and early 2000s had far more "respectable" careers and almost all had been graduated from "name" universities. Soka Gakkai members today reflect Japanese society as a whole, so it is hardly surprising that Komeito began to move away from its politics of confrontation toward being a more cooperative party with a strong stake in the midstream of Japanese politics by the late 1980s.

The "1955 system" began to collapse in the 1980s with the emergence of several alternative conservative parties, which drained many votes from the LDP, and with the decline of the JSP, whose relevance became questionable owing to the decline of labor unions and Japan's emergence as a postindustrial society. The Soka Gakkai-Komeito bloc of roughly 10 percent of the Diet seats represented a key component of the struggle for power, and the organization's membership, as noted above, now more closely resembled that of the whole of Japanese society. These changes, plus a mutual desire for power and influence, led to the formation in 1999 of an alliance between the LDP and Soka Gakkai-Komeito, one of the strangest political partnerships in Japanese political history.

One must question whether this alliance between the core of Japan's establishment and an heir to the country's eight-century-old Nichiren Buddhist tradition will prove to be enduring—or to be a fleeting marriage of convenience with little substance. One must also ask what effect the Soka Gakkai has had on Japan's postwar democratic society.

Japan is unquestionably a far more democratic society at the start of the new century than it was in the immediate postwar era. The Allied Occupation effectively broke the political power monopoly that the conservative establishment had enjoyed until the nation's catastrophic defeat in August 1945. The Supreme Commander of the Allied Powers' (SCAP's) political reforms and new constitution guaranteed the formation of labor unions, gave women the vote, and placed power squarely in the hands of the electorate. Conservative establishment forces consolidated their control over the government with the 1955 creation of the LDP, but a motley grouping of progressive forces, which included the JSP and Soka Gakkai-Komeito, controlled enough votes and seats in the Diet to prevent any amendments to the nation's very liberal constitution. One wonders whether the virtual demise of the JSP[18] and Soka Gakkai-Komeito's decision to join an LDP-led coalition might spell the end to the traditional progressive check on the conservative establishment and an eventual erosion of some of the more liberal aspects of Japanese democracy.

LDP leaders in the past often portrayed the Soka Gakkai's political activities as a threat to the separation of religion and state and to freedom of religion, in general. And it is as a self-styled reform and political movement, rather than as a religious organization, that the Gakkai poses its greatest threat to the political establishment.[19] The Soka Gakkai's political efforts have been generally successful, and with over eight million voters, it represents a sizable voting block that has often worked in opposition to the LDP. The Komeito, which was formed in the mid-1960s, disbanded in 1994, and reconstructed as the New Komeito in 1998, was the first and thus far only religiously based mass party in modern Japanese history. Although the Komeito and Gakkai are officially separate entities, the Gakkai has endorsed the party.[20] Soka Gakkai leaders and members perceive themselves as a people's movement that is dedicated to creating a happy and prosperous society based on Buddhist principles. As has been observed elsewhere, "[a]lthough vocal in its support of religious freedom and its opposition to government intervention in religious affairs, the Soka Gakkai's this worldly asceticism—its commitment to the creation of a good society, and thus its concern for social reform—drives the Soka Gakkai into the arena of political activity."[21]

This concern for social welfare and reform led the Komeito to craft a legislative agenda between the 1970s and 1990s that stressed the need to work for the disadvantaged. For example, the party in its present iteration supports a plan to use revenues from the current consumption tax for social welfare programs. It also suggests that a state-run insurance program needs to be extended to provide nursing care to those elderly who receive such services at home but are not covered by existing plans.[22]

As a party with a strong religious base, the Komeito was difficult to classify in terms of the classical conservative-progressive division of Japanese politics.[23] From the 1950s to the late 1970s, the conservative LDP opted for a low profile on foreign affairs, focusing almost entirely on probusiness policies designed to promote rapid economic growth. The ostensibly progressive JSP, on the other hand, called for unarmed neutrality and the passage of a package of social welfare programs to assist the disadvantaged. The Komeito generally supported the JSP legislative agenda from the mid-1960s to the 1980s, but by the early 1990s, it had shifted its foreign policy stance in favor of the United States–Japan Security Treaty system. That it continued support for a "progressive" social welfare agenda while accepting the LDP-backed security system with the United States led some journalists in the 1990s to call the Komeito a "centrist" party. Even so, most Komeito voters supported the party for religious and not ideological reasons.[24] Voter profile studies in Japan indicate that the vast majority of votes for Komeito candidates were cast by Soka Gakkai members, so the platforms of the candidates had very little bearing on whether they were elected.[25]

Since the 1970s, the Komeito has worked with changing combinations of opposition centrist and progressive parties, and on occasion has made tacit agreements with the LDP. Such tactics played at least an indirect role in persuading the Soka Gakkai to reduce its former exclusivist stance and become a more open and accommodating organization. The Soka Gakkai's bitter divorce from the dogmatic Nichiren Shoshu priesthood[26] in the early 1990s freed the organization to open even more doors to the outside world. Soka Gakkai officials argue that their movement has retained its core religious values,[27] which is probably true in a general sense, but the necessities of political compromise and pragmatism have had a profoundly mellowing effect on the organization.

The Komeito embarked on an active campaign during the 1990s to secure a stronger place in Japan's rapidly changing political system. The slow decline of the LDP led various moderate and conservative splinter parties to foster an alliance that actually governed Japan for eleven months in 1993–1994 and to the formation of a short-lived united front opposition party, the Shinshinto, which fragmented because the only thing that its members could agree on was their opposition to the LDP.

The LDP used the public frenzy over Aum Shinrikyō's terrorist attack on the Tokyo subway in March 1995 to launch both legislation and severe criticism against Aum and the Soka Gakkai in a transparent effort to embarrass and curtail Gakkai leaders, whose political maneuvering had helped to drive the LDP from power and threatened to do so again. An example of the LDP's hostility can be seen in a 1995 statement made by Shizuka Kamei, a right-wing LDP legislator: "Japan is finished if Soka Gakkai takes over. State Shinto will look good by comparison."[28]

The demise of the Shinshinto into a variety of new splinter parties, including a revived Komeito (now called "New Komeito"), and increasing public dissatisfaction with the LDP-created political chaos. This situation was compounded by the LDP's horrendous showing in the July 1998 Upper House elections, in which it lost its majority and failed to capture even a single seat in any of Japan's major urban centers. Anxious to regain some stability, the LDP went shopping for new political partners. The first splinter party to succumb was a former LDP henchman's tiny Conservative Party, but a far bigger prize was necessary to bring dependable stability.

The truly stunning development in 1999 was the agreement by the LDP and the Soka Gakkai-Komeito to form a coalition government that now had an overwhelming majority in both houses of the Diet. The motivation of the LDP was obvious—it would sign a compact perhaps even with the devil if it meant that it could retain power. This attitude had led to a brief alliance with its old nemesis, the JSP, in 1994, and five years later it had now gone to bed with its other archrival, the Soka Gakkai. But why did the Soka Gakkai-Komeito agree to such an alliance?

There are a variety of reasons why the Soka Gakkai and the Komeito may have favored forming a partnership. Perhaps the greatest temptation was actual access to power after so many years in the political wilderness. A legislative aide in the Diet reported overhearing one Komeito legislator telling another in 1999: "We can now have some real power. Nobody can call us 'outsiders' anymore."[29] Except for a few months of shared power in 1993–1994, the Soka Gakkai and Komeito had been on the outside looking in since the Soka Gakkai had begun running candidates for national office in the mid-1950s. While playing the role of loyal opposition may have had a certain appeal for many years, to actually wield power is an important objective of any politician or party.

Access to such has given the Gakkai and Komeito the opportunity to actually influence the passage of legislation and get some of its own ideas enacted into law.

The Soka Gakkai also has been concerned about who will succeed Ikeda and the difficult period of transition that will occur when he passes from the scene. Although Ikeda formally resigned his position as president of the Soka Gakkai in 1979, he is still revered as the movement's spiritual leader and spokesman.[30] Ikeda was born in 1928, and still is very active in Soka Gakkai affairs; however, he is now in his mid-seventies and is said to be concerned about what the future of the movement will be after his retirement or death. One of his desires is to spare the Soka Gakkai from as many outside attacks as possible. Japanese scholars and journalists familiar with the movement speculate that the post-Ikeda Soka Gakkai will be led by a new generation of leaders that includes Ikeda's one surviving son.[31] Observers also believe that the organization might be especially vulnerable to outside attacks during this period of transition.[32] Anson Shupe has written:

> The pressures on any conventional religion to modify its doctrines and activities toward less radical forms are obvious. Respectability and legitimacy ease persecution and rejection, and are beneficial for recruitment and membership retention. Fewer resources need to be expended to repel attacks by opponents and competitors, freeing time and energy for more productive pursuits.[33]

By 2002, it was clear that the formation of this alliance with the LDP had bought the Soka Gakkai at least the semblance of a cold peace. It is too early to tell whether the sect has gained further respect and legitimacy, but attacks in the popular press have been kept to a minimum.[34]

Another obvious concern is the continued ability of the Komeito to win seats in the Diet. The key is the retention of the proportional representation electoral system, which is favored by Komeito candidates. The current election system permits the election of five hundred candidates to the lower house of the Diet. Three hundred candidates are elected through single-member constituencies while the other two hundred candidates are elected through a complicated method of proportional representation. The single-seat constituency system works very well for large, well-financed national parties, such as the LDP, but could prove fatal for smaller parties, such as the Komeito, whose voters are largely confined to such areas as Tokyo, Osaka, and Fukuoka. The LDP's retention of the proportional representation system was an important concession to the Komeito to get it to join the coalition.

Another factor is the Komeito's goal of the Japanese government's implementation of a variety of economic reforms to ease the country's recession, which although by early 2004 seemed to be slowly reversing its downward acceleration, still remained very serious. Drawing an image fresh from popular culture, former Komeito dietman Endo Otohiko compared Japan to the doomed ship *Titanic*, noting that although it looked beautiful inside, it was fated to sink unless something drastic was done to save it. Komeito leaders have proposed a number of policies aimed at reviving the Japanese economy, including structural reform and deregulation intended to create more open markets and various measures meant to create employment possibilities. Speaking with the author on these matters in late 1998, Komeito Deputy Chairperson Hamayotsu Toshiko had suggested that the national budget allocation be changed from "the current overemphasis on construction to a more meaningful allocation in favor of such areas as telecommunications, the environment, social welfare, and culture."[35]

Conclusion

The Komeito has held its own in the three national elections since its decision to join the coalition with the LDP. Its number of seats in the Upper House increased from twenty-two in 1998 to twenty-three in 2001, but its number in the Lower House shrank from the usual mid-forties to thirty-one in the 2000 election—part of this shrinkage can be attributed to the reduction of the number of seats in the Lower House to 480—but grew to thirty-four in the November 2003 election. Thus, it is clear that the Soka Gakkai and Komeito will remain important political forces for years to come.

The Komeito in 2005, however, is a very different entity than it was in 1970 when it was officially separated from the Soka Gakkai. It is now a modern political party, which, while deriving most of its votes and policies from the Soka Gakkai, very jealously guards its autonomy and runs its day-to-day affairs like any other party.[36] But its willingness to dissolve itself in the mid-1990s, and, then, after its rebirth in the late 1990s, its willingness to work as a coalition partner of the LDP are also reflective of the more adaptable "mainstream" behavior of the Soka

Gakkai. The Komeito's decision in 2004 to support the sending of Japanese troops to Iraq, a move that enraged many Soka Gakkai leaders and members, is another sign of the party's growing independence from its traditional socioeconomic base.

Some opposition politicians and journalists argue that the Komeito is not a legitimate political party because it strictly adheres to the interests and doctrines of a specific religious group, but it would be far more correct to say that the Komeito is, at best, a "religiously" based political party. It must develop policies and practices that will appeal not only to Soka Gakkai members but to independently minded voters as well. There are now indications that at least some Soka Gakkai members were so angry with their organization's decision to join the LDP coalition that they either did not vote in the three most recent elections or voted for non-Komeito candidates. This means that Komeito must work independently to broaden its base of support. Its strong gains in the 2003 general elections indicate that the Komeito is winning back more Soka Gakkai voters as well as gaining a few more non-Soka Gakkai votes.

But are the Soka Gakkai and Komeito contributing to the development of Japanese democracy in the early years of the twenty-first century? The answer seems to be a vigorous "yes" for several reasons.

Before the 1990s, most eligible voters in Japan actually cast ballots in Japanese elections, but over the past decade the percentage of Japanese voting in elections has declined rapidly. Figures for the past three elections suggest that only roughly half of Japanese bother to vote and that the percentage of young Japanese voting is much lower. Soka Gakkai voters, however, seem to play very active roles in political campaigns and to vote in high numbers. Thus, while most opinion polls in recent years of all voters give the Komeito about 4 to 5 percent of the vote, it receives between 10 and 15 percent in most elections because Soka Gakkai members vote as a huge bloc. This was the case, again, in the 2003 national elections, despite dissatisfaction on the part of some members with the party's foreign policy in the Middle East. The fact that so many Soka Gakkai members take such a deep interest in competitive electoral politics is a very healthy sign.

Another very positive feature is that the Komeito today is only one of two genuinely mass political parties in Japan—the Japan Communist Party is the other. Its status as a mass party gives it a solid base of support as well as durability, which is something one cannot say for a very fluid political system in which political parties, lacking a strong base of public support, appear out of nowhere, shine for one or two elections, and then disappear almost as quickly. A healthy democracy needs some degree of political stability with durable political parties, and the Soka Gakkai-Komeito is one of only a very few Japanese parties that are.

Finally, the Soka Gakkai-Komeito team will remain its own master. It may or may not decide one day to abandon its marriage with the LDP or it may go on to form some other coalition partnership, but it will always be master of its own house. This team's role in maintaining a competitive political system in Japan and its strong adherence to liberal principles, such as freedom of religion and freedom of expression, mean that it will remain an important pillar of Japanese democracy for years to come.

Notes

1. The Soka Gakkai has been politically active only in Japan. None of its over two hundred foreign chapters has ever engaged in political activities.

2. The Soka Gakkai and Komeito have been separate entities since 1970. The Soka Gakkai strongly endorses the Komeito in every election and a vast majority of Komeito candidates and office holders are Soka Gakkai members, however, Komeito leaders manage the day-to-day affairs of their party independently of direct Gakkai control.

3. Nakano Tsuyoshi, "New Religions and Politics in Postwar Japan," *Sociologica* 14.12, no. 3 (1990): 3.

4. Ibid., 5.

5. Nariyoshi Tamaru, "The Soka Gakkai in Historical Perspective," in *Global Citizens: The Soka Gakkai Buddhist Movement in the World*, ed. Bryan Wilson and David Machacek (Oxford: Oxford University Press, 2000), 24.

6. Bryan Wilson and David Machacek, introduction to *Global Citizens: The Soka Gakkai Buddhist Movement in the World*, ed. Wilson and Machacek (Oxford: Oxford University Press, 2000), 6.

7. Ibid.

8. Tamaru, "The Soka Gakkai in Historical Perspective," 38.

9. *Obutsumyogo* means "the union of worldly matters and Buddhist teaching." The idea is that Buddhism and Buddhist morality-ethics should serve as the foundation of all human activities, including politics.

10. Derived from Tamaru, "The Soka Gakkai in Historical Perspective," 38. The dates reflect the thinking of this writer.

11. *Mappo*, or Latter Day of the Law, is the "last of the three periods following Shakyamuni Buddha's death when Buddhism falls into confusion and Shakyamuni's teachings lose the power to lead people to enlightenment. . . . The *Daishitsu* Sutra predicts that this . . . will be an 'age of conflict,' when monks will disregard the precepts and feud constantly among themselves, heretical views will prevail, and Shakyamuni's Buddhism will perish." The first two eras are *shobo* (true law), which began immediately after the Buddha's death and endured a thousand years, and *zobo*

(imitative law), which lasted during the second millennium following the Buddha's death. During *shobo*, it was said that the world was a contented and peaceful place. The peace was maintained during *zobo*, but the world became an ugly chaotic realm during *mappo*. Asian Buddhist tradition holds that Shakyamuni died in 949 B.C.E. Calculating from this date, Japanese Buddhist scholars in the Kamakura period believed that *mappo* had begun in 1052 C.E. They attributed the chaos of the Kamakura period to this concept. See Nichiren Shoshu International Center (NSIC), *A Dictionary of Buddhist Terms and Concepts* (Tokyo: NSIC, 1983), 244.2.

12. Nichiren, like many Buddhists of his time, asserted that the *Lotus Sutra* represented the final and greatest teachings of the Buddha. "Buddha himself realized that . . . with the coming of *mappo*, this sutra must be spread to the rest of the world to save humanity. . . . [The Lotus is indeed] expounded for the sake of us sinful men living at the beginning of *mappo*" and an all-out effort must be made to introduce the Buddhist Law in the Lotus to all of humanity. Quoted in Murano Senchu, trans., *Nichiren Shorai Metsugo Gohyakusai Shi Kanjin Honzonsho* (Tokyo: Kodansha, 1954), 37.

13. Hiroshi Aruga, "Soka Gakkai and Japanese Politics," in *Global Citizens*, ed. Wilson and Machacek, 103.

14. Ibid.

15. Ibid., 105–6; reprinted by permission of Oxford University Press.

16. Hamayotsu Toshiko, deputy chairman, New Komeito, interview by author, Tokyo, November 28, 1998.

17. Aruga, "Soka Gakkai and Japanese Politics," 113–14. Reprinted by permission of Oxford University Press.

18. Renamed the Social Democratic Party [Shakai Minshuto] in the 1990s.

19. Philip Hammond and David Machacek, *Soka Gakkai in America* (Oxford: Oxford University Press, 1999), 19.

20. Nishiguchi Hiroshi, vice president, Soka Gakkai, interview by author, Tokyo, July 25, 1997.

21. Hammond and Machacek, *Soka Gakkai in America*, 20.

22. Sayumi Daimon and Yoko Hani, "LDP May Have to Walk Political Tightrope," *Japan Times*, July 24, 1999, 3.

23. See Gerald Curtis, *The Japanese Way of Politics* (New York: Columbia University Press, 1988), 1–44, for a discussion of the 1955 system and the transformation process that began in the late 1980s.

24. Ibid., 228. According to a mid-1980s survey cited by Curtis, while less than 10 percent of the followers of most Japanese political parties expressed an interest in active religious practice, nearly half of the Komeito's supporters replied in the affirmative.

25. Hans H. Baerwald, *Party Politics in Japan* (Boston: Allen & Unwin, 1986), 9; Curtis, *Japanese Way*, 157; and Anson Shupe, "Soka Gakkai and the Slippery Slope from Militancy to Accommodation," in *Religion and Society in Modern Japan*, ed. Mark Mullins, Shimazono Susumu, and Paul Swanson (Berkeley, CA: Asian Humanities Press, 1993), 235. When I asked Endo Otohiko, a former Komeito dietman from Tokyo, to define the occupational or social support base for the Komeito, he replied: "Our support comes from all classes because Soka Gakkai members come from all classes. We are essentially, but not entirely, the party of the Soka Gakkai." Endo Otohiko, interview by author at the Diet, Tokyo, July 9, 1992.

26. The Soka Gakkai technically had been the lay organization of the Nichiren Shoshu sect, but the two organizations, in fact, had operated very independently of each other.

27. Akiya Einosuke, president, Soka Gakkai, interview by author, Soka Gakkai headquarters, Tokyo, June 18, 1992, and Ikeda Daisaku, president, Soka Gakkai International, interview by author, Soka University, Tokyo, November 3, 1992.

28. Edward W. Desmond and Irene Kunii, "The Power of Soka Gakkai: Growing Revelations about the Complicated and Sinister Nexus of Politics and Religion," *Time*, November 20, 1995.

29. Legislative aide to Hamada Takujiro, interview by author, Diet office building, Tokyo, July 21, 1999.

30. When I asked Ikeda, in 1984, to define his position in the Soka Gakkai, he replied that he regarded himself to be a spiritual leader and teacher, whose job was to minister to the needs of Soka Gakkai members. Ikeda has spent much of his time in recent years meeting with and lecturing to members both at home and abroad; his monthly guidance messages are discussed at Soka Gakkai study meetings. I asked current Soka Gakkai President Akiya Einosuke in 1992 to define Ikeda's role in the sect in comparison with Akiya's own leadership role. Akiya replied with a smile, "Ikeda sensei is the leader's leader."

31. Watanabe Takesato, professor of journalism, Doshisha University, interview by author, Kyoto, May 31, 1999, and Tsukamoto Akira, television news executive, Nippon Terebi, interview by author, July 31, 1999.

32. Hamada Takujiro, Upper House dietman, interview by author, Tokyo, July 14, 1999, and Watanabe interview, May 31, 1999.

33. Shupe, "Soka Gakkai and the Slippery Slope," 237.

34. Various Soka Gakkai leaders interviewed between 1999 and 2001 doubted the validity of this claim. They insisted that Ikeda was not involved in this train of thought.

35. Endo Interview, July 22, 1999, and Hamayotsu interview, November 25, 1997, in Tokyo.

36. Indeed, many of the other institutions created by the Soka Gakkai have developed their own sense of independence and self-governance. For example, when I inquired into a possible position as a "Visiting Scholar" at Soka University in 1992 to some friends working as Gakkai staffers, I received an enthusiastic response, but it required much effort for them to get Soka University officials to accept me because my college has no official exchange relationship with the university. Today, the university is in charge of its own hiring and recruits many professors who are decidedly not Soka Gakkai members. The Komeito is said to be recruiting more and more candidates in the same manner.

About the Editors and Contributors

David Ambuel is associate professor of philosophy and Leidecker Chair of Asian Studies at the University of Mary Washington. His research and publications primarily concern ancient Greek philosophy and Indian and other Asian philosophies, with special concentration on Buddhism. He received his M.A. from the University of Munich and his Ph.D. from Northwestern University. Ambuel's firsthand Asian experience was enriched by teaching at Thailand's second oldest university, Thammasat University, in Bangkok. Among numerous publications, he co-edited *Philosophy, Religion and the Question of Intolerance*, published by the State University of New York Press in 1997.

Coeli M. Barry is based in Thailand, where she has taught at Thammasat, Chulalongkorn, and Mahidol Universities. She also has taught in the United States at the University of California, Los Angeles, and Cornell University. Currently, she is a research fellow in the Asian Research Institute at the National University of Singapore and a lecturer with the Southeast Asian Studies Program at Thammasat University. Barry specializes in modern Southeast Asian politics. She presently is completing an edited volume of Muslim Filipino short stories, in addition to an intellectual and cultural history of the Philippine Catholic Church from the 1940s through the 1990s.

Greg Barton is a senior lecturer in politics at Deakin University, where he taught religious studies (focusing on Islam and Christianity) for nine years, and now teaches courses in political leadership, global Islamic politics, and society culture in contemporary Asia. His research and published work center on the influence of Islamic and Islamist thought in Indonesia and their contributions to the development of civil society and politics and also to the emergence of Jihadi terrorism. With the support of large grants from the Australian Research Council, Barton has spent extensive time in Indonesia, working closely with researchers from Australia, the United States, France, and Indonesia. He has written three books and edited two others, and written dozens of refereed essays, book chapters, and articles for the international media. His biography of Indonesia's fourth president, *Abdurrahman Wahid, Muslim Democrat, Indonesian President: A View from the Inside* (2002) and his volume, *Indonesia's Struggle: Jemaah Islamiyah and the Soul of Islam* (2004), were published by University of New South Wales Press. *Islamic Liberalism in Indonesia* and *Islam's Other Nation: A Fresh Look at Indonesia* will be published in 2005 and 2006, respectively.

Deborah A. Brown is associate professor in the department of Asian Studies at Seton Hall University. She teaches world religions and modern and contemporary area Asian studies, with special attention to East Asia. She has authored, edited, and co-edited eight books on East Asian affairs and also contemporary religion, including *Christianity in the Twenty-first Century* (Crossroad, 2000). Her research has focused extensively on the critical issues facing Hong Kong society in transition, including church-state relations, and on electoral and other steps away from or toward democratization in Hong Kong and Taiwan, respectively. Brown has edited three special refereed journal volumes on Hong Kong in transition, and authored and co-authored over sixty articles—the majority on matters of democratization in East Asia—in international media publications and scholarly journals. From 1997 through 2003, she was managing editor of the *American Asian Review*. She currently is managing editor of the *Taiwan Journal of Democracy*.

Tun-jen Cheng is Class of 1935 Professor in the Department of Government at the College of William and Mary, Williamsburg, Virginia. He previously taught at the University of California, San Diego, and also was a visiting scholar at the University of Tsukuba, Japan, and an associate visiting professor at the University of Michigan, Ann Arbor. His primary interests are in comparative political economy and East Asian development. He has published numerous journal articles and book chapters, co-authored *Newly Industrializing East Asia in Transition* (Institute of International Studies, University of California, Berkeley, 1987), and co-edited *Political Change in Taiwan* (Lynne Rienner, 1991), *Inherited Rivalry* (Lynne Rienner, 1995), *The Security Environment in the Asian-Pacific* (M.E. Sharpe, 2000), and *New Leadership, New Agenda*

(Center for Asian Studies, St. John's University, 2002). Cheng is the director of the Pacific Asia Program and chair of the East Asian Studies Program at William and Mary, and was editor-in-chief of the *American Asian Review*, 2001–2003. He now serves as editor of the *Taiwan Journal of Democracy*.

Julia Ching regrettably passed away in 2002. She wrote her chapter for this volume during her last year of life. At the time of her death, she was University Professor Emerita and Lee Chair Professor for Chinese Thought and Culture at the University of Toronto. There, she also had been professor of East Asian philosophy and religion. She was born in Shanghai and raised in this city and in Hong Kong. Prior to teaching at the University of Toronto, she had taught at Columbia University, Yale University, the Sorbonne, and in Taiwan and Tübingen, Germany. She also had been a visiting professor at the Chinese Social Science Academy. Professor Ching was an elected member of the American Society for the Study of Religion, and became a member of the Order of Canada in 2000. Her fields of research were religion and spirituality and comparative philosophies and religions. A prolific writer, her many books include *Probing China's Soul: Religion, Politics, and the Protest in the People's Republic* (Harper and Row, 1990), *Chinese Religions* (Macmillan, Orbis Books, 1993), with Hans Kung, *Christianity and Chinese Religions* (SCM Press, Presbyterian Publishing, 1993), *Mysticism and Kingship in China: The Heart of Chinese Wisdom* (Cambridge University Press, 1997), *The Butterfly Healing: A Life between East and West* (Orbis Books, 1998), and *The Religious Thought of Chu Hsi* (Oxford University Press, 2000).

Hyug Baeg Im is professor in the department of political science, Korea University, Seoul, South Korea. He has been a visiting professor at Georgetown University (1995), Duke University (1997), and Stanford University (2002–2003), and a visiting research fellow at the National Endowment for Democracy (1995–1996). His study focuses on the issues related to democracy and democratization in Korea, including the role of civil society in reforming political parties, the impact of external security environment changes on Korean democracy, and political reforms for accountable and transparent governance. His recent publications include "South Korean Democratic Consolidation in Comparative Perspective," in *Consolidating Democracy in South Korea* (2000), and with Byung Kook Kim, "'Crony Capitalism' in South Korea, Thailand, and Taiwan: Myth and Reality," in the *Journal of Asian Studies* 1, no. 1 (2001). His article, "Faltering Democratic Consolidation in South Korea: Democracy at the End of the Three Kims Era," appeared in *Democratization* 11, no. 5 (December 2004).

André Laliberté received his Ph.D. at the University of British Columbia and teaches political science at the University of Quebec in Montreal. He has written on various aspects of democratic consolidation in Taiwan, including the involvement of Buddhist organizations in the creation of an inclusive identity, the development of social services, and the establishment of cross-Strait relief operations. He currently examines the implementation of welfare policies in rural China and, in particular, local governments' cooperation with transnational philanthropic associations. Laliberté's book, *Safeguarding the Faith, Building a Pure Land, Helping the Poor: The Politics of Buddhist Organizations in Taiwan, 1989–2003*, was published by Routledge in 2004.

Patricia Martinez is a Malaysian who is senior research fellow and head of intercultural studies at the Asia-Europe Institute of the University of Malaya. Her Ph.D. specialization is in Islam, and she publishes and presents extensively on Islam in Malaysia and Southeast Asia and on Muslim-Christian interfaith issues and relationships. She has held visiting fellowships at the East-West Center in Hawaii (2003) and at the Asia-Pacific Research Center at Stanford University (2004). She was a Luce Research Scholar (2003) at Ohio University, and was awarded a Fulbright in Islamic Studies in 2003–2004. She employs her training in the study of Islam and Arabic for interdisciplinary research that addresses contemporary issues. One of her research projects defined the cultural identity of "ordinary Muslims" in Malaysia; another traced the genealogies of Islamic state models and the evolution of calls for an "Islamic State" in Malaysia and Southeast Asia. She is the Malaysian collaborator in a current research project to survey ethnic and religious conflict and peace-building capacities in Indonesia, Malaysia, Sri Lanka, and Nigeria. Martinez has held a United Nations consultancy (2001–2002) for an Indonesian education pilot project to overcome the problems of ethnic and religious difference. She is on the International Board of the Asia Foundation's International Center for Islam and Pluralism (ICIP), based in Jakarta.

Daniel A. Metraux is professor of Asian studies at Mary Baldwin College in Staunton, Virginia, and editor of the *Southeast Review of Asian Studies* and *Virginia Review of Asian Studies*. He has written six books and numerous scholarly articles and book chapters on the Soka Gakkai as a religious, social, and political movement in Japan and on the growth of its chapters in Canada, Australia, and Southeast Asia. His books include *The Soka Gakkai Revolution* (1994), and *The International Expansion of a Modern Buddhist Movement: The Soka Gakkai in Southeast Asia and Australia* (2001), both published by University Press of America. He has also written several other books and articles on Japanese history, society, and politics and on contemporary Taiwan. Metraux was a visiting fellow at the Australian National University in 2002.

Murray A. Rubinstein is professor of history at Baruch College of the City University of New York. He has written two monographs, edited four books, and contributed over thirty articles to collections of essays and scholarly journals. Rubinstein is the head of the Taiwan Studies Group of the Association of Asian Studies and is editor of the M.E. Sharpe series, Taiwan in the Modern World. Much of his research and writing has centered on the histories, features, and trends of acculturated Christianity in China and Taiwan.

Index

Abduh, Muhammad, 225, 230
Abdul Aziz Bari, 260
Abdul Hamid Othman, 248, 258
Abines family in the Philippines, 175
Abu Baker Ba'asyir, 232
Abu Hanifa, 251
Abu'l Ala Maududi, 230
Activism, social/political. *See* Political participation/involvement of religious organizations in
Acupuncture and Falun Gong, 43
Aghajari, Hashem, 262
AIDS (acquired immune deficiency syndrome), 130
al-dhimma (non-Muslims) in Malaysia, 249–253
Al-Mawardi, 249–252
Alwi, Mazeni, 262
Ambedkar, D. R., 8
Amnesty International, 51
Anamnesis, 175
Anglican Church in Hong Kong, 183, 186, 188, 195
Anwar, Zainah, 261
Aquino, Corazon, 26, 157, 160, 166–171, 175
Aruga, Hiroshi, 273
Asyari, Hasyim, 229
Aum Shinrikyo, 267, 279
Aung San Suu Kyi, 8
Authority/indebtedness/hierarchy, democracy in Thailand and personal, 86–88, 100–104
Autocratic regimes, three-way race to maintain/seize power among, 246

Bacani, Teodoro, 172
Ba'hais, 75
Band, George, 116
Bangladesh, 10
Benshengren people, 66, 69
 See also Taiwanese democracy, Buddhism for the human realm and
Bernas, Joaquin, 166–167, 169
Bhikkhu Buddhadasa, 18
Bhumibol Adulyadej (King), 90
Bolasco, Marlo, 163, 166
Boxers (Chinese rebels), 45–46
Brahmanism, 90
Bridgman, Elijah, 195
Buddha Light International Organization (BLIA), 56–59, 76
Buddhadasa Bhikkhu, 18
Buddhism, 6–8, 144, 192, 203–204
 See also China and Falun Gong: political implications; Japan and Soka Gakkai's role in postwar politics; Taiwanese democracy, Buddhism for the human realm and; Thailand, Buddhism and democratization in

Cakri dynasty, 90
Carter, Jimmy, 122, 235
Catholic Church, 12–14. *See* Hong Kong's Catholic Church and the challenge of democratization; Korea, Christian churches and democratization in South; Philippines, conservative church reformism and democracy in the

293

Catholic Missionary Society in America, 117, 128
Central Institute of Islamic Research, 234
Chamlong Srimuang, 19, 92, 93–94
Chang Myun, 137–138
Chavalit Yongchaiyudh, 95
Chen Lü'an (Chen Li-an), 56, 58, 66, 71, 72, 75–76
Cheng Yen (Master), 21
Chi Hak-Soon, 141–142, 147, 151
Chiang Ching-kuo, 66, 116, 120, 123
Chiang Kai-shek, 23, 127
China and Falun Gong: political implications
  founder of movement and his teachings, 43–45, 50
  future of the group, 53
  Jiang Zemin leading the charge against the group, 49–50
  opposition's harassment/criticisms of, 45–46
  outlaws movement, Chinese government, 41, 46–47, 50–51
  reactions to the banning of the movement, 47–48
  suicide protests, controversy over the, 51–55
  translating Falun Gong term, 42–43
  Zhongnanhai compound surrounded by followers, 41
  See also Hong Kong's Catholic Church and the challenge of democratization; Taiwanese *listings*
Choi Jang Jip, 136
Christianity, 11–14
  See also Hong Kong's Catholic Church and the challenge of democratization; Korea, Christian churches and democratization in South; Philippines, conservative church reformism and democracy in the; Taiwanese democracy and the Presbyterian Church
Chun Doo Hwan, 143
Chun Tae II, 139–140

Church News, 125–126
Ciji Gongdehui, 20–21, 56, 59, 62, 64, 65, 70, 71, 76
"Clarification on 'The Declaration of Human Rights,'" 124
"Clash of civilizations thesis," 221
Cohen, Marc, 126
Communism and the Philippines, 162–163, 169
  See also China and Falun Gong: political implications; Hong Kong's Catholic Church and the challenge of democratization; Taiwanese *listings*
Confucian tradition, 104, 192, 213
Constitutionalism and the Islamic state in Malaysia, 259–263
Council of Trent (1545–1563), 13
Cummings, Bruce, 136

Dahlan, Ahmad, 225, 229, 230
Dalai Lama, the fourteenth, 8
Decision of the National People's Congress on the Method for the Formation of the First Government and the First Legislative Council of the Hong Kong Special Administrative Region, 188
"Declaration of Human Rights by the Presbyterian Church on Taiwan," 122
Declaration on Freedom of Religion or Belief and Elimination of Intolerance and of Discrimination Based on Religion or Belief, 255
Democracy in America (de Tocqueville), 183–184
Democracy without Democrats? The Revival of Politics in the Muslim World (Salame), 245
Democratization and religion in Asian societies. *See* Religious organizations and Asian democratization
Dhammajayo, 94
Dhammajivo, 94

Dhammakaya Incident, The (Phra Dhammapitaka), 95
al-dhimma (non-Muslims) in Malaysia, 249–253
Diamond, Larry, 9
Ding Renjie (Ting Renchieh), 59
Disillusion and abandonment of cultural suppositions, 103
Duran, Khalid, 244–245

Eastern Catholic Church, 12
Education and modern secular curricula in Indonesia, 225–226
    See also education/schools for the community *under* Hong Kong's Catholic Church and the challenge of democratization
Effendi, Djohan, 234
El Shaddai, 172
Emperor in Japan, politics/religion historically linked under divine authority of the, 268
England, 110–111, 182
Estrada, Joseph, 26, 170
Eun Myunggi, 146
Evangelicals in the Philippines, 172–174

"Facing a Problem of Semantics" (Faruqui), 257
Falun Gong. *See* China and Falun Gong: political implications
Faruqui, Shad S., 254, 256–257
Fisherman's Service Center, 129
Foguangshan monastic order, 56, 57, 62, 64, 65, 70, 72, 75
Formosa Betrayed (Kerr), 114
Formosa magazine movement, 121, 124
Fu Tieshan, Michael, 209–210
Fundamentalists in the Philippines, 172–174

Gao Zhumin, 121, 123, 124, 126–127
Gikong Church, 125
Graham, Billy, 150
Great Britain, 110–111, 182
Gregory VII (Pope), 12
Groups/organizations. *See* Organizations/movements in

Guidelines on Participation of Parishes and Church Organizations in Election Activities, 190
Guoji Foguanghui, 56–59, 76
Guoyu language, 116–117
Gus Dur, 27–29, 224, 228–230, 234, 236, 239

Habibie, B. J., 228, 229
Hadith (sayings of Prophet Muhammad), 251
Hakka people, 66, 110, 113, 114, 119
Han Taiwanese, 110, 113–115
Hao Bocun (Hau Po-tsun), 70
Harding, Andrew, 260–261
Hasyim, Wahid, 229–230
He Zouxiu, 41, 45
Healing and Falun Gong, 43
Health care and Presbyterian Church in Taiwan, 117–118
Hierarchy/personal authority/ indebtedness, democracy in Thailand and, 86–88, 100–104
Hiroshi, Aruga, 274–275
Hokkien dialect, 113–114
Hoklo people, 66, 119
Hong Kong's Catholic Church and the challenge of democratization
    Basic Law guidelines and, 191–192, 204, 207, 210–212
    British rule allowing for religions to flourish, 182
    chief executive controls government decisions and, 211
    commitment to democratization, church's, 209–212
    Document 19, PRC's official policy on religions contained in, 183
    education/schools for the community and conspiracy of government against churches cloaked in democracy/transparency/ accountability, 204–209
    financial accountability issues, 206–207

Hong Kong's Catholic Church and the challenge of democratization education/schools for the community and *(continued)*
    Grant Schools, government criticizes, 200–201
    management committees/supervisory roles, 205–206
    number of school locations by sector/religious background of school, 197
    reforms, sweeping, 196, 198–199
    school-based management, 201–202
    sea change for church-run schools, 201–204
    subsidies, government, 193–196
    summary/conclusions, 214
  independence of religious groups/institutions and, 183–185
  individual, Catholic Church and belief in the primacy of the, 180–181
  modernization in China aided by Catholics/Protestants, 181–182
  not to engage in electoral fairs, church fighting for right, 187–193
  Philippines and Hong Kong, comparing, 25–27
  sanctity of individuals/personal freedoms, church's commitment to, 181
  sovereignty of Hong Kong shifts in 1997, 185–186
  summary/conclusions, 213–215
  Tiananmen Square massacre, commemoration of, 182
  Zen Ze-kiun, beliefs/efforts of, 209–212
"How Democratic is Islam?" (Duran), 244
Hudud legislation in Malaysia, 261–262
Hukum fiqh (laws of Muslim jurisprudence), 249
Huntington, Samuel P., 9, 221
Hutchcroft, Paul, 174

Ibrahim, Ahmad, 258–259

Ibrahim, Saad E., 246
Ikeda, Daisaku, 280
Iman and distinction between Sunni and Shiite Muslims, 10–11
India, 10, 73
Individual, Catholic Church and belief in the primacy of the, 180–181
Individual attitudes/remedies as focus of Buddhist philosophy, 85–86
Indonesia, Islam and democratic transition in
  antiliberal, essentialist view of Islam as, 222–223
  democratic Muslim nations, importance of success for, 221–222
  Islamic thought in Indonesia and, 230–235
  leaders, Islamic, 229–230
  Malaysia and Indonesia, comparing, 27–31
  military as outside of civilian control and, 222
  organizations, Islamic mass, 223–229
  parliamentary elections of 1999/2004 and, 222, 223
  party politics and, 236–239
  political participation/involvement of religious organizations and, 29
  problems to overcome and, 222
  stereotypes of Islamic civilization and, 221
  summary/conclusions, 239–240
International Islamic University, 258
Iran, 9, 10, 245
Iraq, 10
Islam, 9–11, 73
  See also Indonesia, Islam and democratic transition in; Malaysia, democracy/Islamic state in
Islamists, 221, 228, 231–233, 236, 239
  See also Malaysia, democracy/Islamic state in

Jackson, Peter A., 90, 91
Japan, 111, 226

INDEX 297

Japan and Soka Gakkai's role in postwar politics
   Emperor, politics/religion historically linked under divine authority of the, 268
   Great Propagation Campaign launched by Soka Gakkai, 271
   Komeito Party and, 267–269
   Liberal Democratic Party in partnership with Soka Gakkai and, 275–281
   mainstream, Soka Gakkai moves into the, 275–281
   "new religions" activity in politics and, 267–269
   origins of Soka Gakkai as a sociopolitical movement and, 271–275
   political participation/involvement of religious organizations and, 17, 60–61
   Religious Organizations Law of 1939 and, 269
   summary/conclusions, 281–283
   world-reforming sect, Soka Gakkai as, 270–271, 273
Jehovah's Witnesses, 75
Jemaah Islamiyah, 228, 233
Jesus Christ, 12
Jiang Zemin, 43, 46, 49–50, 52
Jihadi Islamists, 221, 232–233
John XXIII (Pope), 141
John Paul II (Pope), 14, 177, 180, 181, 212, 213
Johnson, James, 113
Jong Chul Choi, 149
Josei, Toda, 269, 271, 272

Kamei, Shizuka, 279
Kaohsiung Incident (1979), 124
Karmic Buddhism, 90–91, 97
Khun Yay, 94, 95
Kim Chaejun, 138, 149
Kim Dae Jung, 22, 147
Kim Seung Hun, 143, 148
Kim Su-Hwan, 141

Kim Young Sam, 22
Kissinger, Henry, 116, 120
Kittivuddo, 83
Koran, 9, 244, 253
Korea, Christian churches and democratization in South
   competition for the religious market and, 143–144
   incubator/shelter for democratic activists, the church as, 145–148
   invitation from social movements and, 142–143
   legitimacy, pursuit of spiritual/nonspiritual formulas for, 139–142
   and mobilization of students/young workers by networking, 148–149
   opposition movement, Korean churches join the, 137–139
   overview, 136–137
   political opposition, religious organizations' ties to the, 22–23
   political participation/involvement of religious organizations and, 17, 23
   Taiwan and South Korea, comparing, 21–25
   transition to democracy, contributions in the, 144
   who participated and how did democratic activists acquire hegemony, 149–153
Korean Bishops' Council, 141, 142
Korean Catholic Farmers' Movement (KCFM), 148
Korean Christian Association for Anti-Communism, 150
Korean Christian Center, 143
Korean Christian Presbyterian Church, 149
Korean Christian Women's Association, 140
Korean Council of Christian Churches, 150
Korean National Council of Churches (KNCC), 140, 144, 148, 149–151

Korean Student Christian Federation (KSCF), 140, 146
Kuomintang (KMT) government, 20, 21
    See also Taiwanese *listings*
Kwok Nai Wang, 192
Kyunghyang Daily, 137

Labor issues in South Korea, 139–140, 146
Land reforms in the Philippines, 167–168
Language of the natives, the Presbyterian Church in Taiwan respecting the, 111, 113–114, 116–117
Laothamatas, Anek, 87
Latin America and liberation theology, 13–14
Lau, Emily, 186
Law Fan Chiu-fun, Fanny, 200–201
Lebanon, 10
Lee Teng-hui (Li Denghui), 56, 58, 61, 69, 128
Legge, James, 195
Leo I (Pope), 12
Leung, Anthony K. C., 196, 198, 211
Lewis, Bernard, 9
Li Hongzhi, 42, 43–45, 48, 50, 53
Li Peng, 46
Liang Shuming, 59
Liberal/progressive Islamic intellectuals, 225–226, 229–235, 239–240, 244, 245
Liberation theology, 13–14, 26, 140, 148
    See also Political participation/involvement of religious organizations
Lien Zhan (Lien Chan), 57, 58
Lim, Millard, 170
Lin I-hsiung, 125
Lin Wen-cheng, 126
Lin Yixiong, 125
Lippman, Thomas W., 11
Liu Jianchao, 209
Lo Gan, 49
Lotus Sutra, 271

Luang Po Sod, 94, 95
Luangta Maha Bua, 106
Lust-Okar, Ellen, 16
Luther, Martin, 13

Ma'arif, Syafi'i, 230, 234
Macapagal-Arroyo, Gloria, 173
MacCall, Donal, 125
MacIntire, Carl, 120
MacKay, George L., 113
Madjid, Nurcholish, 234
Maha Chula Buddhist University, 106
Mahanikai sect, 89
Mahathir Mohamad, 247, 257, 260
Mahayana Buddhists, 18
Mahendra, Yusril I., 239
Malaysia, democracy/Islamic state in
    constitutionalism and, 259–263
    declaration that Malaysia is an Islamic state, responses to, 247–249
    hudud legislation and, 261–262
    Indonesia and Malaysia, comparing, 27–31
    Islam as coherent/contiguous with democracy, debate over, 242–247
    non-Muslims, rights of, 249–253
    political opposition, religious organizations' ties to the, 30
    political participation/involvement of religious organizations and, 29–31
    summary/conclusions, 263–264
Malaysia Is an Islamic Nation (Wan Zahidi Wan Teh), 248–250
Malaysiakini, 262
Mappo concept, Buddhism and the, 272
Marcos, Ferdinand, 157, 160
Martyrdom in the cause of Allah, 11
Maryknoll Order, 117, 128
Masyumi, 227, 228
Mater et Magistra, 141
Maududi, Abu'l Ala, 230
Al-Mawardi, 249–252
McGurn, William, 198
Meilidao, 121, 124
Metzger, Thomas, 69

INDEX 299

Middle East, 10, 16
Minjian tradition, 128
Minjung theology, 140, 148, 152
Minnan people, 24
Minnan-Taiwanese dialect, 111
Moderate Islamism, 244
Modernism, Islamic, 225–226, 229–235, 239–240, 244, 245
Mongkut (King), 89, 91, 105
Morgarajah, Jeyagenesh, 262
Mormons in Taiwan, 75
Moussalli, Ahmad S., 244
Muhammad 'Abduh, 225
Muhammad al-Muntazar, 11
Muhammadiyah, 27–28, 224–230, 235
Muhammad (Prophet), 10–11
Myungdong Cathedral, 143, 147–148

Nafi' ibn Sarjis, 251
Nahdlatul Ulama (NU), 27, 224, 226–229, 235
Nasution, Nursanita, 28–29
Natsir, Mohammad, 230
Nichiren Buddhism, 270–272, 274, 276
Nixon, Richard M., 116, 120
Non-Muslims in Malaysia, 249–253
Nonsantri Muslims in Indonesia, 230
North Africa (MENA) countries, 16

Obedience vows and Vatican II, 164
Omotokyo movement, 269
Opium War of 1839–1842, 194
Organizations/movements in
  China
    Boxers, 45–46
    Xinhua, 209
    Yellow Turbans, 45
  Hong Kong
    Anglican Church, 183, 186, 188, 195
    Anglo-Chinese College, 195
    Buddhist Association, 183, 188, 212
    Catholic Bishop's Office, 189–190
    Chinese Muslim Cultural and Fraternal Association, 192

Organizations/movements in
  Hong Kong *(continued)*
    Christian Council, 192
    Education Commission, 199, 202, 203
    Election Committee, 192–193
    National People's Congress, 188
    Parents' Alliance, 198
    Standing Committee of the National People's Congress, 210–212
    Taoist Association, 192
  India
    Jana Sangh, 73
  Indonesia
    Association of Muslim Intellectuals, 228–229
    Jemaah Islamiyah, 228, 233
    Masyumi, 227, 228
    Muhammadiyah, 27–28, 224–230, 235
    Mujahidin Council, 232
    Nahdlatul Ulama, 27, 224, 226–229, 235
    People's Voter Education Network, 235
    Reformasi movement, 235
    Supreme Islamic Council, 226–227
    United Action Front, 233
  Japan
    Aum Shinrikyo, 267, 279
    Kyodan, 269
    Omotokyo movement, 269
    Reiyukai, 269
    Rissho Koseikai, 269
    Seicho-no-Ie, 267
    Sekai Kyuseikai, 269
    Soka Kyoiku Gakkai, 269
    Tenrikyo, 269
    Union of New Religious Organizations, 267, 269
  Korea, South
    Catholic Priests' Association for Justice, 142, 147, 148, 151, 152
    Chundogyo, 144
    Jeunes Ouvriers Catholiques, 140, 148

300   INDEX

Organizations/movements in
  Korea, South *(continued)*
    Justice and Peace Committee, 142
    National League for Democratic
      Youth and Students, 142, 147
    Protestant Christian Professors'
      Conference, 148
    Urban Industrial Mission, 140, 148
    Young Catholic Workers, 140
  Malaysia
    Chinese Association, 248
    Christian Federation, 255, 256
    Consultative Council on Buddhism,
      Christianity, Hinduism and
      Sikhism, 248, 255
    Council of Churches, 255
    Federation of the Evangelical
      Christians, 248
    Reid Commission, 258
    Sisters in Islam, 261
    United Malays National
      Organization, 29–31, 249, 261
  Pakistan
    Central Institute of Islamic
      Research, 234
    United Action Front, 233
  Philippines
    Ateneo de Manila, 169
    Catholic Bishops' Conference, 168,
      170, 175, 189–190
    Couples for Christ, 172
    evangelicals, 172–174
    fundamentalists, 172–174
    Jesus is Lord, 172
    People Power Revolution, 157, 166,
      173–174
  Sri Lanka
    Mavbima Surakime Vyaparaya, 73
  Taiwan
    Assembly Hall Church, 127
    Ba'hais, 75
    Buddha Light International
      Organization, 56–59, 76
    Buddhist Association of the
      Republic of China, 56, 61–65,
      67, 70–71, 75

Organizations/movements in
  Taiwan *(continued)*
    Buddhist Compassion Relief Tzu-
      Foundation, 20–21, 56, 59, 62,
      64, 65, 70, 71, 76
    Chinese Buddhist Association, 20,
      67
    Foguangshan monastic order, 56,
      57, 62, 64, 65, 70, 72, 75
    Formosa magazine movement, 121,
      124
    Gikong Church, 125
    Iguangdao, 46
    Jehovah's Witnesses, 75
    Maryknoll Order, 117, 128
    Mormons, 75
    Solidarity Union, 58
    Yiguandao, 61
  Thailand
    Dhammakaya, 94–96
    Maha Chula Buddhist University,
      106
    Mahanikai sect, 89
    Santi Asoke movement, 19, 91–93
    Thammasat University, 83–84
    Wat Phra Dhammakaya movement,
      94–96
  See also Japan and Soka Gakkai's role
    in postwar politics; Korean
    listings
O'Sullivan, Noel, 70
Osman, Fathi, 244
Otohiko, Endo, 281
Ottoman Empire, 252
"Our Appeal," 122

Pacem in Terris, 141
Pacifism and Taiwanese Buddhism, 75
Pai Daeng (Pramoj), 83
Pakiam, Murphy, 263
Pakistan, 10, 233–235
Park Chong Chul, 147–148
Park Chung Hee, 22, 138, 140, 141, 143,
  146
Park Hyungkyu, 138, 146–147
Parties, political. *See* Political parties in

INDEX   301

Patronage system in Thailand, 85, 86–88
Patten, Christopher, 183
Paul (apostle), 12
People's Republic of China (PRC), 67, 180
  See also China and Falun Gong: political implications; Hong Kong's Catholic Church and the challenge of democratization; Taiwanese *listings*
Pesantren (religious boarding schools), 225–226
Peter (apostle), 12
Philippine Magsaysay Award, 21
Philippines, conservative church reformism and democracy in the
  Aquino, democracy/the church after, 161, 170–174
  Aquino administration and the church/legacies of martial law, 160, 166–170, 175
  democratic paradoxes and the different faces of the church, 168–170
  fundamentalism and new religious movements, 172–174
  historical perspectives on church/state/democracy, 159, 161–163
  Hong Kong and the Philippines, comparing, 25–27
  inequalities in Philippine society, church not addressing roots of, 176–177
  land reform and the triumph of elite democracy, 167–168
  Marcos administration and Vatican II, 160, 163–166, 175
  NGO, church characterized as an, 158
  overview of conservative reformism, 158–159
  prominence of Catholic Church compared to other Southeast/East Asia countries, 157–158
  summary/conclusions, 174–177
  women's activism/rights, lack of, 169–171
Phillips, Steven, 114

Photirak, 91–93
Phra Dhammapitaka, 95
Political opposition in, religious organizations' ties to the
  Indonesia, 228
  Korea (South), 22–23, 137–139, 148–149
  Malaysia, 30
  overview, 5, 16
  Taiwan, 121–125
  See also headings under individual countries
Political participation/involvement of religious organizations in
  China, 51–55
  Hong Kong, 14
  Indonesia, 29
  Japan, 17, 60–61
  Korea, South, 17, 23, 145–148
  liberation theology and, 13–14
  Malaysia, 29–31
  overview, 6
  pacts on limited forms of participation, 245
  Philippines, 14, 25–26, 164–166
  Taiwan, 17, 20–21, 23–25, 61, 128–131
  Thailand, 17, 19–20, 88–91, 93–94, 97–100
  See also headings under individual countries; Organizations/movements in; Taiwanese democracy and the Presbyterian Church
Political parties in
  China
    Communist Party, 180
  India
    Vishwa Hindu Parishad, 73
  Indonesia
    Crescent Moon and Star Party, 233, 239
    Democratic Party of Indonesia, 228
    Golkar Party, 236
    Hizb ut-Tahrir, 232
    Islamic Party, 228
    National Awakening Party, 224, 235, 236

Political parties in
  Indonesia *(continued)*
    National Mandate Party, 224, 235, 236
    Prosperous Justice Party, 233, 239
    Reform Star Party, 233
    Star Party, 233
    United Development Party, 228
  Japan
    Communist Party, 282
    Komeito, 267–269, 275–281
    Liberal Democratic Party, 267, 275–281
    Socialist Party, 275, 278
  Malaysia
    Barisan Nasional, 247
    Democratic Action Party, 255–256
    Islamic Party, 29–31
    Parti Islam SeMalaysia, 242, 247–248, 260
  Taiwan
    Democratic Progressive Party, 56, 57
    Kuomintang, 56, 62, 63, 66–67
    People First Party, 58
    Tuanjie Lianmeng, 58
  Thailand
    Palang Dhamma Party, 93–94
    Thai Rak Thai Party, 94
Poverty, Taiwanese Buddhist perspectives on, 72–73
Poverty and the Catholic Church in the Philippines, 173–174
Pra Buddhadasa, 91
Pramoj, Kugrit, 83
PRC. *See* People's Republic of China
Presbyterian Church. *See* Taiwanese democracy and the Presbyterian Church
Pridi Panomyong, 84
"Principle of Church Unity, The," 152
Progressive/liberal Islamic intellectuals, 225–226, 229–235, 239–240, 244, 245
Prostitution in Taiwan, teenage, 129, 131

Protestant Church, 11–14, 143, 181
  See also Korea, Christian churches and democratization in South; Taiwanese democracy and the Presbyterian Church
Protestant Reformation, 9, 12–13
"Public Statement of Our National Faith," 121

Qigong exercises. *See* China and Falun Gong: political implications
Qur'an, 9, 244, 253

Radical Islamism, 221, 228, 231, 232–233, 236
Rahman, Fazlur, 10, 234, 235
Rais, Amien, 28, 29, 224, 228, 229, 236
Rama IV, 89
Rama IX, 88
Ramkhamhaeng (King), 88
Ramos, Fidel, 26, 170
Red Bamboo (Pramoj), 83, 84
Reformasi movement, 235
Reformation, Protestant, 9, 12–13
Religious organizations and Asian democratization
  doctrines, religious
    Buddhism, 6–8
    Christianity, 11–14
    Islam, 9–11
  inclusion/exclusion of church prior to democratic transition and, 5, 15–16, 20
  legitimacy formula of the prior regime and, 5, 15, 18–19
  overview, 3–6
  paired comparisons
    Buddhist organizations in Thailand and Taiwan, 18–21
    Islam in Indonesia and Malaysia, 27–31
    Protestants in Korea and Taiwan, 21–25
    Roman Catholic Church in the Philippines and Hong Kong, 25–27

Religious organizations and Asian democratization *(continued)*
    See also headings under individual countries; Organizations/movements in; Political opposition, religious organizations' ties to the; Political participation/involvement of religious organizations
Republic of China (ROC). *See* Taiwanese listings
Revivalism and Islamic modernism, 234
Rhee Syng Man, 137
Rida, Rashid, 230
Rissho Ankokuron (Nichiren), 272
Rissho Koseikai, 269
Ro, Paul Marie K., 137
Roberts, Issachar J., 194
Rocamora, Joel, 174
Roman Catholic Church, 12–14
    See also Hong Kong's Catholic Church and the challenge of democratization; Korea, Christian churches and democratization in South; Philippines, conservative church reformism and democracy in the
Rosales, Guadencio, 173

Salame, Ghassan, 245
Santi Asoke Incident, The (Phra Dhammapitaka), 95
Santi Asoke movement, 19, 91–93
Santri Muslims, 230, 233, 234
Sathijaseelan, Shamala, 262, 263
Saudi Arabia, 10
School-based management (SBM). *See* education/schools for the community *under* Hong Kong's Catholic Church and the challenge of democratization
Seventh-Day Adventists, 118
"Shadow over the Catholic Church," 171
Shanghai Communiqué (1972), 120
Shari'a (Islamic law), 221, 253, 260, 262–263

Shari'a (Islamic law) *(continued)*
    See also Malaysia, democracy/Islamic state in
Shi Mingde, 124, 127, 128
Shiite Muslims, 10–11
Shintoism, 268, 269, 272, 279
Shura (consultation) and debates about Islam and democracy, 244–245
Siddhartha Gautama, 8
Siddiq, Ahmad, 228, 230
Sik, Ling L., 248
Sik Kok Kwong, 27, 212
Sin, Jaime L., 169, 173
Sin Chew Kit Poh, 248
Sisters in Islam (SIS), 261
Smith, Carl T., 195
Smith, George, 195
Soka Gakkai. *See* Japan and Soka Gakkai's role in postwar politics
Soka Kyoiku Gakkai (SKG), 269
Somdej Phra Buddhajarn, 105
South America and liberation theology, 13
South China Morning Post, 212
Southern Baptist Convention, 118
Special Administrative Region (SAR). *See* Hong Kong's Catholic Church and the challenge of democratization
Sri Lanka, 60–61, 73
Stanton, Vincent, 195
Suchinda Krapravoon, 93
Suharto, 28, 222, 223, 228, 229, 235
Suicide by self-immolation in South Korea, 139–140
Suicide protests, Falun Gong and controversy over the, 51–55
Sukarno, 223, 227, 228
Sulak Sivaraksa, 18, 60, 91
Sunni Muslims, 9–11
Suzuki-roshi, Shunryu, 60–61
Syafi'i Ma'arif, 234
Syansuri, Bisri, 229
Symbolic importance of Buddhism to government in Thailand, 89–90

Symbolism and moderate Islamists in Indonesia, 232
Syria, 10

Tainan Theological College, 126
Taiwanese democracy, Buddhism for the human realm and
  attitude of Buddhist organizations, understanding the, 59–63
  inclusion/exclusion of Buddhists prior to democratic transition, 20
  muted responses of Buddhist organizations, 63–68
  political participation/involvement of religious organizations, 20–21
  political philosophy, outline of
    Buddhist comparative perspective, 73–76
    conservative views, diversity of, 69–73
    overview, 68–69
  silence from Buddhists during martial law period and throughout the 1990s, 55–59
  summary/conclusions, 76–77
  Thailand and Taiwan, comparing, 18–21
Taiwanese democracy and the Presbyterian Church
  1860s and 1870s: arrival of missionaries, 110–111
  1945–1948: redefinition process, 111–115
  1949–1964: lying low/defending turf, 115–119
  1965–1985: years of confrontation, 120–128
  1986–present: benevolent/charitable works and evolution of democracy, 128–130
  external help for the church and, 61
  health care and, 117–118
  and Kaohsiung Incident (1979), 124
  Korea (South) and Taiwan, comparing, 21–25
  language of the natives respected by Presbyterian Church, 111, 113–114, 116–117

Taiwanese democracy and the Presbyterian Church *(continued)*
  People's Republic of China replaces Taiwan in United Nations, 120
  political participation/involvement of religious organizations and, 17, 23–25
  sociopolitical agenda for the Presbyterian Church and, 109–111
  summary/conclusions, 130–132
  2–28 slaughter by Kuomintang and, 114–115
Taiwanhua, 117
Taiwan Presbyterian Church News, 123, 124
Taixu (Tai Hsu), 59, 60, 63, 72
Tamaru, Nariyoshi, 270
Tan, Christine, 167, 169
Taoism, 42, 192
  See also China and Falun Gong: political implications
Thailand, Buddhism and democratization in
  constitution of 1997 and reforms, 84, 96–100
  coup (military in 1976) and, 83–84
  Dhammakaya movement and, 94–96
  future for the Buddhist spiritual community, 105–106
  ideals of Buddhist democracy, traditional, 103
  individual attitudes/remedies as focus of Buddhist philosophy, 85–86
  judicial system and constitution (1997), 101–102
  Kugrit's government and, 83
  and legitimacy formula of the prior regime, 18–19
  middle class protests (1992) and, 84, 93
  Palang Dhamma Party, 93–94
  personal authority/indebtedness/ hierarchy and, 86–88, 100–104
  and political participation/involvement of religious organizations, 17, 19–20

Thailand, Buddhism and democratization in *(continued)*
  Santi Asoke movement and, 91–93
  and senate system/constitution (1997), 99–102
  and shifting relation of religion to politics, 88–91
  summary/conclusions, 106
  Taiwan and Thailand, comparing, 18–21
  West, democratization in the East as different from democracy in the, 84–86
Thaksin Shinawatra, 94
Thammasat University, 83–84
Thammayut sect, 89, 91
Thanom Kittikachorn, 83
Theology for Self-Determination (Poho), 109
Theravada Buddhists, 18
Third Wave, The (Huntington), 136
Tiananmen Square massacre, 182
Tin, John, 125, 131
Tocqueville, Alexis de, 183–185, 213
Toshiko, Hamayotsu, 274, 281
Tragic Beginning (Myers, Lai & Wou), 114
Treaty of Nanking, 194
Tsunesaburo, Makiguchi, 269
Tsutomu, Shiobara, 271
Tsuyoshi, Nakano, 268–269
Tung Chee-hwa, 198, 203–204, 211
Tung Fong Yat Po, 204
Turkey, 222, 234
21st Century New Taiwan Mission Movement, 109

Ulama (religious scholars), 225, 226, 249
Umar, 251
United Nations, 51, 52, 120
United Reformed Church, 127
United States, South Korea's dependence on, 145–146
United States as colonizer of the Philippines, 161
United States Commission on International Religious Freedom, 209
University of Chicago, 234
University of Malaya, 258

Vatican Council, Second (1961–1965), 13, 141, 163, 164–166, 176
Vellarde, Mike, 172
Vietnamese refugees in Hong Kong, 182
Villanueva, Eddie, 172
Violence and Islamists, 232

Wahid, Abdurrahman, 27–29, 224, 228–230, 234, 236, 239
Waishengren people, 66
Wan Zahidi Wan Teh, 248
Wang Ching-feng, 66
Wang Xianzhi, 125
Wang Youqun, 41
Wang Zhiwen, 41
Women's activism/rights and the Philippines, 169–171
World Council of Churches (WCC), 120, 127, 146
World Hindu Council, 73
World Pentecostal Campaign/Explosion of 1773/1974, 150
Wu, John B., 188
Wu Boxiong (Wu Po-hsiung), 56, 58, 72, 76

Xingyun (Hsing Yun), 20, 57–58, 65, 69–73
Xu Tianxian, 125

Yalung, Crisostomo, 171
Ye Jianying, 46
Yemen, 10
YMCA in Taiwan, 119
Young, Michael, 209
Yuanzhumin people, 66, 110, 113–115, 117, 119, 121, 129, 131

Yuanzhumin people *(continued)*
  See also Taiwanese democracy,
    Buddhism for the human realm and
Yudhoyono, Susilo B., 239
Yun Bo Sun, 147
Yushin authoritarian system in South
  Korea, 146–147, 149

Zartman, I. William, 243
Zen Ze-kiun, Joseph, 26–27, 203,
  209–212

Zhang Bingling, 59
Zhaohui (Chao Fei), 56
Zhengfeng (Lin Qiuwu), 60
Zhengyan (Cheng Yen), 58, 62, 69–73,
  76
Zhong Gong, 46
Zhou Lien-hua, 127
Zhu Rongji, 41, 43
Zhuan Falun (Li Hongzhi), 42, 49–50
Zhumin, Gao, 121, 123, 124, 126–127
Zubaida, Sami, 247

For Product Safety Concerns and Information please contact our EU
representative GPSR@taylorandfrancis.com
Taylor & Francis Verlag GmbH, Kaufingerstraße 24, 80331 München, Germany

www.ingramcontent.com/pod-product-compliance
Lightning Source LLC
Chambersburg PA
CBHW071155300426
44113CB00009B/1221